Programming 2D Games

Charles Kelly

CRC Press
Taylor & Francis Group
Boca Raton London New York

CRC Press is an imprint of the
Taylor & Francis Group, an **informa** business

AN A K PETERS BOOK

Cover image courtesy of Nicholas R. Wilson.

CRC Press
Taylor & Francis Group
6000 Broken Sound Parkway NW, Suite 300
Boca Raton, FL 33487-2742

© 2012 by Taylor & Francis Group, LLC
CRC Press is an imprint of Taylor & Francis Group, an Informa business

No claim to original U.S. Government works

Printed in the United States of America on acid-free paper
Version Date: 20120709

International Standard Book Number: 978-1-4665-0868-2 (Hardback)

Library of Congress Cataloging-in-Publication Data

Kelly, Charles.
    Programming 2D games / Charles Kelly. -- 1st ed.
       p. cm.
    Includes index.
    ISBN 978-1-4665-0868-2 (hardcover : alk. paper)
       1. Computer games--Programming. I. Title.

    QA76.76.C672K46 2012
    794.8'1526--dc23   2012019334

Visit the Taylor & Francis Web site at
http://www.taylorandfrancis.com

and the CRC Press Web site at
http://www.crcpress.com

Programming 2D Games

Table of Contents

Introduction

The chapter material is arranged to take the reader through the process of creating a complete 2D game engine and several game examples. By the end of Chapter 8, the reader should be able to start his or her own game project. The material in Chapters 9 through 11 may be covered during the process of working on the game. Chapter 12 covers network game coding and should only be explored after the reader has a thorough understanding of the material in the previous 11 chapters. In the course I teach, we cover the first 11 chapters in approximately 10 weeks. During that time, the student is working on end-of-chapter exercises and designing his or her game project. The last five weeks of the course is devoted to completing the game project.

Chapter 1: Getting Started

In Chapter 1, we introduce the Microsoft Visual Studio 2010 development environment and briefly describe the DirectX API. The code presented in this book is written in the C++ programming language. A reader who is not familiar with C++ but is familiar with C or Java should be able to understand and use the material because of the extensive examples provided. A brief introduction to the C++ language is included. The role of a game engine is described and then some general programming tips and tools are listed. After completing this chapter, the reader should have a better understanding of the development environment and what purpose a game engine serves.

Chapter 2: Windows Programming Fundamentals

In Chapter 2, we examine the fundamentals of Windows programming. We begin with how to start a new project in Visual Studio. Next, we add a source file and then write our first Windows program, the classic "Hello World." The requirements and operation of a Windows application is explained. We also look at how to get input from a keyboard and how to prevent our program from having more than one running copy. By the end of this chapter, the reader will have successfully created, compiled, and executed a fully functional Windows program.

Chapter 3: Introduction to DirectX

DirectX is an application programming interface (API) for writing programs that need high performance graphics, sound, or specialized interaction with peripheral devices. In this chapter, we take our first look at the DirectX API and how to use it. The DirectX code that we introduce in this chapter will be incorporated into a `Graphics` class. The `Graphics` class will become part of our game engine. We create and configure a Visual Studio project for DirectX programming and then we create our first DirectX programs.

Chapter 4: The Game Engine

In Chapter 4, we begin building our game engine. We create the `Game` class, which is the core of the engine. We incorporate Windows message handling and the high-performance Windows timer. The proper technique for recovering lost Window's devices is explored and the corresponding code is added. Next, we look at the code required by DirectX to draw images to the screen. We wrap up the `Game` class with the main game loop and how it is used to control the speed of our game. Chapter 4 also includes the `Input` class. In the `Input` class, we examine how to get input from the keyboard, mouse, and game controllers. We end Chapter 4 with a first look at the Spacewar game we will be creating throughout the rest of the book. By the end of Chapter 4, the reader will have completed the basic framework for the game engine and will have a better understanding of how real-time applications, such as games, operate in a Windows environment.

Chapter 5: Sprites and Animation

This chapter is all about drawing graphics with sprites and animation. We use DirectX sprites to draw images to the screen. Sprites support drawing images that contain transparent parts. The images drawn by sprites are called *textures*. We look at how to load textures from files and how to manage them once they are loaded into memory with our `Texture Manager` class. The code that actually draws sprites will become part of our `Image` class. The new classes we create in this chapter will be incorporated into our game engine. We end the chapter by looking at how to draw animated sprites. After completing this chapter, the reader will be able to use his or her game engine to draw animated graphics.

Chapter 6: Collisions and Entities

In this chapter, we see how to make our game sprites behave like physical entities. We begin by examining vectors and vector math. DirectX contains many vector operations that we will use to aid in the calculations we need to perform. We thoroughly explain how to detect when game items are colliding on the screen. We then examine how to use physics in a game to make our entities react realistically. Our collision and physics code becomes part of a new `Entity` class, which is added to our game engine. We end Chapter 6 with a functional version of our Spacewar game. By the end of this chapter, the reader will be able to draw animated graphics that can react with each other.

Chapter 7: Sound

In Chapter 7, our game engine gets a voice of its own. We will examine how to create and edit audio files using Audacity. Next, we will look at how to prepare our audio files for game use by using XACT. Then, we see how to play back the sounds using the XACT engine. Our audio code is added to an `Audio` class that we will add to our game engine. By the end of this chapter, the reader will understand how to create, edit, and play back game audio.

Chapter 8: Text

We examine how to use our existing graphics code to create a sprite-based text system and we also see how to use DirectX text. We wrap our text code up in a new `Text` class. We use our new text capabilities to add a console to our game engine. After completing this chapter, the reader will be able to display text messages in his or her game and add commands to the console.

Chapter 9: Enhanced Appearance

In Chapter 9, we look at different techniques for enhancing the appearance of our game. These techniques include giving our game a feeling of depth and adding user interface elements. After completing this chapter, the reader will have learned several techniques for enhancing the appearance of 2D games.

Chapter 10: Tiled Games

Tiled games have been around for quite a while but they are still very relevant today. We examine the advantages of a tiles game. Then we explore using tools to create tile sets and edit game maps. Lastly, we will see how to draw our game screens from the tile sets in interesting ways. By the end of this chapter, the reader will be able to create their own platform-style games.

Chapter 11: Building a Complete Game

It all comes together in this chapter in the creation of a complete game. We cover some of the fundamentals of project management, including how to manage time and resources. Then we step through the different stages of creating our Spacewar game. We also cover how to save and load game states with the help of some space pirates.

Chapter 12: Network Programming

TCP/IP and UDP/IP are useful for more than just web surfing. In Chapter 12, we use Windows sockets to add network communications to our games. We start by describing how Windows sockets work. The socket code is included in a `Net` class that becomes part of our game engine. Our new network code is used to create a simple client/server chat program and then we create a network-playable version of Spacewar.

Acknowledgments

Many people have contributed helpful information and feedback during the development of this book. Special thanks go to Aaron Bolster, Brice Bowman, Zachary Bruck, Aaron Colpaert, Daniel Desloover, Preston Doherty, Gerald Hagerman, Royce Houghton, Nicholas Loar, Ryan Stanley, and Kyle Williams. Very special thanks to Nicholas R. Wilson for the great cover art. Very special thanks also go to Aaron Curley for your help in working out the details of the game engine code. This is a better book because of your contributions.

I would also like to thank Alice Peters, Sarah Chow, Kara Ebrahim, Sunil Nair, and all the people at A K Peters publishing for your help in making this book possible.

1 Getting Started

◼ 1.1 Overview

Welcome to *Programming 2D Games*. This book assumes no previous game programming experience. We are going to start at the beginning with Windows programming and progress all the way through the development of a complete 2D game engine. All along the way we will be creating a classic two-player game. The material in the chapters that follow is presented in a logical and straightforward manner. The topics and code presented in early chapters are used as building blocks in later chapters. All of the code we create in this book will use proper software development methodologies. Great care has been taken to ensure that the methods and techniques discussed in this book are up to date and correct. Thorough testing has been performed on all of the code to make sure it compiles and runs successfully and is free of errors. After completing this book, the reader will have all the knowledge and tools necessary to create his or her own great games.

Some examples of the type of 2D games we can create are:

- side and vertical scrolling,

- classic arcade,

- tiled games,

- animated adventure, and

- puzzles.

■ 1.2 The Development Environment

All of the programs in this book were created with Microsoft Visual Studio 2010 using the C++ programming language. If you don't own Visual Studio and you are a student, find out if your school participates in the MSDN Academic Alliance program. Through the MSDNAA, students are able to obtain Visual Studio and other Microsoft software at little or no cost. Check out the MSDNAA web site for more information: http://msdn. microsoft.com/academic/default.aspx.

The Microsoft DirectX SDK (June 2010) was used for all the programs in this book. All of the examples in this book will compile and run successfully on Windows XP, Windows Vista, Windows 7, and Windows 8.

■ 1.3 What Is DirectX?

DirectX is a collection of application programming interfaces (APIs) that provide low-level access to the Windows operating system. Some of the APIs in DirectX include Direct3D, XACT, DirectInput, and XInput. By utilizing these APIs, programmers are able to create Windows applications that have much better performance than traditional Windows programming techniques allowed.

1.3.1 The APIs

The APIs in DirectX include:

- *Direct3D.* This is the primary graphics API. Contrary to what the name might imply, Direct3D does support the creation of 2D graphics as well as 3D graphics.

- *XACT.* This API supports the loading and playing of multiple WAV files simultaneously with control over most playback attributes. It is useful for sound effects and music.

- *DirectInput.* DirectInput is used to get input from legacy input devices such as joysticks, racing wheels, etc. All new input devices will be accessed via XInput.

- *XInput.* This is a newer input API for Windows and Xbox 360. It works with Windows XP Service Pack 1 and newer; it supports Xbox 360 controllers under Windows; and it does not work with legacy DirectInput devices.

- *DirectPlay.* DirectPlay is a network communications support. It allows writing games that connect with other players via the Internet or LANs.

- *DirectSetup.* This API provides an easy way to support end-user installation of the DirectX runtime required to run your game.

■ 1.4 Why C++?

The C++ programming language has been around for a long time and sometimes gets bashed for being too difficult to learn or too dangerous to use. Despite its critics, C++ is the most popular language currently used for commercial game development. A *Game Developer Magazine* survey reported that 76% of developers were using C++ to make games. With numbers like those, if you are serious about learning to write games, you need to be using C++.

1.4.1 What Level of C++ Skill Is Required?

If you are new to object-oriented programming, there is no need to be concerned; we are going to show you all of the code. Using the object-oriented code presented in this book is very straightforward and many examples are included. A thorough understanding of the C language—or Java—plus the ability to use predefined classes is the level of programming expertise required to be successful in writing the programs presented in this book. Additional discussion and exercises are provided for the accomplished C++ programmer who wishes to modify or enhance the included game engine code.

1.4.2 C++ in 60 Seconds

The following discussion of object-oriented programming techniques is very brief and is in no way meant to explain object-oriented programming (OOP) in detail.

In C++ a *class* is a declaration. When a variable is created from the class declaration, it is called an *object*. Classes may have sections declared as private: or public:. The private: section of the class is typically where the variables are defined. The public: section of the class is where the function prototypes or complete functions are placed. In our code (see Listing 1.1), we will use two files for each class: a header file and a source file. The header file will contain the class declaration, which includes variables and function prototypes. We will, on occasion, place complete functions inside the header file. Those functions are, by default, inline functions, so we will only do this when the functions are very small.

Each time an inline function is called, the compiler inserts all of the function code directly into the program. This makes inline functions slightly faster to call than normal functions. The increased speed comes at the cost of a larger executable file.

The source file will contain the code to implement all of the other functions. As an example, the code in Listing 1.1 is part of graphics.h, where we are defining a Graphics class.

```
class Graphics
{
private:
  // DirectX pointers and stuff

    LP_3D        direct3d;
    LP_3DDEVICE device3d;
    D3DPRESENT_PARAMETERS d3dpp;
  // Other variables

    HRESULT      result;        // Standard Windows return codes
```

```
    HWND        hwnd;
    bool        fullscreen;
    int         width;
    int         height;
// (For internal engine use only. No user-serviceable parts inside.)
// Initialize D3D presentation parameters
    void        initD3Dpp();
public:
// Constructor
    Graphics();
// Destructor
    virtual ~Graphics();
// Releases direct3d and device3d
    void        releaseAll();
// Initialize DirectX graphics
// hw = handle to window
// width = width in pixels
// height = height in pixels
// fullscreen = true for full screen, false for window
// Throws GameError on error
    void        initialize(HWND hw, int width, int height, bool fullscreen);
// Display the offscreen backbuffer to the screen
    HRESULT showBackbuffer();
};
```

Listing 1.1. Defining the Graphics class.

Note the use of extensive comments above each function prototype in the header file! In Visual C++ the comments are displayed in the code completion window. (See Figure 1.1.)

In object-oriented programming, only the public sections of an object are accessible from outside the object. This may be one of the biggest conceptual hurdles for new

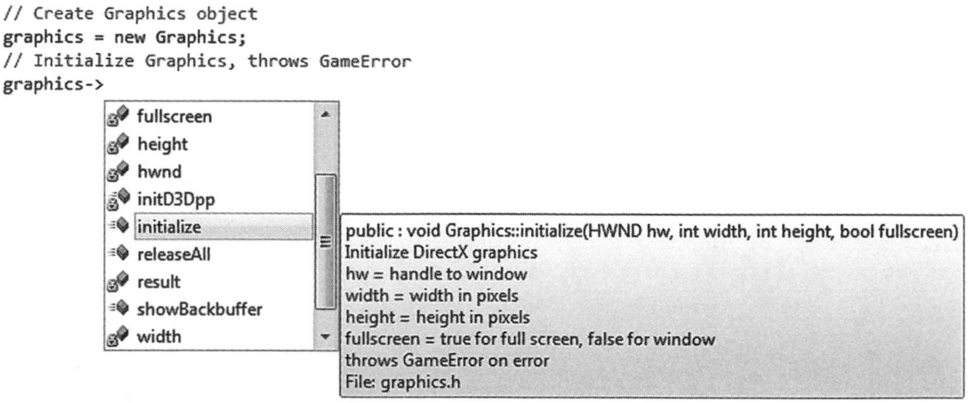

Figure 1.1. The code completion window.

object-oriented programmers to overcome. The only parts of an object our code may use are the public parts and the only parts of an object that are typically public are functions. That means there is no direct access to variables contained inside the object. If we want to interact with a variable contained in an object, we may only do so by using the object's functions.

Restricting access to variables in an object is referred to as "data hiding" or "information hiding."

C++ objects have some "automatic" functions. The *constructor* function is called automatically when a new object is created. It is used to initialize the object's variables. The *destructor* function is called automatically when an object is deleted. It is used to clean up any memory that was reserved by the object. Constructor and destructor functions must meet two criteria: they must be the same name as the class, and there must be no return type, not even void.

In our `Graphics` class in Listing 1.1, the constructor and destructor functions are declared as:

```
// Constructor
Graphics();
// Destructor
virtual ~Graphics();
```

The destructor is designated with the tilde ~ character. The *virtual* keyword is used when this class may be used as a base class to build more advanced classes.

Typically only the function prototype is in the header file. The rest of the function code is in the source file. To indicate that a function is part of a class, `ClassName::` precedes each function name, as in:

```
bool Graphics::initialize(HWND hw, int w, int h, bool full)
{
```

The prefix `Graphics::` tells the compiler that it can find the prototype for the *initialize* function in the `Graphics` class.

`::` *is the scope resolution operator.*

To use objects in our program, we may create an object variable directly or create an object pointer. If we wanted to create an object named `Graphics` from our `Graphics` class, we would do:

```
// Graphics object
Graphics graphics;
```

The public functions are then accessed by using the dot operator in the same way that members of `struct`s are accessed:

```
// Initialize Graphics
graphics.initialize(hwnd, WINDOW_WIDTH, WINDOW_HEIGHT, FULLSCREEN);
```

If a pointer to an object is used, then we might do something like:

```
// Graphics pointer
Graphics *graphics;
```

Then the object is created by using `new`, as in:

```
// Create a Graphics object
graphics = new Graphics;
```

Once the object is created, we can access any of the public functions through the object pointer with the -> operator:

```
// Initialize Graphics
graphics->initialize(hwnd, WINDOW_WIDTH, WINDOW_HEIGHT, FULLSCREEN);
```

Sometimes we declare a function in a class but we are not sure how to implement it at the moment. For example, something that all programmers need to do is draw the game items on the screen. Obviously, a `Game` class should contain such a function, but it cannot possibly know how to draw the game items for every possible game. The solution to this puzzle is to use a *pure virtual function*. A pure virtual function is declared by setting the function prototype equal to 0, as in:

```
virtual void render() = 0;
```

If this declaration is in a `Game` class, then every class that inherits from `Game` must provide the implementation for the `render` function. In other words, a pure virtual function acts as a placeholder for a function.

Class declarations may inherit from existing classes. Inheriting from an existing class copies all of the existing class into the new class. If we have a class named `Game` and we want to create a new class named `Spacewar` that inherits from `Game`, we would program the following:

```
class Spacewar : public Game
{
    // New Spacewar stuff goes here
}
```

The phrase : `public Game` indicates that the `Spacewar` class inherits from the `Game` class. The `Spacewar` class starts with everything that is in `Game`. We may now add, remove, or modify any code we wish in the `Spacewar` class.

Our last bit of C++ instruction is about handling exceptions that may occur during program execution. To accomplish this, we will enclose our methods in a *try/catch* block. Any exceptions that occur in a try/catch block will be handled locally by our code instead of causing our program to crash. As an example, see Listing 1.2 for part of our `WinMain` function.

1. Getting Started

```
try{
    game->initialize(hwnd);        // Throws GameError
    // Main message loop
    int done = 0;
    while (!done)
    {
        if (PeekMessage(&msg, NULL, 0, 0, PM_REMOVE))
        {
            // Look for quit message
            if (msg.message == WM_QUIT)
                done = 1;
            // Decode and pass messages on to WinProc
            TranslateMessage(&msg);
            DispatchMessage(&msg);
        } else
            game->run(hwnd);        // Run the game loop
    }
    SAFE_DELETE(game);        // Free memory before exit
    return msg.wParam;
}
catch(const GameError &err)
{
    game->deleteAll();
    DestroyWindow(hwnd);
    MessageBox(NULL, err.getMessage(), "Error", MB_OK);
}
catch(...)
{
    game->deleteAll();
    DestroyWindow(hwnd);
    MessageBox(NULL, "Unknown error occurred in game.", "Error", MB_OK);
}
```

Listing 1.2. Adding try/catch to WinMain.

The try{ } encloses the code where exception handling is desired. Two catch statements are used in this example. The first, catch(const GameError &err), is looking for GameError exceptions only and will ignore all others. The second, catch(...), will catch any exception that may occur. The code we want to run in the event of an exception is placed between the catch braces.

We may create our own exceptions. This is accomplished with the C++ *throw* statement. The syntax for *throw* is throw(item);.

Almost anything may be used for the item that is thrown. In our code, we will create a GameError class to throw. Creating our own custom class allows us to include any information we wish to convey about the error condition. Our GameError class looks like the code in Listing 1.3.

The data members of our class are an int errorCode and a std::string *message*. The possible errorCode values are defined in the namespace gameErrorNS. The default constructor in our class assigns a default error code of FATAL_ERROR and a default string of "Undefined Error in game." The two-argument constructor allows us to specify different values for the errorCode and message.

```
// Programming 2D Games
// Copyright (c) 2011 by:
// Charles Kelly
// gameError.h v1.0
// Error class thrown by game engine.
#ifndef _GAMEERROR_H            // Prevent multiple definitions if this
#define _GAMEERROR_H            // file is included in more than one place.
#define WIN32_LEAN_AND_MEAN
#include <string>
#include <exception>
namespace gameErrorNS
{
    // Error codes
    // Negative numbers are fatal errors that may require the game to be
    // shutdown.
    // Positive numbers are warnings that do not require the game to be
    // shutdown.
    const int FATAL_ERROR = -1;
    const int WARNING = 1;
}
// Game Error class. Thrown when an error is detected by the game engine.
// Inherits from std::exception
class GameError : public std::exception
{
private:
    int       errorCode;
    std::string message;
public:
    // Default constructor
    GameError() throw() :errorCode(gameErrorNS::FATAL_ERROR),
                        message("Undefined Error in game.") {}
    // Copy constructor
    GameError(const GameError& e) throw(): std::exception(e),
                        errorCode(e.errorCode), message(e.message) {}
    // Constructor with args
    GameError(int code, const std::string &s) throw() :errorCode(code),
    message(s)
    {}
    // Assignment operator
    GameError& operator= (const GameError& rhs) throw()
    {
        std::exception::operator=(rhs);
        this->errorCode = rhs.errorCode;
        this->message = rhs.message;
    }
    // Destructor
    virtual ~GameError() throw() {};
    // Override what from base class
    virtual const char* what() const throw() { return this->getMessage(); }
    const char* getMessage() const throw() { return message.c_str(); }
    int getErrorCode() const throw() { return errorCode; }
};
#endif
```

Listing 1.3. The GameError class.

When we detect a critical error that requires us to halt our game, we will throw the GameError class with parameters for errorCode and message like this:

```
if (FAILED(result))
    throw(GameError(gameErrorNS::FATAL_ERROR,
                    "Error creating Direct3D device"));
```

Our GameError class inherits from the standard exception class std::exception. All exceptions thrown by the standard library are derived from std::exception. Catching std::exception will catch any class derived from std::exception, including our own.

■ 1.5 Naming Conventions

The following are the naming conventions used in this book. These conventions only apply to the code we will be creating. Microsoft has its own naming convention that is used in all of the DirectX code.

- *Variable.* Variables begin with lowercase letters. Multiword variables capitalize the first letter of each additional word:

    - `int variable;`

    - `int multiWordVariable;`

- *Function.* Functions follow the same naming convention used by variables. They begin with lowercase letters and multiword function names have the first letter of each additional word capitalized. Function calls are always followed by parentheses (), which distinguish them from variables.

- *Constant.* Constants are all in uppercase characters. Multiword constants are separated by underscores:

    - `const int CONSTANT = 1;`

    - `const int MULTI_WORD_CONSTANT = 2;`

- *Namespace.* Namespaces have the two-letter suffix "NS." They begin with lowercase letters, and multiword names capitalize the first letter of each additional word.

    - `namespace namesNS`

    - `namespace multiWordNamesNS`

- *Class or struct.* Classes or structs begin with a capital letter. Multiword names capitalize the first letter of each additional word:

    - `class ClassName`

    - `struct StructName`

- *Macro.* Macros are all in uppercase characters. Multiword macros are separated by underscores:

  - ```
    #define SETCOLOR_ARGB(a,r,g,b)
    ```

▌ 1.6 Game Engine

A *game engine* is a collection of source files that comprise the fundamental elements common to most games. Most commercially-produced games are written using a game engine. In order to thoroughly understand what a game engine is and how to use it, we will create our own. Throughout this book, as each new topic of game programming is introduced, it will be incorporated into our own game engine. The result will be a fully functional 2D game engine written in C++. As we build our game engine, we will be using it to create a classic game of Spacewar.

It is not necessary to be an expert in object-oriented programming to comprehend or make use of the code that is developed in this book since most of the heavy lifting will be done for us. Individuals who are more accomplished C++ programmers will be able to add personalized touches to the code.

▌ 1.7 Tips and Tools

As we are about to discover, game programming is rewarding, fun, and challenging. Good fundamentals in program coding will make our journey smoother. There are some lessons many programmers learn the hard way. Here are a few tips and tools that will help you avoid the pitfalls and save you many hours of frustration.

- BACKUP! BACKUP! BACKUP!

  - Storage space is very cheap. Make regular backups of the game project. Give each backup a different version number.

  - DO NOT DELETE THEM. We may inadvertently create a defect in our program that goes unnoticed for a while. By having an archive of previous versions of our game, we can look back in time to find a version before the defect and determine which changes caused the problem.

  - Hard drives fail. The manufacturer is so certain of this they even tell us the average number of hours it takes for the drive to fail. (MTBF—mean time between failures). Backup! Backup! Backup! Is there an echo in here?

- Get WinMerge (http://winmerge.org/). WinMerge is a great open-source tool for comparing and merging differences in files.

- Comment! Comment! Comment!

  - Use good meaningful comments that describe what the code does and why it does it.
    ```

- Modular programming.

  - Don't write the entire game in one huge function.

  - Compile and test each module often and before proceeding to the next.

- Test! Test! Test!

- Don't procrastinate.

  - Many a programmer has underestimated the amount of time required to develop a complete computer game. Allow ample time in the budget for testing and feature changes.

- Start simple.

  - Start with the simplest form of the game, get it working, and save it, then gradually add features as time permits.

  - Do not worry about creating fancy graphics or sound effects. Concentrate on writing the game code first using very simple graphics and sounds. Update the graphics and sounds as time permits once the game code is finished.

- Don't believe everything you read. That goes for what is in this book also. It is too easy for mistakes to make their way into material. Take the time to do your own research.

Chapter Review

This chapter introduced the tools of the trade that we will be using to create our games. The key points covered in this chapter are the following:

- C++ is the predominate language used for commercial game development on Windows and the Xbox 360.

- Microsoft Visual C++ and the Microsoft DirectX API are important tools of the trade.

- The level of programming experience necessary to understand and use the code presented in this book is a good foundation in C++, C, or Java, with an understanding of how to use objects.

- A review of the C++ language refreshes our understanding of the language and helps us gauge our level of understanding.

- Most commercial games today are written using a game engine. We will be creating our own game engine as we progress through this book.

- There are some important tips and tools that can help prevent a disaster.

Review Questions

1. Name two types of 2D computer games.

2. What is an API?

3. What advantage does DirectX provide when writing games?

4. Which part of the DirectX API is used to get input from modern game controllers?

5. Describe the relationship between a class and an object.

6. Any items declared in the `private` part of a class may only be accessed from where?

7. Which C++ operator is used to access elements through a pointer to an object?

8. What mechanism will our code use to handle exceptions?

9. What is the WinMerge program used for?

10. Why is it important to backup computer files?

Exercises

1. Describe the purpose of a game engine.

2. Describe some 2D games you enjoy playing.

3. Describe a 2D game you would like to create.

4. What are the key features in games that make them enjoyable?

2 Windows Programming Fundamentals

2.1 Windows Programming Fundamentals

In this chapter, we will be using the Windows application programming interfaces (API) to write our programs. The Windows API is also referred to as WinAPI and formerly was called the Win32 API or just the Win32. The Windows API provides access to many of the inner workings of Windows. In order for our game to coexist peacefully in a Windows environment, it is important to understand the information presented in this chapter.

2.2 "Hello World" Windows Style

OK, enough talking! It's time to write some code. Let's write a program that displays "Hello World" in the title bar of a window. When it runs, it will look something like the image in Figure 2.1.

2.2.1 Getting Started with Visual Studio

The first thing we need to do is start Visual Studio and create a new project.

The screen images shown here might differ from those on your computer.

Figure 2.1. "Hello World" Windows application.

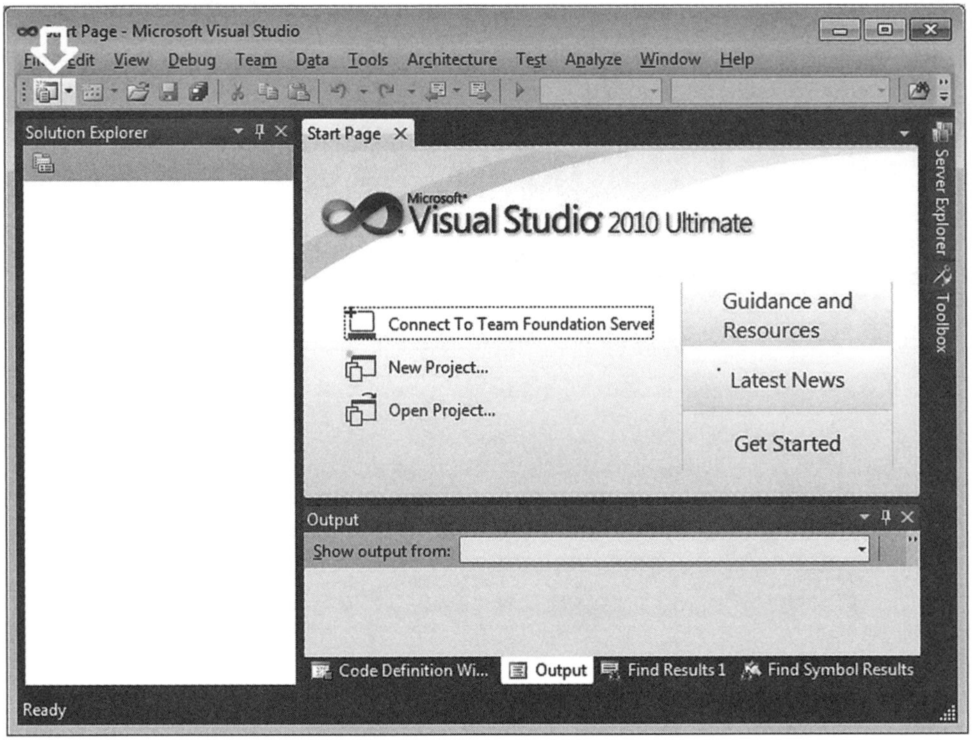

Figure 2.2. Visual Studio with the "New Project" button highlighted.

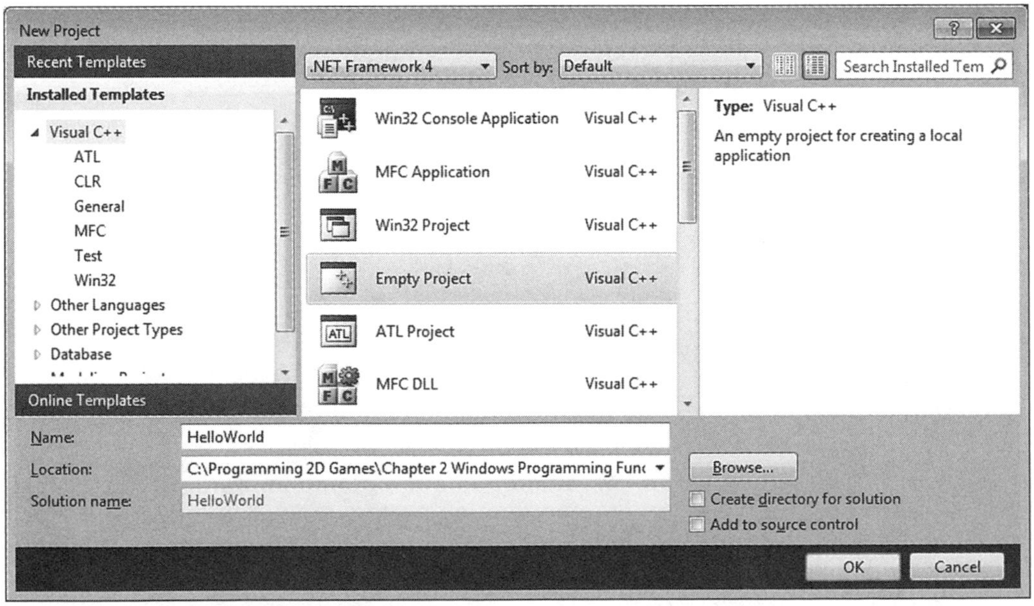

Figure 2.3. Visual Studio's "New Project" screen.

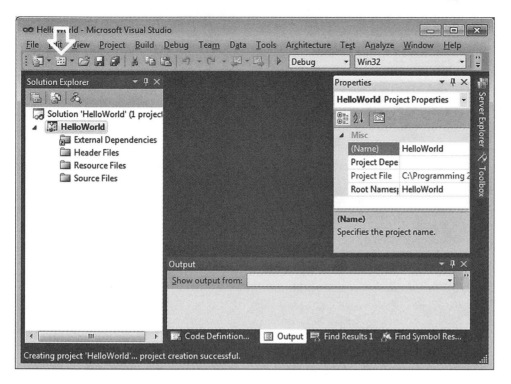

Figure 2.4. Visual Studio with the "Add New Item" button indicated.

- Create a new project by selecting *File → New → Project* from the menu or by clicking the "New Project" button on the toolbar (see Figure 2.2).

- Make sure Visual C++ is selected as the project type in the left pane. In the center pane select "Empty Project" (see Figure 2.3).

- Name the project "HelloWorld." (The project name is also the name given to the executable file when the project is compiled.) The solution name defaults to the project name.

- Clear the check box labeled "Create directory for solution."

- Specify the location where the project should be created and click OK.

- Next, add a source file to the empty project by clicking the "Add New Item" button on the toolbar (see Figure 2.4).

- Select "C++ File (.cpp)" in the center pane (see Figure 2.5(A)).

- Name the item "winmain" (Figure 2.5(B)) and click the "Add" button (Figure 2.5(C)).

The `winmain.cpp` source file is open and ready for us to enter code (see Figure 2.6).

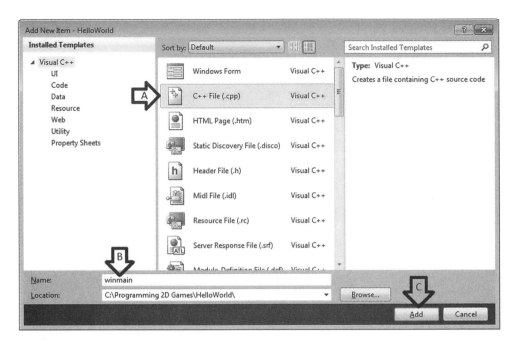

Figure 2.5. Adding a new C++ file to the project.

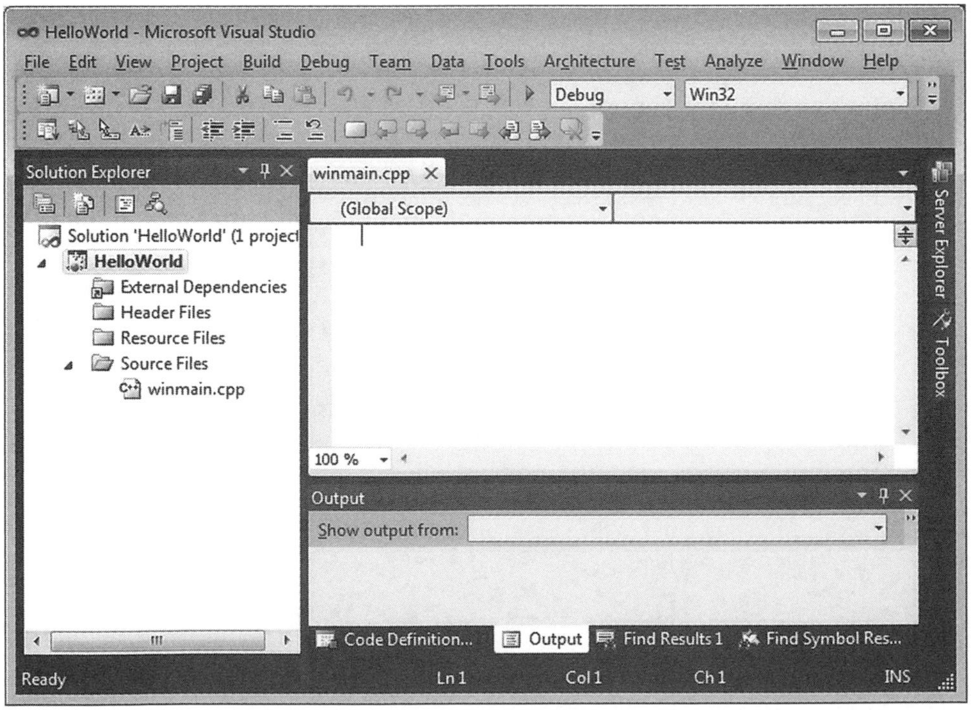

Figure 2.6. Visual Studio with a source file ready for editing.

2. Windows Programming Fundamentals

2.2.2 WinMain Function

If you are not totally new to programming, chances are good that you have written one or two "Hello World" programs. (If you are totally new to programming, you need to find a good book on C++ programming and read that first . . . Don't worry, we'll wait for you . . . OK, you're back—that was fast!)

Just to refresh your memory, "Hello World" in C++ might look something like Listing 2.1.

```cpp
#include <iostream>
int main()
{
  std::cout << "Hello World";
  std::cin.get();           // Wait for Enter key
  return 0;
}
```

Listing 2.1. The Hello World program in C++.

A few lines of code is typically all that is required to display a simple text message because Windows takes care of creating an output window for us. As you are about to see, our Windows version of "Hello World" is a little more involved because we are going to create our own window.

In Listing 2.1, our program included the iostream header file. The iostream header file is required to use cout and cin. In Windows programming, we use the windows.h header file. The windows.h header file includes many definitions and header files we need for our application and some that we do not. A few of the additional header files can actually cause problems later on. To reduce the number of files included, we will use the directive #define WIN32_LEAN_AND_MEAN prior to including windows.h.

In Listing 2.1, our program had a function named main. The main function is where program execution begins. In Windows programming, the main function is replaced with WinMain. The WinMain function looks like the code in Listing 2.2.

```cpp
//============================================================================
// Starting point for a Windows application
int WINAPI WinMain( HINSTANCE hInstance,
                    HINSTANCE hPrevInstance,
                    LPSTR     lpCmdLine,
                    int       nCmdShow)
```

Listing 2.2. The WinMain function.

As you can see, WinMain looks different than the traditional main function. Here is a brief explanation of each part of WinMain.

The return type is int. We will examine the value returned from WinMain in more detail when we look at messages and the message loop later in this chapter. For those of you who can't wait, here is an explanation: `WinMain` typically contains a message loop that runs until a `WM_QUIT` message is received. Upon receiving a `WM_QUIT` message, `WinMain` should return the value contained in the quit message's `wParam` parameter. If `WinMain` terminates before entering the message loop, it should return 0.

Next is the calling convention `WINAPI`. A calling convention defines how the function is called. The order in which parameters are passed, how the stack is cleaned up, etc., is all specified by the calling convention.

The input parameters are:

- `hInstance`. This is essentially a pointer to the application. It is used by some of the Windows functions to identify which application is calling them.

- `hPrevInstance`. Always NULL. It is an obsolete parameter that is only maintained in the parameter list for backwards compatibility with earlier versions of Windows.

- `lpCmdLine`. A pointer to a null-terminated string of command line parameters. Command line parameters are words or symbols that may be passed to an application when it is started.

- `nCmdShow`. How the window is to be shown.

These parameters are all inputs to the `WinMain` function. Typically we do not use them to control the appearance of our window in game programs.

A common point of confusion is trying to change the `WinMain` *parameters to affect the appearance of the window. The parameters for* `WinMain` *are all inputs that are set elsewhere. We will examine how to change the appearance of our window in the following sections.*

2.2.3 Window Class

Before we can display our window we need to create and register a `Window` class. The `Window` class is where we define some of the initial features of our window. We do that by filling in a `WNDCLASSEX` structure. You may think there are a lot of members in the structure, but don't be concerned. Once we have a configuration that we like for our games, we won't need to make many changes, if any. In our example (Listing 2.3) the name of the structure is `wcx`.

```
WNDCLASSEX wcx;
HWND hwnd;

// Fill in the Window class structure with parameters
// that describe the main window.
wcx.cbSize = sizeof(wcx);              // Size of structure
wcx.style = CS_HREDRAW | CS_VREDRAW;   // Redraw if size changes
wcx.lpfnWndProc = WinProc;             // Points to window procedure
wcx.cbClsExtra = 0;                    // No extra class memory
```

```
wcx.cbWndExtra = 0;                     // No extra window memory
wcx.hInstance = hInstance;              // Handle to instance
wcx.hIcon = NULL;
wcx.hCursor = LoadCursor(NULL,IDC_ARROW);   // Predefined arrow
// Background brush
wcx.hbrBackground = (HBRUSH)GetStockObject(BLACK_BRUSH);
wcx.lpszMenuName =  NULL;                // Name of menu resource
wcx.lpszClassName = CLASS_NAME;          // Name of window class
wcx.hIconSm = NULL;                      // Small class icon

// Register the window class
// RegisterClassEx returns 0 on error
if (RegisterClassEx(&wcx) == 0)          // If error
    return false;
```

Listing 2.3. The WNDCLASSEX structure.

Let's take a look at the members of wcx and what they do:

- cbSize. This is the size of the structure. We use sizeof(wcx) to put the size of the wcx structure in cbSize.

- style. Defines various aspects of the window, including how it is updated. Styles may be combined with the OR operator '|'. In our example, we are using CS_HREDRAW | CS_VREDRAW. This causes the window to redraw if the horizontal or vertical size changes.

- lpfnWndProc. A pointer to the function that processes the messages sent to the window. WinProc is a function that we will write to process messages (more on that later).

- cbClsExtra. Specifies how much extra memory the system should reserve for our Window class. We don't need extra, so it is set to 0.

- cbWndExtra. Specifies how much extra memory the system should reserve for each window belonging to our class. Again, we don't need any extra, so it is set to 0.

- hInstance. Identifies the application that registered the class. This identification is used in other Windows function calls to identify our application.

- hIcon. Defines the large icons used by Windows to represent the program. We will look at how to set this later.

- hCursor. Defines the mouse cursor used in the window. In our example, we are using the standard mouse pointer arrow.

- hbrBackground. The color and/or pattern used to fill the background of the window. We are filling our window with black.

- `lpszMenuName`. Defines a default menu for windows that do not define their own. We are not defining a default menu, so the member is set to NULL.

- `lpszClassName`. Identifies this class from other registered classes. This class name must be used again in a call to the CreateWindow function, so we are going to create a constant called CLASS_NAME, like this: `const char* const CLASS_NAME = "WinMain";`

- `hIconSm`. Defines the small icon used in the window's title bar and on the start menu.

- `RegisterClassEx`. The final step in creating the class is to register it with Windows. We do this with the RegisterClassEx function call (Listing 2.4). RegisterClassEx returns 0 on error. Our code checks the return value of RegisterClassEx and returns false if there was an error.

```
// Register the Window class
// RegisterClassEx returns 0 on error
if (RegisterClassEx(&wcx) == 0)      // If error
    return false;
```

Listing 2.4. Registering the Window class.

2.2.4 CreateWindow Function

We have created a Window class, so now we can create an actual window. We do that by calling the CreateWindow function. The CreateWindow function uses the Window class along with additional parameters to define the properties of the new window. The CreateWindow function syntax is:

```
HWND CreateWindow(
    LPCTSTR   lpClassName,
    LPCTSTR   lpWindowName,
    DWORD     dsStyle,
    int       x,
    int       y,
    int       nWidth,
    int       nHeight,
    HWND      hWndParent,
    HMENU     hMenu,
    HINSTANCE hInstance,
    LPVOID    lpParam
);
```

The parameters for CreateWindow are:

- `lpClassName`. A pointer to a NULL-terminated string containing the Window class name. This name must match the name used in the lpszClassName member in the CreateWindowClass function.

- `lpWindowName`. The text that appears in the title bar of the window.

- `dsStyle`. The style of window to create. Many styles are available; some of the styles we will use are:

  - `WS_OVERLAPPEDWINDOW`. Creates a resizable window with the familiar controls.

  - `WS_OVERLAPPED`. Creates a fixed size window with no controls. This is the style we will most often use for windowed games.

  - `WS_EX_TOPMOST | WS_VISIBLE | WS_POPUP`: These are three styles combined with the OR '|' operator. This is the style we will use for full-screen games.

- `x, y`. The coordinates of the top-left corner of the window.

- `nWidth`. The width of the window in pixels.

- `nHeight`. The height of the window in pixels.

- `hWndParent`. The parent window. Normally our games will not have a parent window.

- `hMenu`. The window menu.

- `hInstance`. The application identifier from the `Window` class.

- `lpParam`. Additional window parameters.

The actual function call might look something like Listing 2.5. Some notes about Listing 2.5:

- `CLASS_NAME` is a char constant we declared earlier as "WinMain" (see Listing 2.10).

- `APP_TITLE` is a char constant we declared earlier as "Hello World". `APP_TITLE` is the text that will be displayed in the title bar (see Listing 2.10).

- `WS_OVERLAPPEDWINDOW`. Creates a normal window. Usually for games, we will use a different style. (See `dsStyle` above.)

- `CW_USEDEFAULT`. For this demo, we are using the default size and position.

- `NULL, NULL`. No parent window and no menu.

- `hInstance`. The handle to our application. This is the `hInstance` parameter that is passed to our program in `WinMain`.

- `NULL`. No additional window parameters.

```
// Create window
hwnd = CreateWindow(
    CLASS_NAME,                 // Name of the window class
    APP_TITLE,                  // Title bar text
    WS_OVERLAPPEDWINDOW,        // Window style
    CW_USEDEFAULT,              // Default horizontal position of window
    CW_USEDEFAULT,              // Default vertical position of window
    WINDOW_WIDTH,               // Width of window
    WINDOW_HEIGHT,              // Height of the window
    (HWND) NULL,                // No parent window
    (HMENU) NULL,               // No menu
    hInstance,                  // Handle to application instance
    (LPVOID) NULL);             // No window parameters
```

Listing 2.5. The `CreateWindow` function call.

Next, we need to check the value returned from `CreateWindow` to see if any errors occurred. If the function was successful, the return value is a handle to the new window. If the function failed, the return value is `NULL`. If an error occurred, we cannot proceed, so we simply return `FALSE` and our program ends (Listing 2.6).

```
// If there was an error creating the window
if (!hwnd)
    return FALSE;               // Cannot proceed so exit
```

Listing 2.6. Checking the return value from `CreateWindow`.

`NULL` *in C++ is equal to 0. The result of* (!hwnd) *is* true *when* hwnd *is* NULL.

We are almost there! The next steps are to show the window and send the window a message to paint itself. That code looks like Listing 2.7.

```
    // Show the window
    ShowWindow(hwnd, nCmdShow);
    // Send a WM_PAINT message to the window procedure
    UpdateWindow(hwnd);
    return true;
}
```

Listing 2.7. Displaying the window.

We now have enough code to display a window. To give our program a clean look, we will place the window creation code in a function named `CreateMainWindow` and call it from `WinMain` (see Listing 2.10).

2.2.5 Message Loop

Windows will communicate with our program by sending it messages. These messages may be used to tell us about user operations, such as mouse movements or key presses, or they may be commands from Windows. A loop in `WinMain` is used to check for messages (Listing 2.8). If our application is going to accept character input from the user, it needs to call the `TranslateMessage` function inside the message loop. `TranslateMessage` is a Windows function that translates virtual-key messages into character messages. The messages are sent to our `WinProc` function for processing by the `DispatchMessage` function. `WinMain` remains in this loop until a `WM_QUIT` message is received. When `WinMain` returns to the system, the return value is the `wParam` parameter of the `WM_QUIT` message.

```
// Main message loop
int done = 0;
while (!done)
{
// PeekMessage is a non-blocking method for checking for Windows messages
    if (PeekMessage(&msg, NULL, 0, 0, PM_REMOVE))
    {
        // Look for quit message
        if (msg.message == WM_QUIT)
            done = 1;
        // Decode and pass messages on to WinProc
        TranslateMessage(&msg);
        DispatchMessage(&msg);
    }
}
return msg.wParam;
}
```

Listing 2.8. The main message loop.

Be sure to use `PeekMessage`, *not* `GetMessage`, *in the message loop.* `GetMessage` *waits for messages before returning.* `PeekMessage` *checks for incoming messages but does not wait if no messages are pending. This keeps our message loop running at maximum speed at all times, which is critical for games that have animated graphics.*

2.2.6 WinProc Function

Last but not least is the `WinProc` function. This is the function used to process messages. `WinProc` is typically the name given to this function. The name of this function must match the name specified in the `WNDCLASSEX` structure in the `CreateWindowClass` function we looked at earlier.

A wide assortment of messages may be sent to our program. We may choose to respond to those messages by placing the necessary code in `WinProc`. Any messages we ignore will be handled by Windows. In Listing 2.9, the only message we are responding to is

WM_DESTROY. WM_DESTROY is sent to us by Windows when our window is being destroyed after it has been removed from the screen. If a WM_DESTROY message is received, we call PostQuitMessage(0) to signal Windows that our application has made a request to terminate (quit). This will result in WM_QUIT being added to our message queue. The WM_QUIT message will cause the main message loop in WinMain to exit.

```cpp
//=============================================================================
// Window event callback function
//=============================================================================
LRESULT WINAPI WinProc( HWND hWnd, UINT msg, WPARAM wParam, LPARAM lParam )
{
    switch( msg )
    {
        case WM_DESTROY:
            // Tell Windows to kill this program
            PostQuitMessage(0);
            return 0;
    }
    return DefWindowProc( hWnd, msg, wParam, lParam );
}
```

Listing 2.9. The Window event callback function.

Whew! It was a lot of code just to display "Hello World" but remember that we did all this extra work so we could have more control over the appearance of our window and the message processing of our application. We will need this extra control to write quality games. Listing 2.10 is the complete listing of our "Hello World" example.

```cpp
// Programming 2D Games
// Copyright (c) 2011 by:
// Charles Kelly
// Chapter 2 "Hello World" Windows Style v1.0
// winmain.cpp
#define WIN32_LEAN_AND_MEAN
#include <windows.h>
// Function prototypes
int WINAPI WinMain(HINSTANCE, HINSTANCE, LPSTR, int);
bool CreateMainWindow(HINSTANCE, int);
LRESULT WINAPI WinProc(HWND, UINT, WPARAM, LPARAM);
// Global variable
HINSTANCE hinst;
// Constants
const char CLASS_NAME[]   = "WinMain";
const char APP_TITLE[]    = "Hello World";    // Title bar text
const int  WINDOW_WIDTH  = 400;               // Width of window
const int  WINDOW_HEIGHT = 400;               // Height of window
//=============================================================================
// Starting point for a Windows application
// Parameters are:
//    hInstance. Handle to the current instance of the application
```

```
//   hPrevInstance. Always NULL, obsolete parameter
//   lpCmdLine. Pointer to null-terminated string of command line arguments
//   nCmdShow. Specifies how the window is to be shown
//=============================================================================
int WINAPI WinMain( HINSTANCE hInstance,
                    HINSTANCE hPrevInstance,
                    LPSTR     lpCmdLine,
                    int       nCMdShow)
{
    MSG msg;
    // Create the window
    if (!CreateMainWindow(hInstance, nCmdShow))
        return false;
    // Main message loop
    int done = 0;
    while (!done)
    {
        // PeekMessage is a non-blocking test for Windows messages
        if (PeekMessage(&msg, NULL, 0, 0, PM_REMOVE))
        {
            // Look for quit message
            if (msg.message == WM_QUIT)
                done = 1;
            // Decode and pass messages on to WinProc
            TranslateMessage(&msg);
            DispatchMessage(&msg);
        }
    }
    return msg.wParam;
}
//=============================================================================
// Window event callback function
//=============================================================================
LRESULT WINAPI WinProc( HWND hWnd, UINT msg, WPARAM wParam, LPARAM lParam )
{
    switch( msg )
    {
        case WM_DESTROY:
            // Tell Windows to kill this program
            PostQuitMessage(0);
            return 0;
    }
    return DefWindowProc( hWnd, msg, wParam, lParam );
}
//=============================================================================
// Create the window
// Returns: false on error
//=============================================================================
bool CreateMainWindow(HINSTANCE hInstance, int nCmdShow)
{
    WNDCLASSEX wcx;
    HWND hwnd;

    // Fill in the window class structure with parameters
    // that describe the main window.
    wcx.cbSize = sizeof(wcx);              // Size of structure
    wcx.style = CS_HREDRAW | CS_VREDRAW;// Redraw if size changes
    wcx.lpfnWndProc = WinProc;             // Points to window procedure
```

```
wcx.cbClsExtra = 0;                  // No extra class memory
wcx.cbWndExtra = 0;                  // No extra window memory
wcx.hInstance = hInstance;           // Handle to instance
wcx.hIcon = NULL;
wcx.hCursor = LoadCursor(NULL,IDC_ARROW);   // Predefined arrow
// Background brush
wcx.hbrBackground = (HBRUSH)GetStockObject(BLACK_BRUSH);
wcx.lpszMenuName = NULL;             // Name of menu resource
wcx.lpszClassName = CLASS_NAME;      // Name of window class
wcx.hIconSm = NULL;                  // Small class icon

// Register the window class
// RegisterClassEx returns 0 on error
if (RegisterClassEx(&wcx) == 0)      // If error
    return false;
// Create window
hwnd = CreateWindow(
    CLASS_NAME,              // Name of the window class
    APP_TITLE,               // Title bar text
    WS_OVERLAPPEDWINDOW,     // Window style
    CW_USEDEFAULT,           // Default horizontal position of window
    CW_USEDEFAULT,           // Default vertical position of window
    WINDOW_WIDTH,            // Width of window
    WINDOW_HEIGHT,           // Height of the window
    (HWND) NULL,             // No parent window
    (HMENU) NULL,            // No menu
    hInstance,               // Handle to application instance
    (LPVOID) NULL);          // No window parameters
// If there was an error creating the window
if (!hwnd)
    return false;
// Show the window
ShowWindow(hwnd, nCmdShow);
// Send a WM_PAINT message to the window procedure
UpdateWindow(hwnd);
return true;
}
```

Listing 2.10. Hello World example.

▌ 2.3 Device Context

Windows is designed to work with a wide array of display or output devices. This *device independence* allows applications to access the various output devices in the same manner. The heart of device independence is the graphics device interface (GDI). The GDI is a dynamic-link library that, together with a device driver, enables applications to draw to a printer or to a VGA display.

In order to access a particular device, an application informs the GDI to load the appropriate device driver and prepare the device for drawing operations. This is accomplished by creating a device context (DC). A DC is a structure that defines a `Graphics` object and its properties. Windows created a device context when it created our window. We will see how to access our new window using its device context in the code that follows.

2.4 Keyboard Input with Windows API

There are two types of keyboard input typically used by games. Depending on our game, we may need to use one or both. One input type is text, where the user types characters on the keyboard and we want to know which characters have been pressed and in what order. For example, did the user type the word "north"? The other input type is using the keyboard as a game controller, where we want to know which keys are currently being pressed. For example, is the user currently holding down the "W" key and the right arrow key?

2.4.1 WM_CHAR Message

Windows sends several messages related to key presses. To read characters, we are going to use the WM_CHAR message. A WM_CHAR message will be sent to our game whenever the user types a character on the keyboard. To read the typed characters, all we need to do is add the WM_CHAR message handler to our WinProc function (Listing 2.11).

```
case WM_CHAR:                   // A character was entered by the keyboard
    switch (wParam)             // The character is in wParam
    {
        case 0x08:              // Backspace
        case 0x09:              // Tab
        case 0x0A:              // Linefeed
        case 0x0D:              // Carriage return
        case 0x1B:              // Escape
            MessageBeep((UINT) -1);      // Beep but do not display
            return 0;
        default:                // Displayable character
            ch = (TCHAR) wParam;    // Get the character
            InvalidateRect(hwnd, NULL, TRUE);    // Force WM_PAINT
            return 0;
    }
```

Listing 2.11. The WM_CHAR message handler.

The wParam contains the character code for the key just pressed. We check for non-displayable characters and tell Windows to play a beep sound just to acknowledge the key press. If a displayable character is pressed, we read the value from wParam and save it in the variable ch.

Just for fun, let's display the character on the screen. We will do that by looking for the WM_PAINT message in WinProc. A WM_PAINT message is sent when Windows determines that all or part of our window needs to be repainted. This will occur, for example, if we resize the window. To force an immediate WM_PAINT event, we place a call to the InvalidateRect function at the end of the WM_CHAR message code.

Before we can display text in our window, we need to get its device context. The BeginPaint function prepares a window for painting and returns a handle to the device context. A *handle* is a Windows data type that is used to reference different objects. We create a special variable to hold the handle to the device context with the code in Listing 2.12.

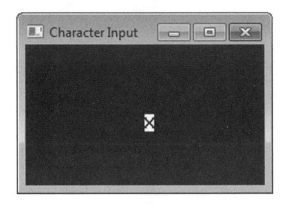

Figure 2.7. The "Character Input" example.

```
HDC     hdc;                    // Handle to device context
```

Listing 2.12. Handle to device context.

Text may be displayed in the window using the TextOut function. We will only be using TextOut in this chapter so that we may test our text input code. In later chapters, we will use different techniques for displaying text in our games. The first parameter in TextOut is our hdc variable. The code in Listing 2.13 is added to our WinProc function.

```
case WM_PAINT:                  // The window needs to be redrawn
    hdc = BeginPaint(hwnd, &ps);    // Get handle to device context
    GetClientRect(hwnd, &rect);     // Get the window rectangle
    // Display the character
    TextOut(hdc, rect.right/2, rect.bottom/2, &ch, 1);
    EndPaint(hwnd, &ps);
    return 0;
```

Listing 2.13. Displaying text.

Figure 2.7 is the output of our program when "X" is pressed. Listing 2.14 is a complete listing of our "Character Input" example.

```
// Programming 2D Games
// Copyright (c) 2011 by:
// Charles Kelly
// Chapter 2 Character Input with Windows API v1.0
// winmain.cpp
#define WIN32_LEAN_AND_MEAN
#include <windows.h>
```

```cpp
// Function prototypes
int WINAPI WinMain(HINSTANCE, HINSTANCE, LPSTR, int);
bool CreateMainWindow(HINSTANCE, int);
LRESULT WINAPI WinProc(HWND, UINT, WPARAM, LPARAM);
// Global variables
HINSTANCE hinst;
HDC     hdc;                 // Handle to device context
TCHAR ch = ' ';             // Character entered
RECT rect;                  // Rectangle structure
PAINTSTRUCT ps;             // Used in WM_PAINT
// Constants
const char CLASS_NAME[]  = "Keyboard";
const char APP_TITLE[]   = "Character Input";
const int  WINDOW_WIDTH  = 400;    // Width of window
const int  WINDOW_HEIGHT = 300;    // Height of window
//=========================================================================
// Starting point for a Windows application
//=========================================================================
int WINAPI WinMain(HINSTANCE hInstance,
                   HINSTANCE hPrevInstance,
                   LPSTR     lpCmdLine,
                   int       nCmdShow)
{
    MSG  msg;
    // Create the window
    if (!CreateMainWindow(hInstance, nCmdShow))
        return false;
    // Main message loop
    int done = 0;
    while (!done)
    {
        if (PeekMessage(&msg, NULL, 0, 0, PM_REMOVE))
        {
            // Look for quit message
            if (msg.message == WM_QUIT)
                done = 1;
            // Decode and pass messages on to WinProc
            TranslateMessage(&msg);
            DispatchMessage(&msg);
        }
    }
    return msg.wParam;
}
//=========================================================================
// Window event callback function
//=========================================================================
LRESULT WINAPI WinProc( HWND hwnd, UINT msg, WPARAM wParam, LPARAM lParam )
{
    switch( msg )
    {
        case WM_DESTROY:
            // Tell Windows to kill this program
            PostQuitMessage(0);
            return 0;
        case WM_CHAR:           // A character was entered by the keyboard
            switch (wParam)     // The character is in wParam
            {
                case 0x08:      // Backspace
```

```
                    case 0x09:              // Tab
                    case 0x0A:              // Linefeed
                    case 0x0D:              // Carriage return
                    case 0x1B:              // Escape
                        MessageBeep((UINT) -1);    // Beep but do not display
                        return 0;
                    default:                // Displayable character
                        ch = (TCHAR) wParam;    // Get the character
                        InvalidateRect(hwnd, NULL, TRUE);    // Force WM_PAINT
                        return 0;
                }
            case WM_PAINT:                  // The window needs to be redrawn
                hdc = BeginPaint(hwnd, &ps);    // Get handle to device context
                GetClientRect(hwnd, &rect);     // Get the window rectangle
                // Display the character
                TextOut(hdc, rect.right/2, rect.bottom/2, &ch, 1);
                EndPaint(hwnd, &ps);
                return 0;
            default:
                return DefWindowProc( hwnd, msg, wParam, lParam );
        }
}
//=============================================================================
// Create the window
// Returns: false on error
//=============================================================================
bool CreateMainWindow(HINSTANCE hInstance, int nCmdShow)
{
    WNDCLASSEX wcx;
    HWND hwnd;

    // Fill in the window class structure with parameters
    // that describe the main window.
    wcx.cbSize = sizeof(wcx);               // Size of structure
    wcx.style = CS_HREDRAW | CS_VREDRAW;    // Redraw if size changes
    wcx.lpfnWndProc = WinProc;              // Points to window procedure
    wcx.cbClsExtra = 0;                     // No extra class memory
    wcx.cbWndExtra = 0;                     // No extra window memory
    wcx.hInstance = hInstance;              // Handle to instance
    wcx.hIcon = NULL;
    wcx.hCursor = LoadCursor(NULL,IDC_ARROW);    // Predefined arrow
    // Black background
    wcx.hbrBackground = (HBRUSH)GetStockObject(BLACK_BRUSH);
    wcx.lpszMenuName = NULL;                // Name of menu resource
    wcx.lpszClassName = CLASS_NAME;         // Name of window class
    wcx.hIconSm = NULL;                     // Small class icon

    // Register the window class
    // RegisterClassEx returns 0 on error
    if (RegisterClassEx(&wcx) == 0)         // If error
        return false;
    // Create window
    hwnd = CreateWindow(
        CLASS_NAME,                 // Name of the window class
        APP_TITLE,                  // Title bar text
        WS_OVERLAPPEDWINDOW,        // Window style
        CW_USEDEFAULT,              // Default horizontal position of window
        CW_USEDEFAULT,              // Default vertical position of window
```

```
        WINDOW_WIDTH,              // Width of window
        WINDOW_HEIGHT,             // Height of the window
        (HWND) NULL,               // No parent window
        (HMENU) NULL,              // No menu
        hInstance,                 // Handle to application instance
        (LPVOID) NULL);            // No window parameters
    // If there was an error creating the window
    if (!hwnd)
        return false;
    // Show the window
    ShowWindow(hwnd, nCmdShow);
    // Send a WM_PAINT message to the window procedure
    UpdateWindow(hwnd);
    return true;
}
```

Listing 2.14. The "Character Input" example.

2.4.2 WM_KEYDOWN, WM_KEYUP message

If we want to use the keyboard like a giant game pad, then we will want to use WM_KEYDOWN and WM_KEYUP events. Each time a key is pressed, a WM_KEYDOWN event is triggered. When the key is released, a WM_KEYUP event occurs. We can use these two events along with their parameters to track the state of each key on the keyboard.

In order to keep track of the state of the keyboard keys, we are going to create an array of Boolean values. Each entry in the array will represent the state of one key on the keyboard. If the Boolean value is true, it means the key is pressed, and if the value is false, then the key is up. We want to allow the player to press multiple keys simultaneously and we might want to allow the use of the shift and control keys as game buttons.

The WM_KEYDOWN and WM_KEYUP message handlers in WinProc look like the code in Listing 2.15.

```
case WM_KEYDOWN:                                 // Key down
    vkKeys[wParam] = true;
    switch(wParam)
    {
        case VK_SHIFT:                           // Shift key
            nVirtKey = GetKeyState(VK_LSHIFT);   // Get state of left
                                                 // shift
            if (nVirtKey & SHIFTED)              // If left shift
                vkKeys[VK_LSHIFT] = true;
            nVirtKey = GetKeyState(VK_RSHIFT);   // Get state of right
                                                 // shift
            if (nVirtKey & SHIFTED)              // If right shift
                vkKeys[VK_RSHIFT] = true;
            break;
        case VK_CONTROL:                         // Control key
            nVirtKey = GetKeyState(VK_LCONTROL);
            if (nVirtKey & SHIFTED)              // If left control
                vkKeys[VK_LCONTROL] = true;
            nVirtKey = GetKeyState(VK_RCONTROL);
```

```
                if (nVirtKey & SHIFTED)                    // If right control
                    vkKeys[VK_RCONTROL] = true;
                break;
        }
        InvalidateRect(hwnd, NULL, TRUE);                  // Force WM_PAINT
        return 0;
        break;
    case WM_KEYUP:                                         // Key up
        vkKeys[wParam] = false;
        switch(wParam)
        {
            case VK_SHIFT:                                 // Shift key
                nVirtKey = GetKeyState(VK_LSHIFT);
                if ((nVirtKey & SHIFTED) == 0)             // If left shift
                    vkKeys[VK_LSHIFT] = false;
                nVirtKey = GetKeyState(VK_RSHIFT);
                if ((nVirtKey & SHIFTED) == 0)             // If right shift
                    vkKeys[VK_RSHIFT] = false;
                break;
            case VK_CONTROL:                               // Control key
                nVirtKey = GetKeyState(VK_LCONTROL);
                if ((nVirtKey & SHIFTED) == 0)             // If left control
                    vkKeys[VK_LCONTROL] = false;
                nVirtKey = GetKeyState(VK_RCONTROL);
                if ((nVirtKey & SHIFTED) == 0)             // If right control
                    vkKeys[VK_RCONTROL] = false;
                break;
        }
        InvalidateRect(hwnd, NULL, TRUE);                  // Force WM_PAINT
        return 0;
        break;
```

Listing 2.15. Key down and key up message handlers.

Each time a key is pressed or released, the Boolean value in vkKeys is changed to reflect the new key state. To test a key, all we need to do is look at the key's corresponding entry in the vkKeys array. The key's index into the array corresponds to its virtual key code. Virtual key codes are different from the character codes we get from WM_CHAR messages. A virtual key code is assigned by Windows. Each key on the keyboard has an assigned virtual key code. For a complete list of virtual key codes, look in the WinUser.h file, which is located in "C:Program Files (x86)\Microsoft SDKs\Windows\v7.0A\Include" on Windows 7 computers. Listing 2.16 is a partial list.

```
#define VK_SHIFT 0x10
#define VK_CONTROL 0x11
#define VK_ESCAPE 0x1B
#define VK_SPACE 0x20
#define VK_LEFT 0x25                                       // Arrow keys
#define VK_UP 0x26
#define VK_RIGHT 0x27
#define VK_DOWN 0x28
```

2. Windows Programming Fundamentals

```
/*
 * VK_0 - VK_9 are the same as ASCII '0' - '9' (0x30 - 0x39)
 * 0x40 : unassigned
 * VK_A - VK_Z are the same as ASCII 'A' - 'Z' (0x41 - 0x5A)
 */

/*
 * VK_L* & VK_R*: left and right Alt, Ctrl and Shift virtual keys.
 * Used only as parameters to GetAsyncKeyState() and GetKeyState().
 * No other API or message will distinguish left and right keys in this way.
 */
#define VK_LSHIFT 0xA0
#define VK_RSHIFT 0xA1
#define VK_LCONTROL 0xA2
#define VK_RCONTROL 0xA3
#define VK_LMENU 0xA4
#define VK_RMENU 0xA5

#define VK_NUMPAD0 0x60
...
#define VK_NUMPAD9 0x69

#define VK_F1 0x70
...
#define VK_F12 0x7B
```

Listing 2.16. Virtual key codes.

To test the state of a specific key—say, for example, the right arrow key—we could do something like in Listing 2.17.

```
if (vkKeys[VK_RIGHT])
    // Right arrow currently pressed
```

Listing 2.17. Testing for the right arrow key press.

Not all keyboards are the same. Some keyboards limit the number of keys that may be pressed simultaneously and some key combinations may not be supported. We can write a little program for testing key combinations. The program displays a "T" if the corresponding key is currently down and "F" if the key is up. In Figure 2.8, we see the output of our program and the result of pressing and holding the "G," "H," "J," and "K" keys, in that order. The two Ts represent the key states for the "G" and "H" keys. The lower case "h" in the top left corner is the last key press entered. As we can see in this picture, the "J" and "K" keys had no effect. The supported key combinations may differ from keyboard to keyboard. This is a very important point to remember when we are designing the input scheme for our game. The best approach is to allow the user to select the keys they wish to use.

The complete keyboard test program with WM_KEYDOWN and WM_KEYUP message handlers is available for download as "Keys Down" from www.programming2dgames.com.

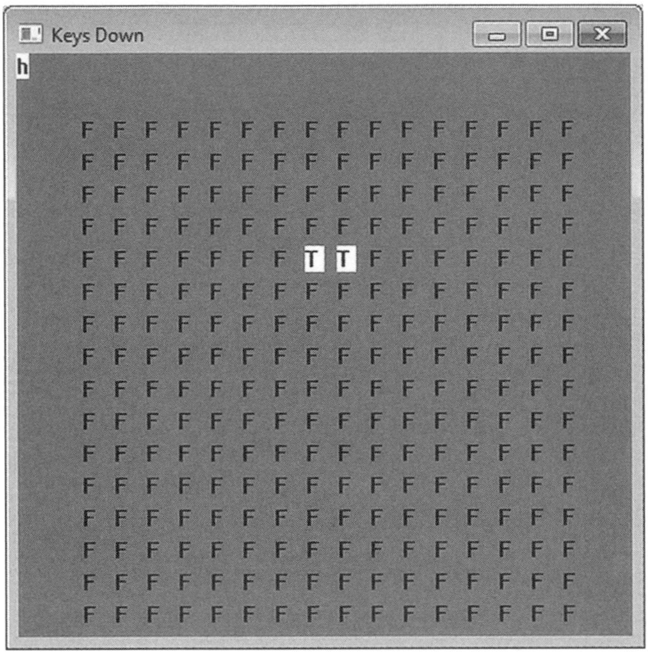

Figure 2.8. KEYDOWN example.

Other functions exist that may be used to read the keyboard. Some of them, such as `GetAsyncKeyState`, are popular choices according to many online game programming sites. Caution would be advised when using any of these other methods. `GetAsyncKeyState`, for example, does not mix well with other Windows applications. It reads the current state of the keyboard even if our application does not have input focus. That would cause our game to respond to key presses entered into a different application. Do thorough research before using any new functions.

▌ 2.5 Using a Mutex to Prevent Multiple Instances

If the person playing our game has had a few too many caffeinated drinks, he or she may get impatient if the game does not start immediately, and he or she may try to start it again. This may result in multiple instances of the game running at the same time. Running multiple instances would use more system resources and might interfere with the performance of our game. The user might not realize multiple instances were running, especially if the game is running in full-screen mode. To prevent multiple instances of our game, we can use a mutex. A *mutex* is an object that may be owned by only one thread at a time. If we create a mutex when our game starts, then any subsequent attempts to create the same mutex will fail. The mutex is created with a call to the `CreateMutex` function. Let's write a function that checks for existing instances of our game and prevents duplicates (Listing 2.18).

```
//==========================================================================
// Checks for another instance of the current application
// Returns: true if another instance is found
//          false if this is the only one
//==========================================================================
bool AnotherInstance()
{
    HANDLE ourMutex;
    // Attempt to create a mutex using our unique string
    ourMutex = CreateMutex(NULL, true,
            "Use_a_different_string_here_for_each_program_48161-XYZZY");
    if (GetLastError() == ERROR_ALREADY_EXISTS)
        return true;            // Another instance was found

    return false;               // We are the only instance
}
```

Listing 2.18. Using a mutex.

▌ 2.6 Multitasking in Windows

Windows is like a conductor of an orchestra. Everything that happens—every program, every process, every task—is controlled by Windows. For this discussion, we will use the term *thread* to describe any task that Windows is trying to perform. There may be other applications running at the same time as our game plus Windows has many processes of its own that are running. All of these programs and processes appear to run at the same time. But how is this possible if there is only one CPU? The answer is *time slicing*, or preemptive multithreading, or whatever we want to call it. It works like this: Windows maintains a queue of threads that want to run. It starts one thread, lets it run for a very short amount of time, suspends the current thread, then starts the next. This process is repeated for all running threads. The exact length of each time slice varies depending on a number of factors. Times of 1 to 20 milliseconds per slice are typical.

In systems with multiple and/or multicored CPUs, it is possible to have more than one thread running at the same time; but even in a quad core system with hyperthreading, there is only room for eight threads. In a typical Windows system, there are dozens of threads running at any given time, so preemptive multithreading is still required.

The multitasking nature of Windows means our game will only be allowed to run in short time slices. We also have very limited control over when the next time slice will occur. This will present some timing issues for games that need smooth animation. We will see how to deal with these issues in later chapters.

Chapter Review

In this chapter we created a Windows version of "Hello World." Then we learned how to get input from the keyboard and how to prevent multiple instances of a program from running.

We also discussed how Windows does multitasking. Here are the main points:

- We created and configured a project in Visual Studio.

- We learned that `WinMain` is the starting point for a Windows application.

- We learned about registering a `Window` class and the `WNDCLASSEX` structure.

- We saw how to use the `CreateWindow` function to create the window and what its parameters do.

- We learned about Windows messages, how to write a message loop, and how to use `PeekMessage` to check for new messages.

- We created a function named `WinProc` to process Windows messages.

- We learned how to use the `WM_CHAR` message to read character input.

- We learned how to use `WM_KEYDOWN` and `WM_KEYUP` messages to use a keyboard like a game controller.

- We wrote a function that can test for a currently running instance of our program.

- We learned that Windows uses multitasking to run programs in short time slices.

Review Questions

1. What is the starting point for a Windows application?

2. What is the role of the `lpfnWndProc` member of the `WNDCLASSEX` structure?

3. What style is most commonly used for the `dsStyle` parameter of the `CreateWindow` function for windowed games?

4. What style value is the `dsStyle` parameter set to for full-screen games?

5. If `hwnd` is equal to `NULL`, does the following if statement display true or false?

```
if(hwnd)
    std::cout << "true";
else
    std::cout << "false";
```

6. How does Windows communicate with our program?

7. When does the message loop end?

8. What happens to messages our program ignores?

9. What is the `WM_CHAR` message used for?

10. What is a virtual key code?

Exercises

1. Modify the "Hello World" program shown in Figure 2.1 so it displays "Hello World by:" followed by your name.

2. Which key presses result in a "beep" from the PC speaker from Listing 2.14?

3. Use the `keyboard2` program shown in Figure 2.8 to test keyboard input.

   a. What is the maximum number of simultaneous key presses allowed?

   b. List key combinations that do not work (maximum of five).

Examples

All examples are available for download from www.programming2dgames.com.

- *Hello World.* A complete Windows application that displays "Hello World" in the title of a window.

  – Demonstrates Windows programming fundamentals.

- *Character Input.* Displays the character typed on the keyboard.

  – Uses the `WM_CHAR` message to get the keyboard input.

- *Keys Down.* Displays a grid that represents the current key press state of every key on the keyboard.

  – Uses the `WM_KEYDOWN` and `WM_KEYUP` messages to determine the state of the keys on a keyboard.

- *Prevent Multiple.* A windows application that allows only one running instance of itself.

  – Demonstrates using a mutex to prevent multiple instances of a program.

3 Introduction to DirectX

3.1 Introduction to DirectX

DirectX is an application programming interface (API) for writing programs that need high performance graphics, sound, or specialized interaction with peripheral devices. The code in this book uses DirectX9, which is compatible with Windows XP, Windows Vista, Windows 7 and Windows 8. (DirectX 9 is also the version used by the Xbox 360, but running our games on an Xbox 360 would require an Xbox 360 Development Kit, which is only available to registered developers.) There are newer versions of DirectX available, so the question might be asked, "Why not use the latest version?" The reason is all about the operating systems used by our target audience. Windows XP continues to maintain a very large share of the PC operating systems in use. The newer versions of DirectX are not compatible with Windows XP. That means XP users would not be able to enjoy our games if we used a newer DirectX version. There are some features in the newer versions of DirectX that we could take advantage of when writing our games, but nothing that we can't do with a little extra coding in DirectX9.

In order to write DirectX applications, we need the Microsoft DirectX SDK installed on the computer. The DirectX SDK is available as a free download from Microsoft at http://msdn.microsoft.com/directx. The SDK includes support for DirectX9 and later versions.

3.2 Initializing DirectX

In order to successfully compile the following code, the `d3d9.h` header file and the `d3d9.lib` library file are required. The first step in writing a DirectX application is to create a `Direct3D` object and get an interface to it. The `Direct3DCreate9` function does just that.

```
IDirect3D9 * Direct3DCreate9(
    UINT SDKVersion
);
```

The `SDKVersion` parameter should be `D3D_SDK_VERSION`. The value of `D3D_SDK_VERSION` is set by the DirectX header files included in the application and is used to ensure that the version of DirectX used during compiling matches the runtime DLLs installed on the target machine. A typical call might look like the code in Listing 3.1.

```
// Initialize Direct3D
direct3d = Direct3DCreate9(D3D_SDK_VERSION);
if (direct3d == NULL)
    throw(GameError(gameErrorNS::FATAL_ERROR, "Error initializing
            Direct3D"));
```

Listing 3.1. Initializing Direct3D.

`Direct3DCreate9` returns a pointer to an `IDirect3D9` interface if it is successful; otherwise, `NULL` is returned. Before our program exits, we must call `direct3d->Release()`. Failure to do so will result in a memory leak. See Section 3.6 for more details.

▐ 3.3 Creating a Device

The second step in writing a DirectX application is to call the `CreateDevice` function. This function returns a working device interface as described by the parameters:

```
HRESULT CreateDevice(
    UINT Adapter,
    D3DDEVTYPE DeviceType,
    HWND hFocusWindow,
    DWORD BehaviorFlags,
    D3DPRESENT_PARAMETERS *pPresentationParameters,
    IDirect3DDevice9 **ppReturnedDeviceInterface
);
```

The parameters are:

- `Adapter`. Number of the display adapter to use. `D3DADAPTER_DEFAULT` is used to specify the primary display adapter.

- `DeviceType`. The valid values are members of the `D3DDEVTYPE` enumerated type. We will make use of two types:

  - `D3DDEVTYPE_REF`. Implements the Direct3D features in software. This is useful for testing purposes only. It will only work on systems that have the DirectX SDK installed, so it should never be used in release code. The `d3dref9.dll` file will need to be installed to use this type. On Windows XP, it will be installed by the DirectX SDK in the Windows\System32 folder. On Windows Vista and 7, it is typically not installed by the DirectX SDK. Copy `d3dref9.dll` into the project folder and it should work. The file may typically be found in "Program Files (x68)\Microsoft DirectX SDK (Month Year)\ Developer Runtime\x86" or a similar name depending on the installation.

- `D3DDEVTYPE_HAL`. Specifies hardware rasterization. If `CreateDevice` fails when `D3DDEVTYPE_HAL` is specified, it means the adapter does not support hardware graphics acceleration, at which point we can politely inform users that they will not be able to play our game until they get a better graphics card.

Rasterization *is the process of converting a graphic shape into pixels (dots) for display.*

- `hFocusWindow`. The focus window informs Direct3D that an application has switched from foreground mode to background mode. For windowed-only applications, this parameter may be `NULL`. We will normally fill in this parameter with the handle to our window.

- `BehaviorFlags`. A wide range of possible flags are available for use but only two are really applicable for our use:

  - `D3DCREATE_HARDWARE_VERTEXPROCESSING`. Specifies that vertex processing be performed by the graphics hardware.

  - `D3DCREATE_SOFTWARE_VERTEXPROCESSING`. Specifies that vertex processing be performed by software run by the system CPU.

Hardware vertex processing will only work if the hardware supports it. We will see how to test the hardware capabilities a little later.

This is not the same thing as hardware rasterization, which we specified earlier.

For now, we will specify software vertex processing. On some systems when DirectX debugging is enabled, the compiler will report a "Direct3D9 (ERROR) ASSERTION FAILED!" when using software vertex processing. After extensive online research we feel safe in ignoring this error report. It is apparently the result of a video card driver that is not 100% compliant with the DirectX specifications.

A vertex *is a point in 3D space described by location, color, texture, and other attributes.*

- *pPresentationParameters. A pointer to a D3DPRESENT_PARAMETERS structure that specifies properties for the device to be created. We will use a separate function to fill this structure (see our initD3Dpp() function below).

- **ppReturnedDeviceInterface. This is a return value. It contains the address of a pointer to the created device.

If CreateDevice succeeds, it returns D3D_OK. If it fails, one of the following error codes is returned: D3DERR_DEVICELOST, D3DERR_INVALIDCALL, D3DERR_NOTAVAILABLE, D3DERR_OUTOFVIDEOMEMORY. A call to CreateDevice and initD3Dpp might look like Listing 3.2.

```
    initD3Dpp();          // Initialize D3D presentation parameters
    // Create Direct3D device
    result = direct3d->CreateDevice(
        D3DADAPTER_DEFAULT,
        D3DDEVTYPE_HAL,
        hwnd,
        D3DCREATE_SOFTWARE_VERTEXPROCESSING,
        &d3dpp,
        &device3d);

    if (FAILED(result))
        throw(GameError(gameErrorNS::FATAL_ERROR,
            "Error creating Direct3D device"));
}
//=============================================================================
// Initialize D3D presentation parameters
//=============================================================================
void Graphics::initD3Dpp()
{
    try{
        ZeroMemory(&d3dpp, sizeof(d3dpp));    // Fill the structure with 0
        // Fill in the parameters we need
        d3dpp.BackBufferWidth   = width;
        d3dpp.BackBufferHeight  = height;
        if(fullscreen)                                 // If fullscreen
            d3dpp.BackBufferFormat  = D3DFMT_X8R8G8B8; // 24-bit color
        else
            d3dpp.BackBufferFormat  = D3DFMT_UNKNOWN;  // Use desktop
                                                       // setting
        d3dpp.BackBufferCount   = 1;
        d3dpp.SwapEffect        = D3DSWAPEFFECT_DISCARD;
        d3dpp.hDeviceWindow     = hwnd;
        d3dpp.Windowed          = (!fullscreen);
        d3dpp.PresentationInterval   = D3DPRESENT_INTERVAL_IMMEDIATE;
    } catch(...)
    {
        throw(GameError(gameErrorNS::FATAL_ERROR,
            "Error initializing D3D presentation parameters"));
    }
}
```

Listing 3.2. Creating a DirectX device.

When checking the return status of DirectX methods, always use the predefined macros `FAILED`
or `SUCCEEDED`. *Never look for specific return values, including* `D3D_OK`. *To test for an error,
use* `if (FAILED(status));` *to test for success, use* `if (SUCCEEDED(status))`, *where*
`status` *is the value returned from the DirectX method.*

Before our program exits, we must call `device3d->Release()`. Failure to do so will
result in a memory leak. See Section 3.6 later in this chapter for more details.

3.4 Clearing a Display Buffer

If all went well, DirectX is initialized and the `device3d` pointer is pointing to the Direct3D
device. We may now use the device to draw our game graphics. For now, we will simply fill
the window with a solid color by using the `Clear` function. The syntax of the `Clear` function
is:

```
HRESULT Clear(
    DWORD Count,
    const D3DRECT *pRects,
    DWORD Flags,
    D3DCOLOR Color,
    float Z,
    DWORD Stencil
);
```

The parameters are:

- `Count`. The number of rectangles to clear, as listed in the array pointed to by
  `pRects`. Must be set to 0 if `pRects` is `NULL`.

- `pRects`. Pointer to an array of `D3DRECT` structures that describe the rectangles to
  clear. To clear the entire buffer, set `pRects` to `NULL` and `Count` to 0.

- `Flags`. One or more flags defined in `D3DCLEAR` that identify the type of surface
  to clear. We will always use `D3DCLEAR_TARGET`, which says we want to clear the
  buffer.

- `Color`. The RGB (red, green, blue) color value to fill the target with. DirectX has
  some predefined macros that make it easier to construct RGB colors. `D3DCOLOR_
  XRGB(0,255,0)` creates a solid RGB color using the specified values for red, green,
  and blue. Each color may be a number from 0 through 255. This example would
  create bright green.

- `Z`. Specifies the *z* value to fill the depth buffer with as a float number from 0 to 1.
  We do not use depth buffers, so 0.0f will do just fine.

- `Stencil`. Specifies the value to fill the stencil buffer with as a number from 0 to
  2^{n-1} (*n* is the bit depth of the stencil buffer). We do not use stencil buffers, so 0 will
  do. Listing 3.3 is what the actual call looks like.

```
device3d->Clear(0, NULL, D3DCLEAR_TARGET, D3DCOLOR_XRGB(0,255,0), 0.0f, 0);
```

Listing 3.3. Clearing the display buffer.

The `Clear` function is accessed through our `device3d` pointer that was returned by the `CreateDevice` function we called earlier.

The `->` operator in C++ is used to access members via a pointer. In this case, `device3d` is a pointer that points to the Direct3D device. We can access any of the member functions in the device by using `device3d->` . In Visual Studio, a code completion window will pop up as soon as we type `device3d->`. All of the available methods are listed.

■ 3.5 Page Flipping

Now we can display the cleared rectangle. To draw the graphics in our game, we will employ a technique known as *page flipping*. With page flipping, we draw to an area of memory that is not currently being displayed. When we have constructed one complete frame, we flip the offscreen and visible buffers. This is done to prevent tearing or distortion of the display. If we were drawing directly to the displayed buffer, we would occasionally see partially erased or partially complete drawings, as shown in Figure 3.1. With page flipping, we complete the drawing before displaying, so no tearing is possible.

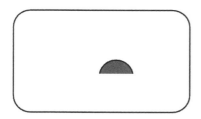

We will refer to the offscreen memory as the *back buffer*. Earlier in the `initD3Dpp` function, we set the `SwapEffect` presentation parameter to `D3DSWAPEFFECT_DISCARD`. This tells Direct3D to discard the contents of the visible buffer when it presents the back buffer as the display. Discarding the old contents of the display buffer is the highest performance mode of page flipping. All that is required is that we create the new back buffer from scratch each time, which we would normally do anyway. Figure 3.2 shows what the buffers might look like before and after flipping.

Figure 3.1. Partial image displayed.

The `Present` function in DirectX does page flipping. Here is the syntax:

```
HRESULT Present(
    const RECT    *PSourceRect,
    const RECT    *pDestRect,
    HWND          hDestWindowOverride,
    const RGNDATA *pDirtyRegion
);
```

We will use `NULL` for all four parameters. In order to be thorough in our coverage, here are the descriptions of the parameters:

- `pSourceRect`. Set to `NULL` to present the entire source rectangle. If a swap chain was created with `D3DSWAPEFFECT_COPY` then set to the address of a `RECT` structure that contains the source rectangle.

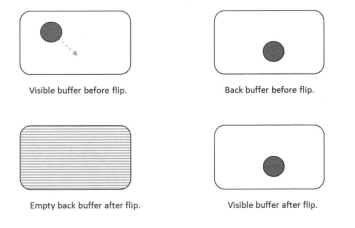

Visible buffer before flip.　　　　Back buffer before flip.

Empty back buffer after flip.　　　Visible buffer after flip.

Figure 3.2. The buffers before and after page flipping.

- pDestRect. Set to NULL to fill the entire destination rectangle. If a swap chain was created with D3DSWAPEFFECT_COPY then set to the address of a RECT structure containing the destination rectangle.

- hDestWindowOverride. A handle to the destination window. If NULL, the hWndDeviceWindow member of D3DPRESENT_PARAMETERS is used.

- pDirtyRegion. NULL unless a swap chain was created with D3DSWAPEFFECT_ COPY. If not NULL, the value specifies the minimal set of pixels that need to be updated and is expressed in back buffer coordinates.

Listing 3.4 is what a typical call will look like.

```
result = device3d->Present(NULL, NULL, NULL, NULL);
```

Listing 3.4. Performing a page flip.

After the call to Present, the former back buffer is now the visible buffer and the former visible buffer is now the back buffer.

3.6 A Clean Exit

Some of the DirectX methods we use require some housekeeping when we are finished with them. In order to free the memory and resources reserved by the previous code, we need to call device3d->Release() and direct3d->Release(). Always release resources in the opposite order of how they were created. It is also important that we do not attempt to call the Release() method on a resource that has not been created.

A simple test of the device pointer will prevent an invalid call to `Release()` (Listing 3.5).

```
if(device3d != NULL)
        device3d->Release();
```

Listing 3.5. Releasing a device.

This is a common operation, so defining a macro might be in order (Listing 3.6).

```
// Safely release pointer referenced item
#define SAFE_RELEASE(ptr)       { if(ptr) { (ptr)->Release(); (ptr)=NULL; } }
```

Listing 3.6. A macro that safely releases a device.

With our new macro, we can write a function to safely release our resources, like in Listing 3.7.

```
//===========================================================================
// Release all
//===========================================================================
void Graphics::releaseAll()
{
    SAFE_RELEASE(device3d);
    SAFE_RELEASE(direct3d);
}
```

Listing 3.7. Releasing resources.

We also need to delete any memory that was reserved with the *new* operator. Listing 3.8 shows a macro that will safely perform the delete.

```
// Safely delete pointer referenced item
#define SAFE_DELETE(ptr)        { if (ptr) { delete (ptr); (ptr)=NULL; } }
```

Listing 3.8. A macro that safely deletes.

We will place our macros in `constants.h` file along with other globally-defined game constants.

A memory leak occurs when a program reserves memory and does not release it.

Visual Studio has the ability to detect memory leaks when we build and run debug versions. To enable this feature, we need to add a few lines of code to `winmain.cpp` (Listing 3.9).

```
#define _CRTDBG_MAP_ALLOC        // For detecting memory leaks
#include <stdlib.h>              // For detecting memory leaks
#include <crtdbg.h>              // For detecting memory leaks
//-----------------------------------------
// Starting point for a Windows application
int WINAPI WinMain(HINSTANCE hInstance,
                   HINSTANCE hPrevInstance,
                   LPSTR     lpCmdLine,
                   int       nCmdShow)
{
    // Check for memory leak if debug build
    #if defined(DEBUG) | defined(_DEBUG)
        _CrtSetDbgFlag( _CRTDBG_ALLOC_MEM_DF | _CRTDBG_LEAK_CHECK_DF );
    #endif
```

Listing 3.9. Detecting memory leaks.

When the program is built and run in debug mode, memory leaks will be displayed in the Visual Studio output window when the program is exited:

```
Detected memory leaks!
Dumping objects ->
```

▌ 3.7 The Graphics Class

We are going to create a `Graphics` class to hold all of the DirectX graphics code we have introduced in this chapter. This type of class is typically referred to as a wrapper class. The wrapper class will wrap the DirectX functions inside our own functions and will redefine the DirectX types with our own types. Our functions and types will be used in place of the DirectX equivalent everywhere else in our code. This will limit the use of DirectX specific code to our wrapper classes, which will make it easier to upgrade our code to use different APIs in the future.

In our object-oriented design, each class will be written in two files: a header `.h` file and a source `.cpp` file. The header file will contain the class declaration, function prototypes, variables, and constants. The source file will contain the bulk of the code. The DirectX defines and class declarations will be placed in `graphics.h`, as shown in Listing 3.10.

The source code for the functions is in `graphics.cpp`. The first two functions are the constructor and destructor. The constructor initializes the variables and the destructor calls the `releaseAll` function (Listing 3.11).

```cpp
// Programming 2D Games
// Copyright (c) 2011 by:
// Charles Kelly
// Chapter 3 graphics.h v1.0
#ifndef _GRAPHICS_H            // Prevent multiple definitions if this
#define _GRAPHICS_H            // file is included in more than one place
#define WIN32_LEAN_AND_MEAN
#ifdef _DEBUG
#define D3D_DEBUG_INFO
#endif
#include <d3d9.h>
#include "constants.h"
#include "gameError.h"
// DirectX pointer types
#define LP_3DDEVICE LPDIRECT3DDEVICE9
#define LP_3D       LPDIRECT3D9
// Color defines
#define COLOR_ARGB DWORD
#define SETCOLOR_ARGB(a,r,g,b) \
    ((COLOR_ARGB)((((a)&0xff)<<24)|(((r)&0xff)<<16)|(((g)&0xff)<<8)|
                               ((b)&0xff)))
class Graphics
{
private:
    // DirectX pointers and stuff
    LP_3D       direct3d;
    LP_3DDEVICE device3d;
    D3DPRESENT_PARAMETERS d3dpp;
    // Other variables
    HRESULT     result;        // Standard Windows return codes
    HWND        hwnd;
    bool        fullscreen;
    int         width;
    int         height;
    // (For internal engine use only. No user serviceable parts inside.)
    // Initialize D3D presentation parameters
    void    initD3Dpp();
public:
    // Constructor
    Graphics();
    // Destructor
    virtual ~Graphics();
    // Releases direct3d and device3d
    void    releaseAll();
    // Initialize DirectX graphics
    // hw = handle to window
    // width = width in pixels
    // height = height in pixels
    // Fullscreen = true for full screen, false for window
    // Throws GameError on error
    void    initialize(HWND hw, int width, int height, bool fullscreen);
    // Display the offscreen backbuffer to the screen
    HRESULT showBackbuffer();
};
#endif
```

Listing 3.10. The graphics.h file.

```
// Programming 2D Games
// Copyright (c) 2011 by:
// Charles Kelly
// Chapter 3 Graphics Class v1.0
// graphics.cpp
#include "graphics.h"
//=============================================================================
// Constructor
//=============================================================================
Graphics::Graphics()
{
    direct3d = NULL;
    device3d = NULL;
    fullscreen = false;
    width = GAME_WIDTH;     // Width & height are replaced in initialize()
    height = GAME_HEIGHT;
}
//=============================================================================
// Destructor
//=============================================================================
Graphics::~Graphics()
{
    releaseAll();
}
```

Listing 3.11. The `Graphics` class constructor and destructor.

The `releaseAll` function uses the `SAFE_RELEASE` macro to free the DirectX resources reserved (Listing 3.12).

```
//=============================================================================
// Release all
//=============================================================================
void Graphics::releaseAll()
{
    SAFE_RELEASE(device3d);
    SAFE_RELEASE(direct3d);
}
```

Listing 3.12. Releases the reserved resources.

The `initialize` function (Listing 3.13) initializes Direct3D and creates a Direct3D device. The parameters are:

- `hw`. Handle to the Windows device returned by our `CreateMainWindow` function in `winmain.cpp`.

- `w`. Width of the display buffer in pixels.

- h. Height of the display buffer in pixels.

- full. true for full screen, false for window.

```
//=============================================================================
// Initialize DirectX graphics
// Throws GameError on error
//=============================================================================
void Graphics::initialize(HWND hw, int w, int h, bool full)
{
    hwnd = hw;
    width = w;
    height = h;
    fullscreen = full;
    // Initialize Direct3D
    direct3d = Direct3DCreate9(D3D_SDK_VERSION);
    if (direct3d == NULL)
        throw(GameError(gameErrorNS::FATAL_ERROR,
                        "Error initializing Direct3D"));
    initD3Dpp();           // Init D3D presentation parameters
    // Create Direct3D device
    result = direct3d->CreateDevice(
        D3DADAPTER_DEFAULT,
        D3DDEVTYPE_HAL,
        hwnd,
        // Reports Direct3D9 (ERROR) ASSERTION FAILED! on some systems
        // But there is really no error
        D3DCREATE_SOFTWARE_VERTEXPROCESSING,
        // Does not work if graphics card lacks hardware vertex processing
        // D3DCREATE_HARDWARE_VERTEXPROCESSING
        &d3dpp,
        &device3d);
    if (FAILED(result))
        throw(GameError(gameErrorNS::FATAL_ERROR,
                        "Error creating Direct3D device"));
}
```

Listing 3.13. Initializes DirectX graphics.

The initD3Dpp function sets up the D3D presentation parameters (see Listing 3.14). It is called by initialize in Listing 3.13.

```
//=============================================================================
// Initialize D3D presentation parameters
//=============================================================================
void Graphics::initD3Dpp()
{
    try{
        ZeroMemory(&d3dpp, sizeof(d3dpp));      // Fill the structure with 0
        // Fill in the parameters we need
```

```
    d3dpp.BackBufferWidth   = width;
    d3dpp.BackBufferHeight  = height;
    if(fullscreen)                              // If fullscreen
        d3dpp.BackBufferFormat  = D3DFMT_X8R8G8B8;// 24-bit color
    else
        d3dpp.BackBufferFormat  = D3DFMT_UNKNOWN; // Use desktop setting
    d3dpp.BackBufferCount   = 1;
    d3dpp.SwapEffect        = D3DSWAPEFFECT_DISCARD;
    d3dpp.hDeviceWindow     = hwnd;
    d3dpp.Windowed          = (!fullscreen);
    d3dpp.PresentationInterval  = D3DPRESENT_INTERVAL_IMMEDIATE;
} catch(...)
{
    throw(GameError(gameErrorNS::FATAL_ERROR,
                    "Error initializing D3D presentation parameters"));
}
}
```

Listing 3.14. Initializes the D3D presentation parameters.

The showBackbuffer function does the page flipping to display the back buffer (Listing 3.15). In this chapter it also clears the back buffer to lime green. The call to device3d->Clear will be moved in later chapters.

```
//=============================================================================
// Display the backbuffer
//=============================================================================
HRESULT Graphics::showBackbuffer()
{
    result = E_FAIL;    // Default to fail, replace on success
    // (This function will be moved in later versions)
    // Clear the backbuffer to lime green
    device3d->Clear(0, NULL, D3DCLEAR_TARGET, D3DCOLOR_XRGB(0,255,0),
            0.0f, 0);
    // Display backbuffer to screen
    result = device3d->Present(NULL, NULL, NULL, NULL);
    return result;
}
```

Listing 3.15. Displays the offscreen buffer.

3.8 Our First DirectX Program

Let's create a project in Visual Studio so we can try all the methods we just covered. Follow the steps outlined in Chapter 2 to create a new empty project. Clear the checkbox labeled "Create directory for solution." Name the project "DirectX Window." Visual Studio will create a new folder named "DirectX Window."

Use Windows Explorer to copy the winmain.cpp file we created in Chapter 2 to the DirectX Window folder that was just created.

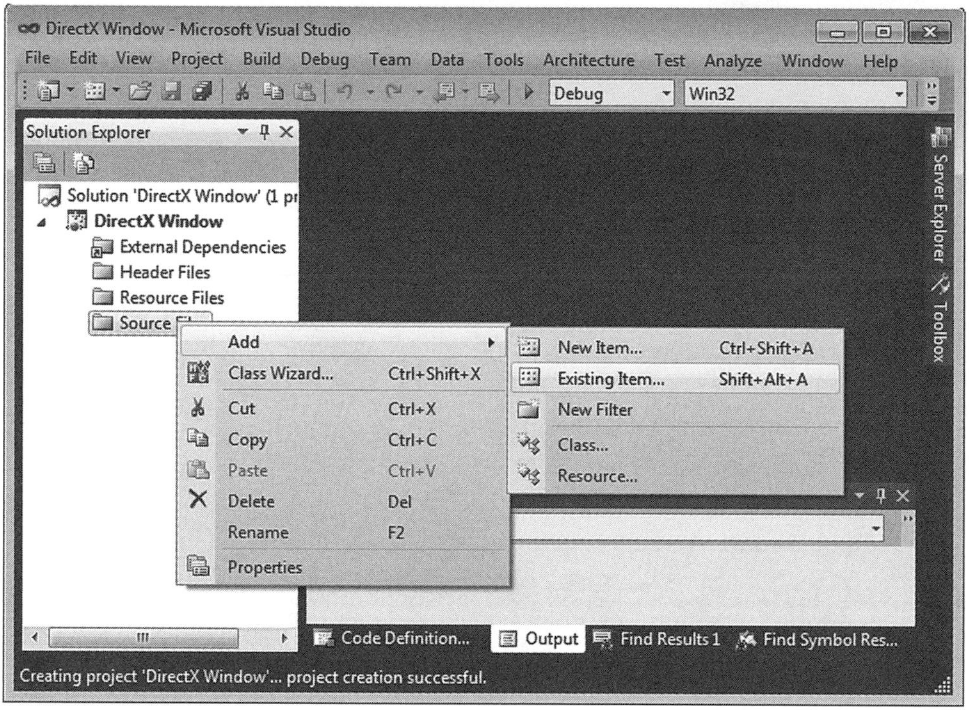

Figure 3.3. Adding an existing item.

Right click the "Source Files" folder in the "Solution Explorer" window. Point to "Add" then select "Existing Item..." (Figure 3.3). Select `winmain.cpp` and click the "Add" button. Double-click `winmain.cpp` in the "Solution Explorer" window to open `winmain.cpp` for editing. Change the APP_TITLE constant from "Hello World" to "DirectX Window."

3.8.1 Configuring a Project for DirectX

Before we can compile DirectX code, we need to configure our project.

Include directories. Right click the project name "DirectX Window" in the "Solution Explorer" and select "Properties."

- Change the "Configuration:" in the top left to "All Configurations."

- Select "VC++ Directories" under "Configuration Properties" in the left pane of the properties page.

- Click "Include Directories" in the right pane.

- Open the drop down menu and select "<Edit...>" (Figure 3.4).

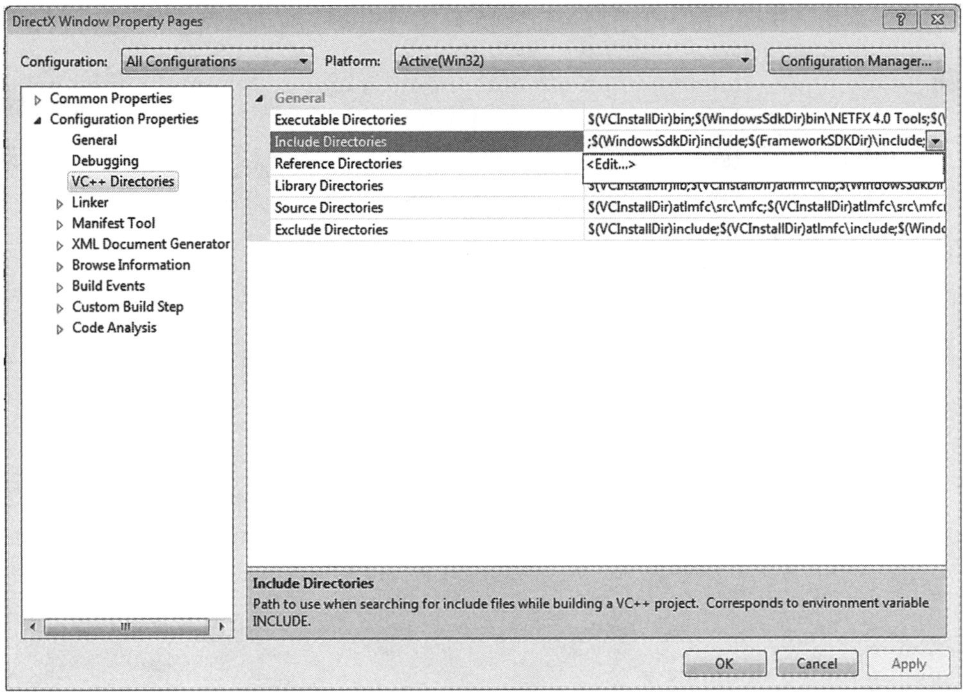

Figure 3.4. "Include Directories."

- Enter "$(DXSDK_DIR)\Include" as shown in Figure 3.5 then click "OK." This tells Visual Studio where to look for the DirectX include files.

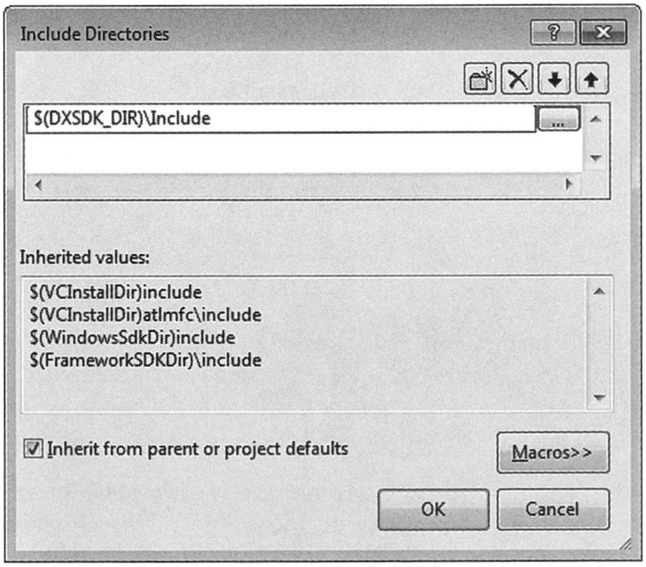

Figure 3.5. Adding the included directory.

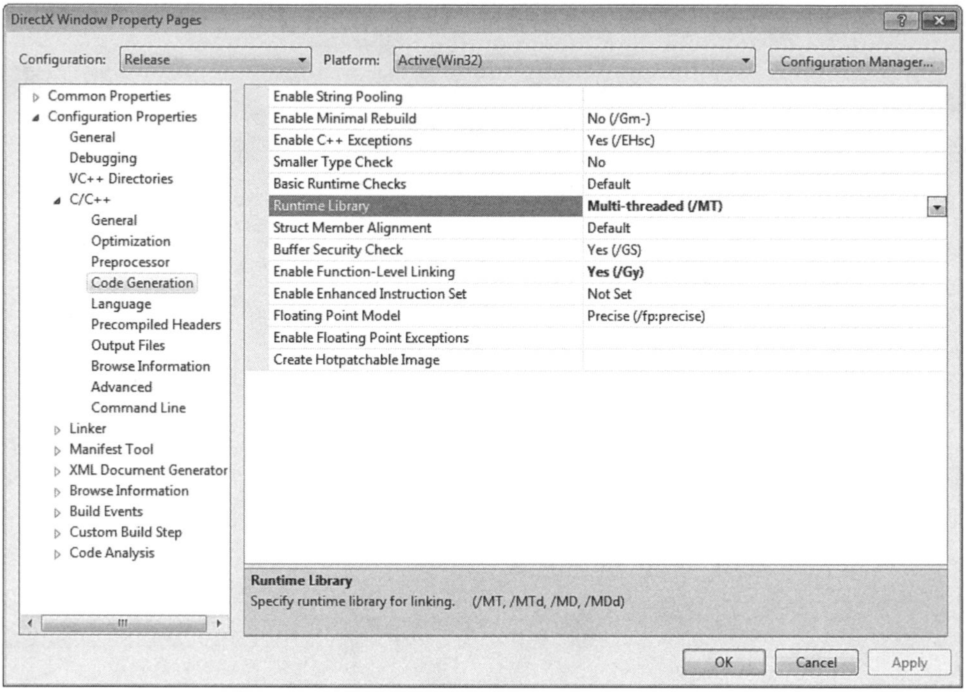

Figure 3.6. "Runtime Library."

Library directories. Next, we need to tell the linker where to look for the DirectX library files.

- Click "Library Directories" in the right pane.

- Open the drop down menu and select "<Edit...>."

- Enter "$(DXSDK_DIR)\Lib\x86" in the same manner as before. Click "OK" in the "Library Directories" window, then click "Apply" in the "DirectX Window Property Pages."

Runtime library.

- Change the "Configuration:" in the top left of the "DirectX Window Property Pages" to "Release" (see Figure 3.6).

- Expand C/C++ and select "Code Generation."

- Change the "Runtime Library" to "Multi-threaded (/MT)." This change will statically link in the C Runtime Libraries, which allows our program to run on systems that do not have the C Runtime Library DLL installed (MSVCP100.DLL or equivalent).

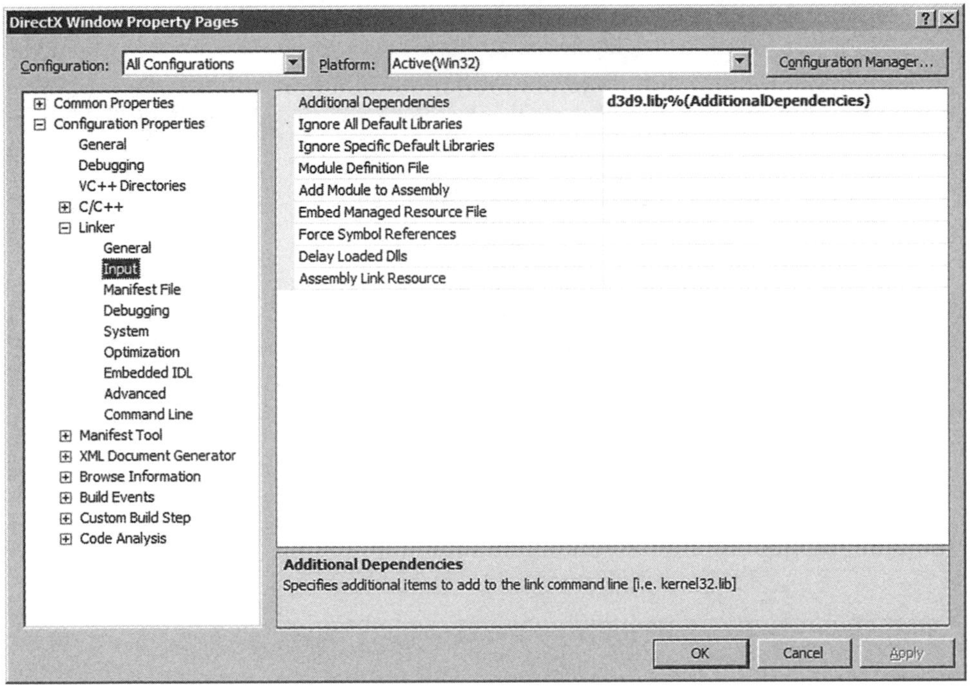

Figure 3.7. "Additional Dependencies" window.

Additional dependencies. Now we tell Visual Studio which DirectX libraries to include.

- Change the "Configuration:" in the top left to "All Configurations."

- Expand "Linker" in the left tab of the properties page.

- Select "Input" in the left pane.

- Click "Additional Dependencies" in the right pane.

- Open the drop down menu and select "<Edit...>."

- Enter "d3d9.lib" and click "OK" in the "Additional Dependencies" window; then click "OK" in the "DirectX Property Pages" window (see Figure 3.7).

The configuration is now complete for this project. In future projects, we will add more .lib files to the "Additional Dependencies" as we add more features from DirectX to our programs. Now we can add our DirectX code to the project.

- Right click the "Source Files" folder in the "Solution Explorer" window. Point to "Add," then select "New Item..."

- Select "C++ File (.cpp)" in the center window and replace "<Enter_name>" with "graphics" then click "Add." This creates a C++ source file where we can enter the code for graphics.cpp, shown earlier. Of course, in the interest of time and to avoid mistakes, just grab the code from the book's web site: www.programming 2dgames.com.

- Right click the "Header Files" folder in the "Solution Explorer" window. Point to "Add" then select "New Item..."

- Select "Header File (.h)" in the center window and replace "<Enter_name>" with "graphics" then click "Add." This creates a C++ header file where we can enter the code for graphics.h, shown earlier. Again, in the interest of time and to avoid mistakes, just grab the code from the book's web site.

- The only step remaining is to modify a few lines in winmain.cpp.

- Add #include graphics.h at the top of winmain.cpp (see Listing 3.16).

```
// Programming 2D Games
// Copyright (c) 2011 by:
// Charles Kelly
// Chapter 3 DirectX Window v1.0
// winmain.cpp
#define _CRTDBG_MAP_ALLOC        // For detecting memory leaks
#define WIN32_LEAN_AND_MEAN
#include <Windows.h>
#include <stdlib.h>              // For detecting memory leaks
#include <crtdbg.h>              // For detecting memory leaks
#include "graphics.h"
// Function prototypes
int WINAPI WinMain(HINSTANCE, HINSTANCE, LPSTR, int);
bool CreateMainWindow(HWND &, HINSTANCE, int);
LRESULT WINAPI WinProc(HWND, UINT, WPARAM, LPARAM);
// Global variable
HINSTANCE hinst;
```

Listing 3.16. Including graphics.h in winmain.cpp.

Create a Graphics pointer above the WinMain function (Listing 3.17).

```
// Graphics pointer
Graphics *graphics;
```

Listing 3.17. Graphics pointer.

Create the Graphics object and call the graphics->initialize function after CreateMainWindow (Listing 3.18). GAME_WIDTH, GAME_HEIGHT and FULLSCREEN are defined in constants.h (Listing 3.21).

```
//==============================================================================
// Starting point for a Windows application
// Parameters are:
//   hInstance. Handle to the current instance of the application
//   hPrevInstance. Always NULL, obsolete parameter
//   lpCmdLine. Pointer to null-terminated string of command line arguments
//   nCmdShow. Specifies how the window is to be shown
//==============================================================================
int WINAPI WinMain( HINSTANCE hInstance,    HINSTANCE hPrevInstance,
                    LPSTR     lpCmdLine,    int       nCmdShow)
{
    // Check for memory leak if debug build
    #if defined(DEBUG) | defined(_DEBUG)
        _CrtSetDbgFlag( _CRTDBG_ALLOC_MEM_DF | _CRTDBG_LEAK_CHECK_DF );
    #endif
    MSG  msg;
    HWND hwnd = NULL;
    // Create the window
    if (!CreateMainWindow(hwnd, hInstance, nCmdShow))
        return 1;
    try{
        // Create Graphics object
        graphics = new Graphics;
        // Initialize Graphics, throws GameError
        graphics->initialize(hwnd, GAME_WIDTH, GAME_HEIGHT, FULLSCREEN);
```

Listing 3.18. Initializing the graphics.

The main message loop is updated to call the `graphics->showBackbuffer()` function if no Windows messages need processing. When the loop exits, we delete the `Graphics` object to release the memory that was reserved (Listing 3.19).

```
        // Main message loop
        int done = 0;
        while (!done)
        {
            // PeekMessage, nonblocking method for checking for Windows
            // messages
            if (PeekMessage(&msg, NULL, 0, 0, PM_REMOVE))
            {
                // Look for quit message
                if (msg.message == WM_QUIT)
                    done = 1;
                // Decode and pass messages on to WinProc
                TranslateMessage(&msg);
                DispatchMessage(&msg);
            } else
                graphics->showBackbuffer();
        }
        SAFE_DELETE(graphics);   // Free memory before exit
        return msg.wParam;
    }
    catch(const GameError &err)
    {
        MessageBox(NULL, err.getMessage(), "Error", MB_OK);
    }
    catch(...)
```

```
    {
        MessageBox(NULL, "Unknown error occurred in game.", "Error", MB_OK);
    }
    SAFE_DELETE(graphics);    // Free memory before exit
    return 0;
}
```

Listing 3.19. Updated message loop.

The WinProc function is unchanged from our Chapter 2 examples. The CreateMainWindow function must be modified to return the handle to the Windows device. The Windows device handle is required by our Graphics::initialize function (Listing 3.13). The handle is returned via the hwnd reference parameter. The complete source code for the DirectX Window example is available for download from www.programming2dgames.com. For those readers who prefer to code in the examples from the book, Listing 3.26 at the end of the next section contains a complete example with support for fullscreen operation.

▌ 3.9 Fullscreen or Windowed

The code we created earlier contained the Boolean variable fullscreen in graphics.cpp. We sort of snuck that in without describing it. Let's take a look at it now and how to create a fullscreen application. In graphics.cpp the fullscreen variable is set by the full parameter in the initialize function. It is used in the initD3Dpp function in graphics.cpp to select the back buffer format (Listing 3.20).

```
//=============================================================================
// Initialize D3D presentation parameters
//=============================================================================
void initD3Dpp()
{
    try{
        ZeroMemory(&d3dpp, sizeof(d3dpp));      // Fill the structure with 0
        // Fill in the parameters we need
        d3dpp.BackBufferWidth   = width;
        d3dpp.BackBufferHeight  = height;
        if(fullscreen)                                  // If fullscreen
            d3dpp.BackBufferFormat  = D3DFMT_X8R8G8B8;  // 24-bit color
        else
            d3dpp.BackBufferFormat  = D3DFMT_UNKNOWN;   // Use desktop
                                                        // setting
        d3dpp.BackBufferCount   = 1;
        d3dpp.SwapEffect        = D3DSWAPEFFECT_DISCARD;
        d3dpp.hDeviceWindow     = hwnd;
        d3dpp.Windowed          = (!fullscreen);
        d3dpp.PresentationInterval  = D3DPRESENT_INTERVAL_IMMEDIATE;
    } catch(...)
    {
        throw(GameError(gameErrorNS::FATAL_ERROR,
                    "Error initializing D3D presentation parameters"));
    }
}
```

Listing 3.20. Fullscreen format.

```
//-----------------------------------------------
//                  Constants
//-----------------------------------------------
// window
const char CLASS_NAME[] = "Spacewar";
const char GAME_TITLE[] = "Game Engine Part 1";
const bool FULLSCREEN = false;                  // windowed or fullscreen
const UINT GAME_WIDTH =  640;                   // width of game in pixels
const UINT GAME_HEIGHT = 480;                   // height of game in pixels
```

Listing 3.21. Constants

```
// Initialize Graphics, throws GameError
graphics->initialize(hwnd, GAME_WIDTH, GAME_HEIGHT, FULLSCREEN);
```

Listing 3.22. Initializing graphics in `Winmain`.

If `fullscreen` is true, we are setting the format of the back buffer to `D3DFMT_X8R8G8B8`. That means 24 bits of color per pixel with no transparency (more on transparency later). When `fullscreen` is false, we set the back buffer format to `D3DFMT_UNKNOWN`, which tells DirectX to use the current desktop format. We also need to make a few changes in `winmain.cpp`. Let's put a constant in `constants.h` for setting windowed or fullscreen mode (Listing 3.21).

We will use the `FULLSCREEN` constant in our call to initialize in `winmain.cpp`, as shown in Listing 3.22. In the `CreateMainWindow` function of `winmain.cpp`, we need to add the highlighted code in Listing 3.23.

```
// Set up the screen in windowed or fullscreen mode?
DWORD style;
if (FULLSCREEN)
    style = WS_EX_TOPMOST | WS_VISIBLE | WS_POPUP;
else
    style = WS_OVERLAPPEDWINDOW;
// Create window
hwnd = CreateWindow(
    CLASS_NAME,              // Name of the window class
    APP_TITLE,              // Title bar text
    style,                  // Window style
    CW_USEDEFAULT,          // Default horizontal position of window
    CW_USEDEFAULT,          // Default vertical position of window
    WINDOW_WIDTH,           // Width of window
    WINDOW_HEIGHT,          // Height of the window
    (HWND) NULL,            // No parent window
    (HMENU) NULL,           // No menu
    hInstance,              // Handle to application instance
    (LPVOID) NULL);         // No window parameters
```

Listing 3.23. Adding fullscreen support in the `CreateMainWindow` function.

And that's it. If we set FULLSCREEN to true, we will get a screen full of bright green when we compile and run the program. WAIT! With a windowed application, we could simply close the window to exit the application. When the application is running in fullscreen mode, there is no close button to click on, so how do we exit? We could use the Windows system key combination Alt + F4 to quit the program.

Want to have a little fun with your friends while playing games online? Just tell them to press Alt + F4 to enable a new feature in the game.

A cleaner solution might be to use a key press to exit, such as the "Esc" key. We saw how to check for a WM_CHAR message in Chapter 2. We can add a few lines of code to our WinProc function in winmain.cpp to check for the "Esc" key. The ESC_KEY constant is defined in constants.h as VK_ESCAPE (Listing 3.24).

```cpp
//=============================================================================
// Window event callback function
//=============================================================================
LRESULT WINAPI WinProc( HWND hWnd, UINT msg, WPARAM wParam, LPARAM lParam )
{
    switch( msg )
    {
        case WM_DESTROY:
            // Tell Windows to kill this program
            PostQuitMessage(0);
            return 0;
        case WM_CHAR:                   // A character was entered by the
                                        // keyboard
            switch (wParam)             // The character is in wParam
            {
                case ESC_KEY:           // Exit program key
                    // Tell Windows to kill this program
                    PostQuitMessage(0);
                    return 0;
            }
    }
    return DefWindowProc( hWnd, msg, wParam, lParam );
}
```

Listing 3.24. Checking for the "Esc" key.

If we specify parameters that are not compatible with the display device, then CreateWindow will fail. For instance, if we change WINDOW_WIDTH to 1, the program will fail. That is because it is impossible to create a fullscreen window that is only one pixel wide. We will see how to test the device capabilities later in this chapter.

The fullscreen example from Chapter 3 may fail to run on systems with multiple monitors. We will see how to correct this issue in Section 4.2.3.

3.9.1 Client Size vs. Window Size

One final issue to address is the way windows are sized. When we create a window, the width and height parameters to the CreateWindow function include the window title bar and borders. This results in the client area of the window being slightly smaller than our desired size. The *client area* is the inside part of the window where our game graphics are drawn. We can correct this by getting the size of the client area from the created window and resizing the window so the client area is the size we want.

To get the size of the client area, we can use the Windows function GetClientRect:

```
BOOL WINAPI GetClientRect(
    HWND hWnd,
    LPRECT lpRect
);
```

The parameters are the window handle and a RECT structure to receive the client size. The top-left corner of the client area is always (0,0).

Once we know the size of the client area, we can calculate how much bigger the actual window needs to be to give us our desired client size. The new width and height will be:

$$\text{new width} = \text{desired width} + (\text{desired width} - \text{client width}),$$
$$\text{new height} = \text{desired height} + (\text{desired height} - \text{client height}).$$

With the new size calculated, we can use the MoveWindow function to resize the window.

```
BOOL WINAPI MoveWindow(
    HWND hWnd,
    int X,
    int Y,
    int nWidth,
    int nHeight,
    BOOL bRepaint
);
```

The parameters are:

- hWnd. The handle to the window.

- X. The new position of the left edge.

- Y. The new position of the top edge.

- nWidth. The new window width.

- nHeight. The new window height.

- bRepaint. The window is repainted if true and not repainted if false.

We will add the code from Listing 3.25 to CreateMainWindow in winmain.cpp to resize the window.

```
if(!FULLSCREEN)                     // If window
{
    // Adjust window size so client area is GAME_WIDTH x GAME_HEIGHT
    RECT clientRect;
    GetClientRect(hwnd, &clientRect);   // Get size of client area of window
    MoveWindow(hwnd,
               0,                                          // Left
               0,                                          // Top
               GAME_WIDTH+(GAME_WIDTH-clientRect.right),   // Right
               GAME_HEIGHT+(GAME_HEIGHT-clientRect.bottom), // Bottom
               TRUE);                                      // Repaint the
                                                           // window
}
```

Listing 3.25. Adjusting the window size.

A complete listing of our new `winmain.cpp` can be found in Listing 3.26.

```
// Programming 2D Games
// Copyright (c) 2011 by:
// Charles Kelly
// Chapter 3 DirectX Fullscreen v1.0
// winmain.cpp
#define _CRTDBG_MAP_ALLOC           // For detecting memory leaks
#define WIN32_LEAN_AND_MEAN
#include <Windows.h>
#include <stdlib.h>                 // For detecting memory leaks
#include <crtdbg.h>                 // For detecting memory leaks
#include "graphics.h"
// Function prototypes
int WINAPI WinMain(HINSTANCE, HINSTANCE, LPSTR, int);
bool CreateMainWindow(HWND &, HINSTANCE, int);
LRESULT WINAPI WinProc(HWND, UINT, WPARAM, LPARAM);
// Global variable
HINSTANCE hinst;
// Graphics pointer
Graphics *graphics;
//=============================================================================
// Starting point for a Windows application
//=============================================================================
int WINAPI WinMain( HINSTANCE hInstance, HINSTANCE hPrevInstance,
                    LPSTR lpCmdLine, int nCmdShow)
{
    // Check for memory leak if debug build
    #if defined(DEBUG) | defined(_DEBUG)
        _CrtSetDbgFlag( _CRTDBG_ALLOC_MEM_DF | _CRTDBG_LEAK_CHECK_DF );
    #endif
    MSG  msg;
    HWND hwnd = NULL;
    // Create the window
    if (!CreateMainWindow(hwnd, hInstance, nCmdShow))
        return 1;
    try{
        // Create Graphics object
```

```
        graphics = new Graphics;
        // Initialize Graphics, throws GameError
        graphics->initialize(hwnd, GAME_WIDTH, GAME_HEIGHT, FULLSCREEN);
        // Main message loop
        int done = 0;
        while (!done)
        {
            // PeekMessage, a non-blocking method for checking for Windows
            // messages
            if (PeekMessage(&msg, NULL, 0, 0, PM_REMOVE))
            {
                // Look for quit message
                if (msg.message == WM_QUIT)
                    done = 1;
                // Decode and pass messages on to WinProc
                TranslateMessage(&msg);
                DispatchMessage(&msg);
            } else
                graphics->showBackbuffer();
        }
        SAFE_DELETE(graphics);   // Free memory before exit
        return msg.wParam;
    }
    catch(const GameError &err)
    {
        MessageBox(NULL, err.getMessage(), "Error", MB_OK);
    }
    catch(...)
    {
        MessageBox(NULL, "Unknown error occurred in game.", "Error", MB_OK);
    }
    SAFE_DELETE(graphics);   // Free memory before exit
    return 0;
}
//=============================================================================
// Window event callback function
//=============================================================================
LRESULT WINAPI WinProc( HWND hWnd, UINT msg, WPARAM wParam, LPARAM lParam )
{
    switch( msg )
    {
        case WM_DESTROY:
            // Tell Windows to kill this program
            PostQuitMessage(0);
            return 0;
        case WM_CHAR:                  // A character was entered by the key
                                       // board
            switch (wParam)           // The character is in wParam
            {
                case ESC_KEY:         // Exit program key
                    // Tell Windows to kill this program
                    PostQuitMessage(0);
                    return 0;
            }
    }
    return DefWindowProc( hWnd, msg, wParam, lParam );
}
//=============================================================================
// Create the window
```

```
    // Returns: false on error
    //=============================================================================
    bool CreateMainWindow(HWND &hwnd, HINSTANCE hInstance, int nCmdShow)
    {
        WNDCLASSEX wcx;

        // Fill in the window class structure with parameters
        // that describe the main window.
        wcx.cbSize = sizeof(wcx);           // Size of structure
        wcx.style = CS_HREDRAW | CS_VREDRAW;// Redraw if size changes
        wcx.lpfnWndProc = WinProc;          // Points to window procedure
        wcx.cbClsExtra = 0;                 // No extra class memory
        wcx.cbWndExtra = 0;                 // No extra window memory
        wcx.hInstance = hInstance;          // Handle to instance
        wcx.hIcon = NULL;
        wcx.hCursor = LoadCursor(NULL,IDC_ARROW);   // Predefined arrow
        // Black background
        wcx.hbrBackground = (HBRUSH)GetStockObject(BLACK_BRUSH);
        wcx.lpszMenuName = NULL;            // Name of menu resource
        wcx.lpszClassName = CLASS_NAME;     // Name of window class
        wcx.hIconSm = NULL;                 // Small class icon

        // Register the window class
        // RegisterClassEx returns 0 on error
        if (RegisterClassEx(&wcx) == 0)     // If error
            return false;
        // Set up the screen in windowed or fullscreen mode?
        DWORD style;
        if (FULLSCREEN)
            style = WS_EX_TOPMOST | WS_VISIBLE | WS_POPUP;
        else
            style = WS_OVERLAPPEDWINDOW;
        // Create window
        hwnd = CreateWindow(
            CLASS_NAME,             // Name of the window class
            GAME_TITLE,             // Title bar text
            style,                  // Window style
            CW_USEDEFAULT,          // Default horizontal position of window
            CW_USEDEFAULT,          // Default vertical position of window
            GAME_WIDTH,             // Width of window
            GAME_HEIGHT,            // Height of the window
            (HWND) NULL,            // No parent window
            (HMENU) NULL,           // No menu
            hInstance,              // Handle to application instance
            (LPVOID) NULL);         // No window parameters
        // If there was an error creating the window
        if (!hwnd)
            return false;
        if(!FULLSCREEN)             // If window
        {
            // Adjust window size so client area is GAME_WIDTH x GAME_HEIGHT
            RECT clientRect;
            GetClientRect(hwnd, &clientRect);   // Get size of client area of
                                                // window
            MoveWindow(hwnd,
                        0,                                  // Left
                        0,                                  // Top
                        GAME_WIDTH+(GAME_WIDTH-clientRect.right),  // Right
```

```
                    GAME_HEIGHT+(GAME_HEIGHT-clientRect.bottom),// Bottom
                    TRUE);                                       // Repaint
                                                                 // the window
    }
    // Show the window
    ShowWindow(hwnd, nCmdShow);
    // Send a WM_PAINT message to the window procedure
    UpdateWindow(hwnd);
    return true;
}
```

Listing 3.26. New `winmain.cpp` with support for fullscreen graphics added.

▌ 3.10   Debug vs. Retail DLLs

In order for this program to build successfully, we need to add `d3dx9.lib` to the project. There is a retail version and a debug version of this library. Add the debug version as follows:

- Right click the project in the "Solution Explorer" window and select "Properties."

- Set the configuration to "Debug."

- Expand "Linker" in the left tab of the "Properties" page.

- Select "Input" in the left pane.

- Click "%(AdditionalDependencies)" in the right pane.

- Open the drop down menu and select "<Edit...>".

- Enter "d3dx9d.lib."

- Set the configuration to "Release" and repeat the above procedure, but this time enter "d3dx9.lib." The debug version of the library has an extra "d" at the end of the name. The debug library provides more detailed messages and performs extra code validation.

The DirectX SDK has the option of installing debug or retail versions of the D3D9 runtime. If the debug runtime is installed, we can switch between retail and debug versions from the DirectX control panel. The DirectX control panel is under Start/All Programs/ Microsoft DirectX SDK (June 2010)/DirectX Utilities/DirectX Control Panel. The Direct3D tab is where we select the version of the runtime.

▌ 3.11   Determining Device Capabilities

As mentioned previously in this chapter, it is possible for DirectX functions to fail if we specify parameters that are incompatible with the system hardware. This is normally only a concern with fullscreen applications and in most cases windowed applications can skip these steps. There are several DirectX functions we may use to get information about the hardware. The first step is to select the device. We will limit our coverage to display adapters, but the same techniques could be applied to any device type.

A display adapter is a physical device in the computer. It may be a peripheral card plugged into a system bus or integrated into the motherboard. A single graphics card may contain multiple adapters, as in the case of dual-headed displays. Determining the number of display adapters installed in a system is done with the function `IDirect3D9::GetAdapterCount();`. If the game is not going to support multiple monitor displays, skip this step and pass `D3DADAPTER_DEFAULT` as the parameter to those DirectX functions that require the adapter number. `GetAdapterCount()` returns the number of display adapters as an unsigned integer.

Each adapter supports multiple display modes. The function `IDirect3D9::Get AdapterModeCount` returns the number of display modes available for the specified adapter:

```
UINT GetAdapterModeCount(
        UINT Adapter,
        D3DFORMAT Format
);
```

The parameters are:

- `Adapter`. The number of the display adapter. Use `D3DADAPTER_DEFAULT` to specify the primary adapter.

- `Format`. The format of the surface type we want our game to use, as defined in `D3DFORMAT`.

And here are the format choices from `D3DFORMAT`, which are compatible with `GetAdapter ModeCount` and `EnumAdapterModes`:

- `D3DFMT_A1R5G5B5`. A 16-bit pixel format with 5 bits for each color.

- `D3DFMT_R5G6B5`. A 16-bit pixel format with 5 bits for red, 6 bits for green, and 5 bits for blue.

- `D3DFMT_A8R8G8B8`. A 32-bit ARGB pixel format with 8 bits for alpha and 8 bits for each color.

- `D3DFMT_X8R8G8B8`. A 32-bit RGB pixel format with 8 bits for each color.

- `D3DFMT_A2B10G10R10`. A 32-bit pixel format using 10 bits for each color and 2 bits for alpha.

Once we have the number of display modes available for the desired format, we can use `IDirect3D9::EnumAdapterModes` to get details about each mode and determine if hardware acceleration is available:

```
HRESULT EnumAdapterModes(
        UINT Adapter,
        D3DFORMAT Format,
        UINT Mode,
        D3DDISPLAYMODE *pMode
);
```

The parameters are:

- Adapter. The number of the display adapter. Use D3DADAPTER_DEFAULT to specify the primary adapter.

- Format. The format of the surface we want our game to use from D3DFORMAT, as listed above.

- Mode. Display mode number between 0 and the value returned by GetAdapter ModeCount − 1.

- *pMode: Pointer to a D3DDISPLAYMODE structure that is filled in by the function with details about the mode.

The HRESULT return value contains the following:

- If the adapter supports the display mode, D3D_OK is returned.

- If the Adapter parameter exceeds the number of display adapters in the system, D3DERR_INVALIDCALL is returned.

- If either surface format is not supported or if hardware acceleration is not available for the specified formats, D3DERR_NOTAVAILABLE is returned.

The D3DDISPLAYMODE structure is defined as

```
typedef struct D3DDISPLAYMODE {
    UINT        Width;
    UINT        Height;
    UINT        RefreshRate;
    D3DFORMAT   Format;
} D3DDISPLAYMODE, *LPD3DDISPLAYMODE;
```

The members are:

- Width. Screen width in pixels.

- Height. Screen height in pixels.

- RefreshRate. Refresh rate in hertz (cycles per second). A value of 0 indicates the adapter default.

- Format. Member of D3DFORMAT, as described above.

Let's add a new function to `graphics.cpp` to check the compatibility of an adapter (see Listing 3.27).

```
//=============================================================================
// Checks the adapter to see if it is compatible with the BackBuffer
// height, width, and refresh rate specified in d3dpp. Fills in the pMode
// structure with the format of the compatible mode, if found.
// Pre: d3dpp is initialized.
// Post: Returns true if compatible mode found and pMode structure is
// filled.
// Returns false if no compatible mode found.
//=============================================================================
bool Graphics::isAdapterCompatible()
{
    UINT modes = direct3d->GetAdapterModeCount(D3DADAPTER_DEFAULT,
                                        d3dpp.BackBufferFormat);
    for(UINT i=0; i<modes; i++)
    {
        result = direct3d->EnumAdapterModes( D3DADAPTER_DEFAULT,
                                        d3dpp.BackBufferFormat,
                                        i, &pMode);
        if( pMode.Height == d3dpp.BackBufferHeight &&
            pMode.Width  == d3dpp.BackBufferWidth &&
            pMode.RefreshRate >= d3dpp.FullScreen_RefreshRateInHz)
            return true;
    }
    return false;
}
```

Listing 3.27. A function to check adapter compatibility.

We must also define the pMode variable and function prototype in our graphics.h file. The pMode variable is declared as a private variable in the Graphics class:

```
class Graphics
{
private:
    // DirectX pointers and stuff
    LP_3D      direct3d;
    LP_3DDEVICE device3d;
    D3DPRESENT_PARAMETERS d3dpp;
    D3DDISPLAYMODE pMode;
```

The function prototype is added to the public section of the class:

```
    // Checks the adapter to see if it is compatible with the BackBuffer height,
    // width and refresh rate specified in d3dpp. Fills in the pMode structure with
    // the format of the compatible mode, if found.
    // Pre: d3dpp is initialized.
    // Post: Returns true if compatible mode found and pMode structure is filled.
    //       Returns false if no compatible mode found.
    bool    isAdapterCompatible();
```

We will call this function from our initialize function after the call to initD3Dpp(). If the game is set to run in fullscreen, we get the RefreshRate returned by isAdapterCompatible() and we set the d3dpp.FullScreen_RefreshRateInHz parameter with it. See Listing 3.28.

The last device capability we will test for is the ability to perform vertex processing in hardware. To determine if the device supports hardware vertex processing, we will use the `IDirect3D9::GetDeviceCaps` method:

```
HRESULT GetDeviceCaps(
    UINT Adapter,
    D3DDEVTYPE DeviceType,
    D3DCAPS9    *pCaps
);
```

The parameters are:

- `Adapter`. Number of the display adapter. Use `D3DADAPTER_DEFAULT` to specify the primary adapter.

- `DeviceType`. Member of `D3DDEVTYPE`.

- `*pCaps`. Pointer to a `D3DCAPS9` structure that is filled in by this function with the device capabilities.

We will add this function to our `initialize` function in `graphics.cpp`. If the device supports hardware vertex processing, we will use it. The new `initialize` function can be seen in Listing 3.28.

```
//=================================================================
// Initialize DirectX graphics
// Throws GameError on error
//=================================================================
void Graphics::initialize(HWND hw, int w, int h, bool full)
{
    hwnd = hw;
    width = w;
    height = h;
    fullscreen = full;
    // Initialize Direct3D
    direct3d = Direct3DCreate9(D3D_SDK_VERSION);
    if (direct3d == NULL)
        throw(GameError(gameErrorNS::FATAL_ERROR,
            "Error initializing Direct3D"));
    initD3Dpp();        // Init D3D presentation parameters
    if(fullscreen)      // If fullscreen mode
    {
        if(isAdapterCompatible())   // Is the adapter compatible
            // Set the refresh rate with a compatible one
            d3dpp.FullScreen_RefreshRateInHz = pMode.RefreshRate;
        else
            throw(GameError(gameErrorNS::FATAL_ERROR,
                            "The graphics device does not support the" \
                            "specified resolution and/or format."));
    }
    // Determine if graphics card supports harware texturing and lighting
    // and vertex shaders
```

```
    D3DCAPS9 caps;
    DWORD behavior;
    result = direct3d->GetDeviceCaps(D3DADAPTER_DEFAULT,
                                     D3DDEVTYPE_HAL, &caps);
    // If device doesn't support HW T&L or doesn't support 1.1 vertex
    // shaders in hardware, then switch to software vertex processing.
    if( (caps.DevCaps & D3DDEVCAPS_HWTRANSFORMANDLIGHT) == 0 ||
            caps.VertexShaderVersion < D3DVS_VERSION(1,1) )
        // Use software-only processing
        behavior = D3DCREATE_SOFTWARE_VERTEXPROCESSING;
    else
        // Use hardware-only processing
        behavior = D3DCREATE_HARDWARE_VERTEXPROCESSING;
    // Create Direct3D device
    result = direct3d->CreateDevice(
        D3DADAPTER_DEFAULT,
        D3DDEVTYPE_HAL,
        hwnd,
        behavior,
        &d3dpp,
        &device3d);
    if (FAILED(result))
        throw(GameError(gameErrorNS::FATAL_ERROR,
                        "Error creating Direct3D device"));
}
```

Listing 3.28. The new `Graphics::initialize` function.

Chapter Review

In this chapter, we introduced DirectX. We learned how to write a complete DirectX application that filled the window with a color. We created a `Graphics` class to hold all of our DirectX graphics code. We also learned how to determine the capabilities of a DirectX device. Here are the main points:

- The first step is using DirectX is to create a DirectX object using Direct3DCreate9.

- The second step is to create a device with the CreateDevice function.

- The Clear function can fill the window with a color.

- "Page flipping" is drawing to an offscreen buffer then making the offscreen buffer the visible buffer. The Present function does the page flipping.

- The Release method is used to free memory and resources reserved by DirectX functions.

- The Graphics class is our wrapper class for the DirectX graphics code.

- The Graphics::initialize function initializes DirectX graphics.

- The Graphics::showBackbuffer function does the page flip.

- We created and configured a DirectX project in Visual Studio.

- We learned how to create a fullscreen DirectX application.

- We wrote the `Graphics::isAdapterCompatible` function to see if the display adapter is compatible with our desired height, width, and refresh rate.

Review Questions

1. Which DirectX header file (`.h`) is required by the example code in this chapter?

2. Which DirectX library file (`.lib`) is required by the example code in this chapter?

3. Which DirectX function is used to initialize Direct3D?

4. What parameter value is assigned to the `Adapter` parameter of the `CreateDevice` function to use the primary display adapter?

5. What is rasterization?

6. What is a vertex?

7. What is the `SUCCEEDED` macro used for?

8. What parameter values would be used in `D3DCOLOR_XRGB(?,?,?)` to create the bright blue color?

9. Why do we use page flipping to display graphics?

10. What is a memory leak?

11. Each of our classes we create is contained in two files. Which file type contains the variables?

12. Which function in our `Graphics` class displays the back buffer?

Exercises

1. Modify this chapter's "DirectX Window" example program so the window color is dark blue (RGB value (0, 0, 128)) and the window is a different size. (Not all window sizes are valid. Try different size combinations until a working size is found.)

2. Modify this chapter's "DirectX Fullscreen" example program. Change the program to make it run in a window instead of in fullscreen mode so it will be easier to debug. Modify it so that pressing the space bar will exit the program.

3. Modify this chapter's "DirectX Window" example program so a new random window color will be displayed each time the space bar is pressed. Hints: Add a `backColor` variable of type `COLOR_ARGB` to the `Graphics` class. Modify the `showBackbuffer` function in the `Graphics` class to use the `backColor` variable when clearing the screen. Add the following function to the `graphics.h` file:

```
// Set color used to clear screen
void setBackColor(COLOR_ARGB c) {backColor = c;}
```

Examples

All examples are available for download from www.programming2dgames.com. The following is a list of what is available and what the examples show.

- *DirectX Window*. Creates a DirectX window application.

  - Contains a Visual Studio project configured for DirectX.

  - Demonstrates how to use the `Graphics` class to create a DirectX window.

- *DirectX Fullscreen*. Creates a fullscreen DirectX application.

  - Demonstrates how to use the `Graphics` class to create a fullscreen DirectX application.

- *DirectX Device Capabilities*. Displays a dialog box if the graphics device does not support the specified resolution and/or format.

  - Demonstrates how to use the `Graphics::isAdapterCompatible` function.

4 The Game Engine

4.1 The Game Engine, Part 1

Now would be a good time to begin incorporating the code we have introduced into a game engine. Our game engine will be an object-oriented design with a class for each major component. For part 1 of our game engine, we will include `Game`, `Graphics`, and `Input` classes. To create a game with our new game engine, we will create a class that inherits from the `Game` class. For example, if we wanted to create a Spacewar game we would create a new `Spacewar` class that inherits from the `Game` class, as shown in Figure 4.1.

The class diagram in Figure 4.1 was created in Visual Studio 2010 by right clicking on the project in the "Solution Explorer" window and selecting "View Class Diagram." The associations for graphics and input are displayed by expanding the `Game` class, right clicking on the property, and selecting "Show As Association."

4.2 The Game Class

The `Game` class will contain variables and functions that are common to many games. The `Game` class is just a starting point. The `Spacewar` class we create for our game inherits from the `Game` class, so it gets everything defined in the `Game` class. We can modify the functions and variables inherited and add new functions and variables if needed.

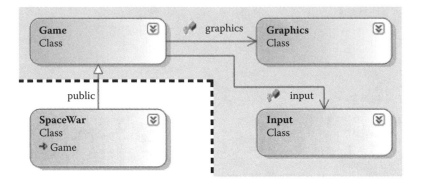

Figure 4.1. Class diagram of the game engine, part 1.

The Game class will have the ability to display graphics and get keyboard input because it will contain objects of the Input class and the Graphics class. The Game class declaration with variables and function prototypes is placed in the game.h file, as shown in Listing 4.1.

```cpp
// Programming 2D Games
// Copyright (c) 2011 by:
// Charles Kelly
// Chapter 4 game.h v1.0
#ifndef _GAME_H                 // Prevent multiple definitions if this
#define _GAME_H                 // file is included in more than one place.
#define WIN32_LEAN_AND_MEAN
#include <windows.h>
#include <Mmsystem.h>
#include "graphics.h"
#include "input.h"
#include "constants.h"
#include "gameError.h"
class Game
{
protected:
    // Common game properties
    Graphics *graphics;         // Pointer to Graphics
    Input    *input;            // Pointer to Input
    HWND     hwnd;              // Window handle
    HRESULT hr;                 // Standard return type
    LARGE_INTEGER timeStart;    // Performance Counter start value
    LARGE_INTEGER timeEnd;      // Performance Counter end value
    LARGE_INTEGER timerFreq;    // Performance Counter frequency
    float    frameTime;         // Time required for last frame
    float    fps;               // Frames per second
    DWORD    sleepTime;         // Milliseconds to sleep between frames
    bool     paused;            // True if game is paused
    bool     initialized;
public:
    // Constructor
    Game();
    // Destructor
```

```
    virtual ~Game();
    // Member functions
    // Window message handler
    LRESULT messageHandler( HWND hwnd, UINT msg, WPARAM wParam, LPARAM
                            lParam );
    // Initialize the game
    // Pre: hwnd is handle to window
    virtual void initialize(HWND hwnd);
    // Call run repeatedly by the main message loop in WinMain
    virtual void run(HWND);
    // Call when the graphics device was lost
    // Release all reserved video memory so graphics device may be reset
    virtual void releaseAll();
    // Recreate all surfaces and reset all entities
    virtual void resetAll();
    // Delete all reserved memory
    virtual void deleteAll();
    // Render game items
    virtual void renderGame();
    // Handle lost graphics device
    virtual void handleLostGraphicsDevice();
    // Return pointer to Graphics
    Graphics* getGraphics() {return graphics;}
    // Return pointer to Input
    Input* getInput()       {return input;}
    // Exit the game
    void exitGame()         {PostMessage(hwnd, WM_DESTROY, 0, 0);}
    // Pure virtual function declarations
    // These functions MUST be written in any class that inherits from Game
    // Update game items.
    virtual void update() = 0;
    // Perform AI calculations
    virtual void ai() = 0;
    // Check for collisions
    virtual void collisions() = 0;
    // Render graphics
    // Call graphics->spriteBegin();
    //   draw sprites
    // Call graphics->spriteEnd();
    //   draw non-sprites
    virtual void render() = 0;
};
#endif
```

Listing 4.1. The game.h file.

The keyword protected: *is similar to private but allows classes that inherit from* Game *direct access to the variables.*

Note the *pure virtual function* declarations for update, ai, collisions, and render. Pure virtual functions act like placeholders. Any class that inherits from Game must override them and provide the complete functions. Pure virtual functions are used here because

```
//============================================================================
// Constructor
//============================================================================
Game::Game()
{
    input = new Input();          // Initialize keyboard input immediately
    // Additional initialization is handled in later call to input->
    // initialize()
    paused = false;               // Game is not paused
    graphics = NULL;
    initialized = false;}
```

Listing 4.2. The Game class constructor.

there is no way for the current Game class to know how to perform the desired operations on the actual game.

The implementation of the Game class is in game.cpp. Let's go through that code by functions with the occasional detour for more detailed explanations of various parts.

The constructor is called automatically whenever a Game object is created. The constructor is typically used to initialize variables. The first thing the Game constructor does is create the Input object so the game has immediate access to the keyboard. A later call to input->initialize finalizes input setup and provides mouse access (see Listing 4.2).

A good practice is to keep constructor code limited to simple variable initialization.

The destructor is called automatically when the Game object is deleted. This is where any memory reserved by the object should be released (see Listing 4.3).

Release the memory in the opposite order it was reserved.

```
//============================================================================
// Destructor
//============================================================================
Game::~Game()
{
    deleteAll();                  // Free all reserved memory
    ShowCursor(true);             // Show cursor
}
```

Listing 4.3. The Game class destructor

4.2.1 Handling Windows Messages

We have moved the Windows message handler code from `winmain.cpp` to the `Game` class to a function named `messageHandler`. Moving this code to the `Game` class, rather than keeping the code in `winmain.cpp`, provides us easier access to code in the `Input` class. (We will examine the `Input` class later in this chapter.) As we saw in Chapter 2, the keyboard communicates with Windows through events. Mouse input is also handled through events. When Windows detects keyboard or mouse events, the `messageHandler` function in the `Game` class will be called to process the messages. The `messageHandler` function will, in turn, call the appropriate function in the `Input` class to process the input data. The `wParam` parameter contains the key data and `lParam` contains the mouse data. See Listing 4.4 for the Windows message handler.

```
//=======================================================================
// Windows message handler
//=======================================================================
LRESULT Game::messageHandler( HWND hwnd, UINT msg, WPARAM wParam,
                              LPARAM lParam )
{
    if(initialized)        // Do not process messages if not initialized
    {
        switch( msg )
        {
            case WM_DESTROY:
                PostQuitMessage(0);    // Tell Windows to kill this program
                return 0;
            case WM_KEYDOWN: case WM_SYSKEYDOWN:// Key down
                input->keyDown(wParam);
                return 0;
            case WM_KEYUP: case WM_SYSKEYUP:    // Key up
                input->keyUp(wParam);
                return 0;
            case WM_CHAR:                       // Character entered
                input->keyIn(wParam);
                return 0;
            case WM_MOUSEMOVE:                  // Mouse moved
                input->mouseIn(lParam);
                return 0;
            case WM_INPUT:                      // Raw mouse data in
                input->mouseRawIn(lParam);
                return 0;
            case WM_LBUTTONDOWN:                // Left mouse button down
                input->setMouseLButton(true);
                input->mouseIn(lParam);
                return 0;
            case WM_LBUTTONUP:                  // Left mouse button up
                input->setMouseLButton(false);
                input->mouseIn(lParam);
                return 0;
            case WM_MBUTTONDOWN:                // Middle mouse button down
                input->setMouseMButton(true);
                input->mouseIn(lParam);
                return 0;
```

```
        case WM_MBUTTONUP:                    // Middle mouse button up
            input->setMouseMButton(false);
            input->mouseIn(lParam);
            return 0;
        case WM_RBUTTONDOWN:                   // Right mouse button down
            input->setMouseRButton(true);
            input->mouseIn(lParam);
            return 0;
        case WM_RBUTTONUP:                     // Right mouse button up
            input->setMouseRButton(false);
            input->mouseIn(lParam);
            return 0;
        case WM_XBUTTONDOWN: case WM_XBUTTONUP: // Mouse X button down/up
            input->setMouseXButton(wParam);
            input->mouseIn(lParam);
            return 0;
        case WM_DEVICECHANGE:                  // Check for controllers
            input->checkControllers();
            return 0;
        }
    }
    return DefWindowProc( hwnd, msg, wParam, lParam ); // Let Windows
                                                        // handle it
}
```

Listing 4.4. Windows message handler in the Game class.

The function WinProc in winmain.cpp now calls messageHandler in the Game class to process Windows messages (Listing 4.5).

```
//=============================================================================
// Window event callback function
//=============================================================================
LRESULT WINAPI WinProc( HWND hWnd, UINT msg, WPARAM wParam, LPARAM lParam )
{
    return (game->messageHandler(hwnd, msg, wParam, lParam));
}
```

Listing 4.5. Calling the message handler.

4.2.2 Time for a Timer

Making graphic items move on the screen or perform other animation is accomplished by displaying a series of still images at the proper interval and location to give the appearance of motion. This is the same technique used by television and motion pictures. If we want to display a spaceship flying smoothly across the screen, we need to know how much time has elapsed since the last image was drawn so the new image may be placed at the correct location onscreen when the new image is drawn. If our timing is off, we will get a spaceship that moves too fast or too slow or that seems to speed up and slow down at random intervals (Figure 4.2).

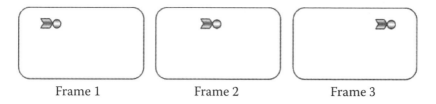

| Frame 1 | Frame 2 | Frame 3 |

Figure 4.2. Animated spaceship.

All modern PCs contain a high-performance timer that is available for program use. The `Game::initialize` function creates a `Graphics` object and initializes graphics (Listing 4.6). It then calls `initialize` for the input object to set up mouse input. Lastly, it sets up the high-performance timer that will be used to regulate the speed of game items. The function `QueryPerformanceFrequency(&timerFreq)` stores the frequency of the high-performance timer in the variable `timerFreq`. The function `QueryPerformanceCounter(&timeStart)` stores the current count from the high-performance timer in the variable `timeStart`. See Section 4.2.5 later in this chapter for more on the timer.

```
//=============================================================================
// Initializes the game
// Throws GameError on error
//=============================================================================
void Game::initialize(HWND hw)
{
    hwnd = hw;                                  // Save window handle
    // Initialize graphics
    graphics = new Graphics();
    // Throws GameError
    graphics->initialize(hwnd, GAME_WIDTH, GAME_HEIGHT, FULLSCREEN);

    // Initialize input, do not capture mouse
    input->initialize(hwnd, false);             // Throws GameError
    // Attempt to set up high resolution timer
    if(QueryPerformanceFrequency(&timerFreq) == false)
        throw(GameError(gameErrorNS::FATAL_ERROR,
                        "Error initializing high resolution timer"));
    QueryPerformanceCounter(&timeStart);        // Get starting time
    initialized = true;
}
```

Listing 4.6. The `Game::initialize` function.

4.2.3 Lost Device

If we run any of the DirectX programs we have created up to this point and then press Ctrl + Alt + Delete, we will observe that the contents of the DirectX window are gone and do not come back, even after returning to the previous environment. This is the result of the Direct3D graphics device being in a lost state. A Direct3D device can be lost to our program any time another event causes rendering to become impossible.

When a device is lost it must be reset and its resources recreated. The sequence to follow when responding to a lost device is as follows:

```
If device is not in a valid state
        If device is lost and not available for reset
                Wait until device can be restored
        Else if the device is available for reset
                attempt to reset the device
                If reset failed
                        return
```

The function `reset` is the only method that may be called on a device that is lost, and it is the only way for an application to regain the use of a lost device. The function `reset` will fail unless all of the resources allocated in `D3DPOOL_DEFAULT` are released prior to calling `reset`.

An application can test a device to see if it is lost by calling the `TestCooperative Level` method. The method is very simple:

```
HRESULT TestCooperativeLevel();
```

There are no parameters. The return value will be `D3D_OK` if the device is operating normally. If the method fails, the return value will be one of the following:

- `D3DERR_DEVICELOST`. The device is lost and cannot be restored at the current time.

- `D3DERR_DEVICENOTRESET`. The device is available for reset.

- `D3DERR_DRIVERINTERNALERROR`. The device is reporting an internal error. There is nothing we can do but report an error to the user.

We will use `TestCooperativeLevel` in our `getDeviceState` method to return the current state of the graphics device. The function in Listing 4.7 will be added to our `Graphics` class.

To reset the graphics device, we need to initialize the D3D presentation parameters again and then call the graphic device's `reset` function. We can add our own `reset` function to the `Graphics` class to perform these tasks (Listing 4.8).

```
//=============================================================================
// Check for lost device
//=============================================================================
HRESULT Graphics::getDeviceState()
{
    result = E_FAIL;    // Default to fail, replace on success
    if (device3d == NULL)
        return result;
    result = device3d->TestCooperativeLevel();
    return result;
}
```

Listing 4.7. Checking for a lost graphics device.

```
//================================================================
// Reset the graphics device
//================================================================
HRESULT Graphics::reset()
{
    result = E_FAIL;      // Default to fail, replace on success
    initD3Dpp();                    // Init D3D presentation parameters
    result = device3d->Reset(&d3dpp);   // Attempt to reset graphics device
    return result;
}
```

Listing 4.8. Reseting the graphics device.

The complete task of checking for and handling a lost graphics device is handled by the handleLostGraphicsDevice function in the Game class, as shown in Listing 4.9.

```
//================================================================
// Handle lost graphics device
//================================================================
void Game::handleLostGraphicsDevice()
{
    // Test for and handle lost device
    hr = graphics->getDeviceState();
    if(FAILED(hr))              // If graphics device is not in a valid state
    {
        // If the device is lost and not available for reset
        if(hr == D3DERR_DEVICELOST)
        {
            Sleep(100);        // Yield CPU time (100 milliseconds)
            return;
        }
        // The device was lost but is now available for reset
        else if(hr == D3DERR_DEVICENOTRESET)
        {
            releaseAll();
            hr = graphics->reset(); // Attempt to reset graphics device
            if(FAILED(hr))          // If reset failed
                return;
            resetAll();
        }
        else
            return;                 // Other device error
    }
}
```

Listing 4.9. Handling a lost graphics device.

4.2.4 Rendering the Game Graphics

DirectX has several different graphic shapes that it can draw. These shapes are referred to as *primitives*. The process of drawing these graphic primitives is called *rendering*. The first step

```
//=============================================================================
// Clear backbuffer and call DirectX BeginScene()
//=============================================================================
HRESULT beginScene()
{
    result = E_FAIL;
    if(device3d == NULL)
        return result;
    // Clear backbuffer to backColor
    device3d->Clear(0, NULL, D3DCLEAR_TARGET, backColor, 1.0F, 0);
    result = device3d->BeginScene();          // Begin scene for drawing
    return result;
}
//=============================================================================
// Call DirectX EndScene()
//=============================================================================
HRESULT endScene()
{
    result = E_FAIL;
    if(device3d)
        result = device3d->EndScene();
    return result;
}
```

Listing 4.10. Beginning and ending a DirectX scene.

in rendering any DirectX primitive is to begin a DirectX scene. A scene is started by calling the DirectX BeginScene function. After all rendering is complete, the scene is ended by calling the DirectX EndScene function. The rendering of primitives outside a scene will fail. We need to add functions to our Graphics class in graphics.h to begin and end a scene. Our new functions are named beginScene and endScene. The beginScene function is also the perfect place to clear the back buffer, so we are relocating the device3d->Clear function call from the showBackbuffer function to beginScene (Listing 4.10).

All rendering of DirectX primitives must be done in a scene.

The renderGame function in the Game class begins a graphics scene and then calls the user-supplied render function. The render function is a pure virtual function that must be part of any class that inherits from the Game class. It is up to the render function to draw the graphics for the current game. Following the call to render, the graphics scene is ended. Next, we test for and handle a lost graphics device. The last step is to display the back buffer to the screen (Listing 4.11).

```
//=============================================================================
// Render game items
//=============================================================================
void Game::renderGame()
```

```
{
    // Start rendering
    if (SUCCEEDED(graphics->beginScene()))
    {
        // Render is a pure virtual function that must be provided in the
        // inheriting class.
        render();                   // Call render in derived class
        // Stop rendering
        graphics->endScene();
    }
    handleLostGraphicsDevice();
    // Display the backbuffer on the screen
    graphics->showBackbuffer();
}
```

Listing 4.11. The Game class renderGame function.

4.2.5 The Game Loop

Most games that contain any sort of animated graphics require a loop to control the animation. The loop is actually the main message loop in the WinMain function of winmain.cpp. The game's run function is repeatedly called from the main message loop in WinMain (Listing 4.12).

The Game::run function checks for a valid graphics pointer and then calls Query PerformanceCounter(&timeEnd), which puts the current count from the high-performance counter in timeEnd. The actual time that has elapsed between calls to the timer is calculated as:

$$frameTime = (timeEnd - timeStart) / timerFreq.$$

This value gives us a very accurate measurement of the time that has elapsed between calls to our game loop. The elapsed time value is saved in the variable frameTime. The frameTime number will be used in later chapters to control the speed of animation in our game.

Our code reads the high-performance timer once per game loop. It then calculates the frameTime as the actual time that has elapsed since the last time the game loop was called. Some game programming books and online examples calculate the frame time value as the amount of time that is required by the game to render one frame. This is typically done by reading the timer at the start and end of the game loop and getting the difference between the two times. This method is incorrect because it fails to account for the time that is spent outside the game loop by Windows and other applications.

Never trust program code from any source. It is too easy for mistakes to make their way into code. Always research the topic and verify the correctness of code before using it.

Next, we have added a few lines of code that can save power. If the time required for the previous frame is less than the time required to achieve our desired frame rate, we put the CPU to sleep during the extra time. Our desired frame rate is specified by the constant

```
// Main message loop
int done = 0;
while (!done)
{
    if (PeekMessage(&msg, NULL, 0, 0, PM_REMOVE))
    {
        // Look for quit message
        if (msg.message == WM_QUIT)
            done = 1;
        // Decode and pass messages on to WinProc
        TranslateMessage(&msg);
        DispatchMessage(&msg);
    } else
        game->run(hwnd);      // Run the game loop
}
```

Listing 4.12. The message loop.

FRAME_RATE in constants.h. The extra time is calculated as sleepTime. A call is made to timeBeginPeriod(1), which requests a 1-millisecond resolution for the Window's timer. The call to Sleep(sleepTime) puts our game to sleep for the specified number of milliseconds. Putting a program to sleep reduces the CPU workload, which saves power and gives us a "green" program. If we need our computer to act as a small space heater, we would leave the power-saving code out.

The power-saving code requires winmm.lib *in "Linker/Input/Additional Dependencies" of the project properties.*

The amount of reduction on the CPU workload can be substantial. Here are the results obtained with the spaceship example program from Chapter 5. It contains a simple animated spaceship moving across the screen. Figure 4.3(a) indicates the CPU usage without the power-saving code. Figure 4.3(b) indicates the CPU usage with the power-saving code. In this particular case, the computer and game settings yielded a reduction in CPU utilization from 73% to 1%.

The amount of power saving obtained depends on several factors, including the complexity of the game, CPU speed, and desired frame rate, to name a few. After the power-saving code, we use the frameTime value to calculate the average frames per second (fps) of the game. We will add the ability to display the fps number in later chapters.

Following the fps calculation, we apply a limit to the frameTime value of MAX_FRAME_TIME. Normally, this limit should never be reached, but it can occur if the computer gets very busy with another task or when we are debugging our game. In those instances, we want to prevent the onscreen characters from making huge jumps in movement that might send them off the screen.

The timeStart variable is updated with the current time. The timeStart value will be used in the frameTime calculation the next time the run function is called. The state of any game controllers is read and saved by input->readControllers. If the game is not paused then update, ai, and collisions functions are called followed by renderGame,

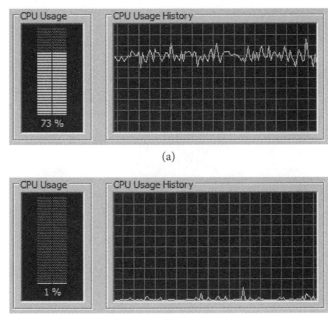

(a)

(b)

Figure 4.3. (a) No power-saving code; (b) with power-saving code.

which is called even when the game is paused. Recall from our earlier description of game.h that update, ai, collisions, and render functions are declared as pure virtual functions and must be implemented in code in the derived class. We will not be able to compile a program that uses the Game class until we provide the code for the pure virtual functions because currently they do not exist. The last operation is to clear the inputs to prepare for the next game loop (Listing 4.13).

```
//=============================================================================
// Call repeatedly by the main message loop in WinMain
//=============================================================================
void Game::run(HWND hwnd)
{
    if(graphics == NULL)                    // If graphics not initialized
        return;
    // Calculate elapsed time of last frame, save in frameTime
    QueryPerformanceCounter(&timeEnd);
    frameTime = (float)(timeEnd.QuadPart - timeStart.QuadPart ) /
                (float)timerFreq.QuadPart;
    // Power-saving code, requires winmm.lib
    // If not enough time has elapsed for desired frame rate
    if (frameTime < MIN_FRAME_TIME)
    {
        sleepTime = (DWORD)((MIN_FRAME_TIME - frameTime)*1000);
        timeBeginPeriod(1);     // Request 1mS resolution for windows timer
        Sleep(sleepTime);       // Release CPU for sleepTime
```

```
        timeEndPeriod(1);        // End 1mS timer resolution
        return;
    }
    if (frameTime > 0.0)
        fps = (fps*0.99f) + (0.01f/frameTime);   // Average fps
    if (frameTime > MAX_FRAME_TIME) // If frame rate is very slow
        frameTime = MAX_FRAME_TIME; // Limit maximum frameTime
    timeStart = timeEnd;
    input->readControllers();        // Read state of controllers
    // update(), ai(), and collisions() are pure virtual functions.
    // These functions must be provided in the class that inherits from
    // Game.
    if (!paused)                     // If not paused
    {
        update();                    // Update all game items
        ai();                        // Artificial intelligence
        collisions();                // Handle collisions
        input->vibrateControllers(frameTime);// Handle controller vibration
    }
    renderGame();                    // Draw all game items
    // Clear input
    // Call this after all key checks are done
    input->clear(inputNS::KEYS_PRESSED);
}
```

Listing 4.13. Power-saving code.

▌▌ 4.3 The Input Class

The Input class has code that is used to handle keyboard, mouse, and game controller input. Two states are stored for each key:

1. Is the key currently down?

2. Was the key pressed during the current game loop?

Those states are stored in two arrays: keysDown and keysPressed, respectively. The two arrays are cleared at the end of each game loop.

Text characters that the user types are stored in the textIn string. The mouse position and button states are stored in the variables, as described by the comments in Listing 4.14. The game controller data is stored in the controllers array.

```
class Input
{
private:
    bool keysDown[inputNS::KEYS_ARRAY_LEN];// True if specified key is dow
    bool keysPressed[inputNS::KEYS_ARRAY_LEN];  // True if specified key was
                                    // pressed
    std::string textIn;                 // User entered text
    char charIn;                        // Last character entered
    bool newLine;                       // True on start of new line
```

```
int   mouseX, mouseY;                // Mouse screen coordinates
int   mouseRawX, mouseRawY;          // High-definition mouse data
RAWINPUTDEVICE Rid[1];               // For high-definition mouse
bool mouseCaptured;                  // True if mouse captured
bool mouseLButton;                   // True if left mouse button down
bool mouseMButton;                   // True if middle mouse button down
bool mouseRButton;                   // True if right mouse button down
bool mouseX1Button;                  // True if X1 mouse button down
bool mouseX2Button;                  // True if X2 mouse button down
ControllerState controllers[MAX_CONTROLLERS]; // State of controllers
```

Listing 4.14. The Input class variables.

The Input constructor clears the key state arrays, textIn string, and mouse data; it also clears controller vibration times. The destructor releases the mouse capture (if captured) (Listing 4.15). Capturing the mouse is done in the initialize function (Listing 4.16).

```
//=============================================================================
// Default constructor
//=============================================================================
Input::Input()
{
    // Clear key down array
    for (size_t i = 0; i < inputNS::KEYS_ARRAY_LEN; i++)
        keysDown[i] = false;
    // Clear key pressed array
    for (size_t i = 0; i < inputNS::KEYS_ARRAY_LEN; i++)
        keysPressed[i] = false;
    newLine = true;                     // Start new line
    textIn = "";                        // Clear textIn
    charIn = 0;                         // Clear charIn
    // Mouse data
    mouseX = 0;                         // Screen X
    mouseY = 0;                         // Screen Y
    mouseRawX = 0;                      // High-definition X
    mouseRawY = 0;                      // High-definition Y
    mouseLButton = false;               // True if left mouse button is down
    mouseMButton = false;               // True if middle mouse button is down
    mouseRButton = false;               // True if right mouse button is down
    mouseX1Button = false;              // True if X1 mouse button is down
    mouseX2Button = false;              // True if X2 mouse button is down
    for(int i=0; i<MAX_CONTROLLERS; i++)
    {
        controllers[i].vibrateTimeLeft = 0;
        controllers[i].vibrateTimeRight = 0;
    }
}
//=============================================================================
// Destructor
//=============================================================================
Input::~Input()
{
```

```
    if(mouseCaptured)
        ReleaseCapture();                   // Release mouse
}
```

Listing 4.15. The `Input` class constructor and destructor.

The `initialize` function sets up the `RAWINPUTDEVICE` array `Rid` in preparation for reading from a high-definition mouse. A standard computer mouse has a resolution of 400 dots per inch (DPI), whereas a high-definition mouse has a resolution of 800 DPI or greater. (High-definition mouse data cannot be obtained through the standard `WM_MOUSEMOVE` message.) The mouse is captured if desired and the controller state array is cleared (Listing 4.16).

Capturing a mouse directs the mouse input to the capturing window. This is typically the behavior wanted in a game if the mouse is being used to control player movement. For normal mouse behavior, do not capture the mouse.

```
//=============================================================================
// Initialize mouse and controller input
// Set capture=true to capture mouse
// Throws GameError
//=============================================================================
void Input::initialize(HWND hwnd, bool capture)
{
    try{
        mouseCaptured = capture;
        // Register high-definition mouse
        Rid[0].usUsagePage = HID_USAGE_PAGE_GENERIC;
        Rid[0].usUsage = HID_USAGE_GENERIC_MOUSE;
        Rid[0].dwFlags = RIDEV_INPUTSINK;
        Rid[0].hwndTarget = hwnd;
        RegisterRawInputDevices(Rid, 1, sizeof(Rid[0]));
        if(mouseCaptured)
            SetCapture(hwnd);               // Capture mouse
        // Clear controllers state
        ZeroMemory( controllers, sizeof(ControllerState) * MAX_CONTROLLERS
                    );
        checkControllers();                 // Check for connected controllers
    }
    catch(...)
    {
        throw(GameError(gameErrorNS::FATAL_ERROR,
                        "Error initializing input system"));
    }
}
```

Listing 4.16. The `Input` class `initialize` function.

4. The Game Engine

4.3.1 Keyboard Input

The `Input` class contains the following functions that are called by the `messageHandler` function to process keyboard input (Listing 4.17).

```
//=============================================================================
// Set true in the keysDown and keysPessed array for this key
// Pre: wParam contains the virtual key code (0-255)
//=============================================================================
void Input::keyDown(WPARAM wParam)
{
    // Make sure key code is within buffer range
    if (wParam < inputNS::KEYS_ARRAY_LEN)
    {
        keysDown[wParam] = true;    // Update keysDown array
        // Key has been pressed, erased by clear()
        keysPressed[wParam] = true; // Update keysPressed array
    }
}
//=============================================================================
// Set false in the keysDown array for this key
// Pre: wParam contains the virtual key code (0-255)
//=============================================================================
void Input::keyUp(WPARAM wParam)
{
    // Make sure key code is within buffer range
    if (wParam < inputNS::KEYS_ARRAY_LEN)
        // Update state table
        keysDown[wParam] = false;
}
//=============================================================================
// Save the char just entered in textIn string
// Pre: wParam contains the char
//=============================================================================
void Input::keyIn(WPARAM wParam)
{
    if (newLine)                            // If start of new line
    {
        textIn.clear();
        newLine = false;
    }
    if (wParam == '\b')                     // If backspace
    {
        if(textIn.length() > 0)             // If characters exist
            textIn.erase(textIn.size()-1);  // Erase last character entered
    }
    else
    {
        textIn += wParam;                   // Add character to textIn
        charIn = wParam;                    // Save last char entered
    }
    if ((char)wParam == '\r')               // If return
        newLine = true;                     // Start new line
}
```

Listing 4.17. The `Input` class functions.

```
// Key mappings
// In this game simple constants are used for key mappings. If variables
// were used it would be possible to save and restore key mappings from a
// data file.
const UCHAR CONSOLE_KEY   = VK_OEM_3;    // ~ key for U.S.
const UCHAR ESC_KEY       = VK_ESCAPE;   // Escape key
const UCHAR ALT_KEY       = VK_MENU;     // Alt key
const UCHAR ENTER_KEY     = VK_RETURN;   // Enter key
const UCHAR SHIP1_LEFT_KEY    = 'A';
const UCHAR SHIP1_RIGHT_KEY   = 'D';
const UCHAR SHIP1_FORWARD_KEY = 'W';
const UCHAR SHIP1_FIRE_KEY    = 'S';
const UCHAR SHIP2_LEFT_KEY    = VK_LEFT;  // Left arrow
const UCHAR SHIP2_RIGHT_KEY   = VK_RIGHT; // Right arrow
const UCHAR SHIP2_FORWARD_KEY = VK_UP;    // Up arrow
const UCHAR SHIP2_FIRE_KEY    = VK_DOWN;  // Down arrow
```

Listing 4.18. Key mappings from the Spacewar game.

Several of the following functions require a vkey parameter. The vkey parameter specifies the key to test. As was described in Chapter 2, each key on the keyboard has an assigned virtual key code. The key code for displayable characters is specified with the ASCII code, which is obtained by using the character inside single quotation marks. For a complete list of virtual key codes, look in the WinUser.h file. The file WinUser.h is located in "C:Program Files (x86)\Microsoft SDKs\Windows\v7.0A\Include" on Windows 7 computers. The example in Listing 4.18 shows some key mappings for our Spacewar game.

```
//==============================================================================
// Returns true if the specified VIRTUAL KEY is down, otherwise false.
//==============================================================================
bool Input::isKeyDown(UCHAR vkey) const
{
    if (vkey < inputNS::KEYS_ARRAY_LEN)
        return keysDown[vkey];
    else
        return false;
}
```

Listing 4.19. The isKeyDown function.

To test if a key is currently pressed, we use the isKeyDown function (Listing 4.19). For example, if we wanted to test for SHIP2_RIGHT_KEY we would follow the code in Listing 4.20.

```
if(input->isKeyDown(SHIP2_RIGHT_KEY))
```

Listing 4.20. Checking for SHIP2_RIGHT_KEY press.

The wasKeyPressed function is used to test if the specified key was pressed at any time during the current game loop (Listing 4.21). We can use the anyKeyPressed function to test for any key that is pressed (Listing 4.22). The getTextIn function returns the text input as a string (Listing 4.23). To get the last character entered, use the getCharIn function (Listing 4.24).

```
//=============================================================================
// Return true if the specified VIRTUAL KEY has been pressed in the most
// recent
// frame. Key presses are erased at the end of each frame.
//=============================================================================
bool Input::wasKeyPressed(UCHAR vkey) const
{
    if (vkey < inputNS::KEYS_ARRAY_LEN)
        return keysPressed[vkey];
    else
        return false;
}
```

Listing 4.21. The wasKeyPressed function.

```
//=============================================================================
// Return true if any key was pressed in the most recent frame.
// Key presses are erased at the end of each frame.
//=============================================================================
bool Input::anyKeyPressed() const
{
    for (size_t i = 0; i < inputNS::KEYS_ARRAY_LEN; i++)
        if(keysPressed[i] == true)
            return true;
    return false;
}
```

Listing 4.22. The anyKeyPressed function.

```
// Return text input as a string
std::string getTextIn() {return textIn;}
```

Listing 4.23. The getTextIn function.

```
// Return last character entered
char getCharIn()          {return charIn;}
```

Listing 4.24. The getCharIn function.

To clear a specific key from the `keysPressed` array, use the `clearKeyPress` function (Listing 4.25). Clear the text input string with the `clearTextIn` function (Listing 4.26). Use the `clearAll` function to clear key presses, mouse, and text input (Listing 4.27).

```
//=====================================================================
// Clear the specified key press
//=====================================================================
void Input::clearKeyPress(UCHAR vkey)
{
    if (vkey < inputNS::KEYS_ARRAY_LEN)
        keysPressed[vkey] = false;
}
```

Listing 4.25. The `clearKeyPress` function.

```
// Clear text input buffer
void clearTextIn() {textIn.clear();}
```

Listing 4.26. The `clearTextIn` function.

```
// Clears key, mouse, and text input data
void clearAll() {clear(inputNS::KEYS_MOUSE_TEXT);}
```

Listing 4.27. The `clearAll` function.

Use the `clear` function to clear the specified input buffer (see Listing 4.28). The valid values for the `what` parameter are:

- `KEYS_DOWN`. Sets all of `keysDown` array to `false`.

- `KEYS_PRESSED`. Sets all of `keysPressed` array to `false`.

- `MOUSE`. Clears mouse `X`, `Y` to 0.

- `TEXT_IN`. Clears text input string.

- `KEYS_MOUSE_TEXT`. Clears all input buffers.

The `what` parameter may be combined with the bitwise OR (|) operator to clear multiple items. For example:

```
input->clear(KEYS_DOWN | KEYS_PRESSED);
```

```
//==============================================================
// Clear specified input buffers
// See input.h for what values
//==============================================================
void Input::clear(UCHAR what)
{
    if(what & inputNS::KEYS_DOWN)        // If clear keys down
    {
        for (size_t i = 0; i < inputNS::KEYS_ARRAY_LEN; i++)
            keysDown[i] = false;
    }
    if(what & inputNS::KEYS_PRESSED)     // If clear keys pressed
    {
        for (size_t i = 0; i < inputNS::KEYS_ARRAY_LEN; i++)
            keysPressed[i] = false;
    }
    if(what & inputNS::MOUSE)            // If clear mouse
    {
        mouseX = 0;
        mouseY = 0;
        mouseRawX = 0;
        mouseRawY = 0;
    }
    if(what & inputNS::TEXT_IN)
        clearTextIn();
}
```

Listing 4.28. Clears the input buffers.

4.3.2 Mouse Input

The mouseIn, mouseRawIn, and setMouseButton functions are called by the messageHandler function to save the mouse input. The mouseIn and mouseRawIn functions are located in input.cpp (Listing 4.29). The functions listed in Listing 4.30 are located in input.h.

```
//==============================================================
// Reads mouse screen position into mouseX, mouseY
//==============================================================
void Input::mouseIn(LPARAM lParam)
{
    mouseX = GET_X_LPARAM(lParam);
    mouseY = GET_Y_LPARAM(lParam);
}
//==============================================================
// Reads raw mouse data into mouseRawX, mouseRawY
// This routine is compatible with a high-definition mouse
//==============================================================
void Input::mouseRawIn(LPARAM lParam)
{
    UINT dwSize = 40;
    static BYTE lpb[40];
```

```
GetRawInputData((HRAWINPUT)lParam, RID_INPUT,
                lpb, &dwSize, sizeof(RAWINPUTHEADER));

RAWINPUT* raw = (RAWINPUT*)lpb;

if (raw->header.dwType == RIM_TYPEMOUSE)
{
    mouseRawX = raw->data.mouse.lLastX;
    mouseRawY = raw->data.mouse.lLastY;
}
}
```

Listing 4.29. Mouse position input functions.

```
// Save state of mouse button
void setMouseLButton(bool b) { mouseLButton = b; }
// Save state of mouse button
void setMouseMButton(bool b) { mouseMButton = b; }
// Save state of mouse button
void setMouseRButton(bool b) { mouseRButton = b; }
// Save state of mouse button
void setMouseXButton(WPARAM wParam)
{
    mouseX1Button = (wParam & MK_XBUTTON1) ? true:false;
    mouseX2Button = (wParam & MK_XBUTTON2) ? true:false;
}
```

Listing 4.30. Mouse button input functions.

When we want to read the mouse position or button status, we use one of the functions in Listing 4.31, all of which are located in input.h. The getMouseX and getMouseY functions return the current screen position of the mouse pointer, where (0,0) is the top-left corner of the screen. Raw mouse data is read with getMouseRawX and getMouseRawY. Raw mouse data returns the x and y position of the mouse relative to its previous position. With raw mouse data, x is negative when moving left and positive when moving right. The position y is negative when moving up and positive when moving down. The button functions return true if the corresponding button is currently pressed and false otherwise.

```
// Return mouse X position
int getMouseX()        const { return mouseX; }
// Return mouse Y position
int getMouseY()        const { return mouseY; }
// Return raw mouse X movement. Left is <0, Right is >0
// Compatible with high-definition mouse
int getMouseRawX()     const { return mouseRawX; }
// Return raw mouse Y movement. Up is <0, Down is >0
// Compatible with high-definition mouse
int getMouseRawY()     const { return mouseRawY; }
```

```
// Return state of left mouse button
bool getMouseLButton() const { return mouseLButton; }
// Return state of middle mouse button
bool getMouseMButton() const { return mouseMButton; }
// Return state of right mouse button
bool getMouseRButton() const { return mouseRButton; }
// Return state of X1 mouse button
bool getMouseX1Button() const { return mouseX1Button; }
// Return state of X2 mouse button
bool getMouseX2Button() const { return mouseX2Button; }
```

Listing 4.31. Returns the mouse data.

4.3.3 Game Controller Input

Our game engine will support input from Xbox 360 controllers (Figure 4.4). In order to use an Xbox 360 controller on a Windows PC, it must be a *wired* controller or the computer must be equipped with an Xbox 360 wireless receiver.

The USB wire that attaches to a wireless controller is only for powering the controller and does not support data transfer.

We need to include `XInput.h` header file in our `input.h` file (Listing 4.32).

We also need to add `xinput.lib` *to "Linker/Input/Additional Dependencies" on the "Project Property" pages.*

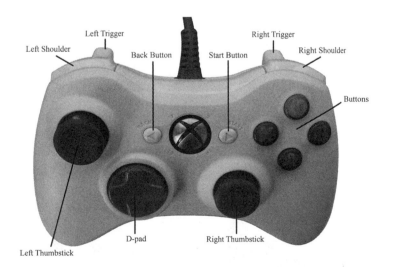

Figure 4.4. An Xbox 360 wired controller.

The Xbox 360 controller input is stored in the `controllers` array (Listing 4.33). `MAX_CONTROLLERS` is defined as 4, which is the maximum number of controllers supported. The structure `ControllerState` is defined, as shown in Listing 4.34. The `state` member contains the state of the buttons, triggers, and thumb sticks. The structure `XINPUT_STATE` is defined in `XInput.h`, as shown in Listing 4.35. The structure `XINPUT_GAMEPAD` is defined in Listing 4.36.

```
#include <XInput.h>
```

Listing 4.32. Including `XInput.h`.

```
ControllerState     controllers[MAX_CONTROLLERS];
```

Listing 4.33. Array of controller data.

```
struct ControllerState
{
    XINPUT_STATE        state;
    XINPUT_VIBRATION    vibration;
    float               vibrateTimeLeft;    // mSec
    float               vibrateTimeRight;   // mSec
    bool                connected;
};
```

Listing 4.34. The `ControllerState` structure.

```
typedef struct _XINPUT_STATE
{
    DWORD               dwPacketNumber;
    XINPUT_GAMEPAD      Gamepad;
} XINPUT_STATE, *PXINPUT_STATE;
```

Listing 4.35. The `XINPUT_STATE` structure.

```
typedef struct _XINPUT_GAMEPAD
{
    WORD                wButtons;
    BYTE                bLeftTrigger;
    BYTE                bRightTrigger;
    SHORT               sThumbLX;
```

```
    SHORT               sThumbLY;
    SHORT               sThumbRX;
    SHORT               sThumbRY;
} XINPUT_GAMEPAD, *PXINPUT_GAMEPAD;
```

Listing 4.36. The `XINPUT_GAMEPAD` structure.

The wButtons member contains the state of the buttons. Each button is defined by one bit in the WORD. The current status of a button may be determined by performing a bitwise AND (&) with a binary number that contains a 1 in the bit corresponding to the desired button. If the result of the AND is `true`, the button is pressed. The definitions in Listing 4.37 are in `input.h` and may be used to test the button status.

```
// Bit corresponding to gamepad button in state.Gamepad.wButtons
const DWORD GAMEPAD_DPAD_UP        = 0x0001;
const DWORD GAMEPAD_DPAD_DOWN      = 0x0002;
const DWORD GAMEPAD_DPAD_LEFT      = 0x0004;
const DWORD GAMEPAD_DPAD_RIGHT     = 0x0008;
const DWORD GAMEPAD_START_BUTTON   = 0x0010;
const DWORD GAMEPAD_BACK_BUTTON    = 0x0020;
const DWORD GAMEPAD_LEFT_THUMB     = 0x0040;
const DWORD GAMEPAD_RIGHT_THUMB    = 0x0080;
const DWORD GAMEPAD_LEFT_SHOULDER  = 0x0100;
const DWORD GAMEPAD_RIGHT_SHOULDER = 0x0200;
const DWORD GAMEPAD_A              = 0x1000;
const DWORD GAMEPAD_B              = 0x2000;
const DWORD GAMEPAD_X              = 0x4000;
const DWORD GAMEPAD_Y              = 0x8000;
```

Listing 4.37. Gamepad button constants.

Controller vibration is controlled by two motors. The speed of each motor may be set in the vibration member of ControllerState. The structure XINPUT_VIBRATION is defined in XInput.h, as shown in Listing 4.38.

```
typedef struct _XINPUT_VIBRATION
{
    WORD wLeftMotorSpeed;
    WORD wRightMotorSpeed;
} XINPUT_VIBRATION, *PXINPUT_VIBRATION;
```

Listing 4.38. The `XINPUT_VIBRATION` structure.

The current state of a game controller may be read with the DirectX function XInputGetState:

```
DWORD XInputGetState(
    DWORD dwUserIndex,
    XINPUT_STATE* pState
)
```

The parameters are:

- dwUserIndex. Number of the controller from 0 to 3.

- pState. Pointer to an XINPUT_STATE structure that receives the state of the controller.

We will call XInputGetState from our readControllers function. Our readControllers function reads the state of each controller and stores it in our controllers array (Listing 4.39). The call to readControllers is added to the Game::run function so it will be called automatically as part of the game loop.

```
//=========================================================================
// Read state of connected controllers
//=========================================================================
void Input::readControllers()
{
    DWORD result;
    for( DWORD i = 0; i <MAX_CONTROLLERS; i++)
    {
        if(controllers[i].connected)
        {
            result = XInputGetState(i, &controllers[i].state);
            if(result == ERROR_DEVICE_NOT_CONNECTED) // If disconnected
                controllers[i].connected = false;
        }
    }
}
```

Listing 4.39. Reads the state of the controllers.

The current state of any controller may be read with the getControllerState function (Listing 4.40).

```
// Return state of specified game controller.
const ControllerState* getControllerState(UINT n)
{
    if(n > MAX_CONTROLLERS-1)
        n=MAX_CONTROLLERS-1;
```

```
    return &controllers[n];
}
```

Listing 4.40. Returns the state of the controllers.

It returns a pointer to a constant `ControllerState` structure in the `controllers` array. To read just the state of a controller's buttons, we have the `getGamepadButtons` function. The number of the controller is passed in parameter n (Listing 4.41).

```
// Return state of controller n buttons.
const WORD getGamepadButtons(UINT n)
{
    if(n > MAX_CONTROLLERS-1)
        n=MAX_CONTROLLERS-1;
    return controllers[n].state.Gamepad.wButtons;
}
```

Listing 4.41. Returns the controller's buttons.

The state of individual buttons may be tested by performing a bitwise AND (&) with the WORD returned and one of the predefined button constants. For example, to test the state of button A from controller 0, we would use the code in Listing 4.42.

```
if(input->getGamepadButtons(0) & GAMEPAD_A)
    // Button A pressed
```

Listing 4.42. Testing button A.

To make it a little easier to test the state of a button, we have included a function for each button. `true` is returned if the button is currently pressed. The code for the functions in Listing 4.43 is in `input.h`. To test the state of button A from controller 0, we would use the code in Listing 4.44.

```
// Return state of controller n D-pad Up.
bool getGamepadDPadUp(UINT n)
// Return state of controller n D-pad Down.
bool getGamepadDPadDown(UINT n)
// Return state of controller n D-pad Left.
bool getGamepadDPadLeft(UINT n)
// Return state of controller n D-pad Right.
bool getGamepadDPadRight(UINT n)
// Return state of controller n Start button.
bool getGamepadStart(UINT n)
// Return state of controller n Back button.
bool getGamepadBack(UINT n)
// Return state of controller n Left Thumb button.
bool getGamepadLeftThumb(UINT n)
```

```
// Return state of controller n Right Thumb button.
bool getGamepadRightThumb(UINT n)
// Return state of controller n Left Shoulder button.
bool getGamepadLeftShoulder(UINT n)
// Return state of controller n Right Shoulder button.
bool getGamepadRightShoulder(UINT n)
// Return state of controller n A button.
bool getGamepadA(UINT n)
// Return state of controller n B button.
bool getGamepadB(UINT n)
// Return state of controller n X button.
bool getGamepadX(UINT n)
// Return state of controller n Y button.
bool getGamepadY(UINT n)
```

Listing 4.43. Button test functions.

```
if(input->getGamepadA(0))
    // Button A pressed
```

Listing 4.44. Testing button A.

The left and right triggers and the thumb sticks are analog controls. The left and right triggers return a BYTE value from 0 to 255, where 0 is released and 255 represents fully depressed. The thumb sticks return a SHORT value for each axis as a signed number between −32,768 and 32,767. The number describes the position of the thumb stick where 0 is centered. Negative numbers indicate left and down; positive numbers indicate right and up.

The analog controls may return values other than 0 when they are fully released. For this reason, applications should use a *dead zone* when processing the analog data. The dead zone is simply a defined threshold value that must be surpassed before movement is considered valid. We have defined two dead zone values in input.h (Listing 4.45).

```
// Default to 20% of range as deadzone
const DWORD GAMEPAD_THUMBSTICK_DEADZONE = 0.20f * float(0X7FFF);
const DWORD GAMEPAD_TRIGGER_DEADZONE = 30;  // Trigger range 0-255
```

Listing 4.45. Dead zones.

The thumb stick dead zone is set to 20% of maximum movement and the trigger dead zone is set to 30 out of the maximum value of 255. The values for the dead zones may need to be adjusted for different controllers. Microsoft's website states, "Please note that some controllers are more sensitive than others, thus the dead zone may vary from unit to unit. It is recommended that you test your games with several Xbox 360 controllers on different systems."[1] The functions in Listing 4.46 for reading the analog controls are located in input.h.

[1] http://msdn.microsoft.com/enus/library/windows/desktop/ee417001(v=vs.85).aspx

```
// Return value of controller n Left Trigger.
BYTE getGamepadLeftTrigger(UINT n)
// Return value of controller n Right Trigger.
BYTE getGamepadRightTrigger(UINT n)
// Return value of controller n Left Thumbstick X.
SHORT getGamepadThumbLX(UINT n)
// Return value of controller n Left Thumbstick Y.
SHORT getGamepadThumbLY(UINT n)
// Return value of controller n Right Thumbstick X.
SHORT getGamepadThumbRX(UINT n)
// Return value of controller n Right Thumbstick Y.
SHORT getGamepadThumbRY(UINT n)
```

Listing 4.46. Functions for reading gamepad analog inputs.

4.3.4 Game Controller Vibration

The Xbox 360 controller contains a left and right vibration motor. The left motor is for creating low frequency vibrations and the right motor for high frequency vibrations. The speed of each motor may be set by specifying a number from 0 to 65,535 in the vibration member of the ControllerState structure. A value of 0 signifies no motor use and a value of 65,535 signifies 100% motor use. In addition to the vibration amount, we also need to control the length of time the motor runs. To make it easier to use the vibration effect, we have included a function to set the rotation rate and rotation time of each motor (Listing 4.47).

```
// Vibrate controller n left motor
// Left is low frequency vibration
// Speed 0=off, 65536=100 percent
// Sec is time to vibrate in seconds
void gamePadVibrateLeft(UINT n, WORD speed, float sec)
{
    if(n > MAX_CONTROLLERS-1)
        n=MAX_CONTROLLERS-1;
    controllers[n].vibration.wLeftMotorSpeed = speed;
    controllers[n].vibrateTimeLeft = sec;
}
// Vibrate controller n right motor
// Right is high frequency vibration
// Speed 0=off, 65536=100 percent
// Sec is time to vibrate in seconds
void gamePadVibrateRight(UINT n, WORD speed, float sec)
{
    if(n > MAX_CONTROLLERS-1)
        n=MAX_CONTROLLERS-1;
    controllers[n].vibration.wRightMotorSpeed = speed;
    controllers[n].vibrateTimeRight = sec;
}
```

Listing 4.47. Controller vibrate functions.

```
//=============================================================================
// Vibrate connected controllers
//=============================================================================
void Input::vibrateControllers(float frameTime)
{
    for(int i=0; i < MAX_CONTROLLERS; i++)
    {
        if(controllers[i].connected)
        {
            controllers[i].vibrateTimeLeft -= frameTime;
            if(controllers[i].vibrateTimeLeft < 0)
            {
                controllers[i].vibrateTimeLeft = 0;
                controllers[i].vibration.wLeftMotorSpeed = 0;
            }
            controllers[i].vibrateTimeRight -= frameTime;
            if(controllers[i].vibrateTimeRight < 0)
            {
                controllers[i].vibrateTimeRight = 0;
                controllers[i].vibration.wRightMotorSpeed = 0;
            }
            XInputSetState(i, &controllers[i].vibration);
        }
    }
}
```

Listing 4.48. Controls the vibration time.

Another function is used to keep track of the vibration time and turn off the motors when the time expires (Listing 4.48). A call to vibrateControllers has been added to the Game::run function (Listing 4.49). The frameTime parameter is used to regulate the vibration time. When the vibration time reaches 0, the corresponding motor speed is set to 0. To vibrate controller 0's left motor at 100% for 1.0 second, we would use the code in Listing 4.50.

```
input->vibrateControllers(frameTime);  // Handle controller vibration
```

Listing 4.49. Calling vibrateControllers.

```
input->gamePadVibrateLeft(0,65535,1.0);
```

Listing 4.50. Vibrating a controller.

4.4 The Spacewar Class

As mentioned earlier, to create a game with the game engine we must create a new class that inherits from the Game class. Let's create a Spacewar class to demonstrate. The Spacewar class is declared in spacewar.h, as shown in Listing 4.51.

```cpp
// Programming 2D Games
// Copyright (c) 2011 by:
// Charles Kelly
// Chapter 4 spacewar.h v1.0
#ifndef _SPACEWAR_H              // Prevent multiple definitions if this
#define _SPACEWAR_H              // file is included in more than one place
#define WIN32_LEAN_AND_MEAN
#include "game.h"
// Spacewar is the class we create; it inherits from the Game class
class Spacewar : public Game
{
private:
    // Variables
public:
    // Constructor
    Spacewar();
    // Destructor
    virtual ~Spacewar();
    // Initialize the game
    void initialize(HWND hwnd);
    void update();         // Must override pure virtual from Game
    void ai();             // "
    void collisions();     // "
    void render();         // "
    void releaseAll();
    void resetAll();
};
#endif
```

Listing 4.51. The Spacewar class declaration.

Notice we must override the pure virtual functions update, ai, collisions, and render declared in the Game class. The bodies of the functions are empty at this time because we have no specific actions for the functions to perform (Listing 4.52).

```cpp
// Programming 2D Games
// Copyright (c) 2011 by:
// Charles Kelly
// Game Engine Part 1
// Chapter 4 spacewar.cpp v1.0
// Spacewar is the class we create
#include "spacewar.h"
//=============================================================
// Constructor
//=============================================================
Spacewar::Spacewar()
```

```
{}
//============================================================================
// Destructor
//============================================================================
Spacewar::~Spacewar()
{
    releaseAll();           // Call onLostDevice() for every graphics item
}
//============================================================================
// Initializes the game
// Throws GameError on error
//============================================================================
void Spacewar::initialize(HWND hwnd)
{
    Game::initialize(hwnd); // Throws GameError
    return;
}
//============================================================================
// Update all game items
//============================================================================
void Spacewar::update()
{}
//============================================================================
// Artificial Intelligence
//============================================================================
void Spacewar::ai()
{}
//============================================================================
// Handle collisions
//============================================================================
void Spacewar::collisions()
{}
//============================================================================
// Render game items
//============================================================================
void Spacewar::render()
{}
//============================================================================
// The graphics device was lost
// Release all reserved video memory so graphics device may be reset
//============================================================================
void Spacewar::releaseAll()
{
    Game::releaseAll();
    return;
}
//============================================================================
// The grahics device has been reset
// Recreate all surfaces
//============================================================================
void Spacewar::resetAll()
{
    Game::resetAll();
    return;
}
```

Listing 4.52. The Spacewar class code.

All our Spacewar game does at this point is display a solid color (boring!). We will add more interesting features in later chapters.

Chapter Review

In this chapter we started constructing our game engine. We learned that each major component of our game engine is contained in a class. We were introduced to the high-performance timer that our game engine will use to control the speed of game elements. The game engine will make calls to render the game graphics and will contain a `run` function that is repeatedly called from the main message loop in `WinMain`. We created an `Input` class to hold the code we need to read from the keyboard, mouse, and game controller. We also learned how to use the vibration feature of a game controller. Here are the key points:

- *A new class.* To create a game with our game engine, we created a new class that inherits from the `Game` class.

- *Direct access.* The `protected:` keyword in the `Game` class allows derived classes direct access to the variables.

- *Keep it simple.* Keep class constructor code limited to simple variable initialization.

- *Releasing resources.* Release resources in the opposite order they are reserved.

- *The lost state.* DirectX devices may become inaccessible and be in what is referred to as a lost state. The device's `Reset` method is the only method that may be called when it is lost.

- *Checking.* The `TestCooperativeLevel` method may be used to check if a device is lost.

- *Scenes.* The rendering (drawing) of DirectX graphics must be done in a scene.

- *The `renderGame` function.* Our `Game` class's `renderGame` function begins a scene, calls our render function, and then ends the scene. It also tests for and handles lost graphics devices and then displays the back buffer to the screen.

- *Actual time elapsed.* The `frameTime` variable in our game engine contains the actual time that has elapsed during the previous frame.

- *The `Input` class.* The `Input` class contains code for using the keyboard, mouse, and game controller.

- *Key press state.* The key press state of a key may be determined with the `isKeyDown` or `wasKeyPressed` function.

- *Pressed keys.* The `anyKeyPressed` function returns `true` if any key was pressed.

- *Input text.* Input text is stored in the `textIn` string.

- *Capturing the mouse.* Capturing the mouse directs all mouse input to the capturing window.

- *Mouse input.* Mouse input consists of x and y movement plus the state of the buttons.

- *Game controller input.* Game controller input consists of buttons, the analog positions of the left and right triggers, and the analog positions of the left and right thumb sticks.

- *High and low frequency vibrations.* The left vibration motor in the game controller is for creating low frequency vibrations and the right motor is for high frequency vibrations.

- *Motor speed.* Each vibration motor's speed is set with a value of 0 to 65,535, where 65,535 represents 100% motor use.

Review Questions

1. To create a game using our game engine, we need to create a new class that inherits from which class?

2. Why do we need to use a timer when displaying animated graphics?

3. What happens to a game if the graphics device becomes lost?

4. What is the first step in rendering any DirectX primitive?

5. How does the message loop in `WinMain` become our game loop?

6. What does putting a program to sleep do?

7. What is the resolution of a high-definition mouse?

8. What does "capturing the mouse" do?

9. What are the virtual key codes for the arrow keys?

10. What is the difference between `getMouseX` and `getMouseRawX` functions?

11. What type of Xbox 360 controller may be used on a Windows PC with no extra hardware?

12. What is the maximum number of Xbox 360 controllers supported by our game engine?

13. What type of vibration does the left motor produce in the Xbox 360 controller?

14. Describe two ways of testing game controller 1 for button B press.

15. Show code that will vibrate controller 1's right motor at 50% for 2.0 seconds.

Exercises

1. Copy the "Engine, Part 1" example to a different folder. Modify the `Spacewar` `update` function to exit the program when the user types the word "exit." Use the `input>getTextIn()` function to read the input string. (Use `PostQuitMessage` `(0)` to end the program.)

2. (Requires Xbox 360 USB controller.) Copy the "Engine, Part 1" example to a different folder. Modify the `Spacewar` `update` function to read the trigger values from a game controller. Use the left trigger value to set the vibration speed of the left motor and the right trigger value to set the vibration speed of the right motor. The trigger value is a `BYTE` and the motor speed is a `WORD`. A trigger value of 0xFF should be converted to a speed value of 0xFF00.

3. Copy the "Engine, Part 1" example to a different folder. Modify the `Spacewar` `update` function to change the background color when a mouse button is clicked. Use `graphics>setBackColor(SETCOLOR_ARGB(255,red,green,blue));` to set the background color, where red, green, and blue specify the intensity of each color as a number from 0 through 255. Display a different color for each mouse button clicked.

Examples

All examples are available for download from www.programming2dgames.com. Included on the website is the following code:

- *Engine, Part 1.*

  - Creates the first part of our game engine.

  - Contains the `Input` class, which supports input from the keyboard, mouse, and game controller.

  - Introduces the `Game` class, which is the heart of the game engine.

  - Demonstrates how to make a new game by creating a class that inherits from `Game`.

5 Sprites and Animation

▌ 5.1 Obtaining Game Graphics

Games need artwork. Fortunately, for some of us, we do not need to be artists to create great looking games. There are several good online resources where we may obtain royalty-free game graphics. Here are a few such sites:

- http://opengameart.org/

- http://freegamearts.tuxfamily.org/

- http://www.reinerstilesets.de/

- http://www.lostgarden.com/search/label/free game graphics

- http://www.widgetworx.com/widgetworx/portfolio/spritelib.html

- http://www.spriteland.com/

- http://www.nasaimages.org/

As with any online resource, always verify the licensing requirements and make sure the material is not violating any copyright laws.

With a little practice, we can create our own game graphics. There are some great free tools available:

- http://blender.org/

- http://www.anim8or.com/

- http://www.gimp.org/

- http://www.makehuman.org/

- http://www.getpaint.net/index.html

- http://www.aseprite.org/

- http://www.ne.jp/asahi/mighty/knight/

▮ 5.2 The Graphics Pipeline

Often in graphics programming, we see references to the *graphics pipeline*. The Direct3D graphics pipeline can be diagrammed, as shown in Figure 5.1.

DirectX contains a complete rendering engine that can perform all the computations required to display complex shapes on the computer screen. The shapes are defined by vertex and primitive data. A *vertex* is a point defined in 3D space. The primitive data defines the type of shape to draw, such as a line, triangle, triangle strip, quad, etc. In addition to location data, a vertex may also contain information about color and texture. A *texture* is a picture that is drawn on the shape.

Basically, we feed vertex and primitive data into one end of the pipeline, throw in some texture data toward the end, and out comes a shape with a picture on it. This process is repeated for every frame rendered in our game.

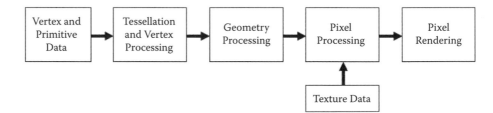

Figure 5.1. The Direct3D graphics pipeline.

▮ 5.3 Drawing with Transparency

In most games, many images are displayed. Sometimes those images overlap on the screen. When images overlap, we typically want part of the top image to be transparent. As an example of what we are referring to, take a look at Figure 5.2.

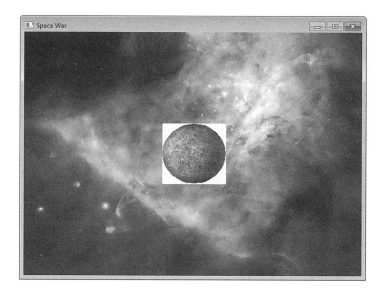

Figure 5.2. Drawing without transparency. Hubble photo of the Orion nebula from NASA. *Courtesy of nasaimages.org.*

The planet in the center was drawn using a technique that did not support transparency. Notice the square border around the image where the background picture is not visible. This is what happens when an image is drawn without transparency.

The transparent parts of an image are designated with a special color key value or with an alpha channel. We may use any color value we wish as the transparent color key, but typically magenta (red = 255, green = 0, blue = 255) is used. Any pixels in the image that match the transparent color are not drawn so they are transparent. If the image is created with software that supports alpha channel transparency then a color key is not required. To draw images with transparency, we will use DirectX sprites.

5.3.1 DirectX Sprites

DirectX *sprites* are comprised of DirectX primitive and texture data. Sprites are part of the DirectX graphics API specifically designed for drawing 2D images. They also support transparency, which makes them perfect for the type of drawing we need to do in our game.

Sprites are created with the `D3DXCreateSprite` function:

```
HRESULT D3DXCreateSprite(
    LPDIRECT3DDEVICE9 pDevice,
    LPD3DXSPRITE *ppSprite
};
```

The parameters:

- `pDevice`. Pointer to an IDirect3DDevice 9 interface.

- `ppSprite`. Returns an address of a pointer to an ID3DXSprite interface.

```
#define LP_SPRITE    LPD3DXSPRITE
```

Listing 5.1. Redefined sprite pointer.

Our design goal is to place all DirectX graphic-specific code in the Graphics class. In keeping with that design idea, we will define the DirectX sprite pointer as LP_SPRITE in graphics.h (Listing 5.1).

All drawing of sprites, performed by our game engine, will be done with one DirectX sprite. The pointer to the sprite is added to the Graphics class in the graphics.h file (Listing 5.2). The sprite creation code is added to the end of our Graphics::initialize function in the graphics.cpp file (Listing 5.3).

```
class Graphics
{
private:
    // DirectX pointers and stuff
    LP_3D       direct3d;
    LP_3DDEVICE device3d;
    LP_SPRITE   sprite;
```

Listing 5.2. Sprite pointer.


```
    // Create Direct3D device
    result = direct3d->CreateDevice(
        D3DADAPTER_DEFAULT,
        D3DDEVTYPE_HAL,
        hwnd,
        behavior,
        &d3dpp,
        &device3d);
    if (FAILED(result))
        throw(GameError(gameErrorNS::FATAL_ERROR,
            "Error creating Direct3D device"));

    result = D3DXCreateSprite(device3d, &sprite);
    if (FAILED(result))
        throw(GameError(gameErrorNS::FATAL_ERROR,
            "Error creating Direct3D sprite"));
}
```

Listing 5.3. Sprite creation.

5.3.2 Sprite Textures

A texture is a picture that is applied to a graphics primitive: a sprite, in this case. The size of the texture image is important. Some older graphics cards do not support very large texture

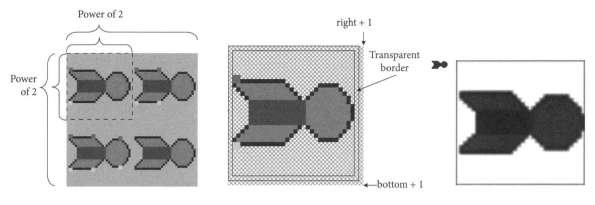

Figure 5.3. Spaceship texture.

Figure 5.4. Sprite border.

Figure 5.5. The border is visible on an enlarged sprite.

files. If the texture is too large to fit in video memory, it will be loaded into system memory, which will result in slower access.

Each individual texture within the picture, and the entire picture, should have width and height that are powers of 2 (see Figure 5.3); that is, 4, 8, 16, 32, 64, 128, etc. Newer graphics cards do support non-power of 2 texture sizes but special code is necessary to check the capabilities of the card and to specify non-power of 2 sizes. The default behavior when a non-power of 2 texture size is used is to round the size up to the nearest power of 2.

Any rectangular portion of the larger texture may be applied to the sprite. This permits us to place multiple sprite textures into one larger image and then select only the texture we want. The `pSrcRect` parameter of the sprite's `Draw` function defines the part of the texture to use. If this parameter is `NULL` the entire image is used as the texture. The rectangle that selects the portion of the source image is defined as follows:

$$\text{left, top, right} + 1, \text{bottom} + 1.$$

It is important to note that the bottom and right must be specified one unit beyond the actual edge of the image desired. The right and bottom edges are easily determined by using the width and height of the sprite as:

$$\text{right} + 1 = \text{left} + \text{width},$$
$$\text{bottom} + 1 = \text{top} + \text{height}.$$

The rectangular region of the source texture should have a minimum one-pixel wide transparent border if the sprite is going to be scaled to a different size (Figure 5.4). This is because DirectX uses bilinear filtering by default when applying the texture to the scaled sprite. Bilinear filtering will sample points outside the specified sprite rectangle, resulting in data being drawn that is not part of the source sprite image.

In Figure 5.5, we see a sprite drawn at a scale factor of 1 and a scale factor of 8. The source image had a solid border one pixel outside the rectangular region of the texture. Note that part of the border is drawn on the scaled sprite but not on the unscaled sprite. See "Sprite Border" in the end-of-chapter examples.

5.3.3 Loading the Texture

The texture that is applied to a sprite will typically be located in a file. We need a function to load the texture image from the file. The DirectX function we will use for this task is `D3DXCreateTextureFromFileEx`. Here is the formal syntax:

```
HRESULT  D3DXCreateTextureFromFileEx(
    LPDIRECT3DDEVICE9 pDevice,
    LPCTSTR pSrcFile,
    UINT Width,
    UINT Height,
    UINT MipLevels,
    DWORD Usage,
    D3DFORMAT Format,
    D3DPOOL Pool,
    DWORD Filter,
    DWORD MipFilter,
    D3DCOLOR ColorKey,
    D3DXIMAGE_INFO *pSrcInfo,
    PALETTEENTRY *pPalette,
    LPDIRECT3DTEXTURE9 *ppTexture
);
```

The parameters:

- `pDevice`. Pointer to an IDirect3DDevice9 interface.

- `pSrcFile`. Pointer to a string that specifies the file name.

- `Width`. Width of the texture in pixels. If 0 or `D3DX_DEFAULT` is specified, the dimensions are taken from the file and rounded up to a power of 2. If the device supports non-power of 2 textures and `D3DX_DEFAULT_NONPOW2` is specified, the size is not rounded.

- `Height`. Height of the texture in pixels. If 0 or `D3DX_DEFAULT` is specified, the dimensions are taken from the file and rounded up to a power of 2. If the device supports non-power of 2 textures and `D3DX_DEFAULT_NONPOW2` is specified, the size is not rounded.

- `MipLevels`. Number of mip levels to make. If 0 or `D3DX_DEFAULT` is specified, a complete mipmap chain is created. Mip levels are used to smooth the transition of textures when moving the player closer or farther away from the textured surface. In 2D games, the surface does not change in distance from the viewer, so mip levels are not used; therefore, we will specify 1 for this parameter.

- `Usage`. We will always use 0. The other choices are `D3DUSAGE_RENDERTARGET`, which specifies that the surface is to be used as a render target, and `D3DUSAGE_DYNAMIC`, which specifies that the surface should be handled dynamically as part of a dynamic texture.

- `Format`. Must be an enumerated type from `D3DFORMAT`, which describes the requested pixel format for the texture. The actual texture returned might have a dif-

ferent format than requested. The actual format is returned in the pSrcInfo structure. Use D3DFMT_UINKNOWN to use the format from the file.

- Pool. Must be an enumerated type from D3DPOOL. Describes the memory class
  into which the texture is loaded.

- Filter. Requires one or more constants from D3DX_FILTER and specifies how
  the image is filtered. We always use D3DX_DEFAULT.

- MipFilter. Requires one or more constants from D3DX_FILTER and specifies
  how the image is filtered. We always use D3DX_DEFAULT.

- ColorKey. The color to treat as transparent, specified as a D3DCOLOR value. All 32
  bits of the color are significant. Pixels in the source image that match ColorKey are
  converted to transparent when the image is loaded. The ColorKey is not required
  for images that support alpha channel transparency.

- pSrcInfo. Pointer to a D3DXIMAGE_INFO structure that is filled with a description of the source image.

- pPalette. Pointer to a PALETTEENTRY structure that represents a 256-color pal-
  ette that is either filled in or NULL. We will always use NULL.

- ppTexture. Address of a pointer to an IDirect3DTexture9 interface that points
  to the created texture.

Check the return value using the FAILED or SUCCEEDED macros. The width and height
of the texture file is obtained with the D3DXGetImageInfoFromFile function:

```
HRESULT D3DXGetImageInfoFromFile(
    LPCSTR pSrcFile,
    D3DXIMAGE_INFO *pSrcInfo
);
```

The parameters:

- pSrcFile. Pointer to the file name of the image.

- pSrcInfo. Pointer to a D3DXIMAGE_INFO structure to be filled with information
  about the image file.

The D3DXIMAGE_INFO structure looks like this:

```
typedef struct D3DXIMAGE_INFO {
    UINT                 Width;
    UINT                 Height;
    UINT                 Depth;
    UINT                 MipLevels;
    D3DFORMAT            Format;
    D3DRESOURCETYPE      ResourceType;
    D3DXIMAGE_FILEFORMAT ImageFileFormat;
} D3DXIMAGE_INFO, *LPD3DXIMAGE_INFO;
```

The members are:

- `Width`. Width of the image in pixels.

- `Height`. Height of the image in pixels.

- `Depth`. Depth of the image in pixels.

- `MipLevels`. Number of mip levels in the image.

- `Format`. A value of `D3DFORMAT` enumerated type that describes the format of the data in the image.

- `ResourceType`. The type of texture in the file defined as either `D3DRTYPE_TEX TURE`, `D3DRTYPE_VOLUMETEXTURE`, or `D3DRTYPE_CubeTexture`.

- `ImageFileFormat`. The format of the image file.

We need to create a function in our `Graphics` class to load textures. Let's name the function `loadTexture`. It receives parameters for the file name and transparent color. The texture width, height, and pointer are returned via the reference parameters. Our complete `loadTexture` function is in Listing 5.4.

```
//=============================================================================
// Load the texture into default D3D memory (normal texture use)
// For internal engine use only. Use the TextureManager class to load game
// textures.
// Pre: filename is name of texture file
//      transcolor is transparent color
// Post: width and height = size of texture
//       texture points to texture
// Returns HRESULT
//=============================================================================
HRESULT Graphics::loadTexture(const char *filename, COLOR_ARGB transcolor,
                              UINT &width, UINT &height, LP_TEXTURE
                              &texture)
{
    // The struct for reading file info
    D3DXIMAGE_INFO info;
    result = E_FAIL;
    try{
        if(filename == NULL)
        {
            texture = NULL;
            return D3DERR_INVALIDCALL;
        }

        // Get width and height from file
        result = D3DXGetImageInfoFromFile(filename, &info);
        if (result != D3D_OK)
            return result;
        width = info.Width;
```

```
        height = info.Height;

        // Create the new texture by loading from file
        result = D3DXCreateTextureFromFileEx(
            device3d,               // 3D device
            filename,               // Image filename
            info.Width,             // Texture width
            info.Height,            // Texture height
            1,                      // Mip-map levels (1 for no chain)
            0,                      // Usage
            D3DFMT_UNKNOWN,         // Surface format (default)
            D3DPOOL_DEFAULT,        // Memory class for the texture
            D3DX_DEFAULT,           // Image filter
            D3DX_DEFAULT,           // Mip filter
            transcolor,             // Color key for transparency
            &info,                  // Bitmap file info (from loaded file)
            NULL,                   // Color palette
            &texture );             // Destination texture
    } catch(...)
    {
        throw(GameError(gameErrorNS::FATAL_ERROR,
                    "Error in Graphics::loadTexture"));
    }
    return result;
}
```

Listing 5.4. The `loadTexture` function.

5.3.4 Drawing the Sprite

The first step in drawing sprites is to begin a DirectX scene. A scene is started for us automatically by the `renderGame` function in the `Game` class (Listing 5.5).

```
//=============================================================================
// Render game items
//=============================================================================
void Game::renderGame()
{
    // Start rendering
    if (SUCCEEDED(graphics->beginScene()))
    {
        render();               // Call render() in derived class
        // Stop rendering
        graphics->endScene();
    }
    handleLostGraphicsDevice();
    // Display the back buffer on the screen
    graphics->showBackbuffer();
}
```

Listing 5.5. The `renderGame` function.

The `renderGame` function calls the pure virtual function `render`. The code for pure virtual functions must be provided in any derived class. When a game is created with our game engine, the class that inherits from the `Game` class must provide the code for the `render` function. The `render` function is where we place our code to draw the game sprites. After all sprite drawing is complete, the `renderGame` function ends the scene by calling `graphics->endScene()`.

The rendering of sprites or any DirectX primitive outside a scene will fail.

Sprite drawing is started by calling the sprite `Begin` function. The `Begin` function is part of the sprite interface returned by the `D3DXCreateSprite(g3ddev,&sprite)` function. A sprite is drawn by calling its `Draw` function. We will configure and draw our game engine sprite as many times as is required for the current scene. A call to the sprite `End` function will add the sprites to the scene.

Between the calls to `sprite->Begin` and `sprite->Draw`, the sprite may be sized, rotated, and positioned on the screen. Positioning of sprites, as with any DirectX primitive, is done using matrix math. For those of us who can't remember how to do matrix math, there is no need to panic—DirectX is going to do the math for us. We just need to know which functions to call.

The DirectX function `D3DMatrixTransformation2D` configures a transformation matrix that can scale, rotate, and position the sprite. The formal function syntax is:

```
D3DXMATRIX * D3DXMatrixTransformation2D(
    D3DXMATRIX *pOut,
    const D3DXVECTOR2 *pScalingCenter,
    FLOAT pScalingRotation,
    const D3DXVECTOR2 *pScaling,
    const D3DXVECTOR2 *pRotationCenter,
    FLOAT Rotation,
    const D3DXVECTOR2 *pTranslation
);
```

The parameters are:

- `pOut`. Pointer to the `D3DXMATRIX` structure where the resulting matrix will be created.

- `pScalingCenter`. Pointer to a `D3DXVECTOR2` structure that identifies the scaling center. A `NULL` value keeps the origin of the sprite at the top-left corner when scaling.

- `pScalingRotation`. The scaling rotation factor.

- `pScaling`. Pointer to a `D3DXVECTOR2` structure that contains the x and y scaling amounts.

- `pRotationCenter`. Pointer to a `D3DXVECTOR2` structure that identifies the rotation center.

- Rotation. The angle of rotation in radians.

- pTranslation. Pointer to a D3DXVECTOR2 structure that contains the x and y position of the sprite.

Once the D3DXMATRIX is configured, a call to the sprite's SetTransform function applies the matrix to the sprite.

```
HRESULT SetTransform(
    const D3DXMATRIX *pTransform
);
```

The sprite Draw function adds the sprite to the scene. Here is the formal function syntax:

```
HRESULT Draw(
    LPDIRECT3DTEXTURE9 pTexture,
    const RECT *pSrcRect,
    const D3DXVECTOR3 *pCenter,
    const D3DXVECTOR3 *pPosition,
    D3DCOLOR Color
);
```

The parameters:

- pTexture. Pointer to an IDirect3DTexture9 interface that contains the picture to draw on the sprite.

- pSrcRect. Pointer to a RECT structure that defines the part of the source texture to use for the sprite.

- pCenter. Pointer to a D3DXVECTOR3 vector that identifies the center of the sprite. A value of NULL identifies the upper-left corner.

- pPosition. Pointer to a D3DXVECTOR3 vector that identifies the position of the sprite. A value of NULL is used to specify the upper-left corner.

- Color. The color of the sprite and alpha channel. The effect is similar to looking through a filter of this color. A value of 0xFFFFFFFF (color constant WHITE) maintains the original color and alpha data. The alpha data is specified by the first two digits of the hexadecimal color value 0xFF------. It affects the transparency of the sprite. A value of 0 is completely transparent and a value of 0xFF (255) is completely opaque. The SETCOLOR_ARGB(a,r,g,b) macro we defined in graphics.h may be used to specify a custom color value, where

  - a = the alpha channel (0 through 255),

  - r = red (0 through 255),

  - g = green (0 through 255), and

  - b = blue (0 through 255).

```
// SpriteData: The properties required by Graphics::drawSprite to draw a
// sprite
struct SpriteData
{
    int         width;      // Width of sprite in pixels
    int         height;     // Height of sprite in pixels
    float       x;          // Screen location (top left corner of sprite)
    float       y;
    float       scale;      // <1 smaller, >1 bigger
    float       angle;      // Rotation angle in radians
    RECT        rect;       // Used to select an image from a larger texture
    LP_TEXTURE  texture;    // Pointer to texture
    bool        flipHorizontal;// True to flip sprite horizontally (mirror)
    bool        flipVertical;  // True to flip sprite vertically
};
```

Listing 5.6. SpriteData properties.

Each time we draw our sprite to the screen, we need to configure its properties. The properties are contained in our SpriteData structure. The structure definition is in graphics.h and looks like the code in Listing 5.6.

The members are:

- width. Width of the sprite in pixels.

- height. Height of the sprite in pixels.

- x, y. Screen location of the top-left corner of the sprite.

- scale. Scaling (zoom) factor. Numbers < 1 reduce the size and numbers > 1 increase the size.

- angle. Rotation angle of the sprite in radians.

- rect. The rectangular portion of a larger texture image to use when drawing this sprite.

- texture. Pointer to the texture image data.

- flipHorizontal. When true, the sprite is flipped horizontally (mirrored).

- flipVertical. When true, the sprite is flipped vertically.

We now have all the functionality we need to draw a sprite. Let's combine the sprite-drawing code into a drawSprite function and add it to our Graphics class. The parameters consist of our SpriteData structure and an optional color. The color parameter allows us to change the color of the entire sprite. The effect is similar to looking through a filter of the specified color. The default color is white, which results in no change to the sprite color. Our function begins as shown in Listing 5.7.

```
//===========================================================================
// Draw the sprite described in SpriteData structure
// Color is optional, it is applied like a filter, white is default (no
// change)
// Pre : sprite->Begin() is called
// Post: sprite->End() is called
// spriteData.rect defines the portion of spriteData.texture to draw
//    spriteData.rect.right must be right edge + 1
//    spriteData.rect.bottom must be bottom edge + 1
//===========================================================================
void Graphics::drawSprite(const SpriteData &spriteData, COLOR_ARGB color)
{
    if(spriteData.texture == NULL)      // If no texture
        return;
```

Listing 5.7. The `drawSprite` function start.

Next, we find the center of the sprite. We need to know where the center is so we can rotate the sprite around that point (Listing 5.8). The X, Y screen position of the sprite is placed in a D3DXVECTOR2 named translate (Listing 5.9). We will use the translate vector later to create a transformation matrix. The D3DXVECTOR2—named scaling—is initialized with the scale value from the spriteData structure. Sprites may be scaled to different sizes in the *x* and *y* dimension. We use the same scaling factor for both (Listing 5.10).

```
// Find center of sprite
D3DXVECTOR2 spriteCenter = D3DXVECTOR2 (
                        (float)(spriteData.width/2*spriteData.scale),
                        (float)(spriteData.height/2*spriteData.scale));
```

Listing 5.8. Finding the center of the sprite.

```
// Screen position of the sprite
D3DXVECTOR2 translate=D3DXVECTOR2((float)spriteData.x,
                                 (float)spriteData.y);
```

Listing 5.9. Creating a translate vector.

```
// Scaling X,Y
D3DXVECTOR2 scaling(spriteData.scale,spriteData.scale);
```

Listing 5.10. Creating a scaling vector.

```
if (spriteData.flipHorizontal)  // If flip horizontal
{
    scaling.x *= -1;                // Negative X scale to flip
    // Get center of flipped image.
    spriteCenter.x -= (float)(spriteData.width*spriteData.scale);
    // Flip occurs around left edge, translate right to put
    // flipped image in same location as original.
    translate.x += (float)(spriteData.width*spriteData.scale);
}
```

Listing 5.11. Adjusting the position of the horizontally-flipped sprite.

If spriteData.flipHorizontal is set to true, we flip the sprite horizontally. This gives us a mirror image of the original sprite (Listing 5.11). If spriteData.flipVertical is set to true, we flip the sprite vertically (Listing 5.12). We create a matrix to rotate, scale, and position the sprite using the code in Listing 5.13. The matrix is applied to the sprite with the SetTransform function (Listing 5.14). The Draw function is called at the end of our drawSprite function (Listing 5.15).

```
if (spriteData.flipVertical)    // If flip vertical
{
    scaling.y *= -1;                // Negative Y scale to flip
    // Get center of flipped image
    spriteCenter.y -= (float)(spriteData.height*spriteData.scale);
    // Flip occurs around top edge, translate down to put
    // flipped image in same location as original.
    translate.y += (float)(spriteData.height*spriteData.scale);
}
```

Listing 5.12. Adjusting the position of the vertically-flipped sprite.

```
// Create a matrix to rotate, scale and position our sprite
D3DXMATRIX matrix;
D3DXMatrixTransformation2D(
    &matrix,                    // The matrix
    NULL,                       // Keep origin at top left when scaling
    0.0f,                       // No scaling rotation
    &scaling,                   // Scale amount
    &spriteCenter,              // Rotation center
    (float)(spriteData.angle),  // Rotation angle
    &translate);                // X,Y location
```

Listing 5.13. Create the transformation matrix.

```
// Tell the sprite about the matrix "Hello Neo"
sprite->SetTransform(&matrix);
```

Listing 5.14. The matrix is applied.

```
// Draw the sprite
sprite->Draw(spriteData.texture,&spriteData.rect,NULL,NULL,color);
}
```

Listing 5.15. Draw the sprite.

To review, the steps involved in drawing a sprite are:

1. Begin a graphics scene.

2. Call the sprite `Begin` function.

3. For each sprite

   a. scale, rotate, and position the sprite with a transformation matrix, and

   b. call the sprite `Draw` function.

4. Call the sprite `End` function.

5. End the graphics scene (Figure 5.6).

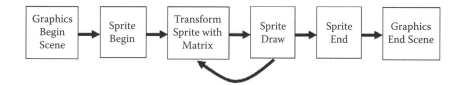

Figure 5.6. Steps involved in drawing a sprite.

5.3.5 Common Colors

We are giving the classes we create their own namespace. The `Graphics` class namespace is `graphicsNS`. To access an item defined in a namespace, we use the namespace followed by the global resolution operator, "`::`"—two colons put together.

A useful item to include in the graphics namespace would be some common color definitions (Listing 5.16).

The last three colors, `FILTER`, `ALPHA25`, and `ALPHA50`, are not really colors at all. The color `FILTER` is a value that may be used as a parameter when drawing images (see Section 5.5.1 later in this chapter); `ALPHA25` and `ALPHA50` may be used to adjust the alpha value of a color by performing a bitwise AND. The alpha value determines how transparent a color appears. A value of 0 is completely transparent and a value of 255 is completely opaque. We will use these alpha values in later examples. To specify the color orange, for example, just use graphicsNS::ORANGE in the code.

```
// Some common colors
// ARGB numbers range from 0 through 255
// A = Alpha channel (transparency where 255 is opaque)
// R = Red, G = Green, B = Blue
const COLOR_ARGB ORANGE = D3DCOLOR_ARGB(255,255,165,  0);
const COLOR_ARGB BROWN  = D3DCOLOR_ARGB(255,139, 69, 19);
const COLOR_ARGB LTGRAY = D3DCOLOR_ARGB(255,192,192,192);
const COLOR_ARGB GRAY   = D3DCOLOR_ARGB(255,128,128,128);
const COLOR_ARGB OLIVE  = D3DCOLOR_ARGB(255,128,128,  0);
const COLOR_ARGB PURPLE = D3DCOLOR_ARGB(255,128,  0,128);
const COLOR_ARGB MAROON = D3DCOLOR_ARGB(255,128,  0,  0);
const COLOR_ARGB TEAL   = D3DCOLOR_ARGB(255,  0,128,128);
const COLOR_ARGB GREEN  = D3DCOLOR_ARGB(255,  0,128,  0);
const COLOR_ARGB NAVY   = D3DCOLOR_ARGB(255,  0,  0,128);
const COLOR_ARGB WHITE  = D3DCOLOR_ARGB(255,255,255,255);
const COLOR_ARGB YELLOW = D3DCOLOR_ARGB(255,255,255,  0);
const COLOR_ARGB MAGENTA = D3DCOLOR_ARGB(255,255,  0,255);
const COLOR_ARGB RED    = D3DCOLOR_ARGB(255,255,  0,  0);
const COLOR_ARGB CYAN   = D3DCOLOR_ARGB(255,  0,255,255);
const COLOR_ARGB LIME   = D3DCOLOR_ARGB(255,  0,255,  0);
const COLOR_ARGB BLUE   = D3DCOLOR_ARGB(255,  0,  0,255);
const COLOR_ARGB BLACK  = D3DCOLOR_ARGB(255,  0,  0,  0);
    // Use to specify drawing with colorFilter
const COLOR_ARGB FILTER = D3DCOLOR_ARGB(  0,  0,  0,  0);
    // AND with color to get 25% alpha
const COLOR_ARGB ALPHA25 = D3DCOLOR_ARGB( 64,255,255,255);
    // AND with color to get 50% alpha
const COLOR_ARGB ALPHA50 = D3DCOLOR_ARGB(128,255,255,255);
```

Listing 5.16. Common colors.

▐ 5.4 The TextureManager Class

The loadTexture function, which we added to the Graphics class, loads the texture data into D3DPOOL_DEFAULT memory. This is normally video memory. If the graphics device is used by another application, it may become unavailable or "lost" to our game. If that happens, we will need to release and reload the texture data as part of the process of recovering the lost graphics device. By creating a separate texture manager class, we can include the code for dealing with a lost device. When we need to use a texture in our game, we will create a TextureManager object to load and manage each texture.

The TextureManager initialize function saves a pointer to the graphics system and loads the specified texture file from disk. The graphics->loadTexture function saves the width, height, and pointer to the texture data (Listing 5.17).

```
//============================================================================
// Loads the texture file from disk
// Post: returns true if successful, false if failed
//============================================================================
bool TextureManager::initialize(Graphics *g, const char *f)
{
    try{
        graphics = g;               // The graphics object
        file = f;                   // The texture file
        hr = graphics->loadTexture(file, TRANSCOLOR, width, height,
                                    texture);
        if (FAILED(hr))
        {
            SAFE_RELEASE(texture);
            return false;
        }
    }
    catch(...) {return false;}
    initialized = true;             // Set true when successfully initialized
    return true;
}
```

Listing 5.17. The TextureManager initialize function.

The onLostDevice and onResetDevice functions are called as part of the mechanism to deal with a lost graphics device (Listing 5.18). There are also functions that return a pointer to the texture data as well as the width and height. These functions are defined in textureManager.h (Listing 5.19).

```
//============================================================================
// Called when graphics device is lost
//============================================================================
void TextureManager::onLostDevice()
{
    if (!initialized)
        return;
    SAFE_RELEASE(texture);
}
//============================================================================
// Called when graphics device is reset
//============================================================================
void TextureManager::onResetDevice()
{
    if (!initialized)
        return;
    graphics->loadTexture(file, TRANSCOLOR, width, height, texture);
}
```

Listing 5.18. The TextureManager onLostDevice and onResetDevice functions.

```
// Returns a pointer to the texture
LP_TEXTURE getTexture() const {return texture;}
// Returns the texture width
UINT getWidth() const {return width;}
// Return the texture height
UINT getHeight() const {return height;}
```

Listing 5.19. Additional `TextureManager` functions.

■ 5.5 The Image Class

All of the code we need to draw and manage a sprite will be incorporated into the `Image` class.

In our game engine design, an Image is the lowest-level object that may be drawn on the screen.

The Image's `initialize` function receives a pointer to the `Graphics` object, the width and height of the image in pixels, the number of columns in the texture, and a pointer to a `TextureManager` that contains the texture.

A width or height value of 0 uses the full texture width or height.

The `initialize` function saves the pointers to `graphics` and `textureManager`. The `spriteData` structure `texture`, `width`, and `height` members are filled in. The number of columns in the texture is saved. The last step in initializing is to configure `spriteData.rect`. The structure `spriteData.rect` specifies a rectangle that may be used to select part of a multi-image texture (Listing 5.20).

```
//=============================================================================
// Initialize the Image
// Post: returns true if successful, false if failed
// Pointer to Graphics
// Width of Image in pixels  (0 = use full texture width)
// Height of Image in pixels (0 = use full texture height)
// Number of columns in texture (1 to n) (0 same as 1)
// Pointer to TextureManager
//=============================================================================
bool Image::initialize(Graphics *g, int width, int height, int ncols,
                       TextureManager *textureM)
{
    try{
        graphics = g;                       // The graphics object
        textureManager = textureM;          // Pointer to texture object
        spriteData.texture = textureManager->getTexture();
        if(width == 0)
```

```
            width = textureManager->getWidth();      // Use full width
        spriteData.width = width;
        if(height == 0)
            height = textureManager->getHeight();    // Use full height
        spriteData.height = height;
        cols = ncols;
        if (cols == 0)
            cols = 1;                    // If 0 cols use 1
        // Configure spriteData.rect to draw currentFrame
        spriteData.rect.left = (currentFrame % cols) * spriteData.width;
        // Right edge + 1
        spriteData.rect.right = spriteData.rect.left + spriteData.width;
        spriteData.rect.top = (currentFrame / cols) * spriteData.height;
        // Bottom edge + 1
        spriteData.rect.bottom = spriteData.rect.top + spriteData.height;
    }
    catch(...) {return false;}
    initialized = true;                  // Successfully initialized
    return true;
}
```

Listing 5.20. The image's `initialize` function.

5.5.1 Drawing the Image

The `Image::draw` function will draw the image to the screen. Images are drawn between calls to `spriteBegin()` and `spriteEnd()`. The `color` parameter is optional because a default value of `WHITE` has been assigned in the prototype (Listing 5.21). The `color` parameter is applied as a filter when the image is drawn. It gives the appearance of viewing the image through a window with `color` shaded glass. The color white (the default) is used for no change. Common color types are defined in `graphics.h`, along with a special color value named `FILTER`. When the color is specified as `FILTER`, the image's `colorFilter` property is used as the color. The `colorFilter` property is a way to specify a color that is always applied when drawing the image (Listing 5.22).

```
// Draw Image using color as filter. Default color is white.
virtual void draw(COLOR_ARGB color = graphicsNS::WHITE);
```

Listing 5.21. Prototype of the `Image::draw` function.

```
//=============================================================================
// Draw the image using color as filter
// The color parameter is optional, white is assigned as default in image.h
// Pre : spriteBegin() is called
// Post: spriteEnd() is called
//=============================================================================
void Image::draw(COLOR_ARGB color)
{
```

```
    if (!visible || graphics == NULL)
        return;
    // Get fresh texture incase onReset() was called
    spriteData.texture = textureManager->getTexture();
    if(color == graphicsNS::FILTER)                // If draw with filter
        graphics->drawSprite(spriteData, colorFilter);// Use colorFilter
    else
        graphics->drawSprite(spriteData, color);       // Use color as filter
}
```

Listing 5.22. The `Image::draw` function.

We have a second version of `draw` that includes a `SpriteData` parameter (Listing 5.23). When `SpriteData` is provided, the `SpriteData.rect` structure is used to select the portion of the texture to draw. This is handy if we want to draw several images using the same sprite setup. For example, suppose we want to draw a spaceship and then draw a shield around it. We will see how to do this in Chapter 6. Images may be flipped horizontally (mirrored) or vertically using the functions in Listing 5.24. Flipping images allows us to use one set of textures in our game for left and right orientation and one set for up and down orientation. The functions in Listing 5.24 are in `image.h`.


```
//=============================================================================
// Draw this image using the specified SpriteData
//   The current SpriteData.rect is used to select the texture
// Pre : spriteBegin() is called
// Post: spriteEnd() is called
//=============================================================================
void Image::draw(SpriteData sd, COLOR_ARGB color)
{
    if (!visible || graphics == NULL)
        return;
    // Use this Images rect to select texture
    sd.rect = spriteData.rect;
    // Get fresh texture incase onReset() was called
    sd.texture = textureManager->getTexture();
    if(color == graphicsNS::FILTER)                // If draw with filter
        graphics->drawSprite(sd, colorFilter);  // Use colorFilter
    else
        graphics->drawSprite(sd, color);        // Use color as filter
}
```

Listing 5.23. The `Image::draw` function with a `SpriteData` parameter.


```
// Flip image horizontally (mirror)
virtual void flipHorizontal(bool flip)
{
```

```
        spriteData.flipHorizontal = flip;
}
// Flip image vertically
virtual void flipVertical(bool flip)
{
        spriteData.flipVertical = flip;
}
```

Listing 5.24. The image's flip functions.

The next three functions are explained in more detail in Section 5.7 later in this chapter. Let's go over them briefly here just to complete the code in the Image class.

- The update function receives the current frameTime as a parameter. The update function is where all code that needs to be synchronized with elapsed time should be placed. The update function sets which frame from the texture image should be displayed, and it calls setRect to select the current frame from the texture image. We will use the update function to draw animated sprites.

- The setCurrentFrame function sets the current frame in a multiple-frame image. This function may be used to change an animation sequence or select a different texture to apply to the image from a multiple-image texture.

- The setRect function sets the spriteData.rect structure used to select the rectangular region of the texture to use for the current sprite.

5.5.2 Image get Functions

A number of get functions are included in image.h (Listing 5.25).

```
// Return reference to SpriteData structure
const virtual SpriteData& getSpriteInfo() {return spriteData;}
// Return visible parameter
virtual bool  getVisible()              {return visible;}
// Return X position
virtual float getX()                    {return spriteData.x;}
// Return Y position
virtual float getY()                    {return spriteData.y;}
// Return scale factor
virtual float getScale()                {return spriteData.scale;}
// Return width
virtual int   getWidth()                {return spriteData.width;}
// Return height
virtual int   getHeight()               {return spriteData.height;}
// Return center X
virtual float getCenterX()              {return spriteData.x + spriteData.
width/2*getScale();}
// Return center Y
virtual float getCenterY()              {return spriteData.y + spriteData.
```

```
width/2*getScale();}
// Return rotation angle in degrees
virtual float getDegrees()          {return spriteData.angle*(180.0f/
                                     (float)PI);}
// Return rotation angle in radians
virtual float getRadians()          {return spriteData.angle;}
// Return delay between frames of animation
virtual float getFrameDelay()       {return frameDelay;}
// Return number of starting frame
virtual int   getStartFrame()       {return startFrame;}
// Return number of ending frame
virtual int   getEndFrame()         {return endFrame;}
// Return number of current frame
virtual int   getCurrentFrame()     {return currentFrame;}
// Return RECT structure of Image
virtual RECT  getSpriteDataRect()   {return spriteData.rect;}
// Return state of animation complete
virtual bool  getAnimationComplete() {return animComplete;}
// Return colorFilter
virtual COLOR_ARGB getColorFilter()  {return colorFilter;}
```

Listing 5.25. The image's get functions.

5.5.3 Image set Functions

A number of set functions are included in image.h (Listing 5.26).

```
// Set X location
virtual void setX(float newX)      {spriteData.x = newX;}
// Set Y location
virtual void setY(float newY)      {spriteData.y = newY;}
// Set scale
virtual void setScale(float s)     {spriteData.scale = s;}
// Set rotation angle in degrees
// 0 degrees is up. Angles progress clockwise
virtual void setDegrees(float deg) {spriteData.angle = deg*((float)
                                                  PI/180.0f);}
// Set rotation angle in radians
// 0 radians is up. Angles progress clockwise
virtual void setRadians(float rad) {spriteData.angle = rad;}
// Set visible
virtual void setVisible(bool v) {visible = v;}
// Set delay between frames of animation
virtual void setFrameDelay(float d) {frameDelay = d;}
// Set starting and ending frames of animation
virtual void setFrames(int s, int e){startFrame = s; endFrame = e;}
// Set current frame of animation
virtual void setCurrentFrame(int c);
// Set spriteData.rect to draw currentFrame
virtual void setRect();
// Set spriteData.rect to r
virtual void setSpriteDataRect(RECT r)   {spriteData.rect = r;}
// Set animation loop. lp = true to loop
virtual void setLoop(bool lp) {loop = lp;}
```

```
// Set animation complete Boolean
virtual void setAnimationComplete(bool a)    {animComplete = a;};
// Set color filter. (use WHITE for no change)
virtual void setColorFilter(COLOR_ARGB color) {colorFilter = color;}
```

Listing 5.26. The image's set functions.

In addition to functions, the image.h file also contains the following properties:

- Graphics *graphics. A pointer to the game's Graphics object will be saved here.

- TextureManager *textureManager. A pointer to the textureManager object will be saved here.

- SpriteData spriteData. A structure that contains the data required by the Graphics::drawSprite function.

- COLOR_ARGB colorFilter. The color to apply as a filter when drawing the sprite if FILTER is specified as the color parameter. The color constant WHITE is used for no change.

- int cols. The number of columns (1 to *n*) in a multiframe sprite.

- int startFrame. The first frame number of a multiframe animation sequence.

- int endFrame. The ending frame number of a multiframe animation sequence.

- int currentFrame. The current frame number of the animation sequence.

- double frameDelay. How long, in seconds, each frame of animation is displayed.

- double animTimer. The variable used to time the animation.

- HRESULT hr. Standard return type.

- bool loop. Set to true to make the animation repeat (the default). When false, the animation will stay on the last frame and animComplete will be set to true.

- bool visible. true when the image is visible.

- bool initialized. true when the image has been successfully initialized.

- bool animComplete. true when a nonlooping animation sequence is complete.

▎ 5.6 Game Engine

Figure 5.7 contains the diagram of our game engine with the new additions.

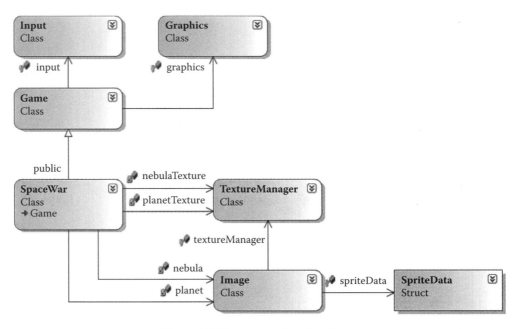

Figure 5.7. The game engine class diagram.

5.6.1   Drawing a Planet

With our new `TextureManager` and `Image` classes, it should be possible to draw a planet with a transparent background.

We will need two `TextureManager` objects and two `Image` objects, one of each for the background nebula and one of each for the planet. The objects are created in `spacewar.h`, as highlighted in Listing 5.27.

```
// Programming 2D Games
// Copyright (c) 2011 by:
// Charles Kelly
// Chapter 5 spacewar.h v1.0
#ifndef _SPACEWAR_H              // Prevent multiple definitions if this
#define _SPACEWAR_H              // file is included in more than one place
#define WIN32_LEAN_AND_MEAN
#include "game.h"
#include "textureManager.h"
#include "image.h"
//=============================================================================
// This class is the core of the game
//=============================================================================
class Spacewar : public Game
{
private:
    // Game items
    TextureManager nebulaTexture;    // Nebula texture
    TextureManager planetTexture;    // Planet texture
```

```
    Image    planet;              // Planet image
    Image    nebula;              // Nebula image
public:
    // Constructor
    Spacewar();
    // Destructor
    virtual ~Spacewar();
    // Initialize the game
    void initialize(HWND hwnd);
    void update();        // Must override pure virtual from Game
    void ai();            // "
    void collisions();    // "
    void render();        // "
    void releaseAll();
    void resetAll();
};
#endif
```

Listing 5.27. Creating `TextureManager` and `Image` objects.

We add the necessary code to initialize the nebula and planet in the `Spacewar::init` `ialize` function (Listing 5.28).

Using values of 0 for width and height will apply the entire texture to the image when it is drawn.

```
//=============================================================================
// Initializes the game
// Throws GameError on error
//=============================================================================
void Spacewar::initialize(HWND hwnd)
{
    Game::initialize(hwnd); // Throws GameError
    // Nebula texture
    if (!nebulaTexture.initialize(graphics,NEBULA_IMAGE))
        throw(GameError(gameErrorNS::FATAL_ERROR,
            "Error initializing nebula texture"));
    // Planet texture
    if (!planetTexture.initialize(graphics,PLANET_IMAGE))
        throw(GameError(gameErrorNS::FATAL_ERROR,
            "Error initializing planet texture"));
    // Nebula
    if (!nebula.initialize(graphics,0,0,0,&nebulaTexture))
        throw(GameError(gameErrorNS::FATAL_ERROR,
                        "Error initializing nebula"));
    // Planet
    if (!planet.initialize(graphics,0,0,0,&planetTexture))
        throw(GameError(gameErrorNS::FATAL_ERROR,
                        "Error initializing planet"));
    // Place planet in center of screen
```

```
        planet.setX(GAME_WIDTH*0.5f  - planet.getWidth()*0.5f);
        planet.setY(GAME_HEIGHT*0.5f - planet.getHeight()*0.5f);
        return;
}
```

Listing 5.28. Initializing the nebula and planet.

The `Spacewar::render` function calls `graphics->spriteBegin()` to begin drawing sprites. Then it calls `nebula.draw()` and `planet.draw()` functions to add the nebula and planet to the scene. Sprite drawing is ended by calling `graphics->spriteEnd()` (Listing 5.29).

The order of drawing is important. We want the planet to appear in front of the nebula so we draw the nebula first and then draw the planet.

We override the `releaseAll` and `resetAll` functions of the `Game` class and fill them with the proper calls to `onLostDevice` and `onResetDevice` for the `TextureManager` objects we created. As mentioned previously, this is necessary when recovering a lost graphics device (Listing 5.30).

```
//=======================================================================
// Render game items
//=======================================================================
void Spacewar::render()
{
    graphics->spriteBegin();            // Begin drawing sprites
    nebula.draw();                      // Add the orion nebula to the scene
    planet.draw();                      // Add the planet to the scene
    graphics->spriteEnd();              // End drawing sprites
}
```

Listing 5.29. Drawing the nebula and planet.

```
//=======================================================================
// The graphics device was lost
// Release all reserved video memory so graphics device may be reset
//=======================================================================
void Spacewar::releaseAll()
{
    planetTexture.onLostDevice();
    nebulaTexture.onLostDevice();
    Game::releaseAll();
    return;
}
```

5. Sprites and Animation

```
//==============================================================
// The grahics device has been reset
// Recreate all surfaces
//==============================================================
void Spacewar::resetAll()
{
    nebulaTexture.onResetDevice();
    planetTexture.onResetDevice();
    Game::resetAll();
    return;
}
```

Listing 5.30. Releasing and resetting the nebula and planet.

The complete program is in this chapter's "Planet" example. It draws the planet with transparency and properly recovers if the graphics device is lost (Figure 5.8).

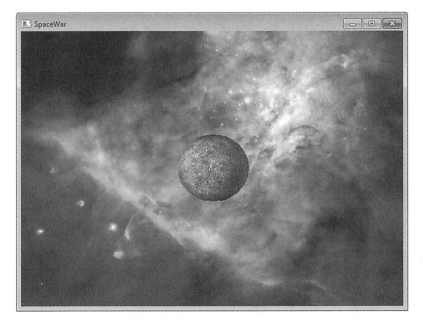

Figure 5.8. Drawing with transparency. Hubble photo of the Orion nebula from NASA. *Courtesy of nasaimages.org.*

▐ 5.7 Simple Animation

5.7.1 Frame by Frame

The update function in our `Image` class contains code to select the current frame of animation based on the elapsed time. Let's examine how to use this to draw some animated spaceships. Our spaceship sprite texture will be comprised of four images of the spaceship. Each

---

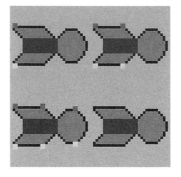

Figure 5.9. Frames of an animated spaceship.

image will have a different sequence of marker lights illuminated. By displaying the images sequentially, the marker lights will appear to blink (Figure 5.9). This type of frame-by-frame animation may be used to animate the game sprites using any number of sequential images. The code in Section 5.7.1 is from the "Spaceship" example.

We add the spaceship to our program by adding a `TextureManager` object for the ship texture and an `Image` object for the ship. The code to initialize the ship texture and `Image` object is placed in the `Spacewar::initialize` function, as shown in Listing 5.31 and Listing 5.32.

```
// Spaceship texture
if (!shipTexture.initialize(graphics,SHIP_IMAGE))
    throw(GameError(gameErrorNS::FATAL_ERROR,
        "Error initializing ship texture"));
```

Listing 5.31. Initializing spaceship `TextureManager`.

```
// Ship
if (!ship.initialize(graphics,SHIP_WIDTH, SHIP_HEIGHT, SHIP_COLS,
                    &shipTexture))
    throw(GameError(gameErrorNS::FATAL_ERROR, "Error initializing ship"));
```

Listing 5.32. Initializing the spaceship Image.

The constants SHIP_WIDTH, SHIP_HEIGHT, and SHIP_COLS were added to `constants.h`. We need to specify these values in the ship initialize function because the ship image contains four separate ship textures. When we draw a ship, we only want to use part of the texture image, not the entire picture, as we did with the nebula and planet. The width, height, and columns data is used by `Image::setRect` to select one of the four ship textures. Next, we set the ship's screen position (Listing 5.33).

```
ship.setX(GAME_WIDTH/4);                    // Start above and left of planet
ship.setY(GAME_HEIGHT/4);
```

Listing 5.33. Setting the spaceship's screen position.

To enable the ship animation, all we need to do is set up the starting and end-ing frames of animation with the `setFrames` function. Set the current frame with the `setCurrentFrame` function and set the animation delay between frames with the `setFrameDelay` function. Animation frames start at 0 in the top left and progress by rows through the image (Listing 5.34). In Figure 5.9, frame 0 is the ship in the top left with one pair of marker lights illuminated, and frame 3 is the ship in the bottom right with the marker lights off.

```
ship.setFrames(SHIP_START_FRAME, SHIP_END_FRAME);   // Animation frames
ship.setCurrentFrame(SHIP_START_FRAME);             // Starting frame
ship.setFrameDelay(SHIP_ANIMATION_DELAY);
ship.setDegrees(45.0f);                             // Angle of ship
```

Listing 5.34. Enabling the spaceship animation and setting angle.

We also made a call to `setDegrees` to demonstrate changing the angle of an image. The resulting program displays the ship with animated lights (Figure 5.10).

The ship's lights are animated because the game engine automatically calls the pure virtual function `update`. We were required to provide the code for the `update` function in our `Spacewar` class. That function calls `ship.update` and passes it the `frameTime` argument (Listing 5.35).

```
//=============================================================================
// Update all game items
//=============================================================================
void Spacewar::update()
{
    ship.update(frameTime);
}
```

Listing 5.35. Calling the ship's `update` function.

Our ship is an `Image` object. The `Image::update` function keeps track of the total elapsed time by adding `frameTime` to `animTimer`. If the total elapsed time is greater than `frameDelay`, the next frame of animation is selected by incrementing the `currentFrame` variable. If the last frame of an animation sequence has been displayed and the `loop` property is `true` (the default), `currentFrame` is reset to `startFrame`. If the image's `loop`

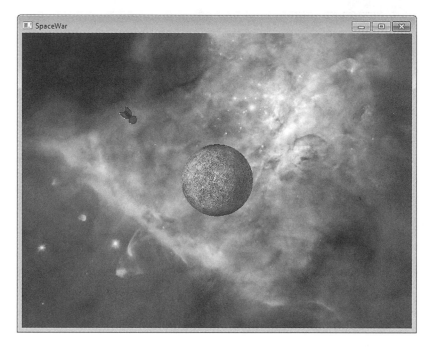

Figure 5.10. The spaceship example.

property is `false`, the animation stays on the last frame and the `animComplete` Boolean is set to `true`. The last step is to call `setRect` (Listing 5.36).

```cpp
//=============================================================================
// Update
// Typically called once per frame
// frameTime is used to regulate the speed of movement and animation
//=============================================================================
void Image::update(float frameTime)
{
    if (endFrame - startFrame > 0)              // If animated sprite
    {
        animTimer += frameTime;                 // Total elapsed time
        if (animTimer > frameDelay)
        {
            animTimer -= frameDelay;
            currentFrame++;
            if (currentFrame < startFrame || currentFrame > endFrame)
            {
                if(loop == true)                // If looping animation
                    currentFrame = startFrame;
                else                            // Not looping animation
                {
                    currentFrame = endFrame;
                    animComplete = true;        // Animation complete
                }
```

```
        }
        setRect();                          // Set spriteData.rect
    }
}
```

Listing 5.36. The `Image::update` function.

The `setRect` function uses the current frame number to calculate the rectangular portion of the texture image to display. The `spriteData.width`, `spriteData.height`, and `cols` data describe the texture image of our spaceship (Listing 5.37).

```
//=================================================================================
//  Set spriteData.rect to draw currentFrame
//=================================================================================
inline void Image::setRect()
{
    // Configure spriteData.rect to draw currentFrame
    spriteData.rect.left = (currentFrame % cols) * spriteData.width;
    // Right edge + 1
    spriteData.rect.right = spriteData.rect.left + spriteData.width;
    spriteData.rect.top = (currentFrame / cols) * spriteData.height;
    // Bottom edge + 1
    spriteData.rect.bottom = spriteData.rect.top + spriteData.height;
}
```

Listing 5.37. Select the rectangular portion of the texture.

The `setCurrentFrame` function sets the current frame in a multiple-frame image. This function may be used to change an animation sequence or to select a different texture to apply to the image from a multiple-texture image (Listing 5.38).

```
//=================================================================================
// Set the current frame of the image
//=================================================================================
void Image::setCurrentFrame(int c)
{
    if(c >= 0)
    {
        currentFrame = c;
        animComplete = false;
        setRect();                          // Set spriteData.rect
    }
}
```

Listing 5.38. Set the current frame.

5.7.2 Movement, Rotation, and Scaling

If we change the x, y coordinates of the image, we can make it move. Changing the angle will make the image rotate and changing the scale will make it get bigger or smaller. The frameTime value is used to regulate the speed of animation. The SpaceWar::update function calls the ship's update function and passes frameTime as a parameter. The angle, scale, and *x* position are adjusted by a constant rate multiplied by frameTime. The code in Listing 5.39 is from the "Spaceship Movement" example at the end of this chapter.

```
//=============================================================================
// Update all game items
//=============================================================================
void Spacewar::update()
{
    ship.update(frameTime);
    // Rotate ship
    ship.setDegrees(ship.getDegrees() + frameTime * ROTATION_RATE);
    // Make ship smaller
    ship.setScale(ship.getScale() - frameTime * SCALE_RATE);
    ship.setX(ship.getX() + frameTime * SHIP_SPEED);    // Move ship right
    if (ship.getX() > GAME_WIDTH)           // If offscreen right
    {
        ship.setX((float)-ship.getWidth());// Position off screen left
        ship.setScale(SHIP_SCALE);          // Set to starting size
    }
}
```

Listing 5.39. Moving and rotating the spaceship.

The constant values above are defined in our constants.h file. The constant ROTATION_RATE is defined as 180, which is equivalent to 180 degrees of rotation per second. The constant SCALE_RATE is defined as 0.2, which yields a 20% reduction in size per second. The constant SHIP_SPEED is defined as 100, which results in 100 pixels of movement per second. The constant SHIP_SCALE is defined as 1.5, which scales the ship to 1.5 times its original size.

The result is a spaceship that constantly flies across the screen while rotating with blinking marker lights; the ship appears to travel into the screen forever, lost in the vastness of the Orion nebula.

Using key presses to move the spaceship is also possible. The code in Listing 5.40 is the update function from the "Spaceship Control" example.

```
//=============================================================================
// Update all game items
//=============================================================================
void Spacewar::update()
{
    if(input->isKeyDown(SHIP_RIGHT_KEY))        // If move right
    {
```

```
            ship.setX(ship.getX() + frameTime * SHIP_SPEED);
            if (ship.getX() > GAME_WIDTH)              // If offscreen right
                ship.setX((float)-ship.getWidth());    // Position offscreen left
        }
        if(input->isKeyDown(SHIP_LEFT_KEY))            // If move left
        {
            ship.setX(ship.getX() - frameTime * SHIP_SPEED);
            if (ship.getX() < -ship.getWidth())        // If offscreen left
                ship.setX((float)GAME_WIDTH);          // Position offscreen right
        }
        if(input->isKeyDown(SHIP_UP_KEY))              // If move up
        {
            ship.setY(ship.getY() - frameTime * SHIP_SPEED);
            if (ship.getY() < -ship.getHeight())       // If offscreen top
                ship.setY((float)GAME_HEIGHT);         // Position offscreen
                                                       // bottom
        }
        if(input->isKeyDown(SHIP_DOWN_KEY))            // If move down
        {
            ship.setY(ship.getY() + frameTime * SHIP_SPEED);
            if (ship.getY() > GAME_HEIGHT)             // If offscreen bottom
                ship.setY((float)-ship.getHeight());   // Position offscreen top
        }
        ship.update(frameTime);
}
```

Listing 5.40. Controlling the spaceship.

In this simple example, the ship stops moving as soon as we release the key. In the next chapter, we will see how to give the ship momentum so it keeps moving.

Chapter Review

In this chapter, we learned about using DirectX sprites to draw game graphics. The picture we want to draw is applied to the sprite as a texture. To make it easier to manage the pictures for our sprites, we created the `TextureManager` class. We also created an `Image` class to hold our sprite code. In Section 5.7, we learned how to animate the sprites. Here are the details:

- Sprites support drawing with transparency.

- Sprites may be sized, rotated, flipped horizontally and vertically, and positioned on the screen.

- Sprite drawing starts by calling the sprite's `Begin` function and ends by calling the `End` function.

- A texture is a picture that is applied to a graphics primitive.

- A texture should have a width and height that are powers of 2.

- Sprite textures should have a minimum one pixel-wide transparent border.

- Sprite textures' right and bottom edges are specified one pixel beyond the actual edge of the image.

- Our `Graphics::drawSprite` function draws the sprite described in our `SpriteData` structure.

- A `TextureManager` object loads and manages one texture file.

- An image is the lowest-level object in our game engine that may be drawn on the screen.

- If the `ImageData` structure contains a width and height of 0, then the entire image will be drawn.

- The `Image::draw` function draws the image.

- If `FILTER` is used as the parameter when calling the `draw` function, then the image's `colorFilter` property is used as the filter color.

- The `Image::draw` function has an optional `SpriteData` parameter, which supports applying different textures to the sprite each time it is drawn.

- The `Image::setCurrentFrame` function sets the current frame in a multiple-frame image.

- The `Image::setRect` function selects the rectangular region of a texture to use for the current sprite.

- To only use part of a texture when drawing an image we need to specify the image's width, height, and number of columns as parameters in the `Image::initialize` function.

- To animate an image, we set the starting and ending frames of animation with the `setFrames` function, set the current frame with `setCurrentFrame`, and set the delay between frames with `setFrameDelay`.

- To make an animation sequence repeat, set the image's `loop` property to `true`.

- An image may be rotated by using the `setDegrees` or `setRadians` function.

- An image may be made smaller or larger with the `setScale` function.

Review Questions

1. What is a vertex?

2. What is a texture?

3. What is the first step in drawing sprites?

4. The rendering of primitives outside a(n) _____ will fail.

5. Textures should have a width and height of _____.

6. If a sprite texture is 32 by 32 pixels square and the top left corner is at (0,0), where is the right edge?

7. Why is it important to provide a transparent border around a sprite's texture?

8. Which function from our `Graphics` class is used to load textures?

9. What is the purpose of the `color` parameter in our `drawSprite` function?

10. What does a `TextureManager` object do?

11. What values are specified for the width and height parameters in the `Image::initialize` function in order to draw the entire image?

12. What is the purpose of the `color` parameter in the `Image::draw` function?

13. Where is the default value assigned to the `color` parameter of the `Image::draw` function?

14. What is the purpose of the optional `SpriteData` parameter in the `Image::draw` function?

15. How can we determine that an image's animation sequence is complete?

16. How do we set an image's animation sequence to not repeat?

17. What is the image's `frameDelay` used for?

18. Which image function is used to set the current frame of an animation sequence?

19. In this chapter's examples, we drew the nebula followed by the planet. What would be displayed if we reversed the order and drew the planet followed by the nebula and why?

Exercises

1. Add a second spaceship to the "Spaceship" example program.

2. Modify the "Spaceship" example program to allow the player to change the angle of the spaceship by pressing keys on the keyboard.

3. Modify the "Spaceship Control" example so the ship keeps moving when the key is released. Do this by creating a float variable for x velocity and one for y velocity. When a movement key is pressed, add or subtract from the corresponding velocity. Here is an example of the code when the "move right" key is pressed:

```
if(input->isKeyDown(SHIP_RIGHT_KEY))          // If move right
    Xvelocity += frameTime * SHIP_SPEED;
```

After the velocities are determined, use them to change the *x* and *y* position of the ship like this:

```
ship.setX(ship.getX() + frameTime * Xvelocity); // Apply X velocity
```

4. (Challenging.) Make the spaceship appear to orbit the planet as viewed from above. That is, the ship should travel in a circle on the screen.

5. (Very challenging.) Make the spaceship appear to orbit the planet as it flies in front of and then behind the planet. Start the ship 1/4 of the way across the screen and centered vertically. Make the ship get bigger in size as it travels from left to right until it is in the center of the screen, then start reducing it in size. When the ship is 3/4 of the way across the screen, make it reverse direction and travel from right to left. When the ship is traveling from right to left, change the order of drawing so the ship is drawn first and then the planet. This will make the ship appear to fly behind the planet. When the ship reaches the center of the screen, start increasing the ship size again. When the ship reaches 1/4 of the way across the screen, start the process over. To enhance the orbital effect even more, give the ship a velocity that starts at 0 and gradually increases in magnitude until the ship is in the center of the screen, and then gradually decreases.

Examples

The following is a list of examples that are available for download from www.programming 2dgames.com.

- *Planet.* Fills the window with the image of a nebula and draws a planet over the nebula.

  - The planet is drawn using transparency.

- *Sprite Border.* Draws a spaceship at 1X scale and a spaceship at 8X scale.

  - The 8X ship has a visible border because the source image does not have a minimum one pixel-wide transparent border.

- *Spaceship.* Adds an animated spaceship to the planet program.

  - Demonstrates how to use the `Image` class to draw animated sprites.

- *Spaceship Movement.* A spaceship flies from left to right across the space scene while rotating and getting smaller.

  - Demonstrates how to move and rotate an image.

  - Demonstrates how to make images wrap around the window.

- *Spaceship Control.* An animated spaceship may be moved around the window by pressing the arrow keys.

  - Demonstrates how to get user input with the `Input` class.

6 Collisions and Entities

In this chapter, we will add a new `Entity` class to the game engine. One of the new features of the `Entity` class is the ability to collide with other entities. In addition to colliding, entities will also have the ability to react to collisions. The code for collision detection and reaction will be part of the `Entity` class. Many of the calculations we need to perform for the collision code will use vectors and vector math, so we will start this chapter by taking a look at vectors.

▌ 6.1 Vectors

A vector represents both length and direction. We will define a vector by the x and y coordinates of its end point. DirectX has `D3DXVECTOR2`, which is a DirectX 2D vector defined as the following code:

```
typedef struct D3DXVECTOR2 {
    FLOAT x;
    FLOAT y;
} D3DXVECTOR2, *LPD3DXVECTOR2;
```

The operators in Listing 6.1 are supported by the DirectX vector `D3DXVECTOR2`.

```
// Assignment operators
D3DXVECTOR2& operator += ( CONST D3DXVECTOR2& );
D3DXVECTOR2& operator -= ( CONST D3DXVECTOR2& );
D3DXVECTOR2& operator *= ( FLOAT );
```

```
D3DXVECTOR2& operator /= ( FLOAT );
// Unary operators
D3DXVECTOR2 operator + () const;
D3DXVECTOR2 operator - () const;
// Binary operators
D3DXVECTOR2 operator + ( CONST D3DXVECTOR2& ) const;
D3DXVECTOR2 operator - ( CONST D3DXVECTOR2& ) const;
D3DXVECTOR2 operator * ( FLOAT ) const;
D3DXVECTOR2 operator / ( FLOAT ) const;
// Comparison operators
BOOL operator == ( CONST D3DXVECTOR2& ) const;
BOOL operator != ( CONST D3DXVECTOR2& ) const;
```

Listing 6.1. Vector operators.

Our game engine design encapsulates the DirectX code. As part of that encapsulation, we will define our own version of D3DXVECTOR2 as VECTOR2 in the `graphics.h` file (Listing 6.2).

```
#define VECTOR2        D3DXVECTOR2
```

Listing 6.2. Our vector type.

6.1.1 Vector Math

DirectX includes vector math functions, which we will also encapsulate in our game engine. Before we see how to do that, let's take a quick look at vector math.

Adding vectors. The sum of two vectors will give the coordinates of the end point that would be reached if both vectors were traveled one after the other (Figure 6.1).

Vector times scalar. Multiplying a vector by a scalar changes the length of the vector (Figure 6.2).

Unit vector. The length of a vector is its *magnitude*. In the case of a velocity vector, for example, the length would represent the speed. If you divide a vector by its length, you

Figure 6.1. The sum of vector V1 and vector V2.

Figure 6.2. The result of multiplying vector V1 by the scalar value 2.

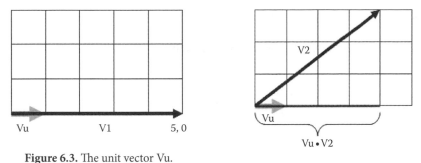

Figure 6.3. The unit vector Vu.

Figure 6.4. Dot product of vectors Vu and V2.

get a *unit vector*, also referred to as a *normalized vector*. A unit vector maintains the same direction as the original, but has a length of 1.

Vector V1 in Figure 6.3 is defined as ($x = 5, y = 0$). The length of vector V1 is 5. Dividing V1 by its length yields ($x = 5/5, y = 0/5$), which is the unit vector Vu ($x = 1, y = 0$).

The dot product. The dot product of two vectors is calculated by multiplying the x values of each and the y values of each and summing the two products. The result is a scalar value:

$$Vdot = (V1x * V2x + V1y * V2y).$$

If a dot product is calculated between a unit vector Vu and a vector V2, the result is a scalar value that represents the portion of V2, which falls along Vu (Figure 6.4).

The dot product of two unit vectors is the cosine of the angle between them.

6.1.2 DirectX Vector Math Functions

Some of the vector math operations we looked at above are performed with standard operators. For example, to multiply a vector by a scalar, we simply use the multiply operator (*):

$$vectorProduct = vector * scalar,$$

where *vectorProduct* and *vector* are vectors and *scalar* is a numeric type.

For more complex operations, we will encapsulate the DirectX vector math functions in `graphics.h`, as shown in Listing 6.3.

```
float Vector2Length(const VECTOR2 *v) {return D3DXVec2Length(v);}
float Vector2Dot(const VECTOR2 *v1, const VECTOR2 *v2)
   {return D3DXVec2Dot(v1, v2);}
void  Vector2Normalize(VECTOR2 *v) {D3DXVec2Normalize(v, v);}
```

Listing 6.3. Our vector math functions.

The functions are as follows:

- `Vector2Length(const VECTOR2 *v)` returns the length of vector V as a float.

- `Vector2Dot(const VECTOR2 *v1, const VECTOR2 *v2)` returns the dot product of vectors V1 and V2 as a float. This is the length of V2 along V1 if V1 is a unit vector.

- `Vector2Normalize(VECTOR2 *v)` converts vector V into a unit vector.

We will see an example of using vector math in our collision code.

▌ 6.2 Collisions

Game collisions occur when two or more "solid" game items occupy the same screen space at the same time. Several different techniques exist for detecting collisions in games. We present the following techniques, in order, from simple to complex: *circle, box, rotated box,* and *rotated box and circle* collision detection. The simpler techniques may not be as accurate as the more complex techniques, but they have the advantage of being the fastest in terms of computation time required. As game designers, we decide which collision detection techniques to use based on the desired accuracy and computation requirements.

6.2.1 Circular Collision Detection

Circular collision detection works by calculating the distance between the centers of two entities and determining if the collision circles defined for each entity overlap. If the circles overlap, then the entities are said to be colliding.

Figure 6.5 illustrates circular collision detection between two spaceships. Notice that the spaceships are not actually colliding even though the circles are overlapping. If circular collision detection were used as shown, it would indicate a collision was occurring, when

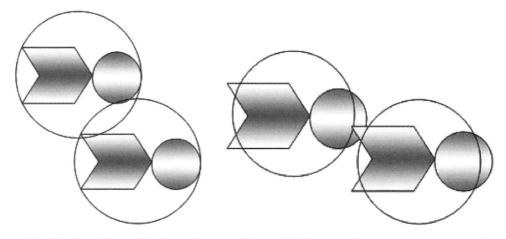

Figure 6.5. Circular collision detection indicating collision when none is occurring.

Figure 6.6. Circular collision detection missing the true collision.

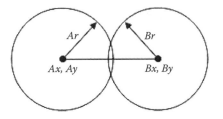

Figure 6.7. Two circles A and B that are colliding.

in reality there was no collision. We could make the collision circle smaller to minimize the false positives for collision. If we did that, we might have a different problem, as illustrated in Figure 6.6. In this case, the ships are colliding but the circles are not overlapping, so no collision would be detected.

A different approach to solving this problem might be to make the game fit the tools we have. What if we simply gave our spaceships shields? A circular shield makes perfect sense. We could even display the shields briefly during a collision to enhance the effect. We will see an example of that code at the end of this chapter.

Two circles are said to be colliding if the distance between their centers is less than or equal to the sum of their radii (Figure 6.7).

The distance between the center of the two circles A and B can be found using the equation:

$$distance = \sqrt{(Ax - Bx)^2 + (Ay - By)^2}.$$

The two circles are colliding if the distance between their centers is less than or equal to the sum of their radii:

$$distance <= (Ar + Br).$$

Combining the two equations yields

$$\sqrt{(Ax - Bx)^2 + (Ay - By)^2} <= (Ar + Br).$$

Calculating squares is generally faster than calculating square roots, so squaring both sides gives us

$$(Ax - Bx)^2 + (Ay - By)^2 <= (Ar + Br)^2.$$

If this comparison is true, the circles are overlapping, which means a collision has occurred. This is the comparison used in the `collideCircle` function (Listing 6.4). The `collideCircle` function receives a reference to the other `Entity` and a reference to a collision vector as parameters. If a collision is detected between this entity and the other entity, the collision vector is calculated and `true` is returned. If no collision is detected, the function returns `false`. The collision vector is the vector between this entity's center and the other entity's center. We will see how to use the collision vector later in this chapter when we look at game physics.

```cpp
//=============================================================================
// Circular collision detection method
// Called by collision(), default collision detection method
// Post: returns true if collision, false otherwise
//       sets collisionVector if collision
//=============================================================================
bool Entity::collideCircle(Entity &ent, VECTOR2 &collisionVector)
{
    // Difference between centers
    distSquared = *getCenter() - *ent.getCenter();
    distSquared.x = distSquared.x * distSquared.x;      // Difference squared
    distSquared.y = distSquared.y * distSquared.y;
    // Calculate the sum of the radii (adjusted for scale)
    sumRadiiSquared = (radius*getScale()) + (ent.radius*ent.getScale());
    sumRadiiSquared *= sumRadiiSquared;                 // Square it
    // If entities are colliding
    if(distSquared.x + distSquared.y <= sumRadiiSquared)
    {
        // Set collision vector
        collisionVector = *ent.getCenter() - *getCenter();
        return true;
    }
    return false;    // Not colliding
}
```

Listing 6.4. The `collideCircle` function returns `true` if the collision circle of the `ent` parameter is colliding with the current entity's collision circle. It also sets the `collisionVector`.

6.2.2 Box Collision Detection

A bounding box is simply a rectangle. An axis-aligned bounding box (AABB) is a rectangle whose edges are parallel with the *x*- and *y*-axis. We will refer to this as *box* collision detection. Figure 6.8 shows box collision detection between two spaceships. Two axis-aligned bounding boxes are colliding when:

- the right edge of *A* is >= left edge of *B*,

- the left edge of *A* is <= right edge of *B*,

- the bottom edge of *A* is >= top edge of *B*, and

- the top edge of *A* is <= bottom edge of *B*.

The function `Entity::collideBox` performs the above collision detection between this entity and the other entity, which is passed in the `ent` parameter (Listing 6.5).

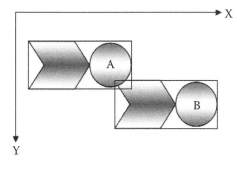

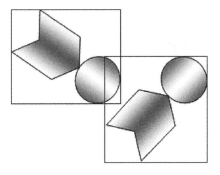

Figure 6.8. Box collision using axis-aligned boxes.

Figure 6.9. Box collision falsely indicating a collision.

The collision vector returned is simply the vector between the centers of each box. Using a vector between the box centers is not technically correct, but it is a compromise we are making to keep the code a little simpler. As we can see in Figure 6.9, the box collision method is not perfect, especially if the entities rotate. To get a better fit between the box and a rotating entity, we can rotate the box.

```
//======================================================================
// Axis-aligned bounding box collision detection method
// Called by collision()
// Post: returns true if collision, false otherwise
//       sets collisionVector if collision
//======================================================================
bool Entity::collideBox(Entity &ent, VECTOR2 &collisionVector)
{
    // If either entity is not active then no collision may occcur
    if (!active || !ent.getActive())
        return false;
    // Check for collision using Axis-Aligned Bounding Box
    if( (getCenterX() + edge.right*getScale() >= ent.getCenterX() +
        ent.getEdge().left*ent.getScale()) &&
        (getCenterX() + edge.left*getScale() <= ent.getCenterX() +
        ent.getEdge().right*ent.getScale()) &&
        (getCenterY() + edge.bottom*getScale() >= ent.getCenterY() +
        ent.getEdge().top*ent.getScale()) &&
        (getCenterY() + edge.top*getScale() <= ent.getCenterY() +
        ent.getEdge().bottom*ent.getScale()) )
    {
        // Set collision vector
        collisionVector = *ent.getCenter() - *getCenter();
        return true;
    }
    return false;
}
```

Listing 6.5. The `collideBox` function returns `true` if the collision box of the `ent` parameter is colliding with the current entity's collision box. It also sets the `collisionVector`.

6.2.3 Rotated Box Collision Detection

In rotated box collision detection, the bounding box is rotated with the entity. Rotating the bounding box with the entity provides a much better fit and thus a more accurate collision detection. Figure 6.10 represents rotated entities with rotated bounding boxes.

Collision occurs if any parts of the bounding boxes overlap. The collision test is performed by projecting each box onto a line. (Visualize the projection as the shadow that would be cast by each box onto the line.) If a line can be found where the projections do not overlap, then the boxes are not colliding. The question now becomes how to choose the lines to project onto. The solution is surprisingly simple. All we need to do is choose any corner from box *A* and any corner from box *B*. Lines parallel to the two edges emanating from the chosen corners serve as the projection lines. In Figure 6.11, the top-left corner of entity *A* was selected as one of the corners. The projection of each entity is shown on one of the lines parallel to the edge of box *A*. As soon as a projection is found where there is no overlap, then the remaining tests may be skipped because the entities are not colliding. The worst case for performance occurs when the entities are colliding, which requires projecting both entities onto four projection lines.

The first published description of this method is believed to be by Mikki Larcombe, Department of Computer Science, Warwick University, England, on comp.graphics.algorithms on October 11, 1995. The complete post is available for viewing in Google Groups archive.

The `collideRotatedBox` function performs the above collision detection between the current entity and a specified entity. `true` is returned if a collision is detected along with a `collisionVector`. The collision vector is simply computed to be the vector between the centers of each entity. Using the centers of each entity is not technically correct with bounding box collisions, and might produce incorrect results if used as part of a physics calculation. We use the simple, yet incorrect, collision vector here to keep the collision detection code as simple as possible (Listing 6.6).

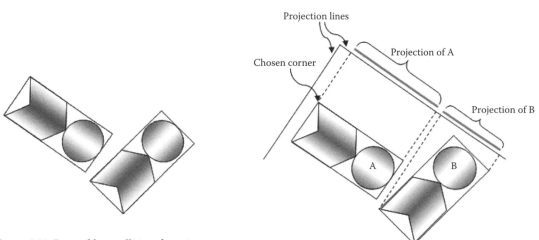

Figure 6.10. Rotated box collision detection.

Figure 6.11. Projecting corners of collision boxes.

```
//============================================================================
// Rotated Box collision detection method
// Called by collision()
// Post: returns true if collision, false otherwise
//       sets collisionVector if collision
// Uses Separating Axis Test to detect collision
// The separating axis test:
// Two boxes are not colliding if their projections onto a line do not
// overlap
//============================================================================
bool Entity::collideRotatedBox(Entity &ent, VECTOR2 &collisionVector)
{
    computeRotatedBox();                    // Prepare rotated box
    ent.computeRotatedBox();                // Prepare rotated box
    if (projectionsOverlap(ent) && ent.projectionsOverlap(*this))
    {
        // Set collision vector
        collisionVector = *ent.getCenter() - *getCenter();
        return true;
    }
    return false;
}
```

Listing 6.6. The `collideRotatedBox` function returns `true` if the rotated collision boxes overlap. It also sets the `collisionVector`.

The corners of the bounding box are contained in the `corners[]` array. They are defined as shown in Figure 6.12.

Corner 0 is always chosen as the base of the projection lines. The location of each corner is calculated using the current rotation angle and position of the entity. Two normalized vectors are created to use as projection lines. They are `edge01` and `edge03`. The current entity is projected onto `edge01` and `edge03`. The minimum and maximum projections are saved as `edge01Min`, `edge01Max` and `edge03Min`, `edge03Max` for the respective projection lines. These calculations are performed in the `computeRotatedBox` function, shown in Listing 6.7(a–e).

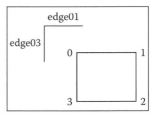

Figure 6.12. The corners of the bounding box.

```
//============================================================================
// Compute corners of rotated box, projection edges and min and max
// projections
// 0---1   corner numbers
// |   |
// 3---2
//============================================================================
void Entity::computeRotatedBox()
{
    if(rotatedBoxReady)
        return;
    float projection;
```

Listing 6.7(a). The `computeRotatedBox` function calculates the corners of the rotated box.

```
VECTOR2 rotatedX(cos(spriteData.angle), sin(spriteData.angle));
VECTOR2 rotatedY(-sin(spriteData.angle), cos(spriteData.angle));
```

Listing 6.7(b). An *x* and *y* vector are created from the current entity angle.

```
const VECTOR2 *center = getCenter();
corners[0] = *center + rotatedX * ((float)edge.left*getScale())   +
                       rotatedY * ((float)edge.top*getScale());
corners[1] = *center + rotatedX * ((float)edge.right*getScale()) +
                       rotatedY * ((float)edge.top*getScale());
corners[2] = *center + rotatedX * ((float)edge.right*getScale()) +
                       rotatedY * ((float)edge.bottom*getScale());
corners[3] = *center + rotatedX * ((float)edge.left*getScale())   +
                       rotatedY * ((float)edge.bottom*getScale());
```

Listing 6.7(c). The corners of the rotated box are calculated.

The current entity angle is used to create two vectors, `rotatedX` and `rotatedY`. These vectors are used to compute the rotated position of the bounding box corners, which can be found in Listing 6.7(b).

The center of the current entity is loaded into a vector named `center`. The bounding box is stored in a `RECT` structure named `edge`. The `edge` structure contains the elements `left`, `right`, `top`, `bottom`. Each element of `edge` is specified as the distance from the entity center. The position of each corner of the bounding box is calculated by multiplying the `rotatedX` and `rotatedY` vectors by the corresponding edge of the bounding box and by adding the result to the entity center vector, as seen in Listing 6.7(c).

For our Spacewar game, we will use the values defined in `ship.h` as the bounding box edges:

```
const int   EDGE_TOP = -8;           // For BOX and ROTATE_BOX collison
const int   EDGE_BOTTOM = 8;         // "    relative to center
const int   EDGE_LEFT = -14;         // "
const int   EDGE_RIGHT = 14;         // "
```

Notice that `EDGE_TOP` and `EDGE_LEFT` are negative numbers because they are relative to the entity center.

The two projection lines are created by building a vector from the corners of each edge connected to corner 0 and normalizing them, as shown in Listing 6.7(d). The current entity is then projected onto the edges. The minimum and maximum projection of the current entity onto both edges is saved into the corresponding `Min` and `Max` variables. A Boolean variable `rotatedBoxReady` is set to `true` to indicate that the rotated box is valid and may be used, as seen in Listing 6.7(e).

```
// Corners[0] is used as origin
// The two edges connected to corners[0] are used as the projection
// lines
```

```
edge01 = VECTOR2(corners[1].x - corners[0].x,
                 corners[1].y - corners[0].y);
graphics->Vector2Normalize(&edge01);
edge03 = VECTOR2(corners[3].x - corners[0].x,
                 corners[3].y - corners[0].y);
graphics->Vector2Normalize(&edge03);
```

Listing 6.7(d). Creating two projection lines.

```
    // This entities min and max projection onto edges
    projection = graphics->Vector2Dot(&edge01, &corners[0]);
    edge01Min = projection;
    edge01Max = projection;
    // Project onto edge01
    projection = graphics->Vector2Dot(&edge01, &corners[1]);
    if (projection < edge01Min)
        edge01Min = projection;
    else if (projection > edge01Max)
        edge01Max = projection;
    // Project onto edge03
    projection = graphics->Vector2Dot(&edge03, &corners[0]);
    edge03Min = projection;
    edge03Max = projection;
    projection = graphics->Vector2Dot(&edge03, &corners[3]);
    if (projection < edge03Min)
        edge03Min = projection;
    else if (projection > edge03Max)
        edge03Max = projection;
    rotatedBoxReady = true;
}
```

Listing 6.7(e). Projecting the entity onto its edges.

The vector dot product is used to project the bounding box onto the projection edge. Let's examine the projection of corner 0 of the current entity and see what the code is actually doing. From our earlier discussion on vector math, we know that taking the dot product of a vector with a unit vector gives us the magnitude of the vector that falls along the unit vector. In Figure 6.13, `edge01` is a unit vector we computed from the bounding box edge between corner 0 and corner 1. A unit vector has a length of 1. Each corner of the bounding box is represented by a vector. Also in Figure 6.13 we can see that the dot product of `corners[0]` and `edge01` gives us the magnitude of `corners[0]` that falls along `edge01`, which we are calling *projection*.

Repeating the dot product for `corners[1]` gives us the minimum and maximum projections of the bounding box along `edge01`. The calculations are repeated with `corners[0]` and `corners[3]` along `edge03`. We only need to project two corners from the current entity onto each edge because the edges are always parallel with the sides of this bounding box (Figure 6.13).

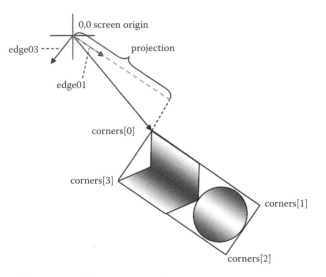

Figure 6.13. The projection of `corners[0]` onto `edge01`.

Now we project the other entity onto `edge01` and `edge03` and compare the minimum and maximum values to the projection of this entity. The other entity will probably have a different rotation angle than the current entity, so we will need to project all four corners onto each edge in order to determine the minimum and maximum projection. The projection of the other entity and comparison to the current entity's projection is performed in the `projectionsOverlap` function (Listing 6.8).

```
//============================================================================
// Projects other box onto this edge01 and edge03
// Called by collideRotatedBox()
// Post: returns true if projections overlap, false otherwise
//============================================================================
bool Entity::projectionsOverlap(Entity &ent)
{
    float projection, min01, max01, min03, max03;
    // Project other box onto edge01
    projection = graphics->Vector2Dot(&edge01, ent.getCorner(0));
    // Project corner 0
    min01 = projection;
    max01 = projection;
    // For each remaining corner
    for(int c=1; c<4; c++)
    {
        // Project corner onto edge01
        projection = graphics->Vector2Dot(&edge01, ent.getCorner(c));
        if (projection < min01)
            min01 = projection;
        else if (projection > max01)
            max01 = projection;
```

```
    }
    // If projections do not overlap
    if (min01 > edge01Max || max01 < edge01Min)
        return false;                     // No collision is possible
    // Project other box onto edge03
    projection = graphics->Vector2Dot(&edge03, ent.getCorner(0));
    // Project corner 0
    min03 = projection;
    max03 = projection;
    // For each remaining corner
    for(int c=1; c<4; c++)
    {
        // Project corner onto edge03
        projection = graphics->Vector2Dot(&edge03, ent.getCorner(c));
        if (projection < min03)
            min03 = projection;
        else if (projection > max03)
            max03 = projection;
    }
    // If projections do not overlap
    if (min03 > edge03Max || max03 < edge03Min)
        return false;                     // No collision is possible
    return true;                          // Projections overlap
}
```

Listing 6.8. The `projectionsOverlap` function projects the other entity's rotated box onto this entity's `edge01` and `edge03`.

If an axis is found where the projections are not overlapping, `false` is returned, which indicates that the entities are not colliding. If the projection of the other entity overlaps the projection of this entity on both edges, then `true` is returned to indicate a collision.

6.2.4 Rotated Box and Circle Collision Detection

If one of the entities is using box or rotated box collision and the other entity is using circle collision, then we need to use a modified form of the rotated box collision detection.

The corners of the collision box are projected onto the edge lines as before. The circle is projected by projecting its center, then adding and subtracting the radius to get the minimum and maximum projection. If the circle is colliding with the box along any edge, then a simple overlap test will detect the collision as is the case with circle *A* in Figure 6.14.

A special case arises if the circle center is outside the projection of the collision box edges. The region outside the projection lines of the box is known as the *Voronoi region*. In Figure 6.14, circle *B* and circle *C* are in Voronoi regions. As we can see, circle *B* and circle *C* would have projections that overlap the collision box, yet only circle *C* is colliding. When a circle's center is in a Voronoi region, we must check for a collision with the circle and the nearest corner of the box. The collision test is performed by comparing the distance from the box corner with the radius of the circle. If the distance to the nearest corner is less than the radius of the circle, then the circle is colliding with the corner of the box. The nearest corner may be determined by comparing the projections of the box corners and circle centers.

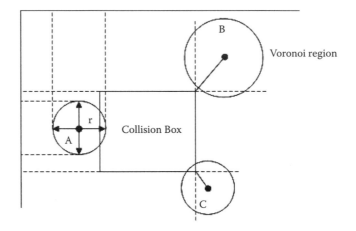

Figure 6.14. Detecting collisions between circles and a box.

Our function that performs this collision test is named `collideRotatedBoxCircle`. The `collideRotatedBoxCircle` function must be called from the entity that is using box or rotated box collision. The other entity must be using circle collision detection. This check is performed in our `collidesWith` function, which then makes the proper call (Listing 6.9).

```
//=============================================================================
// Rotated Box and Circle collision detection method
// Called by collision()
// Uses separating axis test on edges of box and radius of circle
// If the circle center is outside the lines extended from the collision
// box edges (also known as the Voronoi region) then the nearest box corner
// is checked for collision using a distance check.
// The nearest corner is determined from the overlap tests
//
//    Voronoi0 |   | Voronoi1
//          ---0---1---
//            |   |
//          ---3---2---
//    Voronoi3 |   | Voronoi2
//
// Pre: This entity must be box and other entity (ent) must be circle
// Post: returns true if collision, false otherwise
//       sets collisionVector if collision
//=============================================================================
bool Entity::collideRotatedBoxCircle(Entity &ent, VECTOR2 &collisionVector)
{
    float min01, min03, max01, max03, center01, center03;
    computeRotatedBox();                    // Prepare rotated box
    // Project circle center onto edge01
    center01 = graphics->Vector2Dot(&edge01, ent.getCenter());
    // Min and max are Radius from center
    min01 = center01 - ent.getRadius()*ent.getScale();
    max01 = center01 + ent.getRadius()*ent.getScale();
```

```
        if (min01 > edge01Max || max01 < edge01Min) // If projections do not
                                                     // overlap
            return false;                            // No collision is possible

        // Project circle center onto edge03
        center03 = graphics->Vector2Dot(&edge03, ent.getCenter());
        // Min and max are Radius from center
        min03 = center03 - ent.getRadius()*ent.getScale();
        max03 = center03 + ent.getRadius()*ent.getScale();
        if (min03 > edge03Max || max03 < edge03Min) // If projections do not
                                                     // overlap
            return false;                            // No collision is possible
        // Circle projection overlaps box projection
        // Check to see if circle is in voronoi region of collision box
        if(center01 < edge01Min && center03 < edge03Min)    // If circle in
                                                            // Voronoi0
            return collideCornerCircle(corners[0], ent, collisionVector);
        if(center01 > edge01Max && center03 < edge03Min)    // If circle in
                                                            // Voronoi1
            return collideCornerCircle(corners[1], ent, collisionVector);
        if(center01 > edge01Max && center03 > edge03Max)    // If circle in
                                                            // Voronoi2
            return collideCornerCircle(corners[2], ent, collisionVector);
        if(center01 < edge01Min && center03 > edge03Max)    // If circle in
                                                            // Voronoi3
            return collideCornerCircle(corners[3], ent, collisionVector);
        // Circle not in voronoi region so it is colliding with edge of box
        // Set collision vector, uses simple center of circle to center of box
        collisionVector = *ent.getCenter() - *getCenter();
        return true;
}
```

Listing 6.9. The `collideRotatedBoxCircle` function checks for collisions between circles and rotated boxes.

If the circle lies in the Voronoi region, then `collideCornerCircle` is called to test for a collision between the circle and the specified corner (Listing 6.10).

```
//=============================================================================
// The box corner is checked for collision with circle using a distance
// check
// Called by collideRotatedBoxCircle()
// Post: returns true if collision, false otherwise
//       sets collisionVector if collision
//=============================================================================
bool Entity::collideCornerCircle(VECTOR2 corner, Entity &ent, VECTOR2
                                 &collisionVector)
{
    distSquared = corner - *ent.getCenter();           // Corner - circle
    distSquared.x = distSquared.x * distSquared.x;     // Difference squared
    distSquared.y = distSquared.y * distSquared.y;
    // Calculate the sum of the radii, then square it
    sumRadiiSquared = ent.getRadius()*ent.getScale();  // (0 + circleR)
```

```
    sumRadiiSquared *= sumRadiiSquared;                    // Square it
    // If corner and circle are colliding
    if(distSquared.x + distSquared.y <= sumRadiiSquared)
    {
        // Set collision vector
        collisionVector = *ent.getCenter() - corner;
        return true;
    }
    return false;
}
```

Listing 6.10. The `collideCornerCircle` function is used when a circle is in the Voronoi region of a box.

▌ 6.3 The Entity Class

The collision code we have been creating is part of the new `Entity` class. The `Entity` class inherits from the `Image` class and adds the following:

- The ability to collide with other entities.

- Health property and related functions.

- Velocity and delta velocity for movement control.

- Mass property and gravity functions.

- Artificial intelligence shell function.

When we want to create a game item that has any of these new properties or capabilities, we will create a new class that inherits from `Entity`. Since the `Entity` class inherits from the `Image` class, all of the properties and functions of `Image` are also part of `Entity`.

The new `Entity` properties are as follows:

- `entityNS::COLLISION_TYPE  collisionType`. The collision type: NONE, CIRCLE, BOX, or ROTATED_BOX.

- `VECTOR2 center`. The center of the entity.

- `float radius`. Defines the radius of the circle used for circular collision detection.

- `RECT edge`. The rectangular region used by BOX or ROTATED_BOX collision detection. The edge members are `left`, `right`, `top`, and `bottom`. The collision box is specified relative to the entity center. A collision box that is 16 pixels tall and 28 pixels wide would be specified as: `top = -8; edge.bottom = 8; edge.left = -14; edge.right = 14;`

- `VECTOR2 velocity`. The vector containing the current entity velocity.

- float mass. The mass of the entity.

- float health. Health of the entity from 0 to 100.

- bool active. The current state of this entity; only active entities may collide.

The entity class also contains a number of variables used during collision detection. The entity.h header file contains some simple set and get functions for the new variables. The other functions are in entity.cpp. The constructor does simple variable initialization (Listing 6.11).

The function Entity::initialize receives a pointer to the current game engine, the width, the height, and number of columns in the texture image, and a pointer to a TextureManager object. The gamePtr pointer is used to retrieve the current input system, which is saved to the local input pointer. Image::initialize is called inside a return statement, which passes the return value from Image::initialize back to the caller of Entity::initialize (Listing 6.12).

```
// Programming 2D Games
// Copyright (c) 2011 by:
// Charles Kelly
// Chapter 6 entity.cpp v1.0
#include "entity.h"
//=============================================================================
// Constructor
//=============================================================================
Entity::Entity() : Image()
{
    radius = 1.0;
    edge.left = -1;
    edge.top = -1;
    edge.right = 1;
    edge.bottom = 1;
    mass = 1.0;
    velocity.x = 0.0;
    velocity.y = 0.0;
    deltaV.x = 0.0;
    deltaV.y = 0.0;
    active = true;                  // The entity is active
    rotatedBoxReady = false;
    collisionType = entityNS::CIRCLE;
    health = 100;
    gravity = entityNS::GRAVITY;
}
```

Listing 6.11. The Entity class constructor.

```
//=============================================================================
// Initialize the Entity
// Pre: *gamePtr = pointer to Game object
```

```
//         width = width of Image in pixels  (0 = use full texture width)
//         height = height of Image in pixels (0 = use full texture height)
//         ncols = number of columns in texture (1 to n) (0 same as 1)
//         *textureM = pointer to TextureManager object
// Post: returns true if successful, false if failed
//===============================================================================
bool Entity::initialize(Game *gamePtr, int width, int height, int ncols,
                        TextureManager *textureM)
{
    input = gamePtr->getInput();               // The input system
    return(Image::initialize(gamePtr->getGraphics(),width,height,ncols,
           textureM));
}
```

Listing 6.12. The `Entity::initialize` function.

The default behavior of the `Entity::activate` function is simply to set `active` to `true`. The function is provided in case a user-created entity requires a more complex logic to activate (Listing 6.13).

```
//===============================================================================
// Activate the entity
//===============================================================================
void Entity::activate()
{
    active = true;
}
```

Listing 6.13. The simple `Entity::activate` function may be overridden for more complex entities.

The `Entity::update` function adds `deltaV` to the velocity vector and then clears `deltaV`. The `deltaV` variable is set in `Entity::bounce` (see Listing 6.20). Classes that derive from `Entity` should use the `velocity` vector to update the position. The `Image::update` function is called and `rotatedBoxReady` is set to `false` to indicate that BOX and ROTATED_BOX collision detection need to call `computeRotatedBox` before using the bounding box for collision detection (Listing 6.14).

```
//===============================================================================
// Update
// Typically called once per frame
// frameTime is used to regulate the speed of movement and animation
//===============================================================================
void Entity::update(float frameTime)
{
    velocity += deltaV;
    deltaV.x = 0;
    deltaV.y = 0;
    Image::update(frameTime);
```

```
        rotatedBoxReady = false;      // For rotatedBox collision detection
}
```

Listing 6.14. Updating the entity's `velocity` and `Image`.

```
//=============================================================================
// ai (artificial intelligence)
// Typically called once per frame
// Performs ai calculations, ent is passed for interaction
//=============================================================================
void Entity::ai(float frameTime, Entity &ent)
{}
```

Listing 6.15. The `Empty::ai` function allows `Entity` objects to be created.

The `Entity::ai` function is a simple placeholder. The entity has no default artificial intelligence. We chose to use an empty function here instead of a pure virtual function. A pure virtual function would require any derived class to provide the function code. Providing the empty function, as we do here, allows objects of the `Entity` class to be instantiated. That allows us to create objects from the `Entity` class directly. The ability to create `Entity` objects might be handy if we want to do some rapid prototyping for our game (Listing 6.15).

The `Entity::collidesWith` function (Listing 6.16) checks to see if this entity is colliding with the entity passed in the `ent` parameter. The collision type used by each entity is determined and the appropriated collision function is called. Entities default to `CIRCLE` collision. To change the collision method used by derived classes of entity, set the `collisionType` variable to one of the following collision types:

`entityNS::CIRCLE`, `entityNS::BOX` or `entityNS::ROTATED_BOX`.

```
//=============================================================================
// Perform collision detection between this entity and the other Entity
// Each entity must use a single collision type. Complex shapes that
// require multiple collision types may be done by treating each part as a
// separate entity.
// Typically called once per frame
// The collision types: CIRCLE, BOX, or ROTATED_BOX
// Post: returns true if collision, false otherwise
//       sets collisionVector if collision
//=============================================================================
bool Entity::collidesWith(Entity &ent, VECTOR2 &collisionVector)
{
    // If either entity is not active then no collision may occcur
    if (!active || !ent.getActive())
        return false;
    // If both entities are CIRCLE collision
    if (collisionType == entityNS::CIRCLE &&
```

```
            ent.getCollisionType() == entityNS::CIRCLE)
            return collideCircle(ent, collisionVector);
    // If both entities are BOX collision
    if (collisionType == entityNS::BOX && ent.getCollisionType()
                    == entityNS::BOX)
            return collideBox(ent, collisionVector);
    // All other combinations use separating axis test
    // If neither entity uses CIRCLE collision
    if (collisionType != entityNS::CIRCLE &&
            ent.getCollisionType() != entityNS::CIRCLE)
            return collideRotatedBox(ent, collisionVector);
    else        // One of the entities is a circle
        // If this entity uses CIRCLE collision
        if (collisionType == entityNS::CIRCLE)
            return ent.collideRotatedBoxCircle(*this, collisionVector);
        else        // The other entity uses CIRCLE collision
            return collideRotatedBoxCircle(ent, collisionVector);
    return false;
}
```

Listing 6.16. Does this entity collide with the `ent` entity?

The `Entity::outsideRect` function returns `true` if the current entity is outside the specified rectangle. This function might be useful to test if our player is inside a special area of the game (Listing 6.17).

```
//=============================================================================
// Is this Entity outside the specified rectangle
// Post: returns true if outside rect, false otherwise
//=============================================================================
bool Entity::outsideRect(RECT rect)
{
    if( spriteData.x + spriteData.width*getScale() < rect.left ||
        spriteData.x > rect.right ||
        spriteData.y + spriteData.height*getScale() < rect.top ||
        spriteData.y > rect.bottom)
        return true;
    return false;
}
```

Listing 6.17. Is the entity outside the specified rectangle?

The `Entity` class includes an empty `damage` function. The `damage` function will be called when the entity is damaged by a weapon. Currently, the `Entity` class has no idea about the details of the entity, so the function is empty. Normally this function will be overridden by the deriving class to provide appropriate damage. Providing an empty function in the `Entity` class permits `Entity` objects to be instantiated if desired (Listing 6.18).

```
//===========================================================
// Damage
// This entity has been damaged by a weapon
// Override this function in the inheriting class
//===========================================================
void Entity::damage(int weapon)
{}
```

Listing 6.18. The damage function is designed to be overridden.

6.4 Physics for 2D Games

Now that our game entities are colliding, we need some way to make them react to the collisions. Physics to the rescue! In this section, we will examine some simple physics that may be applied to 2D games. This section is in no way meant to be a comprehensive coverage of physics.

6.4.1 Bouncing off the Walls

In many games, we want to confine the game entities to the screen space. We can add some simple checks in the update function that will make the entity bounce off the screen edges. When we want to modify the behavior of a game entity, we should do so in a derived class. In our Spacewar game, we will create a Ship class that inherits from Entity. The code to make the ship bounce off the walls is added to our Ship::update function. The code in Listing 6.19 is from this chapter's "Bounce" example.

```
//===========================================================
// Update
// Typically called once per frame
// frameTime is used to regulate the speed of movement and animation
//===========================================================
void Ship::update(float frameTime)
{
    Entity::update(frameTime);
    spriteData.angle += frameTime * shipNS::ROTATION_RATE;  // Rotate the
                                                            // ship
    spriteData.x += frameTime * velocity.x;  // Move ship along X
    spriteData.y += frameTime * velocity.y;  // Move ship along Y
    // Bounce off walls
    // If hit right screen edge
    if (spriteData.x > GAME_WIDTH-shipNS::WIDTH*getScale())
    {
        // Position at right screen edge
        spriteData.x = GAME_WIDTH-shipNS::WIDTH*getScale();
        velocity.x = -velocity.x;          // Reverse X direction
    }
    else if (spriteData.x < 0)             // Else if hit left screen edge
    {
        spriteData.x = 0;                  // Position at left screen edge
        velocity.x = -velocity.x;          // Reverse X direction
```

```
    // If hit bottom screen edge
    if (spriteData.y > GAME_HEIGHT-shipNS::HEIGHT*getScale())
    {
        // Position at bottom screen edge
        spriteData.y = GAME_HEIGHT-shipNS::HEIGHT*getScale();
        velocity.y = -velocity.y;              // Reverse Y direction
    }
    else if (spriteData.y < 0)                 // Else if hit top screen edge
    {
        spriteData.y = 0;                      // Position at top screen edge
        velocity.y = -velocity.y;              // Reverse Y direction
    }
}
```

Listing 6.19. The `update` function with code added to make the spaceship bounce off the screen edges.

In the `update` function above, `spriteData.x += frameTime * velocity.x;` moves the ship along the *x*-axis at velocity *x* and `spriteData.y += frameTime * velocity.y;` moves the ship along the *y*-axis at velocity *y*. We make the ship bounce off the walls by comparing its new *x* and *y* position with the screen edges. If we determine the ship is off-screen, we reverse its direction by inverting the sign of the velocity. So, in the code from Listing 6.19, `if (spriteData.x > GAME_WIDTH - shipNS::WIDTH*getScale())` tests to see if the ship's current *x* position is off the right edge of the screen. An entities position X, Y is defined at its top-left corner, which is why we subtract `shipNS::WIDTH*getScale()` as part of the test (see Figure 6.15).

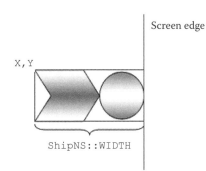

Figure 6.15. A spaceship at the edge of the screen.

6.4.2 Getting Stuck

When a collision with the screen edge or another entity is detected, we must take steps to resolve the collision. That is, the actions taken must lead to a state where the two items are no longer colliding. In the update function (see Listing 6.19), when a collision with the screen edge is detected, the ship is repositioned to place it at the edge of the screen but no longer colliding with it:

```
// If hit right screen edge

if (spriteData.x > GAME_WIDTH-shipNS::WIDTH*getScale())
{
    // Position at right screen edge
    spriteData.x = GAME_WIDTH-shipNS::WIDTH*getScale();
    velocity.x = -velocity.x;              // Reverse X direction

}
```

If this extra step were not taken, it would be possible for the ship to get stuck on the edge of the screen. Here is how that could happen. The distance the ship moves each frame is determined by the speed of the ship and the value of `frameTime`. The time between frames can vary greatly depending on the other tasks Windows is performing. If `frameTime` happens to be a large number just as the ship is approaching the edge of the screen, we could end up with a collision, as shown in Figure 6.16(a). Here a large portion of the ship is beyond the edge of the screen. When the collision is detected, the x velocity would be reversed and during the next frame the ship would move left, as shown in Figure 6.16(b). In (b), the `frameTime` was not unusually large, so the distance the ship moved was not as far. This results in the ship still being in a state of collision with the screen edge. At this point, the code simply says to reverse the direction of the x velocity, which would cause the ship to move to the right during the next frame. This process would repeat over and over, resulting in the ship being stuck to the edge of the screen. This same effect can also occur between two colliding entities.

Different techniques may be used to resolve the collision. For example, instead of repositioning the ship, we could check the current direction and only reverse the x velocity if necessary:

```
if (spriteData.x > GAME_WIDTH - shipNS::WIDTH)  // If hit right screen edge
{
    if (velocity.x > 0)                         // If moving right
        velocity.x = -velocity.x;               // Reverse X direction
}
```

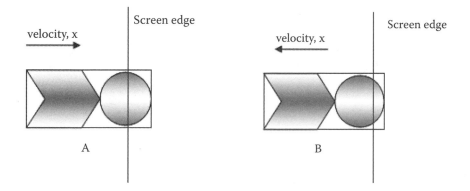

Figure 6.16. Varying `frameTime` resulting in a ship that is stuck to the edge of the screen.

6.4.3 Collision Physics

When two game entities collide, the *conservation of linear momentum* law of nature should be followed. It states that the combined momentum of the two entities must be the same before and after the collision, assuming no loss of energy. The momentum of an entity is equal to its velocity multiplied by its mass:

$$momentum = velocity * mass.$$

If a circle collides with a stationary plane, it should bounce off at the same angle it intersected. In Figure 6.17, V1 represents the velocity vector of the circle before colliding and V1', the velocity vector after colliding. The length of the vector represents the linear speed and is the same for V1 and V1'.

What if the collision was between our spaceship and a stationary circle (like a planet) and we wanted the ship to bounce off? If we treat the contact point between the two circles like a plane, then the problem is the same. Now all we need to do is figure out how to calculate vector V1'.

We know the current velocity of the ship, V1, in Figure 6.18. Our `collideCircle` function returns the collision vector represented by cV. We can use some vector math to calculate V1'.

A little rearranging of the vectors from Figure 6.18 will give us Figure 6.19. The unit vector of the collision vector cV is calculated as cUV:

$$cUV = Vector2Normalize(cV).$$

The dot product of −V1 with the collision unit vector cUV gives us the magnitude of the velocity change that will be applied to the ship after the collision. To get it in the form of a vector, we multiply it with the collision unit vector cUV. Let's name this the reaction vector and designate it rV:

$$rV = (cUV \bullet (-V1)) * cUV.$$

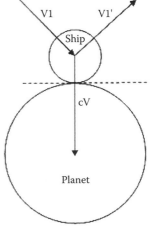

We are assuming that a planet has virtually infinite mass compared to the ship. When the ship hits the planet, the portion of the ship's velocity that is along the collision vector will go to 0 and then the reaction velocity we have just calculated will be added to get the new ship velocity V1'. Calculating the ship's velocity that stops travel along

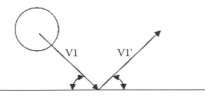

Figure 6.17. Velocity of the ball before and after collision with the wall.

Figure 6.18. Velocity of the ship before and after collision with the planet and collision vector (cV).

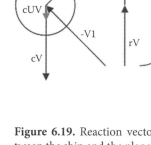

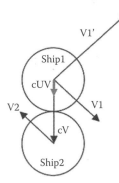

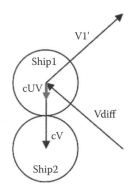

Figure 6.19. Reaction vector (rV) between the ship and the planet.

Figure 6.20. Collision between two ships.

Figure 6.21. The difference in velocities between two colliding ships.

the collision vector is easy; all we need to do is add the reaction vector (rV). So we need to add rV twice—once to stop the ship and a second time to get the new velocity V1'. We can also get the same result by multiplying rV by 2 and then adding to V1 to calculate the ships new velocity V1' (Figure 6.19):

$$V1' = V1 + 2 * rV, \text{ or}$$
$$V1' = V1 + 2 * (cUV \cdot (-V1)) * cUV.$$

This calculation works only if the other entity has virtually infinite mass, but what if the other entity is a ship? In that case, we need to consider the energy that may be transferred between the ships. Figure 6.20 represents the two ships with their respective velocities V1 and V2. The collision unit vector is cUV and the new velocity of Ship1 after the collision is V1'.

If we use a little relativity, we can treat Ship2 as being stationary and calculate a new value for the velocity as the difference between the two ships' velocities. We will label this as Vdiff (Figure 6.21).

$$Vdiff = V2 - V1.$$

This yields the same diagram we had in Figure 6.19. Now all we need to do is factor in the effects of the mass of each ship into our calculation. When the collision was with an entity that had virtually infinite mass, the scalar value of 2 was used as a multiplier. We can compute a new value of the scalar multiplier by using the ratio of the ships masses to get

$$massRatio = 2 * mass2 /(mass1 + mass2).$$

Substituting into our equation for V1', we get:

$$V1' = V1 + massRatio * rV, \text{ or}$$
$$V1' = V1 + massRatio * (cUV \cdot Vdiff) * cUV.$$

In our game code we don't want to change the velocity of the ship until all of the other collisions have been calculated. The change in the ship's velocity, we just calculated, is added to the ship's `deltaV` vector. The `deltaV` vector is added to the ship's velocity in the update function which is not called until all of the other collisions have been calculated.

$$\text{deltaV} = \text{deltaV} + \text{massRatio} * (\text{cUV} \bullet \text{Vdiff}) * \text{cUV},$$
$$\text{V1'} = \text{Vdiff} + \text{deltaV}.$$

The following code is from the "Planet Collision" example. The calculation of `deltaV` is performed in the `Entity::bounce` function (Listing 6.20).

```
//===========================================================================
// Entity bounces after collision with another entity
//===========================================================================
void Entity::bounce(VECTOR2 &collisionVector, Entity &ent)
{
    VECTOR2 Vdiff = ent.getVelocity() - velocity;
    VECTOR2 cUV = collisionVector;              // Collision unit vector
    Graphics::Vector2Normalize(&cUV);
    float cUVdotVdiff = Graphics::Vector2Dot(&cUV, &Vdiff);
    float massRatio = 2.0f;
    if (getMass() != 0)
        massRatio *= (ent.getMass() / (getMass() + ent.getMass()));
    // If entities are already moving apart then bounce must
    // have been previously called and they are still colliding.
    // Move entities apart along collisionVector
    if(cUVdotVdiff > 0)
    {
        setX(getX() - cUV.x * massRatio);
        setY(getY() - cUV.y * massRatio);
    }
    else
        deltaV += ((massRatio * cUVdotVdiff) * cUV);
}
```

Listing 6.20. This entity bounces off the entity `ent`.

The bounce function prevents entities from getting stuck together by making sure that entities in collision are always moving apart. The variable cUVdotVdiff is computed as (cUV • Vdiff). A positive value indicates that the entities are moving apart. If the entities are moving apart when the bounce function is called, then we assume that bounce was called previously and a deltaV was already calculated that caused the entities to move apart. If the entities did not move apart enough during the previous frame and are still colliding, we do not want to compute another deltaV value. Instead, the bounce function moves the current entity away from the other entity along the collision vector.

If two ships collide, we need to call the bounce function twice—once from each ship. The collisionVector is relative to the ship that detected the collision, so when we call the bounce function from the other ship we need to change the direction of the `collisionVector`. We do this by multiplying by a scalar value of –1. Our "Planet Collision" example demonstrates two ships bouncing off the planet and each other. The `collisions` function in `spacewar.cpp` looks like the code in Listing 6.21.

```cpp
//=============================================================================
// Handle collisions
//=============================================================================
void Spacewar::collisions()
{
    VECTOR2 collisionVector;
    // If collision between ship and planet
    if(ship1.collidesWith(planet, collisionVector))
    {
        // Bounce off planet
        ship1.bounce(collisionVector, planet);
        ship1.damage(PLANET);
    }
    if(ship2.collidesWith(planet, collisionVector))
    {
        // Bounce off planet
        ship2.bounce(collisionVector, planet);
        ship2.damage(PLANET);
    }
    // If collision between ships
    if(ship1.collidesWith(ship2, collisionVector))
    {
        // Bounce off ship
        ship1.bounce(collisionVector, ship2);
        ship1.damage(SHIP);
        // Change the direction of the collisionVector for ship2
        ship2.bounce(collisionVector*-1, ship1);
        ship2.damage(SHIP);
    }
}
```

Listing 6.21. Handling collisions between ships, and between ships and the planet.

If a collision is detected, the ship's `damage` function is called. In this example, we are using the `damage` function to enable the display of the ship's shield. In our actual Spacewar game, the `damage` function will inflict damage on the ship that is appropriate to the weapon type.

6.4.4 Shields Up!

As was mentioned previously, we can draw a circular shield around our spaceship to make the shape of our ship conform to the circular collision detection we are using. Figure 6.22 shows the shield being displayed around each ship.

The shield is an `Image` class object that we have added to the `Ship` class. The `shield` object is declared in the `ship.h` file (Listing 6.22). We have also added a Boolean to keep track of when the shield is being displayed.

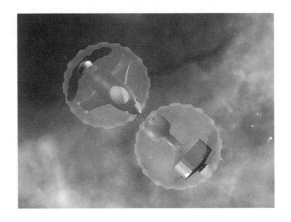

Figure 6.22. Displaying shields after the collision between ships.

```
// Inherits from Entity class
class Ship : public Entity
{
private:
    bool    shieldOn;
    Image   shield;
```

Listing 6.22. The shield variables in the Ship class.

The shield image is initialized in the ship's initialize function. The shield is animated using four individual images. The number of animation frames and the amount of time each frame is displayed are set using constants that are declared in ship.h (Listing 6.23).

```
//=============================================================================
// Initialize the ship
// Post: returns true if successful, false if failed
//=============================================================================
bool Ship::initialize(Game *gamePtr, int width, int height, int ncols,
                      TextureManager *textureM)
{
    shield.initialize(gamePtr->getGraphics(), width, height, ncols,
                     textureM);
    shield.setFrames(shipNS::SHIELD_START_FRAME, shipNS::SHIELD_END_FRAME);
    shield.setCurrentFrame(shipNS::SHIELD_START_FRAME);
    shield.setFrameDelay(shipNS::SHIELD_ANIMATION_DELAY);
    shield.setLoop(false);                      // Do not loop animation
    return(Entity::initialize(gamePtr, width, height, ncols, textureM));
}
```

Listing 6.23. Initializing the shield.

6. Collisions and Entities

```
//=====================================================================
// Draw the ship
//=====================================================================
void Ship::draw()
{
    Image::draw();                  // Draw ship
    if(shieldOn)
        // Draw shield using colorFilter 50% alpha
        shield.draw(spriteData, graphicsNS::ALPHA50 & colorFilter);
}
```

Listing 6.24. Drawing the shield.

```
    if(shieldOn)
    {
        shield.update(frameTime);
        if(shield.getAnimationComplete())
        {
            shieldOn = false;
            shield.setAnimationComplete(false);
        }
    }
```

Listing 6.25. Animating the shield.

The ship's `draw` function takes care of drawing the shield. The shield is drawn by using a 50% alpha channel value that is AND'ed with the `colorFilter` property. The default color

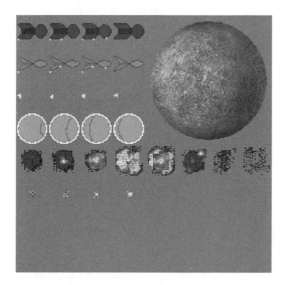

Figure 6.23. The sprite images for the Spacewar game.

of `colorFilter` is white, which does not alter the original color of the shield. If we set the `colorFilter` property of a ship to a different color, it would change the color of the shield also. The shield is drawn using the ship's `spriteData` structure. This draws the shield in the same position as the ship, using the ship's orientation and scale (Listing 6.24).

The shield is animated by calling its `update` function (Listing 6.25). If the shield's animation sequence is complete, the `shieldOn` Boolean is set to `false`, which turns off the display of the shield.

For this example, we have combined all of the game textures into one texture file (Figure 6.23). The shield is the fourth row of images. Additional images are included that will be used in our finished game.

6.4.5 Gravity

Gravity effects are typically applied in a 2D game to make the game items fall down the screen as if they are actually affected by the force of gravity. We can easily simulate this effect by adding one line of code to our object's `update` function:

$$velocity.y = frameTime * GRAVITY.$$

The constant `GRAVITY` is defined in `constants.h` as:

```
const float GRAVITY = 2000.0f;  // Acceleration of gravity pixels/sec
```

This addition will make the object accelerate toward the bottom of the screen. See "Gravity" in the end-of-chapter examples for the complete source.

A more interesting type of gravitational effect is the gravitational attraction between two bodies. The formula to calculate the force exerted between two bodies A and B is:

$$force = GRAVITY * mass\ of\ A * mass\ of\ B\ /\ r^2.$$

Where GRAVITY is the gravitational constant and r^2 is the square of the distance between the center points, which may be calculated using the formula:

$$r^2 = (Ax - Bx)^2 + (Ay - By)^2.$$

The code to perform this calculation is in the entity's `gravityForce` function and looks like the code in Listing 6.26(a).

```
//================================================================================
// Force of gravity on this entity from other entity
// Adds the gravitational force to the velocity vector of this entity
// Force = GRAVITY * m1 * m2 / r*r
//                    2            2
//   r*r  =    (Ax - Bx)   +  (Ay - By)
//================================================================================
void Entity::gravityForce(Entity *ent, float frameTime)
{
    // If either entity is not active then no gravity effect
```

```
if (!active || !ent->getActive())
    return ;
rr = pow((ent->getCenterX() - getCenterX()),2) +
        pow((ent->getCenterY() - getCenterY()),2);
force = gravity * ent->getMass() * mass/rr;
```

Listing 6.26(a). The `gravityForce` function calculates the force of gravity exerted on this entity from the entity `ent`.

The force of gravity is applied to our ship by creating a vector between the ship and planet with a magnitude equal to the force of gravity. This vector will be added to the ship's velocity vector to alter its path through space. To create the gravity vector, we create a vector between the planet and the ship, as seen in Listing 6.26(b).

```
// --- Using vector math to create gravity vector ---
// Create vector between entities
VECTOR2 gravityV(ent->getCenterX() - getCenterX(),
                 ent->getCenterY() - getCenterY());
```

Listing 6.26(b). Creating a vector between two entities.

Then, we normalize the vector, as shown in Listing 6.26(c). Normalizing the vector makes its length equal to 1 and maintains the direction. Multiplying the normalized vector by the force of gravity gives us a gravity vector. That is, it gives us a vector in the direction of the gravitational attraction with a magnitude equal to the force of gravity.

```
// Normalize the vector
Graphics::Vector2Normalize(&gravityV);
// Multipy by force of gravity to create gravity vector
gravityV *= force * frameTime;
```

Listing 6.26(c). Creating a gravity vector.

The last step is to add the gravity vector to the ship's velocity vector to alter the direction of the ship, as shown in the code of Listing 6.26(d).

```
// Add gravity vector to moving velocity vector to change direction
velocity += gravityV;
}
```

Listing 6.26(d). Adding the gravity vector to the velocity vector.

In the real universe, the gravitational constant is 6.67384×10^{-11} N(m/kg)^2. In our game universe, we can use whatever value we want. The most important thing is making our game fun to play, not making it behave by the laws of physics—apologies to all the physics majors in the audience. Besides, it's our universe, so we can make up our own laws. In this example, the value for GRAVITY was set at 6.67384e-11. The planet's mass is 1.0e14 and the ship's mass is 300.0. Increasing any of the values will make the objects be more attracted and decreasing the values will yield less attraction.

The "Orbit" example demonstrates how to use the gravityForce function. In the Spacewar::update function, we call the ship's gravityForce function prior to updating the ship (Listing 6.27).

```
//============================================================================
// Update all game items
//============================================================================
void Spacewar::update()
{
    ship.gravityForce(&planet, frameTime);
    planet.update(frameTime);
    ship.update(frameTime);
}
```

Listing 6.27. Updating the game items.

The gravityForce function changes the ship's velocity vector. The velocity is used to change the ship's position in the Ship::update function (Listing 6.28). Please refer to the "Orbit" example of this chapter for the complete source.

```
//============================================================================
// Update
// Typically called once per frame
// frameTime is used to regulate the speed of movement and animation
//============================================================================
void Ship::update(float frameTime)
{
    Entity::update(frameTime);
    spriteData.angle += frameTime * shipNS::ROTATION_RATE;  // Rotate the
                                                            // ship
    spriteData.x += frameTime * velocity.x; // Move ship along X
    spriteData.y += frameTime * velocity.y; // Move ship along Y
    // Bounce off walls
    // If hit right screen edge
    if (spriteData.x > GAME_WIDTH-shipNS::WIDTH*getScale())
    {
        // Position at right screen edge
        spriteData.x = GAME_WIDTH-shipNS::WIDTH*getScale();
        velocity.x = -velocity.x;              // Reverse X direction
    }
    else if (spriteData.x < 0)                // Else if hit left screen edge
    {
```

```
            spriteData.x = 0;                    // Position at left screen edge
            velocity.x = -velocity.x;            // Reverse X direction
    }
    // If hit bottom screen edge
    if (spriteData.y > GAME_HEIGHT-shipNS::HEIGHT*getScale())
    {
            // Position at bottom screen edge
            spriteData.y = GAME_HEIGHT-shipNS::HEIGHT*getScale();
            velocity.y = -velocity.y;            // Reverse Y direction
    }
    else if (spriteData.y < 0)                  // Else if hit top screen edge
    {
            spriteData.y = 0;                    // Position at top screen edge
            velocity.y = -velocity.y;            // Reverse Y direction
    }
}
```

Listing 6.28. Using the velocity to change the ship screen position.

Chapter Review

This chapter was about detecting collisions and game physics. We started with a little vector math to help us understand the DirectX vector math operations. Next, we looked at four different techniques for performing collision detection: circular, box, rotated box, and rotated box vs. circular. We created the `Entity` class to hold our collision code. We finished up the chapter by looking at how to make our entities bounce and simulate the effects of gravity. Here are the finer points:

- *Vectors.* A vector represents length and direction.

- *Vector math.* Vector math supports unary + -, binary + - * /, and comparison == !=.

- *Definitions.* We define the DirectX 2D vector as `VECTOR2`.

- *Adding.* Adding two vectors results in a vector.

- *Multiplication.* A vector multiplied by a scalar changes the length of the vector.

- *Unit vectors.* A unit vector has a length of 1.

- *Dot products.* The dot product of a vector with a unit vector results in a scalar value that represents a portion of the vector, which falls along the unit vector.

- *Vector math code.* We encapsulated the DirectX vector math code in our `Graphics` class.

- *Circular collision detection.* Circular collision detection performs a distance check between entity centers.

- *Box collision detection.* Box collision detection compares the edges of boxes that are always aligned with the *x*- and *y*-axis.

- *Rotated box collision detection.* Rotated box collision detection looks for any edge where the boxes do not overlap.

- *Rotated box and circle collision detection.* Rotated box and circle collision detection looks for overlap on the box edges and does distance checks on the box corners.

- *Collision detection code.* The `Entity` class contains the collision detection code.

- *Specifying collision type.* Each `Entity` object specifies a collision type from `CIRCLE`, `BOX`, or `ROTATED_BOX`.

- *Testing.* The `Entity::collidesWith` function is used to test for collisions.

- *Getting stuck.* Collision code needs to prevent entities from getting stuck.

- *Bouncing.* The `Entity::bounce` function performs the physics calculations to cause an entity to bounce after colliding with another entity.

- *Gravity.* The `Entity::gravityForce` function calculates the force of gravity applied to the entity from another entity.

Review Questions

1. What are the two members of a `VECTOR2` structure?

2. What is the result of adding two vectors?

3. What happens to a vector when it is multiplied by a scalar?

4. How is a vector converted into a unit vector?

5. What is the result of the dot product between a vector and a unit vector?

6. Which `Graphics` class function performs a vector dot product?

7. Which `Graphics` class function is used to normalize a vector?

8. Two circles will collide if the distance between their centers is what amount?

9. Describe the difference between box and rotated box collision detection.

10. What is an advantage of rotated box collision detection?

11. When does the worst case performance occur for rotated box collision detection?

12. What does it mean if a projection is found where the two rotated boxes are not overlapping?

13. What is the special case when detecting collisions between a rotated box and a circle?

14. What collision test is used between a circle and a box when the circle is in the Voronoi region of the box?

15. What features does the `Entity` class have that are not in the `Image` class?

16. Which property in an entity defines its collision type?

17. What are the possible collision types for an entity?

18. Which `Entity` function is used to check for a collision with another entity?

19. How could a game entity get stuck to the screen edge?

20. How does the `Entity::bounce` function prevent entities from getting stuck?

Exercises

1. Add a third spaceship to the "Planet Collision" example. Make sure that the third ship starts in a different location from the other two. Be sure to check for collisions between all the ships.

2. Modify the "Planet Collision" example to use an array of 10 ships. (Hint: Use a nested loop when performing the collision checks.)

```
for (int i=0; i<MAX_SHIPS; i++)
{
    if(ships[i].collidesWith(planet, collisionVector))
        // Bounce off planet
        ships[i].bounce(collisionVector, planet);
    // If collision between ships
    // For all other ships
    for (int j=i+1; j<MAX_SHIPS; j++)
    {
        if(ships[i].collidesWith(ships[j], collisionVector))
        {
            // Bounce off ship
```

3. Add user control of the spaceship and collision detection to the "Orbit" example.

4. Add a second user-controlled spaceship to your results from exercise 3. Include collision detection between both ships and the planet.

5. Create a simple game of your own design. You may modify one of the chapter examples or create your own. The game must include some sort of user control and collision detection. KEEP IT SIMPLE! The goal here is to practice some of the techniques we have been covering, not create the world's greatest video game. We'll save that for a later chapter.

Examples

The following examples are available for download from www.programming2dgames.com:

- *Bounce.* One spaceship bounces off the edges of the window.

    - Demonstrates collisions with the edge of the game screen.

- *Planet Collision.* Two spaceships fly around, bouncing off a planet and each other.

    – Demonstrates how to call the `bounce` function for the two entities involved in a collision.

    – The planet is assumed to have infinite mass relative to the spaceship.

    – Demonstrates displaying semitransparent images using the alpha channel.

- *Gravity.* A yellow ball bounces inside a blue box.

    – Simulates how gravity affects a falling object.

    – Energy is lost on each bounce.

- *Orbit.* A spaceship orbits a planet.

    – Demonstrates the `Entity::gravityForce` function to calculate the force applied by gravity between two entities.

7 Sound

Sound adds an amazing dimension to games. Even the simplest sound can bring an otherwise dull game to life. Sounds can set the mood, warn the player of danger, celebrate victory, and humiliate the defeated.

The latest Microsoft audio technology for games is XAudio2 and XACT. XAudio2 is a lower-level API that could be used to create an audio engine. XACT is a higher-level API that contains its own audio engine and the Microsoft cross-platform audio creation tool. The audio creation tool in XACT is an application that is used to create special XACT data files. The XACT engine and data files work together to provide an audio solution that is perfect for our game programming needs and we will utilize it exclusively for our game audio.

To add sounds to our game, we need to do the following:

1. Create or obtain audio files.

2. Process the audio files (if necessary).

3. Create a sound bank and a wave bank using XACT.

4. Add the code to our game engine to play audio using the XACT audio engine.

7.1 Obtaining Audio Files

There are several good online resources where we may obtain royalty-free sound effects. Here are a few such sites:

- http://www.freesound.org

- http://www.mediacollege.com/downloads/sound-effects

- http://www.downlopedia.com/sound-effects-collection

Third party audio files may need to be converted into a format that is compatible with XACT. See Section 7.2.2 for details. As with any online resource, always verify the licensing requirements and make sure the material is not violating any copyrights.

▊ 7.2 Creating Audio Files

Many audio editing and processing programs are available. In this book, we have decided to use Audacity (http://audacity.sourceforge.net/). Audacity is a free open-source application. It has an intuitive user interface and all of the features we need to record and process our game audio files. Audacity supports a wide range of file formats and processing options.

7.2.1 Recording Audio with Audacity

Recording our own sound effects can be a lot of fun. There are many sources of sounds all around us—all it takes is a microphone and a little imagination. External microphones generally produce better quality results than built-in microphones. When recording sounds with a microphone, we must be aware of our surroundings. Microphones can easily pick up background sounds that we do not want in our game.

Start Audacity and click the microphone on the toolbar to activate the input level meter. Try adjusting the recording level slider while speaking into the microphone. The input level bar graph should move in response to sounds (Figure 7.1).

To record audio, click the "Record" button on the toolbar. Click the "Stop" button to end recording (Figure 7.2). The recorded sound is now visible in the audio editor. In Figure 7.3, we have selected "Fit in Window" from the "View" menu and we have enlarged the waveform by clicking on the "0.0" as indicated.

Save the audio to a file by selecting "Export..." in the "File" menu. Save as type: WAV (Microsoft) signed 16-bit PCM, and save each sound effect in a separate WAV file. Choose a simple name for each file that reflects its intended use: "beep1.wav," "hit.wav," etc.

The entire recording may be saved or we can select just the portion we want by dragging the mouse across the waveform in the editor and choose "Export Selection" in the "File" menu.

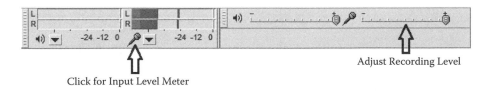

Adjust Recording Level

Click for Input Level Meter

Figure 7.1. Adjusting the recording level in Audacity.

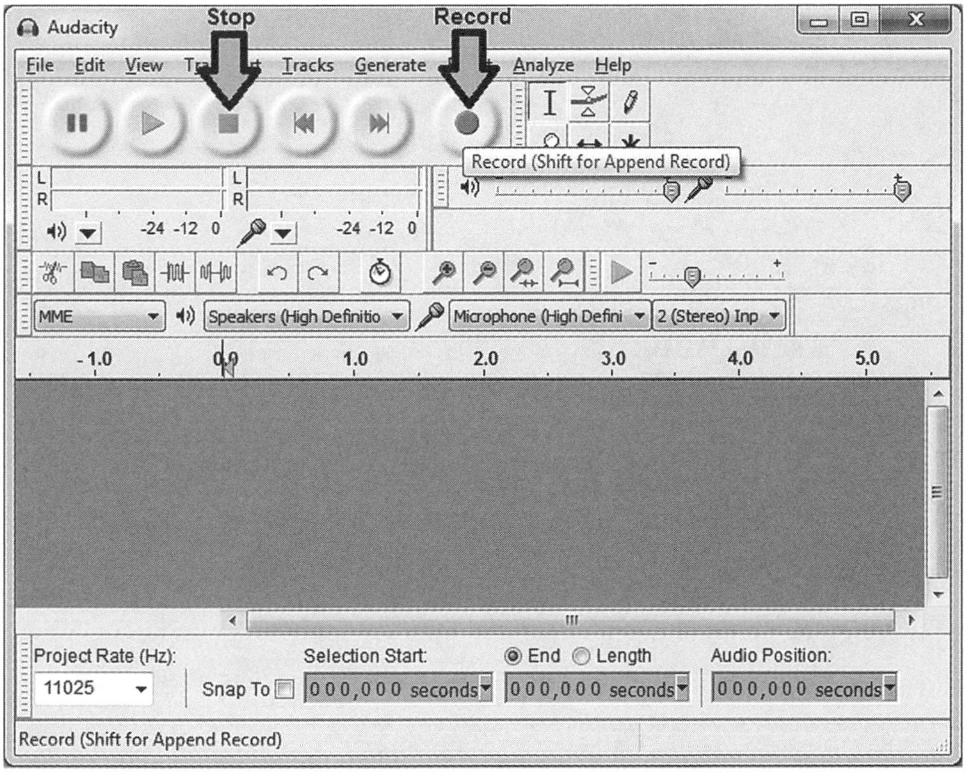

Figure 7.2. Audacity's "Stop" and "Record" buttons.

7.2.2 Audio Processing

Audacity may be used to convert audio files between different formats. To convert an audio file into a format that is compatible with XACT, open the file to be converted and select "Export…" in the "File" menu. Save as type: WAV (Microsoft) signed 16-bit PCM.

Audacity offers a wide array of audio processing features. We will go over just a few basic commands here. Audacity's built-in help does a very good job of explaining how to use all of the features, so there is no point in repeating that information here. From the main toolbar we have the following tools:

 Cut the selected audio.

 Copy the selected audio to the clipboard.

Paste audio from the clipboard to the selected location in the waveform.

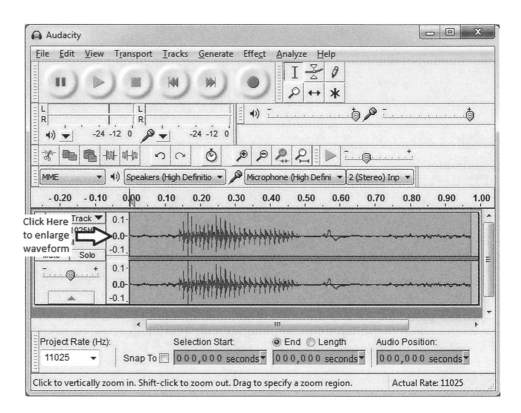

Figure 7.3. Viewing the recorded audio.

Trim (delete) the audio outside the selected region.

Silence the audio in the selected region.

To insert an audio file into the current waveform, open the second audio file, select the desired portion, copy it to the clipboard, click the location to paste it into the current waveform, and click the "Paste" button.

To change the volume level in a waveform, select the portion of the waveform to process and select "Amplify..." under the "Effect" menu. Adjust the slider to increase or decrease the volume. Use the "Preview" button to hear the changes before they are applied.

Dig into Audacity and play with the editing tools it has. With this great tool and a little creativity, we can create some very interesting sound effects.

▌▌ 7.3 Using XACT

To prepare the WAV files for use in our game, we will use the Microsoft cross-platform audio creation tool, or XACT. XACT is normally found in "Start/Microsoft DirectX SDK

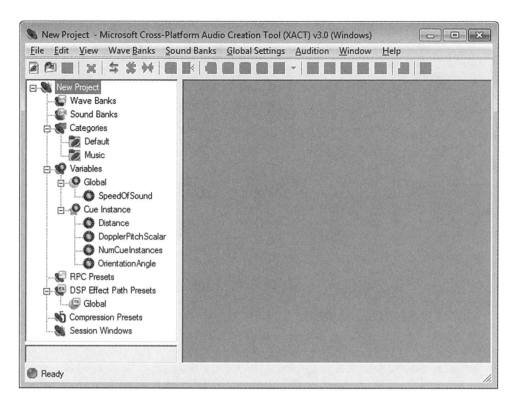

Figure 7.4. The Microsoft cross-platform audio creation tool (XACT).

(date)/DirectX Utilities/Microsoft Cross-Platform Audio Creation Tool (XACT)." Start XACT and select "New Project" from the "File" menu (Figure 7.4).

Give the project a name and select the project location. The project location does not need to be in the same folder as the game code. In Figure 7.5, the project is named "Sound-Example1." After the project is created, perform the following steps to add the WAV files to the project:

1. Right click "Wave Banks" in the left pane and select "New Wave Bank."

2. Right click the newly created wave bank under "Wave Banks," then select "Insert Wave File(s)..." Navigate to the folder containing the WAV files and select the desired files. The wave files appear in the right pane (Figure 7.5).

3. Right click "Sound Banks" in the left pane and select "New Sound Bank."

4. Select all of the wave bank files and drag them into the "Sound Name" portion of the sound bank window. The result is shown in Figure 7.6.

5. Select all of the files that were just added to the sound bank window and drag them into the lower half of the window to create "Cue Names." *Cues* are how the game code references a particular sound. The cues may be renamed if desired (see Figure 7.7).

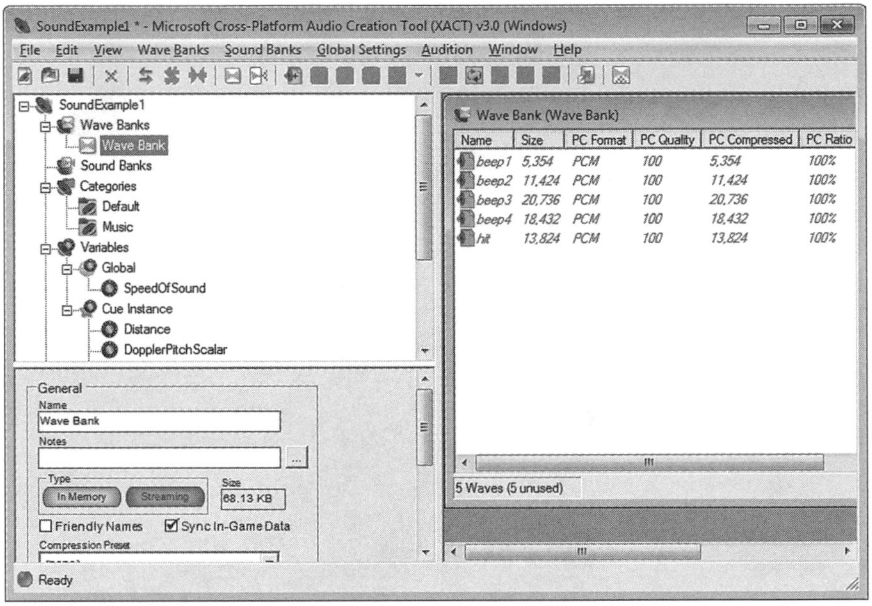

Figure 7.5. The wave bank after wave files have been added.

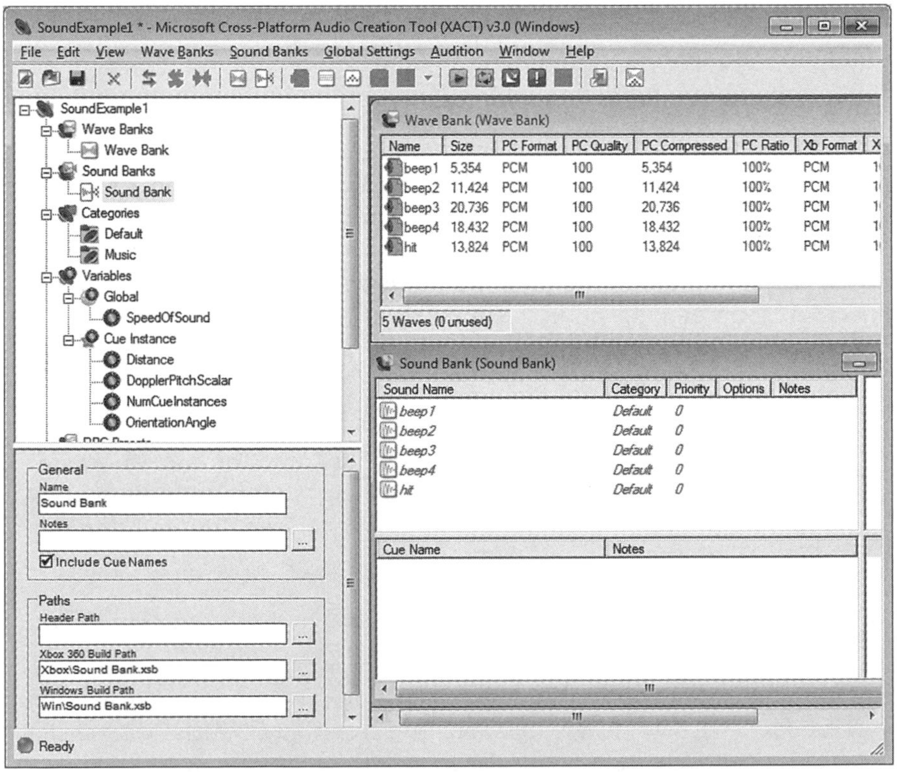

Figure 7.6. The sound bank after dragging in the wave bank files.

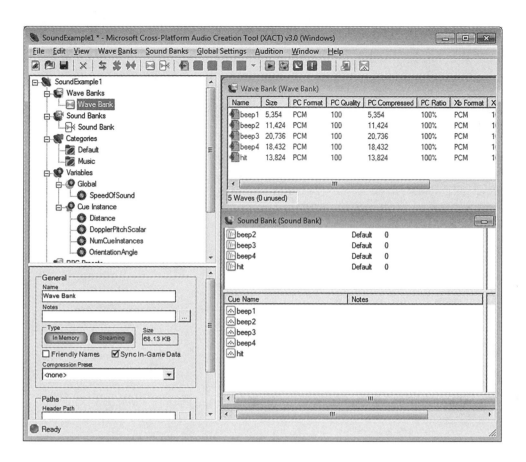

Figure 7.7. The result of dragging the sound bank files into the "Cue Name" area.

6. Select "Build" from the "File" menu and click "Finish."

7. Select "Save Project" from the "File" menu.

If the project builds successfully, the folder where we saved the project will contain the project file—SoundExample1.xap in this example—and two new folders, "Win" and "Xbox." The "Win" folder contains:

- Sound Bank.xsb

- SoundExample1.xgs

- Wave Bank.xwb

The two files Sound Bank.xsb and Wave Bank.xwb are what we need for our game. Copy these files into a folder named "Audio" in the game code folder.

7.3.1 Playing Sounds from XACT GUI

To play sounds directly from the XACT GUI, we need to run "All Programs\Microsoft DirectX SDK (date)\DirectX Utilities\Audio Console." This will start a Windows auditioning server that is required by XACT.

Sounds may be played by selecting the sound name or the cue name and clicking the "Play" or "Repeat Play" button on the toolbar.

▌ 7.4 Adding Audio to the Game Engine

Playing sound cues in our game with the XACT audio engine is fairly straightforward. The steps required are the following:

1. Initialize the XACT engine.

2. Create the XACT wave bank(s) we want to use.

3. Create the XACT sound bank(s) we want to use.

4. Play the sounds using the sound cue.

5. Call the XACT engine's `DoWork()` function periodically.

6. Clean up when we are done.

Let's examine each of the required steps and the DirectX code used to accomplish it. We are going to create an `Audio` class to contain all of the required DirectX audio code. Our `Audio` class is in two files: `audio.h` and `audio.cpp`.

7.4.1 Initialize the XACT Engine

The function `XACT3CreateEngine` creates an instance of the `IXACT3Engine` interface. This interface provides access to the `XACT` object. The formal function description is:

```
HRESULT XACT3CreateEngine(
    DWORD dwCreationFlags,
    IXACT3Engine **ppEngine
)
```

The parameters are:

- `dwCreationFlags`. Specifies how the engine should be created. We will normally use 0 for this parameter. Valid values are:

  - `0`. Normal creation mode.

  - `XACT_FLAG_API_AUDTION_MODE`. Specifies that auditioning should be enabled.

  - `XACT_FLAG_API_DEBUG_MODE`. Specifies that debug mode should be enabled.

- `ppEngine`. Output address that receives a pointer to the created engine.

We will create an `IXACT3Engine` pointer in `audio.h`, as shown in Listing 7.1.

```
IXACT3Engine* xactEngine;
```

Listing 7.1. The pointer to the XACT engine.

The call to `XACT3CreateEngine` will be included in the `initialize` function of our `Audio` class, as Listing 7.2 describes.

```
result = XACT3CreateEngine( 0, &xactEngine );
if( FAILED( result ) || xactEngine == NULL )
    return E_FAIL;
```

Listing 7.2. Creating the XACT engine.

After the engine is created, it must be initialized by calling the `IXACT3Engine` `Initialize` method:

```
HRESULT Initialize(
        const XACT_RUNTIME_PARAMETERS *pParams
)
```

The only parameter is a pointer to an `XACT_RUNTIME_PARAMETERS` structure that contains the desired initialization parameters. The only member of the structure we will use is `lookAheadTime`, which specifies how far ahead the XACT engine will look when transitioning to another sound. `XACT_ENGINE_LOOKAHEAD_DEAFULT` is a good value to use for this parameter. This code is also part of our `initialize` function in the `Audio` class, and looks like Listing 7.3.

```
// Initialize & create the XACT runtime
XACT_RUNTIME_PARAMETERS xactParams = {0};
xactParams.lookAheadTime = XACT_ENGINE_LOOKAHEAD_DEFAULT;
result = xactEngine->Initialize( &xactParams );
if( FAILED( result ) )
    return result;
```

Listing 7.3. Initializing the XACT engine.

Next, we will create an "in memory" XACT wave bank file using the wave bank we created with the XACT GUI tool. This code is basically the same as the XACT example provided by Microsoft. The `WAVE_BANK` parameter in the `CreateFile` function is defined in our `constants.h` file to point to our wave bank we created earlier. Note the use of a relative path name. In our example, the game project folder contains an audio folder (see Listing 7.4). The create code is also added to the `initialize` function of our `Audio` class, as shown in Listing 7.5.

```
// WAVE_BANK must be location of .xwb file
const char WAVE_BANK[]  = "audio\\Win\\WavesExample1.xwb";
```

Listing 7.4. Defining the `WAVE_BANK` constant.

```
// Create an "in memory" XACT wave bank file using memory mapped file IO
result = E_FAIL; // Default to failure code, replaced on success
hFile = CreateFile( WAVE_BANK, GENERIC_READ, FILE_SHARE_READ, NULL,
                    OPEN_EXISTING, 0, NULL );
if( hFile != INVALID_HANDLE_VALUE )
{
    fileSize = GetFileSize( hFile, NULL );
    if( fileSize != -1 )
    {
        hMapFile = CreateFileMapping( hFile, NULL, PAGE_READONLY, 0,
                                      fileSize, NULL );
        if( hMapFile )
        {
            mapWaveBank = MapViewOfFile( hMapFile, FILE_MAP_READ, 0, 0,
                                         0 );
            if( mapWaveBank )
                result = xactEngine->CreateInMemoryWaveBank(
                                        mapWaveBank, fileSize, 0, 0,
                                        &waveBank );
            // mapWaveBank maintains a handle on the file
            // Close this unneeded handle
            CloseHandle( hMapFile );
        }
    }
    // mapWaveBank maintains a handle on the file so close this unneeded
    // handle
    CloseHandle( hFile );
}
if( FAILED( result ) )
    return HRESULT_FROM_WIN32( ERROR_FILE_NOT_FOUND );
```

Listing 7.5. Creating an "in memory" XACT wave bank file.

Next, we read and register the sound bank file we created earlier with XACT. Again, this code is basically the same as the DirectX example. The addition of this code completes our `Audio` class's `initialize` function (Listing 7.6).

```
    // Read and register the sound bank file with XACT
    result = E_FAIL;      // Default to failure code, replaced on success
    hFile = CreateFile( SOUND_BANK, GENERIC_READ, FILE_SHARE_READ, NULL,
                        OPEN_EXISTING, 0, NULL );
    if( hFile != INVALID_HANDLE_VALUE )
    {
        fileSize = GetFileSize( hFile, NULL );
        if( fileSize != -1 )
        {
            soundBankData = new BYTE[fileSize];   // Reserve memory for
                                                  // sound bank

            if( soundBankData )
            {
                if(0 != ReadFile( hFile, soundBankData, fileSize,
                    &bytesRead, NULL))
                    result = xactEngine->CreateSoundBank( soundBankData,
                                                          fileSize,
                                                          0, 0, &soundBank
                                                          );
            }
        }
        CloseHandle( hFile );
    }
    if( FAILED( result ) )
        return HRESULT_FROM_WIN32( ERROR_FILE_NOT_FOUND );
    return S_OK;
}
```

Listing 7.6. Reading and registering the sound bank file.

The SOUND_BANK parameter is defined in constants.h to point to our sound bank. We also need to define the sound cues in constants.h. The sound cues are defined as constant char arrays. The text in the arrays must match the names used in the XACT tool (see Listing 7.7).

```
// Audio files required by audio.cpp
// WAVE_BANK must be location of .xwb file
const char WAVE_BANK[]  = "audio\\Win\\WavesExample1.xwb";
// SOUND_BANK must be location of .xsb file
const char SOUND_BANK[] = "audio\\Win\\SoundsExample1.xsb";
// Sound cues
const char BEEP1[] = "beep1";
const char BEEP2[] = "beep2";
const char BEEP3[] = "beep3";
const char BEEP4[] = "beep4";
const char HIT[]   = "hit";
```

Listing 7.7. Defining the SOUND_BANK constant.

7.4.2 Playing a Sound

To play a sound, we call the GetCueIndex method of the sound bank and give it one of our sound cues as a parameter. The value returned is an index into the sound bank of the actual sound. This index is used as a parameter in the call to the `Play` function. The `playCue` function of our `Audio` class accepts the name of the audio `cue` and plays the corresponding sound (see Listing 7.8).

```
//=============================================================================
// Play sound specified by cue from sound bank
// If cue does not exist no error occurs, there is simply no sound played
//=============================================================================
void Audio::playCue(const char cue[])
{
    if (soundBank == NULL)
        return;
    cueI = soundBank->GetCueIndex( cue );   // Get cue index from sound bank
    soundBank->Play( cueI, 0, 0, NULL );
}
```

Listing 7.8. The `playCue` function plays the sound specified by `cue`.

To play a sound, call `playCue` with the cue name of the desired sound as a parameter. For example, look at the code in Listing 7.9.

```
    audio->playCue(BEEP1);                              // Play sound
```

Listing 7.9. Playing the `BEEP1` sound.

7.4.3 Stopping a Sound

To stop a currently playing sound, we call the `GetCueIndex` method of the sound bank and give it one of our sound cues as a parameter. The value returned is an index into the sound bank of the actual sound. This is used as a parameter in the `Stop` function to stop the sound. The second parameter to `Stop` specifies when the sound should be stopped. If 0 is used, the sound is played to completion according to the design specifications set in the XACT audio tool. If `XACT_FLAG_SOUNDBANK_STOP_IMMEDIATE` is used as the parameter, the sound is stopped immediately. Our `stopCue` function stops the specified sound immediately (see Listing 7.10).

```
//=============================================================================
// Stop a playing sound specified by cue from sound bank
// If cue does not exist no error occurs
//=============================================================================
void Audio::stopCue(const char cue[])
{
    if (soundBank == NULL)
        return;
    cueI = soundBank->GetCueIndex( cue );   // Get cue index from sound bank
    soundBank->Stop( cueI, XACT_FLAG_SOUNDBANK_STOP_IMMEDIATE);
}
```

Listing 7.10. The `stopCue` function stops a playing sound.

To stop a sound, call `stopCue` with the cue name of the desired sound as a parameter. See Listing 7.11 for an example.

```
audio->stopCue(BEEP1);                      // Stop sound
```

Listing 7.11. Stopping the `BEEP1` sound.

7.4.4 XACT Engine DoWork

The XACT engine requires that we call its `DoWork` function periodically. We will create a run function in our `Audio` class that calls `DoWork`. The call to the `Audio::run` function is added to our main game loop. The `Audio::run` function looks like the code in Listing 7.12.

```
//=============================================================
// Perform periodic sound engine tasks
//=============================================================
void Audio::run()
{
    if (xactEngine == NULL)
        return;
    xactEngine->DoWork();
}
```

Listing 7.12. Calling the `DoWork` function.

7.4.5 Audio Cleanup

Cleanup of the audio system is performed in the `Audio` destructor. This code shuts down the XACT engine and releases the memory resources reserved in the `Audio` class (Listing 7.13). The necessary pointers and function prototypes are contained in `audio.h`. Listing 7.14 contains the complete listing.

```
//=============================================================
// Destructor
//=============================================================
Audio::~Audio()
{
    // Shutdown XACT
    if( xactEngine )
    {
        xactEngine->ShutDown(); // Shut down XACT engine and free resources
        xactEngine->Release();
    }
    if ( soundBankData )
        delete[] soundBankData;
    soundBankData = NULL;
```

```
                // After xactEngine->ShutDown() returns, release memory mapped files
                if( mapWaveBank )
                    UnmapViewOfFile( mapWaveBank );
                mapWaveBank = NULL;
                if( coInitialized )              // If CoInitializeEx succeeded
                    CoUninitialize();
        }
```

Listing 7.13. Shutting down the XACT engine and releasing memory resources.

```
// Programming 2D Games
// Copyright (c) 2011 by:
// Charles Kelly
// audio.h v1.0
#ifndef _AUDIO_H                    // Prevent multiple definitions if this
#define _AUDIO_H                    // file is included in more than one place
#define WIN32_LEAN_AND_MEAN
#include <xact3.h>
#include "constants.h"
class Audio
{
    // Properties
  private:
    IXACT3Engine* xactEngine;       // Pointer to XACT sound engine
    IXACT3WaveBank* waveBank;       // Pointer to XACT wave bank
    IXACT3SoundBank* soundBank;     // Pointer to XACT sound bank
    XACTINDEX cueI;                 // XACT sound index
    void* mapWaveBank;              // Call UnmapViewOfFile() to release file
    void* soundBankData;
    bool coInitialized;             // Set true if coInitialize is successful
  public:
    // Constructor
    Audio();
    // Destructor
    virtual ~Audio();
    // Member functions
    // Initialize Audio
    HRESULT initialize();
    // Perform periodic sound engine tasks
    void run();
    // Play sound specified by cue from sound bank
    // If cue does not exist no error occurs, there is simply no sound
    // played
    void playCue(const char cue[]);
    // Stop a playing sound specified by cue from sound bank
    // If cue does not exist no error occurs
    void stopCue(const char cue[]);
};
#endif
```

Listing 7.14. The audio.h file.

7.4.6 Incorporating the Audio Class

The last step is to add our new Audio class to the game engine. We will add an Audio pointer to game.h (Listing 7.15). This pointer is initialized in the Game::initialize function. If the WAVE_BANK and SOUND_BANK constants are defined, then the Audio::initialize function is called (Listing 7.16).

```
Audio    *audio;                         // Pointer to Audio
```

Listing 7.15. Adding a pointer to an Audio class object in our game.h file.

```
//=============================================================================
// Initializes the game
// Throws GameError on error
//=============================================================================
void Game::initialize(HWND hw)
{
    hwnd = hw;                               // Save window handle
    // Initialize graphics
    graphics = new Graphics();
    // Throws GameError
    graphics->initialize(hwnd, GAME_WIDTH, GAME_HEIGHT, FULLSCREEN);
    // Initialize input, do not capture mouse
    input->initialize(hwnd, false);          // Throws GameError
    // Init sound system
    audio = new Audio();
    if (*WAVE_BANK != '\0' && *SOUND_BANK != '\0')// If sound files defined
    {
        if( FAILED( hr = audio->initialize() ) )
        {
            if( hr == HRESULT_FROM_WIN32( ERROR_FILE_NOT_FOUND ) )
                throw(GameError(gameErrorNS::FATAL_ERROR,
                "Failed to initialize sound system" \
                "because media file not found."));
            else
                throw(GameError(gameErrorNS::FATAL_ERROR,
                "Failed to initialize sound system."));
        }
    }
    // Attempt to set up high resolution timer
    if(QueryPerformanceFrequency(&timerFreq) == false)
        throw(GameError(gameErrorNS::FATAL_ERROR,
        "Error initializing high resolution timer"));
    QueryPerformanceCounter(&timeStart);       // Get starting time
    initialized = true;
}
```

Listing 7.16. Initializing the audio system in the Game class initialize function.

In the Game class run function, we add a call to Audio class run function (Listing 7.17). In Game::deleteAll(), we will delete the audio pointer (Listing 7.18).

```
audio->run();                   // Perform periodic sound engine tasks
```

Listing 7.17. Calling the Audio class run function.

```
SAFE_DELETE(audio);
```

Listing 7.18. Deleting the audio pointer.

To make the function call to play a sound a little cleaner, we added an Audio pointer to the Entity class as well (Listing 7.19). This pointer is initialized in the Entity::initialize function (Listing 7.20).

```
Audio    *audio;                // Pointer to audio system
```

Listing 7.19. Adding an Audio pointer to the entity.h file.

```
//=============================================================================
// Initialize the Entity
// Pre: *gamePtr = pointer to Game object
//      width = width of Image in pixels  (0 = use full texture width)
//      height = height of Image in pixels (0 = use full texture height)
//      ncols = number of columns in texture (1 to n) (0 same as 1)
//      *textureM = pointer to TextureManager object
// Post: returns true if successful, false if failed
//=============================================================================
bool Entity::initialize(Game *gamePtr, int width, int height, int ncols,
                        TextureManager *textureM)
{
    input = gamePtr->getInput();                 // The input system
    audio = gamePtr->getAudio();                 // The audio system
    return(Image::initialize(gamePtr->getGraphics(), width, height, ncols,
                        textureM));
}
```

Listing 7.20. Initializing the audio pointer.

That completes the incorporation of the Audio class into the game engine.

7.5 Adding Sound to the Game

To play a sound in the game, all we need to do is call `playCue` from the `Audio` class. Let's add some sounds to our "Bounce" example from Chapter 6. We'll play a different sound when the spaceship bounces off each edge of the window (Listing 7.21). See "Sound Example 1" from this chapter for the complete program.

```cpp
//=============================================================================
// Update
// Typically called once per frame
// frameTime is used to regulate the speed of movement and animation
//=============================================================================
void Ship::update(float frameTime)
{
    Entity::update(frameTime);
    spriteData.angle += frameTime * shipNS::ROTATION_RATE;  // Rotate the
                                                            // ship
    spriteData.x += frameTime * velocity.x; // Move ship along X
    spriteData.y += frameTime * velocity.y; // Move ship along Y
    // Bounce off walls
    // If hit right screen edge
    if (spriteData.x > GAME_WIDTH-shipNS::WIDTH*getScale())
    {
        // Position at right screen edge
        spriteData.x = GAME_WIDTH-shipNS::WIDTH*getScale();
        velocity.x = -velocity.x;           // Reverse X direction
        audio->playCue(BEEP1);              // Play sound
    }
    else if (spriteData.x < 0)              // Else if hit left screen edge
    {
        spriteData.x = 0;                   // Position at left screen edge
        velocity.x = -velocity.x;           // Reverse X direction
        audio->playCue(BEEP2);              // Play sound
    }
    // If hit bottom screen edge
    if (spriteData.y > GAME_HEIGHT-shipNS::HEIGHT*getScale())
    {
        // Position at bottom screen edge
        spriteData.y = GAME_HEIGHT-shipNS::HEIGHT*getScale();
        velocity.y = -velocity.y;           // Reverse Y direction
        audio->playCue(BEEP3);              // Play sound
    }
    else if (spriteData.y < 0)              // Else if hit top screen edge
    {
        spriteData.y = 0;                   // Position at top screen edge
        velocity.y = -velocity.y;           // Reverse Y direction
        audio->playCue(BEEP4);              // Play sound
    }
}
```

Listing 7.21. Playing sounds in the game.

▐ 7.6 Adjusting Audio Playback

The XACT audio environment has several adjustable properties that affect how the sounds are played back. These adjustments are made with the XACT GUI tool and require no modifications to our game code. This gives us more flexibility when creating our games because we are able to make changes to the game audio directly. With this type of system, the audio designers are able to make changes to the game audio without involving the game programmers.

7.6.1 Sound Properties

In the XACT GUI tool, open a sound bank and select one of the sounds from the sound bank window. The audio properties window is displayed. The audio properties in Figure 7.8 are:

- *Name.* The name of the sound.

- *Notes.* Add comments about the sound; this is only visible in the GUI tool.

- *Category.* Specifies the type of sound (global, default, music).

- *Volume.* Adjust the volume of the sound.

- *Pitch.* Adjust the pitch of the sound.

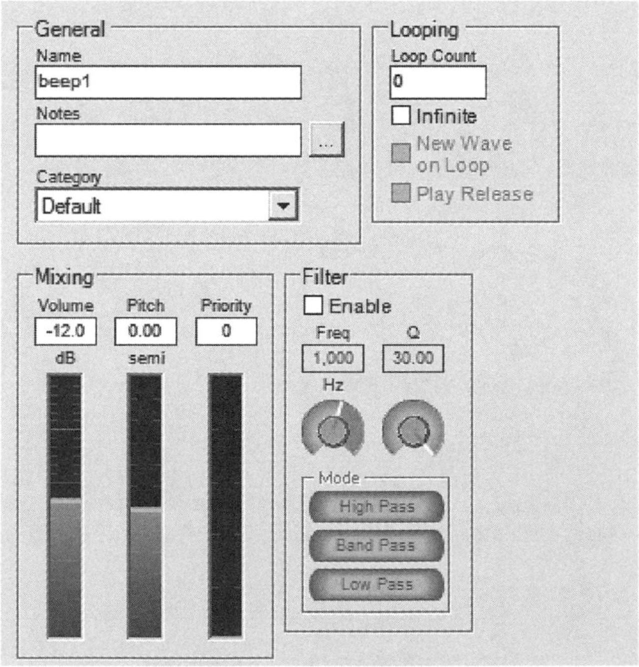

Figure 7.8. XACT audio properties.

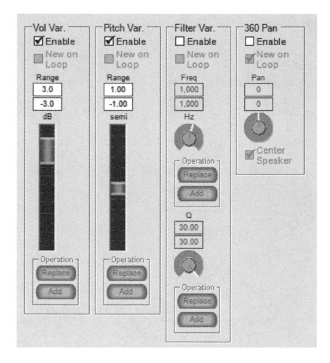

Figure 7.9. Additional XACT audio properties.

- *Priority.* Specifies the priority of the sound where 0 is highest and 255 is lowest. This is only used if the maximum number of allocated voices is used.

- *Loop count.* The number of additional times to play the sound. A value of 1 means the sound is played twice.

Loop count is useful for music sequences that we wish to repeat. The sound will repeat automatically until we stop it.

- *Infinite.* When the sound is started, it plays in a continuous loop.

- *New wave on loop.* A new wave variation is played on the next loop when checked.

- *Play release.* Play any release envelopes or fades when the sound loops.

- *Enable.* Enables filtering.

- *Freq.* Sets the center of the filter frequency.

- *Q.* Sets the roll-off speed of the filter.

- *Mode.* Sets the mode of filtering.

The audio properties in Figure 7.9 are:

- *Vol Var.*

  - *Enable.* Use a random volume when the sound is played.

  - *New on loop.* A new volume is used each time the sound loops.

  - *Range.* The minimum and maximum values of the random volume.

  - *Operation.* How this setting behaves relative to other settings.

- *Pitch Var.*

  - *Enable.* Use a random pitch when the sound is played.

  - *New on loop.* A new pitch is used each time the sound loops.

  - *Range.* The minimum and maximum values of the random pitch.

  - *Operation.* How this setting behaves relative to other settings.

- *Filter Var.*

  - *Enable.* Use a random filter frequency when the sound is played.

  - *New on loop.* A new pitch is used each time the sound loops.

  - *Freq.* The minimum and maximum values of the random frequency.

  - *Operation (Freq).* How this setting behaves relative to other settings.

  - *Q.* The minimum and maximum values of the random Q.

  - *Operation (Q).* How this setting behaves relative to other settings.

The "360 Pan" properties are more applicable to 3D games, so we will not cover them here.

7.6.2 Cues

Cues are used in our game code to play sounds. A cue may trigger the playback of one or more sounds. We created cues earlier by dragging the sound names into the "Cue Name" window. We can also create new cues by right clicking in the "Cue Name" window, pressing Ctrl + "U," or by selecting "New Cue" in the sounds bank menu. The new cue may be renamed by right clicking on it and selecting "Rename."

Sounds are added to a cue by dragging them from the "Sound Name" window and dropping them on the cue. In Figure 7.10, we have created a new cue named "beep1and2" and added "beep1" and "beep2" sounds to it.

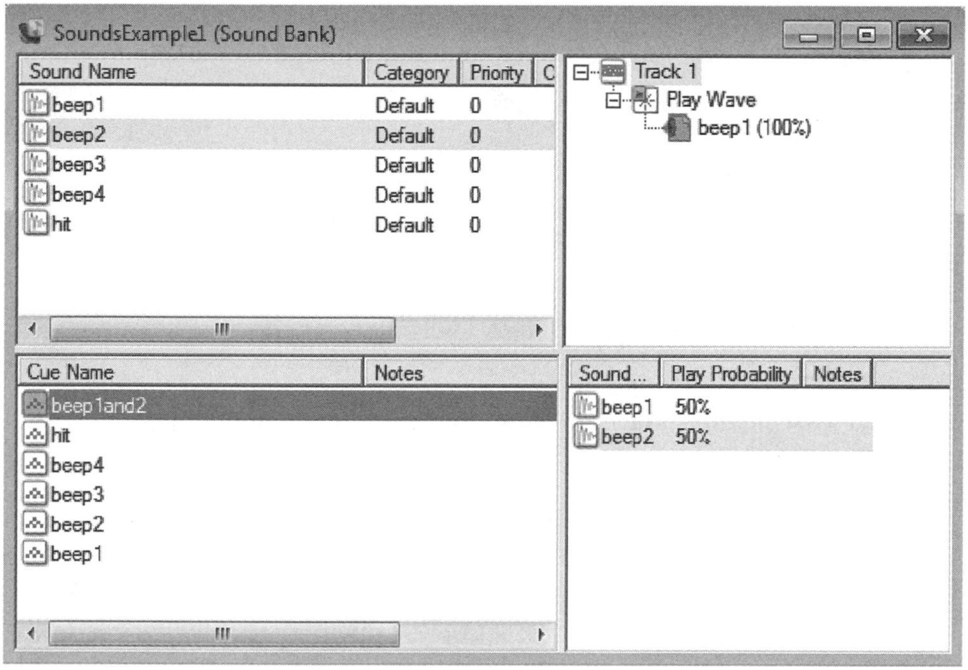

Figure 7.10. Creating a new cue.

7.6.3 Cue Properties

We can adjust a cue's properties to control how its associated sounds are played. The properties of a selected cue are displayed in the lower-left window of the XACT GUI tool. The cue properties from Figure 7.11 are:

- *Name.* The name of the cue.

- *Notes.* Designer notes.

- *Playlist type.* How the sounds are played: ordered, ordered from random, random, random (no immediate repeats), shuffle, interactive.

- *Variations.* The sliders may be used to adjust the probability that a sound may be played.

- *Limit instances.* Limit the number of instances of this sound that can be played at the same time.

Limit instances is a very useful feature that saves us from writing extra code to prevent multiple simultaneous playbacks when playing sounds. See the "Limit Instances" example in this chapter for a demonstration.

- *Maximum.* The maximum number of instances of this sound.

- *Fade in.* Fade in the sound from zero volume to full volume in the time specified.

- *Fade out.* Fade out the sound from full volume to zero volume in the time specified.

- *Behavior at max.* What to do if the maximum number of instances of a sound is reached.

- *Replace instance.* Which playing instance to replace with the new instance.

- *Crossfade type.* How the new instance should replace the old.

We have only examined a few of the features available in the XACT GUI tool. For more detailed information, refer to "All Programs\Microsoft DirectX SDK (date)\DirectX Documentation for C++."

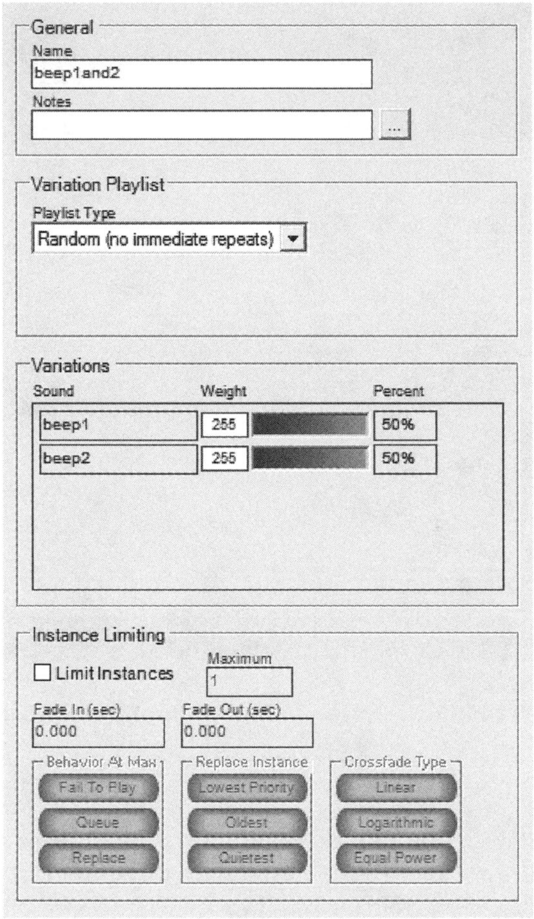

Figure 7.11. XACT cue properties.

Chapter Review

We learned how to make our games stimulate our sense of hearing in this chapter by giving them the ability to make sounds. Good sound effects and music are just as important in a video game as they are in any motion picture. The details from the chapter are the following:

- *Audio sources.* Several good royalty-free sources of game audio are available online.

- *Audacity.* The open-source application Audacity is a great tool for creating and editing game audio.

- *XACT.* We prepared our audio files for use in our game with the Microsoft cross-platform audio creation tool, or XACT.

- *Saving time.* The XACT tool allows us to change sounds used in our game or alter their properties without involving any C++ code changes.

- *Needed files.* The two files `Sound Bank.xsb` and `Wave Bank.xwb` created by XACT are what we need for our game.

- *XACT audio engine.* Our game engine plays the sounds by using the XACT audio engine.

- *Cues.* Each sound has an associated cue that is used to select the sound for playback.

- *DoWork().* The XACT engine's `DoWork()` function must be called periodically.

- `Audio` *class.* The `Audio` class contains the DirectX code required to add the XACT engine to our game engine.

- *Playing sounds.* Sounds are played by calling the `audio->playCue(cue)` function with a cue name of the desired sound as a parameter.

- *Stopping sounds.* To stop a currently playing sound, call the `audio->stopCue (cue)` function with the cue name of the desired sound as a parameter.

- *Sound engine tasks.* The `audio->run()` function must be called periodically to perform sound engine tasks.

- *Multiple sounds.* Cues may be used to play more than one sound.

- *Associated sounds.* Cue properties control how the associated sounds are played.

- *Preventing playbacks.* The cue's "Limit instances" property is useful for preventing multiple simultaneous playbacks of the same sound.

Review Questions

1. (True/False) XACT is a higher-level API than XAudio2.

2. (True/False) The XACT program is used to create processed audio files.

3. (True/False) The two files that contain the game audio are "Sound Bank" and "Cue Bank."

4. (True/False) The open-source program Audacity may be used to edit audio files, but it does not have the ability to record new audio files.

5. What is the recommended audio file type to use when saving audio files?

6. How is the volume level of a waveform changed in Audacity?

7. Which function in the XACT audio engine must be called periodically?

8. What is the purpose of a sound cue?

9. Give an example of a sound being played using a sound cue.

10. What does the cue property "Limit instances" do?

Exercises

1. Modify the "Limit Instances" example program so the sound played by pressing "B" is also limited to one instance. Use only the XACT program to make this change. No code changes are necessary.

2. Modify the "Sound Example 1" example program to use your own sound effects.

3. Add sound effects to the "Planet Collision" example from Chapter 6.

4. Add sound effects to the simple game you created for exercise 5 in Chapter 6.

Examples

The following examples are available for download from www.programming2dgames.com:

*   *Sound Example 1.* One spaceship bounces off the edges of the window. A different sound effect is played for each edge.

    –   Demonstrates using the XACT audio engine to play game sounds.

*   *Limit Instances.* Two spaceships are displayed, ship A and ship B. Pressing the "A" key plays a sound effect that is limited to one instance by setting the "Limit instances" cue property to 1 in the XACT GUI tool. Pressing the "B" key plays a sound effect that has unlimited instances.

    –   Demonstrates using the XACT GUI tool to control the playback of sound effects.

8 Text

There are several ways we may add text to our games. One simple technique that we used in earlier examples is to display a picture that contains prerendered text. Displaying text as part of a picture works just fine for an opening screen, a winning or losing message, or simple dialogs. In this chapter, we will examine two different techniques for displaying text. The first technique we will examine uses sprites to display individual letters from a larger texture image.

8.1 Sprite Text

In a sprite text system, individual letters are contained in a larger texture image. The program determines which part of the larger texture image to display when rendering each character. This technique is essentially the same thing we were doing to display individual frames of a multiframe image in previous chapters. Because of the similarity, we will be able to reuse most of the code we have already written.

A sprite-based text has some advantages. Here are a few of them in no particular order:

- *Create custom fonts*. The characters are simple images, so it is easy to create custom fonts. (Many fonts are copyrighted, so there might be licensing issues if you want to use them in a commercial game.)

- *New characters*. You may want to display characters that do not exist in current fonts, such as Klingon, for example.

- *Fast display*. Sprite text display is very fast.

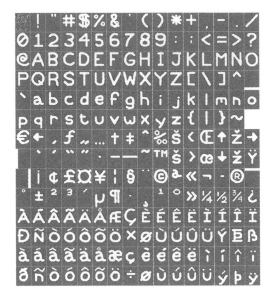

Figure 8.1. A texture image used for sprite text.

Figure 8.2. The effects of scale on a sprite-based font.

- *Manipulate properties.* The properties of individual letters may be manipulated in the same way we can manipulate game images, including rotating, scaling, color change, etc.

Figure 8.1 is an example of a sprite-based font. Our example font contains 224 characters. Each individual character is 48 pixels wide and 62 pixels high. It is important in a sprite-based font to start with large images. If the font is scaled down to produce smaller characters, the quality of each character will be high. If the font is scaled up to produce larger characters, the curved edges of the characters will not be as smooth.

In Figure 8.2, the letter "C" is displayed in heights of 122 pixels, 62 pixels, and 15 pixels, respectively. The 62-pixel-high letter "C" has a scale factor of 1, so the quality is the same as the original texture image. At 122 pixels high, the texture image is scaled up by a factor of 2, which produces noticeable jagged edges. The 15-pixel-high image looks better because the small imperfections in the original image are lost at the smaller scale.

8.1.1 Sprite Text Functions

The functions we are going to create to display the individual character sprites should make displaying text in our game as simple as printing text in any program. The text functions and properties will be incorporated into a `Text` class. Here are the functions that may be used with our sprite-based text:

- `void setXY(int x, int y)`

  Set the display position to `X`, `Y`. The next character displayed will be displayed with its top-left corner at `X`, `Y`, where `X`, `Y` represents pixel coordinates on the game screen. Printing text repositions the display position X, Y to the end of the displayed string. The following escape sequences may also be used to change the display position:

- \n (new line). Returns X to its starting position and advances Y down 1 line. (Note: X is not positioned at the left edge of the window.)

- \r (return). Returns X to its starting position; Y is unchanged.

- \t (tab). Sets X to the start of the next tab position; Y is unchanged. The tab size constant TAB_SIZE = 8 is located in text.h.

- \b (backspace,). Moves X left 1 character.

- \v (vertical tab). Moves Y down 1 row.

Text is displayed with the print function. The print function must be used between calls to spriteBegin and spriteEnd. (See the next section for an example.)

- `void print(const std::string &str)`

Print the string at the current X, Y location.

- `void print(const std::string &str, int x, int y)`

Set the display position to X, Y and then print the string.

- `void print(const std::string &str, int x, int y, textNS::Alignment align)`

Set the display position to X, Y and print the string using the alignment specified. The valid values for align are:

- LEFT. Left justifies the text at X, Y.

- CENTER. Centers the text at X and aligns the top of the text to Y.

- RIGHT. Right justifies the text at X, Y.

- CENTER_MIDDLE. Centers the text at X and the vertical middle to Y.

- CENTER_BOTTOM. Centers the text at X and aligns the bottom to Y.

- LEFT_BOTTOM. Left justifies at X and aligns the bottom to Y.

- RIGHT_BOTTOM. Right justifies at X and aligns the bottom to Y.

- `void setFontHeight(UINT height)`
  `UINT getFontHeight()`

Set or get the current font height in pixels. A height of 62 pixels results in a scaling factor of 1/1 with our example font texture.

- `void getWidthHeight(const std::string &str, UINT &width, UINT &height)`

Get the width and height that would be required to display the string using the current font height. The width and height is in pixels. Nothing is displayed by this function.

- `void setFontColor(COLOR_ARGB c)`
  `COLOR_ARGB getFontColor()`

Set or get the current font color. The default color is `white`. The `graphics.h` file contains a number of predefined color values, or we may use the `SETCOLOR_ARGB` macro to specify a color.

- `void setBackColor(COLOR_ARGB bc)`
  `COLOR_ARGB getBackColor()`

Set or get the current background color. The default background color is `TRANSCOLOR`. The color `TRANSCOLOR` is defined in `constants.h` as `SETCOLOR_ARGB(0,255,0,255)`, which is magenta. Our sprite texture image has a magenta background, which results in the letter being displayed, but not the background.

- `void setProportional(bool p)`
  `bool getProportional()`

Set or get the state of proportional spacing. Use `setProportional(true)` to enable proportional spacing and `setProportional(false)` to disable.

- `void setProportionalSpacing(UINT s)`
  `UINT getProportionalSpacing()`

Set or get the distance between characters when proportional spacing is true. The default value is in `text.h` as `PROPORTIONAL_SPACING = 5;`.

- `void setUnderline(bool u)`
  `bool getUnderline()`

Set or get the state of underline. Use `setUnderline(true)` to enable underline and `setUnderline(false)` to disable.

- `void setBold(bool b)`
  `bool getBold()`

Set or get the state of bold. Use `setBold(true)` to enable bold and `setBold(false)` to disable. Bold printing is accomplished by printing each character twice with a horizontal offset between the characters. The amount of the offset is declared in `text.h` as BOLD_SIZE = 4;.

- ```
  void setTabSize(UINT size)
  bool getTabSize()
  ```

  Set or get the tab size. The default tab size is declared in `text.h` as TAB_SIZE = 8;.

Changes to font properties remain in effect until changed.

- ```
  bool initialize(Graphics *g, const char *file)
  ```

  Initialize the Text object. The parameters are:

  - `*g`. Pointer to the Graphics object.

  - `*file`. Name of the file containing the font texture.

  The Text class inherits from the Image class so we may also use member function from Image to control the display of text such as:

- ```
  float getX()
  float getY()
  ```

  Get the current X or Y location.

- ```
  void setDegrees(float deg)
  void setRadians(float rad)
  ```

  Set the rotation angle of the character. The rotation occurs around the center of each character.

8.1.2 Displaying Sprite Text

Let's take a look at how to use sprite-based text in our programs. We will be looking at code from this chapter's "Three Cs" example. The complete source code may be downloaded from www.programming2dgames.com. We start by including the `text.h` header file in our main Game class header file (Listing 8.1).

```
// Programming 2D Games
// Copyright (c) 2011 by:
// Charles Kelly
// Chapter 8 threeCs.h v1.0
#ifndef _THREECS_H            // Prevent multiple definitions if this
#define _THREECS_H            // file is included in more than one place
#define WIN32_LEAN_AND_MEAN
#include "game.h"
```

```
#include "image.h"
#include "text.h"
#include "constants.h"
```

Listing 8.1. Adding `text.h` to `game.h`.

Next, we create a pointer to a `Text` object. In this example, we named the pointer `fontCK` (Listing 8.2). In the class constructor in `threeCs.cpp`, we create a new `Text` object (Listing 8.3). We delete the `Text` object in the destructor (Listing 8.4). In our initialize function, we call the `Text` object's `initialize` function. `FONT_IMAGE` is defined in `constants.h` (Listing 8.5). We also need to add the appropriate calls to deal with a lost graphics device (Listing 8.6). Printing text is typically done inside the `render` function of the main `Game` class along with all the other game elements (Listing 8.7).

```
class ThreeCs : public Game
{
private:
    // Game items
    Text        *fontCK;               // Sprite-based font
```

Listing 8.2. Creating a `Text` pointer.

```
//==========================================================================
// Constructor
//==========================================================================
ThreeCs::ThreeCs()
{
    fontCK = new Text();        // Sprite-based font
}
```

Listing 8.3. Creating a `Text` object.

```
//==========================================================================
// Destructor
//==========================================================================
ThreeCs::~ThreeCs()
{
    releaseAll();                 // Call deviceLost() for every graphics item
    SAFE_DELETE(fontCK);
}
```

Listing 8.4. Deleting the `Text` object.

```
//===========================================================================
// Initializes the game
// Throws GameError on error
//===========================================================================
void ThreeCs::initialize(HWND hwnd)
{
    Game::initialize(hwnd);
    graphics->setBackColor(graphicsNS::WHITE);
    // Init text
    if (!fontCK->initialize(graphics,FONT_IMAGE))
        throw(GameError(gameErrorNS::FATAL_ERROR,
                        "Error initializing CKfont"));
```

Listing 8.5. Initializing the Text object.

```
//===========================================================================
// The graphics device was lost
// Release all reserved video memory so graphics device may be reset
//===========================================================================
void ThreeCs::releaseAll()
{
    fontCK->onLostDevice();
    Game::releaseAll();
    return;
}
//===========================================================================
// The grahics device has been reset
// Recreate all surfaces and reset all entities
//===========================================================================
void ThreeCs::resetAll()
{
    fontCK->onResetDevice();
    Game::resetAll();
    return;
}
```

Listing 8.6. Releasing and resetting the Text object.

```
//===========================================================================
// Render game items
//===========================================================================
void ThreeCs::render()
{
    graphics->spriteBegin();
    fontCK->setProportional(false);
    fontCK->setFontColor(graphicsNS::BLACK);
    fontCK->setBackColor(TRANSCOLOR);
    fontCK->setFontHeight(FONT_HEIGHT*2);
    fontCK->print("C",20,100);
    fontCK->setFontHeight(FONT_HEIGHT);
```

```
    fontCK->print("C",114,148);
    fontCK->setFontHeight(FONT_HEIGHT/4);
    fontCK->print("C",164,184);
    graphics->spriteEnd();
}
```

Listing 8.7. Printing text.

∎ 8.2 Creating Custom Fonts

Custom fonts may be created using any paint program. The font texture includes a grid that aids in designing the characters. In Figure 8.3, we see the letters "A" and "j" from our texture. In the texture image, the border is yellow. It is shown in black here to make it more visible. The small gap on the side of the border near the bottom of the letter indicates the baseline. The area below the baseline is used by characters with a descender. The characters in CKfont were drawn in white on a black background using a paint program that blends the edges, which results in the gray border around each character. The black background was then replaced with our transparent color magenta. A transparent color would not be required if we used a paint program that supported alpha transparency.

The Text class sets the font color by applying a color filter to the sprite as it is drawn. The texture image should always use white to form the characters in order for the color filter to work as expected.

Care must be taken to ensure that the font texture matches the settings in the Text class. The following are the constants defined in text.h and how they relate to the font texture:

- FONT_BORDER = 3;. The size of the border around each character. Recall from our earlier discussion about sprites that we need to provide a one-pixel-wide transparent border around our sprite textures. One pixel on each side accounts for a border size of 2. To that we add our visible grid on the right and bottom of each character for a total of 3. The visible grid is only drawn on the right and bottom edge of each character. When placed together, they form a complete grid.

- FONT_HEIGHT = 62;. The height of the characters in pixels.

- GRID_WIDTH = 48 + FONT_BORDER;. The width of each character grid in pixels, including the FONT_BORDER. Each grid in this example is 51 pixels wide.

Figure 8.3. Examples of character textures.

- `GRID_HEIGHT = FONT_HEIGHT + FONT_BORDER;`. The height of each character grid in pixels, including the `FONT_BORDER`. Each grid is 65 pixels tall.

- `COLUMNS = 16;`. The number of columns in the font image.

- `ROWS = 14;`. The number of rows in the font image.

- `FRAMES = 1;`. The number of frames of animation for each character (1 = not animated).

- `ANIM_DELAY = 0.0;`. The delay between animation frames.

- `MAX_FONT_HEIGHT = 1000;`. The maximum font height.

- `MIN_CHAR = 0x0020;`. The character code of the top-left character. The top-left character in the font texture is not normally displayable and is assumed to be a space. Hex 0x0020 = 32 decimal.

- `MAX_CHAR = 0x00FF;`. The character code of the bottom-right character. Hex 0x00FF = 255 decimal.

- `PROPORTIONAL_SPACING = 5;`. The pixel spacing between proportionally-spaced characters at 1:1 scaled size. Proportional spacing is scaled for different font sizes.

- `TAB_SIZE = 8;`. The size of a tab stop as represented by character positions.

- `UNDERLINE = '_';`. The character that is used to display an underline. The ASCII value of '_' is 0x5F or 95 decimal. If the underline texture is moved to a different grid position, then the `UNDERLINE` constant must be changed to indicate the grid position. Underline printing is accomplished by printing the underline character followed by the displayed character.

- `SOLID = 0x7F;`. The character that is used to display a solid block. The solid block character is used to display a background color. The decimal value of 0x7F is 127. The value of 127 is calculated by counting the number of characters from the top-left corner of the font texture and adding the value of `MIN_CHAR`, which is hex 0x20 or 32 decimal.

- `BOLD_SIZE = 4;`. Bold printing is accomplished by printing each character twice with a horizontal offset between each print. This is the number of pixels of offset applied for a 1:1 scaled character. Bold spacing is scaled for different font sizes.

▊ 8.3 Text Class Details

The key to proportional spacing in our `Text` class is contained in the `initialize` function. When the font texture is loaded, it is examined pixel by pixel to determine where the left and right edges of each character is located. This information is saved in a `fontData` array. When the character is displayed, the data from the `fontData` array is used to precisely select the character from the texture image. Let's examine the `initialize` function in detail now and look at printing later.

Normally we load textures with our `Graphics::loadTexture` function. The `loadTexture` function loads textures into default D3D memory, which is usually video memory. In order to examine a texture at the pixel level, we are going to load the texture into system memory. We will add a new function to our `Graphics` class for this purpose. We'll name it `Graphics::loadTextureSystemMem`. Listing 8.8 displays the code in all its glory. We specify system memory pool with the parameter `D3DPOOL_SYSTEMMEM`, as shown in the highlighted line in Listing 8.8.

```
//=============================================================================
// Load the texture into system memory (system memory is lockable)
// Provides direct access to pixel data. Use the TextureManager class to
// load textures for display.
// Pre: filename is name of texture file
//      transcolor transparent color
// Post: width and height = size of texture
//       texture points to texture
// Returns HRESULT and fills TextureData structure
//=============================================================================
HRESULT Graphics::loadTextureSystemMem(const char *filename, COLOR_ARGB
                                       transcolor, IINT &width, UINT
                                       &height, LP_TEXTURE &texture)
{
    // The struct for reading bitmap file info
    D3DXIMAGE_INFO info;
    result = E_FAIL;        // Standard Windows return value
    try{
        if(filename == NULL)
        {
            texture = NULL;
            return D3DERR_INVALIDCALL;
        }

        // Get width and height from bitmap file
        result = D3DXGetImageInfoFromFile(filename, &info);
        if (result != D3D_OK)
            return result;
        width = info.Width;
        height = info.Height;
        // Create the new texture by loading a bitmap image file
        result = D3DXCreateTextureFromFileEx(
            device3d,               // 3D device
            filename,               // Bitmap filename
            info.Width,             // Bitmap image width
            info.Height,            // Bitmap image height
            1,                      // Mip-map levels (1 for no chain)
            0,                      // Usage
            D3DFMT_UNKNOWN,         // Surface format (default)
            D3DPOOL_SYSTEMMEM,      // System is lockable
            D3DX_DEFAULT,           // Image filter
            D3DX_DEFAULT,           // Mip filter
```

```
            transcolor,          // Color key for transparency
            &info,               // Bitmap file info (from loaded file)
            NULL,                // Color palette
            &texture );          // Destination texture
    } catch(...)
    {
        throw(GameError(gameErrorNS::FATAL_ERROR,
            "Error in Graphics::loadTexture"));
    }
    return result;
}
```

Listing 8.8. The `loadTextureSystemMem` function is used to load textures into system memory.

8.3.1 Initialize

The `loadTextureSystemMem` function is used to load the font texture into system memory in our `Text::initialize` function. The `Graphics *g` parameter points to our `Graphics` object and the `char *file` parameter is the name of the font texture file (Listing 8.9). We need to lock the font texture before we may access the pixel data (Listing 8.10).

```
//=============================================================================
// Initialize the Text
// Find the left and right edge of each character in the font image
// Post: returns true if successful, false if failed
//       fontData array contains left and right edge of each character
//=============================================================================
bool Text::initialize(Graphics *g, const char *file)
{
    try {
        graphics = g;           // Pointer to graphics object
        //-------------------------------------------------------------
        // Load the font texture and examine it pixel by pixel to find
        // the exact position of each character
        //-------------------------------------------------------------
        // Load font texture into system memory so it may be locked
        UINT w,h;
        HRESULT result = graphics->loadTextureSystemMem(file, TRANSCOLOR,
                                                        w, h, textureData);
        if (FAILED(result))
        {
            SAFE_RELEASE(textureData);
            return false;
        }
```

Listing 8.9. The font texture is loaded into system memory.

```
// textureData.width & textureData.height contain size of entire
// font texture
// Each character has a 1-pixel-wide border
// There are ROWS * COLS characters
// Lock the font texture, which is required to access the pixel
// data
D3DLOCKED_RECT rect;
result = textureData->LockRect(0, &rect, NULL, D3DLOCK_READONLY);
if(FAILED(result))                              // If lock failed
{
    SAFE_RELEASE(textureData);
    return false;
}
```

Listing 8.10. Locking the font texture so we may access the pixel data.

Now we go through the font texture character by character. We process each character pixel by pixel, looking for the left and right edges of each character. The character edges are saved in the fontData array (Listing 8.11).

After we have found the edges of each character, we unlock the texture and release it to free the memory used (Listing 8.12). Our initialize function concludes by loading the texture again, only this time we load it into a texture manager so we may use it to draw characters (Listing 8.13).

```
// for each row of characters in font
for(DWORD row=0; row<textNS::ROWS; row++)
{
  // for each col of characters in font
  for(DWORD col=0; col<textNS::COLUMNS; col++)
  {
    fontData[row][col].left = MAXINT;     // Initialize fontData
    fontData[row][col].right = 0;
    // Process each character pixel by pixel
    // for y = top pixel; y <= bottom pixel; y++
    for(DWORD y=row*textNS::GRID_HEIGHT+1; y<(row+1)*
       textNS::GRID_HEIGHT-1; y++)
    {
      // Get a pointer to the start of this scanline in the texture
      DWORD* pBits = (DWORD*)((BYTE*)rect.pBits + y*rect.Pitch);
      // Process this line of pixels
      for(DWORD x=col*textNS::GRID_WIDTH+1; x<(col+1)*
         textNS::GRID_WIDTH-1; x++)
      {
        // Get this pixel
        DWORD dwPixel = pBits[x];
        // If the alpha is not transparent
        if((dwPixel & 0xff000000) != 0x00)
        {
          if(x < fontData[row][col].left)     // If this pixel is more
                                              // left
             fontData[row][col].left = x;     // Save as left edge of
                                              // character
```

```
        if(x > fontData[row][col].right)    // If this pixel is more
                                            // right
            fontData[row][col].right = x;   // Save as right edge of
                                            // character
        }
      }
    }
  }
}
```

Listing 8.11. Finding the left and right edges of each character.

```
        // Done with the texture, so unlock it
        textureData.texture->UnlockRect(0);

        // Release this font texture, we just needed it to get font
        // spacing
        SAFE_RELEASE(textureData.texture);
```

Listing 8.12. Unlocking the texture and releasing it.

```
    //------------------------------------------------------------
    // Load the font image into a texture manager for use
    //------------------------------------------------------------
    if (!fontTexture.initialize(graphics, file))
        return false;                // If error loading font texture
    // Prepare the font image
    if (!Image::initialize(graphics, textNS::FONT_WIDTH,
        textNS::FONT_HEIGHT, 0, &fontTexture))
        return false;                // If failed
  }
  catch(...)
  {
      return false;
  }
  return true;                       // Successful
}
```

Listing 8.13. Loading the font texture into a texture manager for use.

8.3.2 Print

One `print` function does all of the actual printing. The print function is overloaded to provide three different variations. The other varieties of print call this `print` function. This `print` handles proportional spacing and the escape sequences. Let's take a look at it in detail (Listing 8.14).

```
//============================================================================
// Print string at X,Y
// Pre: spriteBegin()
// Post: spriteEnd()
//============================================================================
void Text::print(const std::string &str, int x, int y)
{
    UCHAR ch = 0, chN = 0;
    std::string str2;
    width = textNS::FONT_WIDTH;
    int scaledWidth = static_cast<int>(textNS::FONT_WIDTH*
                                       spriteData.scale);
    float saveY=0;
    int tabX=0, tabW=0;

    spriteData.x = (float)x;
    spriteData.y = (float)y;
    doAlign(str);
    for(UINT i=0; i<str.length(); i++)
    {
        ch = str.at(i);
```

Listing 8.14. This functions prints a character to the screen at X, Y.

The function parameters are the string to print and the X, Y screen location. The `width` variable is set equal to the width of one character in the sprite texture. The `scaledWidth` variable contains the width of the scaled character, which is the width of the character after printing. The `doAlign(str)` function sets the X and Y locations so the string will be aligned, as specified by the `align` setting. We will examine the `align` function later. The `for` statement loops through each character in the string.

If the character from the string has a matching image in the font texture, then the character is displayable. The index of the current character in the font texture is calculated as `chN` where 0 is the index of the top-left character. The `spriteData.rect` structure is used to select the rectangular portion of the font texture to display for the current character. The top of the selection rectangle is equal to the character index (`chN`) divided by the number of columns in the texture image, and this is multiplied by the height of one row (`GRID_HEIGHT`) plus 1. The bottom of the selection rectangle is equal to the top plus the font height (Listing 8.15).

```
// If displayable character
if (ch > textNS::MIN_CHAR && ch <= textNS::MAX_CHAR)
{
    chN = ch - textNS::MIN_CHAR;            // Make min_char index 0
    spriteData.rect.top = chN / textNS::COLUMNS *
                          textNS::GRID_HEIGHT + 1;
    spriteData.rect.bottom = spriteData.rect.top + textNS::FONT_HEIGHT;
```

Listing 8.15. Calculating where the character is in the font texture.

If proportional printing is enabled, the left and right edges of `spriteData.rect` are loaded from the `fontData` array we filled in earlier. The `proportionalSpacing` variable is added to `width` to provide spacing between each proportional character unless the character occupies the full character width (Listing 8.16).

```
if(proportional)
{
    spriteData.rect.left = fontData[chN/textNS::COLUMNS]
                                 [chN % textNS::COLUMNS].left;
    // DirectX wants right + 1
    spriteData.rect.right = fontData[chN/textNS::COLUMNS]
                                 [chN % textNS::COLUMNS].right + 1;
    width = spriteData.rect.right - spriteData.rect.left;
    // If full width character do not add spacing
    if(width >= textNS::FONT_WIDTH)
    {
        width = textNS::FONT_WIDTH;          // Limit width
        spriteData.rect.left = chN % textNS::COLUMNS *
                            textNS::GRID_WIDTH + 1;
        spriteData.rect.right = spriteData.rect.left +
                             textNS::FONT_WIDTH;
    }
    else    // Not full width so add spacing between characters
        width += proportionalSpacing;
    scaledWidth = static_cast<int>(width*spriteData.scale);
    drawChar(ch);
}
```

Listing 8.16. Calculating the character's screen position when proportional spacing is enabled.

If proportional printing is not enabled, the left edge of `spriteData.rect` is calculated by the modulus of the character index (`chN`) and the number of columns multiplied by the width of one character plus 1. The right edge of `spriteData.rect` is equal to the left edge plus the width of one character minus the border size. The actual display of the character is handled by the `drawChar(ch)` function. The current screen X location is advanced by the width of one scaled character (Listing 8.17).

```
else  // Fixed pitch
{
    width = textNS::FONT_WIDTH;
    spriteData.rect.left = chN % textNS::COLUMNS *
                        textNS::GRID_WIDTH + 1;
    spriteData.rect.right = spriteData.rect.left +
                         textNS::FONT_WIDTH; drawChar(ch);
}
spriteData.x += scaledWidth;
}
```

Listing 8.17. Calculating the character's screen position for fixed pitch spacing.

```
else  // Non displayable character
{
    switch(ch)
    {
    case ' ':                                        // Space
        if(proportional)
        {
            width = textNS::FONT_WIDTH/2;
            scaledWidth = static_cast<int>(width*spriteData.scale);
        }
        drawChar(' ');
        spriteData.x += scaledWidth;
        break;
```

Listing 8.18. Handling nondisplayable characters.

If the character is not displayable, a switch statement is used to check for escape sequences. If the character is a space and proportional spacing is enabled, the width and scaledWidth of a proportional space are calculated. The space is displayed by drawChar(' ') and the screen X location is advanced (Listing 8.18). If the character is a new line \n, the Y screen location is advanced one line down and the X screen location is set to the last X starting position (Listing 8.19).

New line \n and return \r characters return to the last X starting position, not to the left edge of the window.

If the character is a return \r, the X screen location is set to the last X starting position (Listing 8.20). If the character is a tab \t, the screen X position is calculated for the next tab stop position and is based on the scaled width of the font (Listing 8.21).

If the character is a backspace \b, the screen X location is moved left by the width of one scaled character. Backspace does not erase the previous character from the screen (Listing 8.22).

```
// Newline advances 1 line down and sets left edge to starting X screen
// position,
// not left edge of screen
case '\n':                                           // Newline
    spriteData.x = (float)x;
    spriteData.y += static_cast<int>(height*spriteData.scale);
    saveY = spriteData.y;
    str2 = str.substr(i,str.length());
    doAlign(str2);
    spriteData.y = saveY;
    break;
```

Listing 8.19. Handling the new line character.

```
case '\r':                          // Return to starting X position
    spriteData.x = (float)x;
    str2 = str.substr(i,str.length());
    doAlign(str2);
    break;
```

Listing 8.20. Handling the return character.

```
case '\t':          // Tab
    width = textNS::FONT_WIDTH;
    scaledWidth = static_cast<int>(width*spriteData.scale);
    tabX = static_cast<int>(spriteData.x) / (scaledWidth * tabSize);
    tabX = (tabX+1) * scaledWidth * tabSize;
    tabW = tabX - static_cast<int>(spriteData.x);
    while(tabW > 0)
    {
        if(tabW >= scaledWidth)
        {
            drawChar(' ');
            spriteData.x += scaledWidth;
        }
        else
        {
            // Fractional part of character to align with tab stop
            width = tabW;
            drawChar(' ');
            spriteData.x += tabW;
        }
        tabW -= scaledWidth;
    }
    break;
```

Listing 8.21. Handling the tab character.

```
case '\b':                  // Backspace
    spriteData.x -= scaledWidth;
    if(spriteData.x < 0)
        spriteData.x = 0;
    break;
```

Listing 8.22. Handling the backspace character.

If the character is a vertical tab \v, the screen Y location is moved down by the height of one scaled character (Listing 8.23). If the character code is 01, the font signature character in the top-left corner of the font texture is displayed (Listing 8.24).

```
case '\v':                      // Vertical tab
  spriteData.y += static_cast<int>(height*spriteData.scale);
  break;
```

Listing 8.23. Handling the vertical tab character.

```
case 0x01:                      // Font signature character
  spriteData.rect.top = 1;
  spriteData.rect.bottom = 1 + textNS::FONT_HEIGHT;
  spriteData.rect.left = 1;
  spriteData.rect.right = 1 + textNS::FONT_WIDTH;
  draw(spriteData);
  spriteData.x += scaledWidth;
  break;
```

Listing 8.24. Displaying the font signature character.

8.3.3 Aligning Text

The doAlign function sets the screen X,Y position so the string will be displayed according to the align property. The possible values for the align property are: LEFT, CENTER, RIGHT, CENTER_MIDDLE, CENTER_BOTTOM, LEFT_BOTTOM, and RIGHT_BOTTOM. The default alignment is LEFT (Listing 8.25).

```
//==============================================================================
// Set spriteData.x,spriteData.y for current string and alignment
// The default alignment is LEFT
//==============================================================================
void Text::doAlign(const std::string &str)
{
    if(spriteData.texture == NULL)  // If no texture
        return;
    UINT w, h;
    switch(align) {
    case textNS::CENTER:                // Center at X and align top to Y
        getWidthHeight(str,w,h);
        spriteData.x -= w/2;
        break;
    case textNS::RIGHT:                 // Right justify at X,Y
        getWidthHeight(str,w,h);
        spriteData.x -= w;
        break;
    case textNS::CENTER_MIDDLE:         // Center at X and vertical middle to Y
        getWidthHeight(str,w,h);
        spriteData.x -= w/2;
        spriteData.y -= h/2;
        break;
    case textNS::CENTER_BOTTOM:         // Center at X and align bottom to Y
        getWidthHeight(str,w,h);
```

```
            spriteData.x -= w/2;
            spriteData.y -= h;
            break;
    case textNS::LEFT_BOTTOM:          // Left justify at X and align bottom
                                       // to Y
            getWidthHeight(str,w,h);
            spriteData.y -= h;
            break;
    case textNS::RIGHT_BOTTOM:         // Right justify at X and align bottom
                                       // to Y
            getWidthHeight(str,w,h);
            spriteData.x -= w;
            spriteData.y -= h;
            break;
    }
}
```

Listing 8.25. Calculating the screen position of text for each alignment choice.

8.3.4   Get Width and Height

The getWidthHeight function returns the width and height of the string in pixels for the current font size. The string is not displayed. The code is very similar to the print function, so we will dispense with a detailed explanation (Listing 8.26).

```
//=========================================================================
// getWidthHeight
// Determines width and height of string in pixels for current font size
// Does not display the string
//=========================================================================
void Text::getWidthHeight(const std::string &str, UINT &w, UINT &h)
{
    if (spriteData.texture == NULL)          // If no texture
        return;
    UCHAR ch = 0, chN = 0;
    width = textNS::FONT_WIDTH;
    int scaledWidth = static_cast<int>(width*spriteData.scale);
    int strW = 0;
    h = 0;
    int stringWidth = 0;
    for(UINT i=0; i<str.length(); i++)
    {
        ch = str.at(i);
        // If displayable character
        if (ch > textNS::MIN_CHAR && ch <= textNS::MAX_CHAR)
        {
            chN = ch - textNS::MIN_CHAR;      // Make min_char index 0
            if(proportional)
            {
                spriteData.rect.left =
                    fontData[chN/textNS::COLUMNS]
                    [chN % textNS::COLUMNS].left;
                // +1 for DirectX sprite width
```

```
                spriteData.rect.right =
                    fontData[chN/textNS::COLUMNS]
                    [chN % textNS::COLUMNS].right + 1;
                width = spriteData.rect.right - spriteData.rect.left +
                        proportionalSpacing;
                scaledWidth = static_cast<int>(width*spriteData.scale);
            }
            else    // Fixed pitch
            {
                width = textNS::FONT_WIDTH;
                spriteData.rect.left = chN % textNS::COLUMNS *
                                    textNS::GRID_WIDTH+1;
                spriteData.rect.right = spriteData.rect.left +
                                    textNS::FONT_WIDTH;
            }
            stringWidth += scaledWidth;
    }
    else    // Else, nondisplayable character
    {
        switch(ch)
        {
        case ' ':    // Space
            if(proportional)
            {
                width = (textNS::FONT_WIDTH)/2;
                scaledWidth = static_cast<int>(width*spriteData.scale);
            }
            stringWidth += scaledWidth;
            break;
        case '\n':    // Newline
            if(strW == 0)
                strW = stringWidth;
            stringWidth = 0;
            h += static_cast<int>(height*spriteData.scale);
            break;
        case '\r':    // Return
            if(strW == 0)
                strW = stringWidth;
            stringWidth = 0;
            break;
        case '\t':    // Tab
            {
                width = textNS::FONT_WIDTH;
                scaledWidth = static_cast<int>(width*spriteData.scale);
                int tabX = static_cast<int>(spriteData.x) /
                        (scaledWidth * tabSize);
                tabX = (tabX+1) * scaledWidth * tabSize;
                int tabW = tabX - static_cast<int>(spriteData.x);
                while(tabW > 0)
                {
                    if(tabW >= scaledWidth)
                        stringWidth += scaledWidth;
                    else
                    {
                        // Fractional part of character to align with
                        // tab stop
                        width = tabW;
                        stringWidth += tabW;
```

```
                    }
                    tabW -= scaledWidth;
                }
            }
            break;
        case '\b':        // Backspace
            stringWidth -= scaledWidth;
            if(stringWidth < 0)
                stringWidth = 0;
            break;
        case 0x01:        // Special
            stringWidth += scaledWidth;
            break;
        }
    }
}
if(strW==0)
    strW = stringWidth;
w = strW;
return;
}
```

Listing 8.26. The `getWidthHeight` function calculates the screen space required to display the string.

8.3.5 Draw a Character

The `drawChar` function does the actual drawing of characters to the screen. It also displays background color and does underline and bold. If `backColor` is set to a color other than `TRANSCOLOR`, the character defined by the constant `SOLID` is displayed using `backColor` and followed by the character `ch`. Underline displays the character defined by the `UNDERLINE` constant followed by the character `ch`. Bold displays the character `ch`, moves the X screen location to the right by `BOLD_SIZE`, and displays the character `ch` again. Displaying a background color, underline, or bold requires two draws for each character (Listing 8.27).

```
//=============================================================================
// drawChar
// Display character sprite described by spriteData using color and fill
// Does underline and bold
//=============================================================================
void Text::drawChar(UCHAR ch)
{
    SpriteData sd2 = spriteData;      // Copy sprite data
    // Display backColor color
    if(backColor != TRANSCOLOR)       // If backColor is not transparent
    {
        spriteData.rect.top = (textNS::SOLID-textNS::MIN_CHAR) /
                        textNS::COLUMNS * textNS::GRID_HEIGHT + 1;
        spriteData.rect.bottom = spriteData.rect.top +
                          textNS::GRID_HEIGHT - 2;
        spriteData.rect.left = (textNS::SOLID-textNS::MIN_CHAR) %
                        textNS::COLUMNS * textNS::GRID_WIDTH + 1;
```

```
                spriteData.rect.right = spriteData.rect.left + width;
                draw(backColor);            // Draw backColor
                spriteData.rect = sd2.rect;      // Restore character rect
        }
        // Display underline
        if(underline)
        {
                spriteData.rect.top = (textNS::UNDERLINE-textNS::MIN_CHAR) /
                                    textNS::COLUMNS * textNS::GRID_HEIGHT + 1;
                spriteData.rect.bottom = spriteData.rect.top +
                                      textNS::GRID_HEIGHT - 2;
                spriteData.rect.left = (textNS::UNDERLINE-textNS::MIN_CHAR) %
                                    textNS::COLUMNS * textNS::GRID_WIDTH + 1;
                spriteData.rect.right = spriteData.rect.left + width;
                draw(color);
                spriteData.rect = sd2.rect;      // Restore character rect
        }
        // Display character
        if(ch > textNS::MIN_CHAR && ch <= textNS::MAX_CHAR) // If displayable
                                                             // character
        {
                draw(spriteData, color);
                if (bold)    // Bold is done by displaying the character twice with
                             // offset X
                {
                        spriteData.x += textNS::BOLD_SIZE*spriteData.scale;
                        draw(spriteData, color);
                        spriteData.x = sd2.x;
                }
        }
    }
}
```

Listing 8.27. The `drawChar` function displays one formatted character.

▋ 8.4 DirectX Text

DirectX includes text display that uses Window's fonts. Some of the advantages of DirectX text are:

- It does not require a texture image so it will work even if the user deletes all of a game's textures.

- It uses Window's fonts, so large size characters do not have jagged edges like the sprite-based font.

Some of the disadvantages of DirectX text are:

- We have no way of knowing in advance which fonts the user has installed on his or her computer.

- DirectX text display is slower than sprite-based text.

- DirectX text requires a different font for each size character.

- DirectX text does not have as many display options as sprite text.

Figure 8.4 is the output from our "Three Cs DX" example program. The letter "C" is displayed in heights of 122 pixels, 62 pixels, and 15 pixels, respectively. The actual screen size of the letters may differ from the same height letters displayed with our sprite-based text. Notice the smoother edges on the large letter "C" as compared to our sprite example in Figure 8.2.

Figure 8.4. DirectX text in three font sizes.

8.4.1 DirectX Text Functions

Our support for DirectX text is contained in the class TextDX. The member functions are:

- `bool initialize(Graphics *g, int height, bool bold, bool italic,`
  `const std::string &fontName)`

  Initialize a textDX font. A separate textDX object must be created for each font size, style, and name. Dynamic sizing and style is not supported. The parameters are:

  - `*g`. Pointer to the Graphics object.

  - `height`. Height of the font in pixels.

  - `bold`. True for bold.

  - `italic`. True for italic.

  - `&fontName`. Name of the font family. If the desired font is not available, an available font is automatically substituted.

  Text is displayed with the print function. The print function must be used between calls to the spriteBegin and spriteEnd functions. (See the next section for an example.)

- `int print(const std::string &str, int x, int y)`

  Print the string at location X,Y. It returns 0 on fail or the height of the text on success. The parameters are:

  - `&str`. The string containing the text to display.

  - `x, y`. The screen location of the top-left corner of the text.

- `int print(const std::string &str, RECT &rect, UINT format)`

  Print the string in a rectangular region with the specified alignment. It returns 0 on fail or the height of the text on success. The parameters are:

– &str. The string containing the text to display.

– &rect. The rectangular region of the screen that will contain the text.

– format. How the text should be formatted. It may be any combination of the following:

  ◆ DT_BOTTOM. Justifies the text to the bottom of the rectangle.

  ◆ DT_CALCRECT. Calculates the size of the required rectangle but does not display any text.

  ◆ DT_CENTER. Centers the text horizontally.

  ◆ DT_EXPANDTABS. Expands the tab characters. The default is eight characters per tab.

  ◆ DT_LEFT. Left justifies the text.

  ◆ DT_NOCLIP. Draws the text without clipping. Text is drawn faster.

  ◆ DT_RIGHT. Right justifies the text.

  ◆ DT_RTLREADING. Displays the text from right to left.

  ◆ DT_SINGLELINE. The text is displayed in a single line.

  ◆ DT_TOP. Justifies the text to the top of the rectangle.

  ◆ DT_VCENTER. Centers the text vertically if DT_SINGLELINE is specified.

  ◆ DT_WORDBREAK. Lines are broken between words.

- `float getDegrees()      {return angle*(180.0f/(float)PI);}`

  Returns the rotation angle of the text in degrees.

- `float getRadians()      {return angle;}`

  Returns the rotation angle of the text in radians.

- `COLOR_ARGB getFontColor() {return color;}`

  Returns the current font color.

- `float setDegrees(float deg) {angle = deg*((float)PI/180.0f);}`

  Sets the rotation angle of the text in degrees.

> *The rotation angle of DirectX text is applied to the entire string, not character by character as it was with sprite text. The rotation point is the current X, Y text display coordinate.*

- `float setRadians(float rad) {angle = rad;}`

  Sets the rotation angle of the text in radians.

- `void setFontColor(COLOR_ARGB c)`

  Sets the font color. The parameter is:

  - c. The color of the font. The default color is white. The graphics.h file contains a number of predefined color values or we may use the SETCOLOR_ARGB macro to specify a color.

8.4.2 Displaying DirectX Text

Let's take a look at how to use DirectX-based text in our programs. We will be looking at code from this chapter's "Three Cs DX" example. The complete source code may be downloaded from www.programming2dgames.com.

We start by including the textDX.h header file in our main Game class header file (Listing 8.28). Next, we create an object pointer for each desired font (Listing 8.29).

```
// Programming 2D Games
// Copyright (c) 2011 by:
// Charles Kelly
// Chapter 8 threeCsDX.h v1.0
#ifndef _THREECS_H                  // Prevent multiple definitions if this
#define _THREECS_H                  // ..file is included in more than one place
#define WIN32_LEAN_AND_MEAN
#include "game.h"
#include "textDX.h"
#include "constants.h"
```

Listing 8.28. Including textDX.h in game.h.

```
class ThreeCsDX : public Game
{
private:
    // Game items
    TextDX  *dxFontSmall;           // DirectX fonts
    TextDX  *dxFontMedium;
    TextDX  *dxFontLarge;
```

Listing 8.29. Creating a TextDX object pointer for each font.

```
//============================================================================
// Constructor
//============================================================================
ThreeCsDX::ThreeCsDX()
{
    dxFontSmall  = new TextDX();     // DirectX fonts
    dxFontMedium = new TextDX();
    dxFontLarge  = new TextDX();
}
```

Listing 8.30. Creating the TextDX objects.

The TextDX objects are created in our constructor (Listing 8.30). We always need to delete what we create (Listing 8.31). The TextDX objects are then initialized with the desired font (Listing 8.32).

```
//============================================================================
// Destructor
//============================================================================
ThreeCsDX::~ThreeCsDX()
{
    releaseAll();                // Call deviceLost() for every graphics item
    SAFE_DELETE(dxFontSmall);
    SAFE_DELETE(dxFontMedium);
    SAFE_DELETE(dxFontLarge);
}
```

Listing 8.31. Deleting the TextDX objects.

We also need to add the appropriate calls to deal with a lost graphics device (Listing 8.33). The display of the text occurs in the render function (Listing 8.34).

```
//============================================================================
// Initializes the game
// Throws GameError on error
//============================================================================
void ThreeCsDX::initialize(HWND hwnd)
{
    Game::initialize(hwnd);
    graphics->setBackColor(graphicsNS::WHITE);
    // Initialize DirectX fonts
    // 15 pixel high Arial
    if(dxFontSmall->initialize(graphics, 15, true, false, "Arial") ==
        false)
        throw(GameError(gameErrorNS::FATAL_ERROR,
            "Error initializing DirectX font"));
    // 62 pixel high Arial
    if(dxFontMedium->initialize(graphics, 62, true, false, "Arial") ==
        false)
```

```
        throw(GameError(gameErrorNS::FATAL_ERROR,
                "Error initializing DirectX font"));
    // 124 pixel high Arial
    if(dxFontLarge->initialize(graphics, 124, true, false, "Arial") ==
        false)
        throw(GameError(gameErrorNS::FATAL_ERROR,
                "Error initializing DirectX font"));
    reset();                // Reset all game variables
    fpsOn = true;           // Display frames per second
    return;
}
```

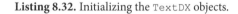

Listing 8.32. Initializing the TextDX objects.

```
//========================================================================
// The graphics device was lost
// Release all reserved video memory so graphics device may be reset
//========================================================================
void ThreeCsDX::releaseAll()
{
    dxFontSmall->onLostDevice();
    dxFontMedium->onLostDevice();
    dxFontLarge->onLostDevice();
    Game::releaseAll();
    return;
}
//========================================================================
// The grahics device has been reset
// Recreate all surfaces and reset all entities
//========================================================================
void ThreeCsDX::resetAll()
{
    dxFontSmall->onResetDevice();
    dxFontMedium->onResetDevice();
    dxFontLarge->onResetDevice();
    Game::resetAll();
    return;
}
```

Listing 8.33. Releasing and resetting the TextDX objects.

```
//========================================================================
// Render game items
//========================================================================
void ThreeCsDX::render()
{
    graphics->spriteBegin();
    dxFontSmall->setFontColor(graphicsNS::BLACK);
    dxFontMedium->setFontColor(graphicsNS::BLACK);
    dxFontLarge->setFontColor(graphicsNS::BLACK);
    dxFontLarge->print("C",20,100);
```

```
    dxFontMedium->print("C",114,148);
    dxFontSmall->print("C",164,184);
    graphics->spriteEnd();
}
```

Listing 8.34. Displaying some text.

8.5 TextDX Class Details

Let's examine the functions from our `TextDX` class in more detail.

8.5.1 Initialize

The `initialize` function creates a DirectX font with the parameter data we provide. It also initializes the transformation matrix. The DirectX function that we are using to create the font is `D3DXCreateFont`. Here is the formal syntax:

```
HRESULT D3DXCreateFont(
    LPDIRECT3DDEVICE9 pDevice,
    INT Height,
    UINT Width,
    UINT Weight,
    UINT MipLevels,
    BOOL Italic,
    DWORD CharSet,
    DWORD OutputPrecision,
    DWORD Quality,
    DWORD PitchAndFamily,
    LPCTSTR pFacename,
    LPD3DXFONT *ppFont
);
```

The parameters are:

- `pDevice`. A pointer to an IDirect3DDevice9 interface. We have access to that from our `Graphics` class via the `get3Ddevice` function.

- `Height`. The height of the characters in pixels.

- `Width`. The width of the characters in pixels. We use 0 for this parameter, which gives the `Height` parameter exclusive control of the font size.

- `Weight`. Typeface weight. We use this to create bold fonts.

- `MipLevels`. The number of mipmap levels. We always set this to 1.

- `Italic`. True for italic font, false otherwise.

- `CharSet`. We always use DEFAULT_CHARSET, which specifies a character set based on the current system locale. Some other possible values are:

- – ANSI_CHARSET. Same as DEFAULT_CHARSET for English locale systems.

- – SYMBOL_CHARSET. Creates a set of symbols.

- – MAC_CHARSET. Creates the Apple Macintosh character set.

- OutputPrecision. Specifies how Windows matches the desired font characteristics with actual fonts. We always use OUT_DEFAULT_PRECIS.

- Quality. Specifies how Windows matches the desired font with the real font when using raster fonts and does not affect TrueType fonts. We always use DEFAULT_QUALITY.

- PitchAndFamily. Pitch may be DEFAULT_PITCH, FIXED_PITCH, or VARIABLE_PITCH. Family may be FF_DECORATIVE, FF_DONTCARE, FF_MODERN, FF_ROMAN, FF_SCRIPT, or FF_SWISS. The pitch and family parameters are combined with the bitwise OR operator "|". We always use DEFAULT_PITCH | FF_DONTCARE.

- pFacename. String that contains the name of the typeface.

- ppFont. Returns a pointer to an ID3DXFont interface.

The code in Listing 8.35 is our initialize function in the TextDX class that calls D3DXCreateFont.

```
//===========================================================================
// Create DirectX Font
//===========================================================================
bool TextDX::initialize(Graphics *g, int height, bool bold, bool italic,
                        const std::string &fontName)
{
    graphics = g;                       // The graphics system
    UINT weight = FW_NORMAL;
    if(bold)
        weight = FW_BOLD;
    // Create DirectX font
    if(FAILED(D3DXCreateFont(graphics->get3Ddevice(), height, 0, weight, 1,
                            italic,
        DEFAULT_CHARSET, OUT_DEFAULT_PRECIS, DEFAULT_QUALITY,
        DEFAULT_PITCH | FF_DONTCARE, fontName.c_str(),
        &dxFont))) return false;
    // Initialize the tranformation matrix
    D3DXMatrixTransformation2D(&matrix, NULL, 0.0f, NULL, NULL, 0.0f,
                              NULL);
    return true;
}
```

Listing 8.35. The TextDX::initialize function.

8.5.2 Print

The print functions display text to the screen. There are two versions of print. The version of print in Listing 8.36 prints the string at the X,Y screen location. The X,Y location specifies the top-left corner of the text. The text is rotated with a transformation matrix to the specified angle.

The version of print in Listing 8.37 prints the string in the rectangular region rect with the alignment specified in format. The format choices are the same as those supported by the DirectX DrawText function.

```
//=============================================================================
// Print text at x,y
// Return 0 on fail, height of text on success
// Pre: spriteBegin()
// Post: spriteEnd()
//=============================================================================
int TextDX::print(const std::string &str, int x, int y)
{
    if(dxFont == NULL)
        return 0;
    // Set font position
    fontRect.top = y;
    fontRect.left = x;
    // Rotation center
    D3DXVECTOR2 rCenter=D3DXVECTOR2((float)x,(float)y);
    // Setup matrix to rotate text by angle
    D3DXMatrixTransformation2D(&matrix, NULL, 0.0f, NULL, &rCenter, angle,
                              NULL);
    // Tell the sprite about the matrix "Hello Neo"
    graphics->getSprite()->SetTransform(&matrix);
    return dxFont->DrawTextA(graphics->getSprite(), str.c_str(), -1,
                             &fontRect, DT_LEFT, color);
}
```

Listing 8.36. Displays text at X, Y that is rotated to angle.

```
//=============================================================================
// Print text inside RECT using DirectX text format
// Return 0 on fail, height of text on success
// Pre: spriteBegin()
// Post: spriteEnd()
//=============================================================================
int TextDX::print(const std::string &str, RECT &rect, UINT format)
{
    if(dxFont == NULL)
        return 0;
    // Setup matrix to not rotate text
    D3DXMatrixTransformation2D(&matrix, NULL, 0.0f, NULL, NULL, NULL,
                              NULL);
    // Tell the sprite about the matrix "Hello Neo"
    graphics->getSprite()->SetTransform(&matrix);
```

```
    return dxFont->DrawTextA(graphics->getSprite(), str.c_str(), -1, &rect,
                             format, color);
}
```

Listing 8.37. Prints text in a rectangular region that is aligned as specified by the `format` parameter.

Both versions of `print` use `DrawText` to print the text. Here is the syntax for `Draw Text`:

```
INT DrawText(
    LPD3DXSPRITE pSprite,
    LPCTSTR pString,
    INT Count,
    LPRECT pRect,
    DWORD Format,
    D3DCOLOR Color
);
```

The parameters are:

- `pSprite`. A pointer to an `ID3DXSprite` object that contains the string. It can be `NULL`, which results in Direct3D using its own sprite object. For improved performance, a sprite object should be specified if `DrawText` is called more than once in a row.

- `pString`. A pointer to the string to draw. If the `Count` parameter is –1, the string must be null-terminated.

- `Count`. The length of the string. If `Count` is –1, then `pString` must point to a null-terminated string.

- `pRect`. Pointer to a `RECT` structure that defines the screen region in which the text is formatted.

- `Format`. How the text should be formatted. It may be any combination of the following:

  - `DT_BOTTOM`. Justifies the text to the bottom of the rectangle.

  - `DT_CALCRECT`. Calculates the size of the required rectangle but does not display any text. The `pRect.bottom` is adjusted to fit the text.

  - `DT_CENTER`. Centers the text horizontally.

  - `DT_EXPANDTABS`. Expands the tab characters. The default is eight characters per tab.

  - `DT_LEFT`. Left justifies the text.

- DT_NOCLIP. Draws the text without clipping. Text is drawn faster.

- DT_RIGHT. Right justifies the text.

- DT_RTLREADING. Displays the text from right to left.

- DT_SINGLELINE. The text is displayed in a single line.

- DT_TOP. Justifies the text to the top of the rectangle.

- DT_VCENTER. Centers the text vertically if DT_SINGLELINE is specified.

- DT_WORDBREAK. Lines are broken between words.

■ 8.6 Adding an FPS Display

Let's use our new text capabilities to add a frames per second display to our game engine. We will use DirectX text because we want our display to always be available no matter which texture files the user may delete (those darn users!). The frames per second (fps) is not normally displayed, so we don't need the fancy features and speed of sprite text anyway. We need to add a TextDX object to our game.h file. The code in Listing 8.38 is from this chapter's "Text Demo" example. We also added a Boolean variable fpsOn, which will control the fps display.

```
float    fps;                   // Frames per second
TextDX   dxFont;                // DirectX font for fps
bool     fpsOn;                 // True to display fps
```

Listing 8.38. Declaring variables required to display fps.

The fpsOn variable gets initialized in the Game constructor. We also set the fps variable to a reasonable starting value. This last step is not necessary, but it does help the fps number settle in to its final range faster (Listing 8.39).

```
//=============================================================================
// Constructor
//=============================================================================
Game::Game()
{
    input = new Input();        // Initialize keyboard input immediately
    // Additional initialization is handled in later call to input>
    // initialize()
    paused = false;             // Game is not paused
    graphics = NULL;
    audio = NULL;
    console = NULL;
```

```
    fps = 100;
    fpsOn = false;                  // Default to fps display off
    initialized = false;
}
```

Listing 8.39. Initializing the fps variables.

The `dxFont` is initialized in the `Game::initialize` function (Listing 8.40). The font constants are defined in `game.h`, as shown in Listing 8.41.

The display of `fps` is done in the `Game::renderGame` function. The `fps` number is converted to a string and displayed in the lower-right corner of the screen. Placing the `fps` display after the call to `render` will make sure the `fps` number is drawn on top of any game items (Listing 8.42). To turn on the fps display, just set `fpsOn` to true (Listing 8.43).

```
// Initialize DirectX font
if(dxFont.initialize(graphics, gameNS::POINT_SIZE, false, false,
                     gameNS::FONT)
    == false)
     throw(GameError(gameErrorNS::FATAL_ERROR,
           "Failed to initialize DirectX font."));
dxFont.setFontColor(gameNS::FONT_COLOR);
```

Listing 8.40. Initializing `dxFont`.

```
namespace gameNS
{
    const char FONT[] = "Courier New";  // Font
    const int POINT_SIZE = 14;          // Point size
    const COLOR_ARGB FONT_COLOR = SETCOLOR_ARGB(255,255,255,255);  // White
}
```

Listing 8.41. The fps constants.

```
//=============================================================================
// Render game items
//=============================================================================
void Game::renderGame()
{
    const int BUF_SIZE = 20;
    static char buffer[BUF_SIZE];
    // Start rendering
    if (SUCCEEDED(graphics->beginScene()))
    {
        render();                       // Call render() in derived object
        graphics->spriteBegin();        // Begin drawing sprites
```

```
        if(fpsOn)                    // If fps display requested
        {
            // Convert fps to Cstring
            _snprintf_s(buffer, BUF_SIZE, "fps %d ", (int)fps);
            dxFont.print(buffer,GAME_WIDTH-100,GAME_HEIGHT-28);
        }
        graphics->spriteEnd();       // End drawing sprites
        console->draw();             // Console is drawn here so it appears
                                     // on top of game

        // Stop rendering
        graphics->endScene();
    }
    handleLostGraphicsDevice();
    // Display the back buffer on the screen
    graphics->showBackbuffer();
}
```

Listing 8.42. Adding the fps display to the renderGame function.

```
fpsOn = true;
```

Listing 8.43. Enabling the fps display.

▌ 8.7 Adding a Console

A console supports text input and output. It is typically used as a diagnostic tool to display messages and to enter commands to control game play. This can be very useful when we are testing our games. For example, we might want to make the player invincible, give him or her extra ammunition, etc. We can use the console to change parameters in the game without involving the C++ compiler. These commands are sometimes referred to as "cheat codes" although that is usually not their intended purpose. Their real purpose is to make it more convenient to test and adjust game play.

In Figure 8.5, we see an example of our console from the Spacewar game. The console has a translucent gray background with white text. Commands are entered on the keyboard and displayed at the prompt ">." As we did for the display of the frames per second, we want to display the console without relying on any external texture files. This will make sure the console always works no matter what those pesky users do. The console characters will be displayed using DirectX text, but what can we do to display the gray background? We can't use a sprite because sprites require an external texture. Why don't we use this opportunity to look at some of the built-in primitives that DirectX can draw and see if any of them will work for our background?

8.7.1 DirectX Primitives

DirectX includes a DrawPrimitive function that can render geometric primitives. The DrawPrimitive function looks like this:

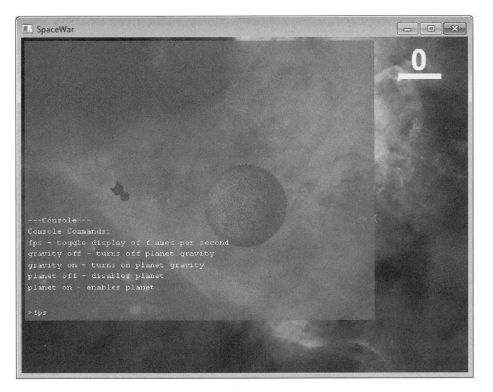

Figure 8.5. The console being used in a game.

```
HRESULT DrawPrimitive(
    D3DPRIMITIVETYPE PrimitiveType,
    UINT StartVertex,
    UINT PrimitiveCount
);
```

The parameters are:

- `PrimitiveType`. A member of the `D3DPRIMITIVETYPE` enumerated type that describes the type of primitive to render.

- `StartVertex`. The index of the first vertex to use from the vertex buffer.

- `PrimitiveCount`. The number of primitives to render.

The `D3DPRIMITIVETYPE` types are:

- `D3DPT_POINTLIST`. Renders the vertices as individual points.

- `D3DPT_LINELIST`. Renders the vertices as individual line segments.

- `D3DPT_LINESTRIP`. Renders the vertices as a continuous polyline.

- D3DPT_TRIANGLELIST. Renders the vertices as individual triangles.

- D3DPT_TRIANGLESTRIP. Renders the vertices as a strip of triangles. The first three vertices define one triangle and each additional vertex defines the third vertex of a new triangle that uses one edge of the existing triangle.

- D3DPT_TRIANGLEFAN. Renders the vertices as a triangle fan. The first three vertices define one triangle and each additional vertex defines a third vertex of a new triangle that uses one edge of the existing triangle. All triangles in a triangle fan share one common vertex.

Triangle strips and triangle fans are more efficient than triangle lists. We will use a triangle fan to draw our background rectangle because it might be slightly easier to visualize the arrangement of the vertices than a triangle strip. To draw a rectangle with a triangle fan, we arrange the vertices as follows:

8.7.2 Drawing a Quad

We will create a new function in our Graphics class to draw the rectangle. In graphic terms, two triangles that form a rectangle are referred to as a *quad,* so we will name our new function drawQuad (Listing 8.44).

```
//===========================================================================
// Display a quad with alpha transparency using Triangle Fan
// Pre: createVertexBuffer was used to create vertexBuffer containing four
//      vertices defining the quad in clockwise order.
//      g3ddev->BeginScene was called
// Post: Quad is drawn
//===========================================================================
bool Graphics::drawQuad(LP_VERTEXBUFFER vertexBuffer)
{
    HRESULT result = E_FAIL;    // Standard Windows return value
    if(vertexBuffer == NULL)
        return false;

    device3d->SetRenderState(D3DRS_ALPHABLENDENABLE, true); // Enable alpha
                                                            // blend
    device3d->SetStreamSource(0, vertexBuffer, 0, sizeof(VertexC));
    device3d->SetFVF(D3DFVF_VERTEX);
    result = device3d->DrawPrimitive(D3DPT_TRIANGLEFAN, 0, 2);
    device3d->SetRenderState(D3DRS_ALPHABLENDENABLE, false); // Alpha blend
                                                             // off

    if(FAILED(result))
        return false;
    return true;
}
```

Listing 8.44. The drawQuad function.

```
    // Configure for alpha blend of primitives
    device3d->SetRenderState(D3DRS_BLENDOP, D3DBLENDOP_ADD);
    device3d->SetRenderState(D3DRS_SRCBLEND, D3DBLEND_SRCALPHA);
    device3d->SetRenderState(D3DRS_DESTBLEND, D3DBLEND_INVSRCALPHA);
}
```

Listing 8.45. The code that enables alpha blending of primitives.

The quad will be drawn using alpha blending to make it semitransparent. Alpha blending is enabled or disabled as part of the current render state. The current render state is set with the `SetRenderState` function. We use it to set the render state parameter `D3DRS_ALPHABLENDENABLE` to true.

The vertices that define the corners of the quad are contained in a vertex buffer. We tell DirectX about the vertex buffer with the `SetStreamSource` function. The parameters used to call the function in Listing 8.44 are:

- 0. The stream number.

- `vertexBuffer`. The name of our vertex buffer.

- 0. The offset in bytes from the beginning of the stream to the beginning of the vertex data.

- `sizeof(VertexC)`. The size of one vertex. We defined `VertexC` as a structure in `graphics.h`. It defines one vertex.

We will draw the quad with `DrawPrimitive` and then turn off alpha blending. Alpha blending must also be configured in our `Graphics::initialize` function by adding the following code at the end (Listing 8.45). We also need to add the same code to our `Graphics::reset` function so that alpha blending will remain enabled after a reset (Listing 8.46).

```
//=============================================================================
// Reset the graphics device
//=============================================================================
HRESULT Graphics::reset()
{
    result = E_FAIL;      // Default to fail, replace on success
    initD3Dpp();                        // Init D3D presentation parameters
    sprite->OnLostDevice();
    result = device3d->Reset(&d3dpp);   // Attempt to reset graphics device
    // Configure for alpha blend of primitives
    device3d->SetRenderState(D3DRS_BLENDOP, D3DBLENDOP_ADD);
    device3d->SetRenderState(D3DRS_SRCBLEND, D3DBLEND_SRCALPHA);
    device3d->SetRenderState(D3DRS_DESTBLEND, D3DBLEND_INVSRCALPHA);
    sprite->OnResetDevice();
    return result;
}
```

Listing 8.46. The `reset` function modified to support alpha blending of primitives.

8.7.3 Create a Vertex Buffer

The vertex buffer is created with the DirectX function `CreateVertexBuffer`. Here is the syntax:

```
HRESULT CreateVertexBuffer(
    UINT Length,
    DWORD Usage,
    DWORD FVF,
    D3DPOOL Pool,
    IDirect3DVertexBuffer9 **ppVertexBuffer,
    HANDLE *pSharedHandle
);
```

The parameters are:

- `Length`. The size of the vertex buffer in bytes.

- `Usage`. Identifies how the vertex buffer will be used. We use `D3DUSAGE_WRITEONLY`, which indicates that we only write to the vertex buffer. This allows the driver to choose the best memory location to give us the optimum performance.

- `FVF`. Describes the vertex format. We use `D3DFVF_VERTEX`, which is defined in `graphics.h` as a combination of `D3DFVF_XYZRHW | D3DFVF_DIFFUSE`. The member `D3DFVF_XYZRHW` indicates that the vertex position has already been transformed. In other words, X,Y,Z are the screen coordinates of the vertices. Here, `D3DFVF_DIFFUSE` indicates that the vertex includes a diffuse color component. The gray color of our quad is defined as part of each vertex. If each vertex were a different color, DirectX would blend the colors together when rendering the quad.

- `Pool`. Which memory pool to place the buffer in. We use `D3DPOOL_DEFAULT`, which usually results in video memory.

- `ppVertexBuffer`. Address of a pointer to an IDirect3DVertexBuffer9 interface. This pointer points to the vertex buffer if the call is successful.

- `pSharedHandle`. Reserved. Set to `NULL`.

We call the DirectX `CreateVertexBuffer` function from our own `Graphics::createVertexBuffer` function, as seen in Listing 8.47.

```
//=============================================================================
// Create a vertex buffer
// Pre: verts[] contains vertex data
//      size = size of verts[]
// Post: &vertexBuffer points to buffer if successful
//=============================================================================
HRESULT Graphics::createVertexBuffer(VertexC verts[], UINT size,
                                     LP_VERTEXBUFFER &vertexBuffer)
{
```

```
        // Standard Windows return value
        HRESULT result = E_FAIL;
        // Create a vertex buffer
        result = device3d->CreateVertexBuffer(size, D3DUSAGE_WRITEONLY,
                                    D3DFVF_VERTEX, D3DPOOL_DEFAULT,
                                    &vertexBuffer, NULL);
        if(FAILED(result))
            return result;
        void *ptr;
        // Must lock buffer before data can be transferred in
        result = vertexBuffer->Lock(0, size, (void**)&ptr, 0);
        if(FAILED(result))
            return result;
        memcpy(ptr, verts, size);    // Copy vertex data into buffer
        vertexBuffer->Unlock();      // Unlock buffer
        return result;
}
```

Listing 8.47. Our function that creates a vertex buffer.

After the buffer is created, we lock it with a call to `vertexBuffer->Lock`. (Vertex buffers must be locked before data is transferred.) Then we copy our vertex data into the buffer with `memcpy`. Finally, we unlock the buffer so it may be used by DirectX.

▍ 8.8 Console Class

All of the new `Graphics` class functions are used to display our console as part of our new `Console` class. The `console.h` file contains constants that define the console properties. They are:

- WIDTH. The width of the console rectangle in pixels. The default value is 500.

- HEIGHT. The height of the console rectangle in pixels. The default value is 400.

- X,Y. The screen location of the top-left corner of the console. The default is 5,5.

- MARGIN. The text margin from the console edge. The default is 4 pixels.

- FONT[]. The font use for the console text. The default is "Courier New."

- FONT_HEIGHT. Height of the console font. The default is 14.

- FONT_COLOR. The color of the console font. The default is white.

- BACK_COLOR. The color of the console background. The default is SETCOLOR_ARGB (192,128,128,128), which is a semitransparent gray.

- MAX_LINES. The maximum number of lines of displayable text in the text buffer.

8.8.1 Console Functions

The console functions are used to display the console, add text to the console display, and handle console commands. Here are the console functions:

- `const void draw();`

  The console is drawn on the game screen.

- `void showHide();`

  The visible property of the console is reversed. A visible console is made invisible and an invisible console is made visible.

- `bool getVisible() {return visible;}`

  Return the current visible property.

- `void show() {visible = true;}`

  Make the console visible.

- `void hide() {visible = false;}`

  Make the console invisible.

- `void print(const std::string &str);`

  Add the text string to the console display.

- `std::string getCommand();`

  Handles console single key commnds. Returns a user-entered command string.

- `std::string getInput() {return inputStr;}`

  Returns the console input text.

- `void clearInput()    {inputStr = "";}`

  Clears the console input text.

8.8.2 Console Class Details

The constructor initializes the console's variables (Listing 8.48).

```
//=============================================================================
// Constructor
//=============================================================================
```

```
Console::Console()
{
    initialized = false;             // Set true when successfully initialized
    graphics = NULL;
    visible = false;                 // Not visible
    fontColor = consoleNS::FONT_COLOR;
    backColor = consoleNS::BACK_COLOR;
    x = consoleNS::X;                // Starting console position
    y = consoleNS::Y;
    textRect.bottom = consoleNS::Y + consoleNS::HEIGHT - consoleNS::MARGIN;
    textRect.left = consoleNS::X + consoleNS::MARGIN;
    textRect.right = consoleNS::X + consoleNS::WIDTH - consoleNS::MARGIN;
    textRect.top = consoleNS::Y + consoleNS::MARGIN;
    vertexBuffer = NULL;
    rows = 0;
    scrollAmount = 0;
}
```

Listing 8.48. The console's constructor.

8.8.3 Initialize

The console's `initialize` function creates the vertex buffer that defines the corners of the background rectangle. It also initializes the DirectX font used to display text (Listing 8.49).

```
//=========================================================================
// Initialize the console
//=========================================================================
bool Console::initialize(Graphics *g, Input *in)
{
    try {
        graphics = g;                        // The graphics system
        input = in;
        // Top left
        vtx[0].x = x;
        vtx[0].y = y;
        vtx[0].z = 0.0f;
        vtx[0].rhw = 1.0f;
        vtx[0].color = backColor;
        // Top right
        vtx[1].x = x + consoleNS::WIDTH;
        vtx[1].y = y;
        vtx[1].z = 0.0f;
        vtx[1].rhw = 1.0f;
        vtx[1].color = backColor;
        // Bottom right
        vtx[2].x = x + consoleNS::WIDTH;
        vtx[2].y = y + consoleNS::HEIGHT;
        vtx[2].z = 0.0f;
        vtx[2].rhw = 1.0f;
        vtx[2].color = backColor;
        // Bottom left
        vtx[3].x = x;
        vtx[3].y = y + consoleNS::HEIGHT;
        vtx[3].z = 0.0f;
```

```
        vtx[3].rhw = 1.0f;
        vtx[3].color = backColor;
        graphics->createVertexBuffer(vtx, sizeof vtx, vertexBuffer);
        // Initialize DirectX font
        if(dxFont.initialize(graphics, consoleNS::FONT_HEIGHT, false,
                            false, consoleNS::FONT) == false)
            return false;           // If failed.
        dxFont.setFontColor(fontColor);
    } catch(...) {
        return false;
    }
    initialized = true;
    return true;
}
```

Listing 8.49. The console's `initialize` function.

The `vtx` array contains the vertex data. The `X` and `Y` coordinates specify the screen location of the vertex. The `Z` coordinate is the depth into the screen. The `rhw` member is always set to 1.0. The color of the vertex defines the color of the quad. If we used different colors for each vertex, the colors would gradually change from one vertex to the next.

The member `rhw` *stands for reciprocal homogenous w. It is a term used in matrix math when transforming vertices in 3D. With 2D graphics, we are working with pretransformed vertices so setting* `rhw` *to 1 effectively removes the term from the calculations.*

The order of the vertices is important. Notice that we are placing the vertices in the vertex buffer in clockwise order (top left, top right, bottom right, bottom left). If this order is not followed, the quad will not be visible. Normally, when DirectX draws triangles, they are only visible from one side. If we viewed the triangle from behind, we would be able to see through it. This is called *back face culling*. It is a common technique used to speed up the rendering of 3D surfaces. DirectX uses the order of the vertices to determine which side of the triangle is visible. If we arranged the vertices in a counterclockwise order, we would be viewing the triangles from the back so they would not be visible.

8.8.4 Draw the Console

The draw function displays the console on the screen. We draw the background quad first, as shown in Listing 8.50(a).

```
//=============================================================================
// Draw console
// Pre: Inside BeginScene/EndScene
//=============================================================================
const void Console::draw()
{
    if (!visible || graphics == NULL || !initialized)
```

```
    return;
graphics->drawQuad(vertexBuffer);          // Draw backdrop
if(text.size() == 0)
    return;
```

Listing 8.50(a). Drawing the console background.

Next, we display the text. There is no mechanism in DirectX to scroll text, so we do it on our own—see Listing 8.50(b) for details. The height of one row of text is calculated in `rowHeight`.

We then calculate how many rows of text will fit on the console by dividing the displayable height of the console by `rowHeight`, as shown in Listing 8.50(c). Then we display the text row by row starting from the bottom of the console and working our way up, as you can see in Listing 8.50(d).

```
graphics->spriteBegin();                   // Begin drawing sprites
// Display text on console
textRect.left = 0;
textRect.top = 0;
// Sets textRect bottom to height of 1 row
dxFont.print("|",textRect,DT_CALCRECT);    // "|" is used as full height
                                           // character
int rowHeight = textRect.bottom + 2;       // Height of 1 row (+2 is row
                                           // spacing)
if(rowHeight <= 0)                          // This should never be true
    rowHeight = 20;                        // Force a workable result
```

Listing 8.50(b). Calculating the height of one row of text.

```
// Number of rows that will fit on console
rows = (consoleNS::HEIGHT - 2*consoleNS::MARGIN) / rowHeight;
rows -= 2;                                 // Room for input prompt at bottom
if (rows <= 0)                             // This should never be true
    rows = 5;                              // Force a workable result
```

Listing 8.50(c). Calculating the number of rows that will fit on the console.

```
// Set text display rect for one row
textRect.left = (long)(x + consoleNS::MARGIN);
textRect.right = (long)(textRect.right + consoleNS::WIDTH -
consoleNS::MARGIN);
// -2*rowHeight is room for input prompt
textRect.bottom = (long)(y + consoleNS::HEIGHT - 2*consoleNS::MARGIN -
                         2*rowHeight);
```

```
// For all rows (max text.size()) from bottom to top
for(int r=scrollAmount; r<rows+scrollAmount && r<(int)(text.size());
    r++)
{
    // Set text display rect top for this row
    textRect.top = textRect.bottom - rowHeight;
    // Display one row of text
    dxFont.print(text[r],textRect,DT_LEFT);
    // Adjust text display rect bottom for next row
    textRect.bottom -= rowHeight;
}
```

Listing 8.50(d). Displaying console text row by row.

The last step is to display the command prompt and any command the user is entering, as Listing 8.50(e) shows.

```
// Display command prompt and current command string
// Set text display rect for prompt
textRect.bottom = (long)(y + consoleNS::HEIGHT - consoleNS::MARGIN);
textRect.top = textRect.bottom - rowHeight;
std::string prompt = ">";                  // Build prompt string
prompt += input->getTextIn();
dxFont.print(prompt,textRect,DT_LEFT);     // Display prompt and command
graphics->spriteEnd();                     // End drawing sprites
}
```

Listing 8.50(e). Displaying the console command prompt.

8.8.5 Show/Hide the Console

The showHide function changes the state of the visible parameter to make the console visible or invisible. It also clears the input buffer in preparation for new console commands or to remove old console commands before returning to the game (Listing 8.51).

```
//=============================================================================
// Show/hide console
//=============================================================================
void Console::showHide()
{
    if (!initialized)
        return;
    visible = !visible;
    input->clear(inputNS::KEYS_PRESSED|inputNS::TEXT_IN);// Erase old input
}
```

Listing 8.51. The console's showHide function.

8.8.6 Adding Text to the Console

The console text is stored in a deque of strings. A *deque* is part of the C++ standard template library. It supports fast random access to elements and efficient insertion and deletion at the front or back. Each line of console text is saved as a string in the deque. The deque is named text and is declared in `console.h`, as seen in Listing 8.52.

```
std::deque<std::string> text;          // Console text
```

Listing 8.52. The `deque` used to hold console text.

The `print` command is used to add text to the console. The new text string is pushed onto the front of the deque. If the maximum number of text lines has been added, the oldest line is deleted from the deque. Only the first line of text in the string will be displayed (Listing 8.53).

```
//===========================================================================
// Add text to console
// Only the first line of text in str will be displayed
//===========================================================================
void Console::print(const std::string &str)    // Add text to console
{
    if (!initialized)
        return;
    text.push_front(str);                       // Add str to deque of text
    if(text.size() > consoleNS::MAX_LINES)
        text.pop_back();                        // Delete oldest line
}
```

Listing 8.53. Text is added to the console with the `print` function.

8.8.7 Console Command

The console will be displayed by pressing the designated key. The `CONSOLE_KEY` constant is defined in `constants.h` as the tilde "~" key (Listing 8.54).

While the console is visible, we may enter commands. The commands include scrolling the console display with the arrow keys or "Page Up," "Page Down," and other text commands. This is all handled in the `getCommand` function. Some of the commands are performed immediately; all others are returned to the game (Listing 8.55).

```
const UCHAR CONSOLE_KEY = VK_OEM_3;        // ~ key for U.S.
```

Listing 8.54. The default key used to display the console.

```
//=============================================================================
// Return console command
// Handles console single key commands
// Returns all other commands to game
//=============================================================================
std::string Console::getCommand()
{
    // If console not initialized or not visible
    if (!initialized || !visible)
        return "";
    // Check for console key
    if (input->wasKeyPressed(CONSOLE_KEY))
        hide();                                     // Turn off console
    // Check for Esc key
    if (input->wasKeyPressed(ESC_KEY))
        return "";
    // Check for scroll
    if (input->wasKeyPressed(VK_UP))                // If up arrow
        scrollAmount++;
    else if (input->wasKeyPressed(VK_DOWN))         // If down arrow
        scrollAmount--;
    else if (input->wasKeyPressed(VK_PRIOR))        // If page up
        scrollAmount += rows;
    else if (input->wasKeyPressed(VK_NEXT))         // If page down
        scrollAmount -= rows;
    if (scrollAmount < 0)
        scrollAmount = 0;
    if (scrollAmount > consoleNS::MAX_LINES-1)
        scrollAmount = consoleNS::MAX_LINES-1;
    if (scrollAmount > (int)(text.size())-1)
        scrollAmount = (int)(text.size())-1;
    commandStr = input->getTextIn();               // Get user entered text
    // Do not pass keys through to game
    input->clear(inputNS::KEYS_DOWN|inputNS::KEYS_PRESSED|inputNS::MOUSE);
    if (commandStr.length() == 0)                  // If no command entered
        return "";
    if (commandStr.at(commandStr.length()-1) != '\r') // If 'Enter' key not
                                                      // pressed
        return "";                                    // Return, can't be
                                                      // command
    commandStr.erase(commandStr.length()-1);       // Erase '\r' from end of
                                                   // command
    input->clearTextIn();                          // Clear input line
    return commandStr;                             // Return command
}
```

Listing 8.55. Use the `getCommand` function to return the user-entered text.

The user-entered command is returned as a string. The \r escape sequence is removed from the end of the command prior to returning.

■ 8.9 Incorporating the Console into the Game Engine

We will define a pointer to the console in `game.h` (Listing 8.56).

```
Console *console;                   // Pointer to Console
```

Listing 8.56. A `Console` pointer.

We will also define a new `consoleCommand` function in our `Game` class. It is used to process commands entered on the console. The prototype is added to `game.h` (Listing 8.57). The `Game` constructor sets the console pointer to `NULL` (Listing 8.58). The console is initialized in the `Game::initialize` function (Listing 8.59). We call the console's `draw` function from our `Game::renderGame` function. The call is placed after the call to `render` so the console will always be drawn on top of the current game screen (Listing 8.60).

```
// Process console commands
virtual void consoleCommand();
```

Listing 8.57. The prototype for the `consoleCommand` function.

```
console = NULL;
```

Listing 8.58. Console code that is added to the game constructor.

```
// Initialize console
console = new Console();
console->initialize(graphics, input);      // Prepare console
console->print("---Console---");
```

Listing 8.59. Initializing the console.

```
// Start rendering
if (SUCCEEDED(graphics->beginScene()))
{
    render();               // Call render() in derived object
    graphics->spriteBegin();     // Begin drawing sprites
    if(fpsOn)               // If fps display requested
    {
        // Convert fps to string
        _snprintf_s(buffer, BUF_SIZE, "fps %d ", (int)fps);
        dxFont.print(buffer,GAME_WIDTH-100,GAME_HEIGHT-28);
    }
    graphics->spriteEnd();       // End drawing sprites
    console->draw();    // Console is drawn here so it appears on top
                        // of game
```

Listing 8.60. Adding the code to draw the console.

```
// Check for console key
if (input->wasKeyPressed(CONSOLE_KEY))
{
    console->showHide();
    paused = console->getVisible();   // Pause game when console is
                                      // visible
}
consoleCommand();                     // Process user entered console command
```

Listing 8.61. Console code that is added to the Game::run function.

We add the code in Listing 8.61 to our Game::run function. It checks to see if the user has pressed the console key and calls the showHide function from the console. We pause the game if the console is visible. It then processes the commands that the user entered on the console. Console commands are processed in Game::consoleCommand (Listing 8.62).


```
//=============================================================================
// Process console commands
// Override this function in the derived class if new console commands are
// added
//=============================================================================
void Game::consoleCommand()
{
    command = console->getCommand();    // Get command from console
    if(command == "")                   // If no command
        return;
    if (command == "help")              // If "help" command
    {
        console->print("Console Commands:");
        console->print("fps - toggle display of frames per second");
        return;
    }
    if (command == "fps")
    {
        fpsOn = !fpsOn;                 // Toggle display of fps
        if(fpsOn)
            console->print("fps On");
        else
            console->print("fps Off");
    }
}
```

Listing 8.62. The default console commands are processed here.

The only commands currently available are help and fps. This function should be overridden in the derived class if new console commands are added. Just copy the existing function to the derived class and add the new commands. The required console functions are also added to release memory used by the console (Listing 8.63).

```
//=============================================================================
// The graphics device was lost
// Release all reserved video memory so graphics device may be reset
//=============================================================================
void Game::releaseAll()
{
    SAFE_ON_LOST_DEVICE(console);
    dxFont.onLostDevice();
    return;
}
//=============================================================================
// Recreate all surfaces and reset all entities
//=============================================================================
void Game::resetAll()
{
    dxFont.onResetDevice();
    SAFE_ON_RESET_DEVICE(console);
    return;
}
//=============================================================================
// Delete all reserved memory
//=============================================================================
void Game::deleteAll()
{
    releaseAll();               // Call onLostDevice() for every graphics item
    SAFE_DELETE(audio);
    SAFE_DELETE(graphics);
    SAFE_DELETE(input);
    SAFE_DELETE(console);
    initialized = false;
}
```

Listing 8.63. Releasing and resetting the console.

A console will now be in every game we create with our game engine.

Chapter Review

The ability to display text is something we tend to take for granted in programming. As we saw in this chapter, displaying text has its own set of challenges when we are creating DirectX games. From displaying something as simple as player scores to a complete in-game dialog, text is a part of practically every game. We used our new text display ability to add a frames per second display to our game engine. We also added a console to our game engine, which required using some DirectX primitives. Some of the key points from the chapter are:

- *Prerendered text.* Simple text may be displayed using a picture that contains pre-rendered text.

- *Sprites.* Sprites may be used to display text in much the same way that game textures are displayed.

- *Sprite-based fonts.* A sprite-based font uses an image to create each character.

- *Creating new fonts.* It is easy to create custom sprite fonts.

- *Speed of sprite text.* Sprite text display is very fast.

- *Tweaking the text.* Sprite text may be rotated, scaled, and displayed in different colors.

- *Bigger is better.* Sprite text looks best when larger texture images are scaled down to smaller font sizes.

- *The* `Text` *class.* The `Text` class contains the functions and properties used to display sprite-based text in our games.

- *Proportional or fixed pitch characters.* The `Text` class supports the display of proportional or fixed pitch characters from the same font texture.

- *Additional text effects.* Additional font properties include underline, bold, color, and background color.

- *Font properties.* Changes to font properties remain in effect until they are changed.

- *The* `print` *function.* Text is displayed with the `print` function.

- *DirectX preferred.* DirectX text does not require a texture image. This makes it the preferred choice for displaying error and system messages.

- *Standard Windows fonts.* DirectX text uses standard Windows fonts so large character sizes do not have jagged edges like sprite-based fonts.

- *Speed of DirectX text.* DirectX text display is slower than sprite-based text.

- *Different fonts for different sizes.* DirectX text requires a different font for each size character.

- *Display options.* DirectX text does not have as many display options as sprite text.

- *Text alignment.* Text alignment is supported for both sprite and DirectX text.

- *Calculations and capabilities.* The game engine includes a frames per second calculation and display capability.

- *Console.* The game engine includes a console that supports text input and output.

- *Console background.* The console background is created by displaying a triangle fan with alpha blending to make it semitransparent.

- *Adding text to the console.* Text is added to the console with the console's print function.

- *Displaying the console.* The console is displayed by pressing the "~" key.

- *Additional commands.* The console includes the commands `help` and `fps`. Additional commands may be added.

Review Questions

1. What are the three methods for displaying text described in the chapter?

2. Which text display method is faster, sprite text or DirectX text?

3. List two advantages of sprite text over DirectX text.

4. Which function is used to set the display position of sprite text?

5. Write a function call that displays sprite text contained in the string `str` at screen position 10,30.

6. Write a function call that displays sprite text contained in the string `str` at screen position 40,50, which centers the text at X and aligns the top of the text to Y.

7. Write a function call that sets the sprite font color to blue.

8. What does the `getWidthHeight` function return?

9. How does the sprite font system display bold characters?

10. List two advantages of DirectX text over sprite text.

Exercises

1. Modify the "Planet Collision" example from Chapter 6 to display a count of the number of collisions with the planet. Display the count using the sprite-based font system.

2. Modify the "Planet Collision" example from Chapter 6 to display a count of the number of collisions with the planet. Display the count using the DirectX-based font system.

3. Create a program that displays your name in bold letters using the sprite-based font system.

   a. Make your name scroll up the screen.

4. Create a program that displays your name in bold letters using the DirectX-based font system.

   a. Make your name scroll up the screen.

5. Add a score display to the game you created for exercise 3 from Chapter 6.

6. Add a console to the game you created for exercise 3 from Chapter 6.

Examples

The following examples are available for download from www.programming2dgames.com.

- *Three Cs.* The letter "C" is displayed in three different sizes using the sprite-based font system.

    – Demonstrates how to display text using the sprite font system.

    – Demonstrates the effect on quality when enlarging a sprite font.

- *Three Cs DX.* The letter "C" is displayed in three different sizes using the DirectX font system.

    – Demonstrates how to display text using the DirectX font system.

    – Demonstrates the effect on quality when enlarging a DirectX font.

- *Text Demo.* Text is displayed using different fonts, colors, and styles. Pressing a key switches the display between DirectX fonts and sprite fonts. The current frames per second is displayed in the lower-right corner of the screen.

    – Demonstrates how to display text using both sprite fonts and DirectX fonts.

    – Demonstrates the different display effects available for each font type.

    – The performance difference between the two font systems is compared.

9 Enhanced Appearance

In Chapter 9, we look at different techniques for enhancing the appearance of our game. These techniques include giving our game a feeling of depth and adding user interface elements. After completing this chapter, the reader will have learned several techniques for enhancing the appearance of 2D games.

▌ 9.1 Bitmap Scrolling

In our previous space-scene examples, the background image is stationary and the ship moves around on the screen. A different visual appearance can be achieved by keeping the ship stationary in the middle of the screen and scrolling the background. The background will scroll forever in whatever direction we want. To accomplish an infinitely scrolling background, we could try to use an infinitely large picture of space or we can choose a more practical approach of using a smaller image that wraps around at the edges.

9.1.1 Wrapping at the Edges

Figure 9.1 represents a bitmap image that is wrapping around horizontally. If our spaceship is stationary in the center of the screen and the background image is moving to the left, our ship will appear to fly through space to the right. It is generally best to use an image that is larger than the screen and contains no easily discernable patterns so the viewer cannot tell that the same image is repeating over and over. We also want to make sure the edges of the image do not create a visible seam where they meet. We are going to replace the nebula picture we were using for the background with a picture of a star field. A picture of random

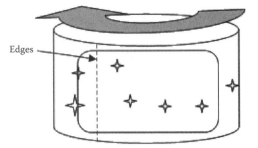

Figure 9.1. Wrapping an image.

stars will help hide the repeating nature of the background and empty space on the edges will hide the seams when we wrap the image. We will also scroll and wrap the image vertically so the star field may be scrolled infinitely in any direction.

There are two ways we can get a star field that is larger than the screen. We could use a high-resolution image that has dimensions larger than our screen or we could use a smaller image and scale it up to make it larger. In this example, we chose to scale up a smaller image. Our star field image is a 640 × 480 pixel image named `space.jpg`.

The following code is from this chapter's "Scrolling Bitmap" example. We load the image into a `TextureManager` as always. In the `Spacewar::initialize` function, we have the code, as shown in Listing 9.1.

```
// Space texture
if (!spaceTexture.initialize(graphics,SPACE_IMAGE))
    throw(GameError(gameErrorNS::FATAL_ERROR,
        "Error initializing space texture"));
```

Listing 9.1. Initializing the `space` texture in `spacewar.cpp`.

The space background will be an `Image` object. The `Image` object is named `space` in our example. After we initialize it with the space texture, we use the `setScale` function to make it bigger. The constant `SPACE_SCALE` is defined in `constants.h` as 2, which will result in the image being two times taller and two times wider (Listing 9.2). If we make our game screen 640 × 480, we will have a space image that is twice as tall and twice as wide as our game screen (see Figure 9.2).

```
// Space image
if (!space.initialize(graphics,0,0,0,&spaceTexture))
    throw(GameError(gameErrorNS::FATAL_ERROR,
        "Error initializing space"));
space.setScale((float)SPACE_SCALE);
```

Listing 9.2. Initializing the `space` `Image` object in `spacewar.cpp`.

Figure 9.2. The scaled space image is larger than the game screen (gray border).

9.1.2 Moving the Background

When the ship moves, we move the location of the space image in the opposite direction. Our code that moves the space image is in `Spacewar::update` and is shown in Listing 9.3.

```
// Update the entities
ship1.update(frameTime);
// Move space in X direction opposite ship
space.setX(space.getX() - frameTime * ship1.getVelocity().x);
// Move space in Y direction opposite ship
space.setY(space.getY() - frameTime * ship1.getVelocity().y);
// Wrap space image around at edge
// If left edge of space > screen left edge
if (space.getX() > 0)
    // Move space image left by SPACE_WIDTH
    space.setX(space.getX() - SPACE_WIDTH);
// If space image offscreen left
if (space.getX() < -SPACE_WIDTH)
    // Move space image right by SPACE_WIDTH
    space.setX(space.getX() + SPACE_WIDTH);
// If top edge of space > screen top edge
if (space.getY() > 0)
    // Move space image up by SPACE_HEIGHT
    space.setY(space.getY() - SPACE_HEIGHT);
// If space image offscreen top
if (space.getY() < -SPACE_HEIGHT)
    // Move space image down by SPACE_IMAGE
    space.setY(space.getY() + SPACE_HEIGHT);
```

Listing 9.3. Moving the space image.

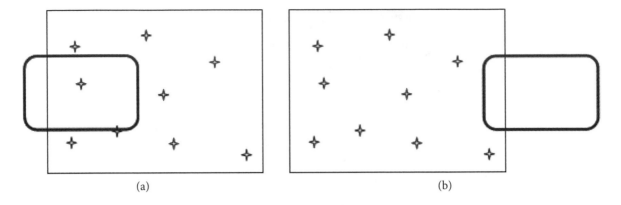

(a)   (b)

Figure 9.3. (a) The space image moving right; (b) the space image moving left.

The space image X and Y are moved in the opposite direction of the ship. If the space image moves to the right until its left edge is visible on the screen, as in Figure 9.3(a), we move the space image to the left, as in Figure 9.3(b). If the space image moves left until it is completely offscreen, we move it to the right. We do the same thing for vertical movement, making sure the space image is either covering the entire screen or is to the left of and/or above the screen. The only part of the screen that is not covered by the space image will be the right and/or bottom edges.

Drawing the background. Eventually, the space image will move far enough so it does not cover the entire screen. When that happens, we will draw the space image, move it, and draw it again until the entire screen is covered. Drawing the background image takes place in our SpacWar::render function (Listing 9.4).

```
//=============================================================================
// Render game items
//=============================================================================
void Spacewar::render()
{
    float x = space.getX();
    float y = space.getY();
    graphics->spriteBegin();                    // Begin drawing sprites
    // Wrap space image around at edges
    space.draw();                               // Draw at current location
    // If space image right edge visible
    if (space.getX() < -SPACE_WIDTH + (int)GAME_WIDTH)
    {
        space.setX(space.getX() + SPACE_WIDTH); // Wrap around to left edge
        space.draw();                           // Draw again
    }
    // If space image bottom edge visible
    if (space.getY() < -SPACE_HEIGHT + (int)GAME_HEIGHT)
    {
        space.setY(space.getY() + SPACE_HEIGHT);// Wrap around to top edge
```

```
        space.draw();                          // Draw again
        space.setX(x);                         // Restore X position
        // If space image right edge visible
        // wrap around to left edge
        if (space.getX() < -SPACE_WIDTH + (int)GAME_WIDTH)
            space.draw();                      // Draw again
    }
    space.setY(y);          // Restore Y position
    ship1.draw();           // Draw the spaceship
    if(menuOn)
        menu.draw();
    if(countDownOn)
    {
        _snprintf_s(buffer, spacewarNS::BUF_SIZE, "%d", (int)
                    (ceil(countDownTimer)));
        fontBig.print(buffer,spacewarNS::COUNT_DOWN_X,
                    spacewarNS::COUNT_DOWN_Y);
    }
    graphics->spriteEnd();                      // End drawing sprites
}
```

Listing 9.4. Drawing the space background.

There are four possible drawing scenarios we need to consider.

1. The space image may completely cover the screen, as in Figure 9.2. In that case, we only need to draw the space image at its current location.

2. The space image's right edge may be visible onscreen, as in Figure 9.4. In that case, we draw the space image, move it to the right, and draw it again.

3. The space image's bottom edge may be visible onscreen, as in Figure 9.5. In that case, we draw the space image, move it down, and draw it again.

4. The space image's bottom and right edges may be visible onscreen, as in Figure 9.6. This is the worst-case scenario and requires drawing the space image four times.

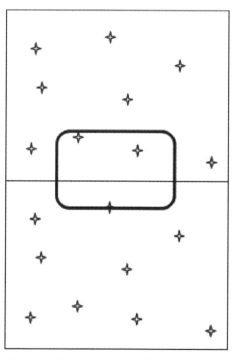

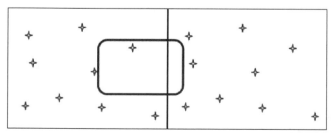

Figure 9.4. The space image is drawn twice when a left or right edge is visible.

Figure 9.5. The space image is drawn twice when a top or bottom edge is visible.

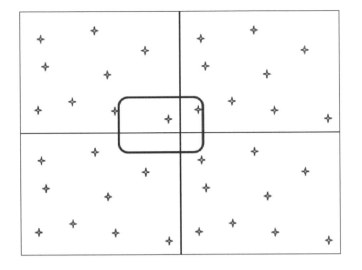

Figure 9.6. The space image is drawn four times when a corner is visible.

The four possible draws of the space image are highlighted in the `render` function. The spaceship is always drawn after the space images so it appears on top of the background.

▌ 9.2 Painter's Algorithm

In a 3D game, the graphics system uses the coordinates of items so that nearby items are always drawn in front of far away items. In a 2D game, the items typically only have a horizontal and a vertical position but no depth. When we display overlapping 2D items, we need some way to determine which items are drawn in front and which items are drawn in back. For that we will rely on a simple technique called the *painter's algorithm*.

The painter's algorithm states that items drawn early will be covered by items that are drawn later. This is the same technique many artists use when creating a picture. The background scenery is painted first and the closer items are painted on top of the background.

We had our first experience with the painter's algorithm in the planet program from Chapter 5 where we displayed a planet image on top of a nebula image. We need to remember this simple algorithm when we are drawing the items in our games.

9.2.1 Layers

One way to make sure our game items are drawn in the proper order is to assign them to layers. The layers are represented by numbers from 0 through *n*. The layer number determines the order in which items are drawn. Typically, the items on layer 0 are drawn first, and then layer 1, etc. Items on the same layer may be items that can collide, in which case they should never overlap or we may not care about the order in which they overlap. An array or list data structure could be used to keep track of the items by layer. Drawing the items would be a matter of iterating through the list and drawing the items by layers.

■ 9.3 Parallax Scrolling

The painter's algorithm allows us to display 2D items based on their depth. We can enhance the appearance of depth with a technique known as *parallax scrolling*. Parallax scrolling adds the appearance of depth to 2D games by scrolling across the background images more slowly than the foreground images.

According to Wikipedia, parallax scrolling was used in video games as early as 1982.

9.3.1 Determining Scroll Rate

The farther an item is from the viewer, the slower the scroll rate. We can clearly see this in Figure 9.7. If our two chickens are crossing the road at the same speed, the chicken crossing at B will have less screen space to travel than the chicken crossing at A. The difference in screen speed between the two chickens is the ratio of distance A to distance B:

$$\text{screen speed } B = \text{screen speed } A * \text{length } B / \text{length } A.$$

This calculation does not need to be precise for most 2D games because we are only using the effect for improved visual appearance. We may also want to assign a minimum scroll speed to the most distant items. This may not be technically correct, but it usually produces a more visually-appealing game.

We can add a planet and some moons to our "Bitmap Scroll" example to demonstrate parallax scrolling (see

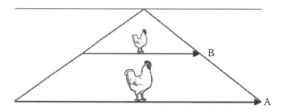

Figure 9.7. The screen speed of distant objects is less than nearby objects.

Figure 9.8. Parallax scrolling of the planet and moons.

Figure 9.8). The planet and moons move in the opposite direction of the ship just as the space background does. The planet is the closest item to the ship so it moves the fastest. The scroll speed of the moons decreases as the moons get progressively farther away from the ship. The complete source code is in this chapter's "Parallax Scroll" example.

The code that moves the planet and moons is added to the Spacewar::update function just above the code that moves the space background (Listing 9.5). This example does not use a precise calculation to determine the scroll rate of the moons; it simply reduces the scroll speed by 20% for each moon.

```
// Update the entities position for parallax scroll
ship1.update(frameTime);
// Move planet along X
planet.setX(planet.getX() - frameTime * ship1.getVelocity().x);
// Move planet along Y
planet.setY(planet.getY() - frameTime * ship1.getVelocity().y);
planet.update(frameTime);
for(int i=0; i<4; i++)        // Move moons
{
    // Reduce scroll speed by 20% for each moon
    moons[i].setX(moons[i].getX() - frameTime * ship1.getVelocity().x
                                    * 0.2f * (4-i));
    moons[i].setY(moons[i].getY() - frameTime * ship1.getVelocity().y
                                    * 0.2f * (4-i));
}
// Move space along X
space.setX(space.getX() - frameTime * ship1.getVelocity().x*0.1f);
// Move space along Y
space.setY(space.getY() - frameTime * ship1.getVelocity().y*0.1f);
// Wrap space image around at edge
// If left edge of space > screen left edge
if (space.getX() > 0)
    // Move space image left by SPACE_WIDTH
    space.setX(space.getX() - SPACE_WIDTH);
// If space image offscreen left
if (space.getX() < -SPACE_WIDTH)
    // Move space image right by SPACE_WIDTH
    space.setX(space.getX() + SPACE_WIDTH);
// If top edge of space > screen top edge
if (space.getY() > 0)
    // Move space image up by SPACE_HEIGHT
    space.setY(space.getY() - SPACE_HEIGHT);
// If space image offscreen top
if (space.getY() < -SPACE_HEIGHT)
    // Move space image down by SPACE_IMAGE
    space.setY(space.getY() + SPACE_HEIGHT);
```

Listing 9.5. Parallax scroll code in Spacewar update function.

Drawing of the planet and moons is handled in the Spacewar::render function. The planet and moons are drawn from back to front using the painter's algorithm (Listing 9.6).

9. Enhanced Appearance

```
for (int i=3; i>=0; i--)
    moons[i].draw();                        // Draw moons, back to front
planet.draw();                              // Draw the planet
ship1.draw();                               // Draw the spaceships
```

Listing 9.6. Drawing the planet and moons.

▌ 9.4 Shadows and Reflections

Shadows and reflections may be used as a general way to enhance the appearance of our games, but they may also serve a more important role. In games involving flying craft, a shadow may be used to provide a visual indicator of a craft's relationship to the surface below it. In Figure 9.9, the shadow or reflection helps us gauge the airplane's altitude. The shadow would also be helpful as an alignment aid if our game play involved dropping items from the plane.

In this example, the airplane is described by a `Plane` class that inherits from the `Entity` class. The shadow is an `Image` object that is contained in the `Plane` class. Making the shadow part of the `Plane` class is the logical approach because obviously there cannot be a shadow without a plane and we want the shadow to move with the plane.

The shadow is always drawn directly under the plane at its X,Y location. Changes in the plane's altitude do not affect the position of the shadow. This example uses a scrolling background with the plane's shadow always in the center. The coordinates of the plane and shadow and other constants are declared in `plane.h`. The code in Listing 9.7 is from the "Shadow" example. The shadow `Image` object declaration is highlighted.

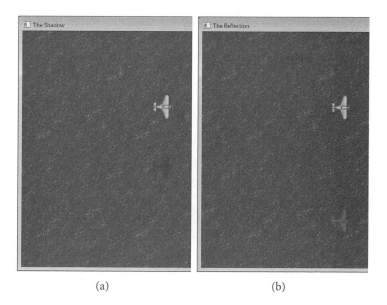

(a)   (b)

Figure 9.9. A plane with (a) shadow or (b) reflection.

```
// Programming 2D Games
// Copyright (c) 2011 by:
// Charles Kelly
// Chapter 9 plane.h v1.0
#ifndef _PLANE_H                    // Prevent multiple definitions if this
#define _PLANE_H                    // file is included in more than one place
#define WIN32_LEAN_AND_MEAN
#include "entity.h"
#include "constants.h"
namespace planeNS
{
    const int   PLANE_SIZE = 64;         // The texture size
    const int   PLANE_START_FRAME = 0;// Frame numbers
    const int   PLANE_END_FRAME = 1;
    const int   SHADOW_FRAME = 2;
    const int   TEXTURE_COLS = 2;        // Number of columns in texture image
    const int   PLANE_VERTICAL_SPEED = 64;  // Climb/descend rate
    const int   SHADOW_Y = GAME_HEIGHT/2;   // The shadow's Y coordinate
    const int   PLANE_MAX_Y = SHADOW_Y - 10;// The plane's maximum Y
                                            // coordinate
    const int   X = GAME_WIDTH/2;           // The plane's starting
                                            // location
    const int   Y = GAME_HEIGHT/4;
    const float ROTATION_RATE = (float)PI;  // Radians per second
    const float SPEED = 100;                // 100 pixels per second
    const float ANIMATION_DELAY = 0.01f;    // Time between frames
}
// Inherits from Entity class
class Plane : public Entity
{
private:
    Image     shadow;          // The plane's shadow
    float     planeY;          // Temp storage for plane Y
public:
    // Constructor
    Plane();
    // Inherited member functions
    // Draw the plane and shadow
    virtual void draw();
    // Initialize the plane
    // Pre: *gamePtr = pointer to Game object
    //      width = width of Image in pixels  (0 = use full texture width)
    //      height = height of Image in pixels (0 = use full texture
    //      height)
    //      ncols = number of columns in texture (1 to n) (0 same as 1)
    //      *textureM = pointer to TextureManager object
    virtual bool initialize(Game *gamePtr, int width, int height,
                            int ncols, TextureManager *textureM);
    // Update the plane's animation and position
    void update(float frameTime);
};
#endif
```

Listing 9.7. Adding an Image object for the plane's shadow.

```
//=============================================================================
// Draw the plane and shadow
//=============================================================================
void Plane::draw()
{
    // Draw shadow
    planeY = spriteData.y;              // Save plane Y
    spriteData.y = planeNS::SHADOW_Y;
    // Draw shadow using colorFilter 25% alpha
    shadow.draw(spriteData, graphicsNS::ALPHA25 & graphicsNS::BLACK);
    spriteData.y = planeY;              // Restore plane Y
    // Draw plane
    Entity::draw();
}
```

Listing 9.8. Drawing the plane and shadow.

The plane's `draw` function draws the shadow then the plane. We draw the shadow first because we want the plane to always appear on top of the shadow. The code that draws the shadow saves the plane's screen Y location (`spriteData.y`) to `planeY`. It then replaces the plane's Y with `SHADOW_Y`, the constant that defines the Y location of the shadow. The shadow is drawn using the plane's `spriteData`. This gives the shadow the same orientation and position as the plane but with a Y value of `SHADOW_Y`. The second parameter to the `shadow.draw` function makes the shadow black with a 25% alpha value. Recall that the alpha value specifies the amount of transparency. An alpha value of 25% produces a shadow that makes the area darker but still allows the underlying image to remain visible (Listing 9.8).

If we had more than one plane, we would need to draw all of the shadows first and then draw all of the planes.

Drawing a reflection would be similar to drawing the shadow, but the vertical position of the reflection moves opposite the plane. If the plane moves up the screen, the reflection moves down, and vice versa. The vertical position of the reflection is calculated by subtracting the plane's altitude above the water from the minimum reflection Y value.

Another technique for displaying a shadow or reflection is to change the frame of the current sprite instead of creating a separate `Image` object. The "Reflection" demo uses this technique. The current frame of the plane sprite is saved. The reflection frame of the sprite texture is selected by adding the `REFLECTION_FRAME_OFFSET` to the current frame. This selects an image of the plane as seen from underneath. The reflection is drawn and the plane sprite is restored to its original frame.

The code in Listing 9.9 is from the "Reflection" demo program.

```
//=============================================================================
// Draw the plane and reflection
//=============================================================================
void Plane::draw()
{
```

```
        // Draw reflection
        planeY = spriteData.y;            // Save plane Y
        spriteData.y = planeNS::RELECTION_MIN_Y + planeNS::PLANE_MAX_Y -
                spriteData.y;
        frame = getCurrentFrame();        // Current frame of plane sprite
        // Set frame for reflection
        setCurrentFrame(frame + planeNS::REFLECTION_FRAME_OFFSET);
        // Draw reflection using 25% alpha
        Entity::draw(spriteData, graphicsNS::ALPHA25);
        setCurrentFrame(frame);           // Restore plane's frame
        spriteData.y = planeY;            // Restore plane Y
        // Draw plane
        Entity::draw();
}
```

Listing 9.9. Drawing the plane and reflection.

The texture image for the "Shadow" demo contains two textures for the plane and one texture for the shadow. The "Reflection" demo includes two textures for the plane and two textures for the reflection (see Figure 9.10).

There is one more interesting tidbit about our "Shadow" and "Reflection" demo programs. The scrolling ocean is drawn using an image that is smaller than the screen. We said in our earlier discussion about scrolling bitmaps that a larger image produces better results. By paying close attention to the surface of the water, it might be possible to see the same wave patterns in multiple places onscreen.

The complete source code is available from www.programming2dgames.com.

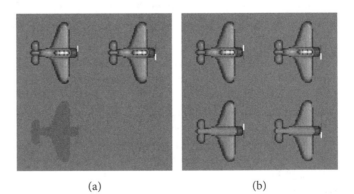

(a)   (b)

Figure 9.10. (a) The shadow texture image and (b) the reflection texture image.

▌ 9.5 Message Dialog

We are probably all familiar with dialog boxes. They come in various forms and provide a useful way to display text messages to users. Most of us are probably also aware that Windows has dialog boxes built in that we may use when writing Windows applications. Using

Figure 9.11. An example of our message dialog.

the standard Windows dialogs inside fullscreen DirectX applications is possible, but not without its own set of issues (more on that later).

The `Console` class we created in the previous chapter supported the display of text on a DirectX surface. We should be able to extend that idea to create our own message dialog class. Figure 9.11 shows a sample of our dialog in action. This is, of course, a rather generic dialog. We could make a much fancier one by displaying a bitmap image as a background and displaying text on top of it.

The following code is from the "messageDialog Demo" example. The `messageDialog` `.h` file contains the namespace `messageDialogNS` where the dialog constants are declared (Listing 9.10).

```
namespace messageDialogNS
{
    const UINT WIDTH = 400;              // Default width of dialog
    const UINT HEIGHT = 100;             // Default height
    const UINT BORDER = 5;
    const UINT MARGIN = 5;               // Text margin from border
    const char FONT[] = "Arial";         // Font
    const int FONT_HEIGHT = 18;          // Font height
    const COLOR_ARGB FONT_COLOR = graphicsNS::WHITE;       // Text color
    const COLOR_ARGB BORDER_COLOR = D3DCOLOR_ARGB(192,192,192,192);
                                         // Border color
    const COLOR_ARGB BACK_COLOR = SETCOLOR_ARGB(255,100,100,192);
                                         // Backdrop color
    const UINT X = GAME_WIDTH/2 - WIDTH/2; // Default location
    const UINT Y = GAME_HEIGHT/4 - HEIGHT/2;
    const UINT BUTTON_WIDTH = (UINT)(FONT_HEIGHT * 4.5);
    const UINT BUTTON_HEIGHT = FONT_HEIGHT + 4;
    const int MAX_TYPE = 2;
    const int OK_CANCEL = 0;             // OK Cancel button type
    const int YES_NO = 1;                // Yes No button type
    static const char* BUTTON1_TEXT[MAX_TYPE] = {"OK", "YES"};
    static const char* BUTTON2_TEXT[MAX_TYPE] = {"CANCEL", "NO"};
    const byte DIALOG_CLOSE_KEY = VK_RETURN;    // Enter key
    const COLOR_ARGB BUTTON_COLOR = graphicsNS::GRAY; // Button background
    const COLOR_ARGB BUTTON_FONT_COLOR = graphicsNS::WHITE; // Button text
                                                        // color
}
```

Listing 9.10. Declaration of the message dialog constants.

```
// Message Dialog
class MessageDialog
{
protected:
    Graphics      *graphics;              // Graphics system
    Input         *input;                 // Input system
    TextDX        dxFont;                 // DirectX font
    float          x,y;                   // Screen location
    UINT          height;                 // Dialog height, calculated in
                                          // print()
    UINT          width;                  // Dialog width
    std::string text;                     // Dialog text
    RECT          textRect;               // Text rectangle
    RECT          buttonRect;             // Button rectangle
    RECT          button2Rect;            // Button2 rectangle
    COLOR_ARGB    fontColor;              // Font color (a,r,g,b)
    COLOR_ARGB    borderColor;            // Border color (a,r,g,b)
    COLOR_ARGB    backColor;              // Background color (a,r,g,b)
    COLOR_ARGB    buttonColor;            // Button color
    COLOR_ARGB    buttonFontColor;        // Button font color
    VertexC vtx[4];                       // Vertex data
    LP_VERTEXBUFFER dialogVerts;          // Dialog vertex buffer
    LP_VERTEXBUFFER borderVerts;          // Border vertex buffer
    LP_VERTEXBUFFER buttonVerts;          // Button vertex buffer
    LP_VERTEXBUFFER button2Verts;         // Button2 vertex buffer
    int buttonClicked;                    // Which button was clicked (1 or 2)
    int buttonType;                       // 0 = OK/Cancel, 1 = Yes/No
    bool     initialized;                 // True when initialized successfully
    bool     visible;                     // True to display
    HWND     hwnd;                        // Handle to window
    float    screenRatioX, screenRatioY;
```

Listing 9.11. The message dialog variables.

The class declaration follows the constants. Most of the comments adequately describe the purpose of each variable. The `height` is calculated in the `print` function to make the dialog taller or shorter based on the requirements of the text string being displayed. The `width` is not automatically adjusted. The `screenRatio` variables are used in the code that checks for a mouse click on the buttons. The `buttonType` variable is used to select the text defaults for the buttons. There are currently two choices available: 0 for OK/CANCEL and 1 for YES/NO (see Listing 9.11).

The function prototypes follow the variables. We can adjust the color of the font, border, background, button, and button font. The dialog can be hidden or made visible. Text is added using the `print` function. We'll see how to use these functions in Listing 9.12.

```
public:
    // Constructor
    MessageDialog();
    // Destructor
```

```cpp
    virtual ~MessageDialog();
    // Initialize the MessageDialog
    // Pre: *g points to Graphics object
    //      *in points to Input object
    //      hwnd = window handle
    bool initialize(Graphics *g, Input *in, HWND hwnd);
    // Prepare vertex buffers
    void prepareVerts();
    // Display the MessageDialog
    const void draw();
    // Return button clicked
    // 0 = no button clicked
    // 1 is left button, 2 is right button
    int getButtonClicked()   {return buttonClicked;}
    // Return visible
    bool getVisible() {return visible;}
    // Set font color
    void setFontColor(COLOR_ARGB fc)      {fontColor = fc;}
    // Set border color
    void setBorderColor(COLOR_ARGB bc)   {borderColor = bc;}
    // Set background color
    void setBackColor(COLOR_ARGB bc)      {backColor = bc;}
    // Set button color
    void setButtonColor(COLOR_ARGB bc)   {buttonColor = bc;}
    // Set button font color
    void setButtonFontColor(COLOR_ARGB bfc) {buttonFontColor = bfc;}
    // Set visible;
    void setVisible(bool v) {visible = v;}
    // Set button type 0 = OK/CANCEL, 1 = YES/NO
    void setButtonType(UINT t)
    {
        if(t < messageDialogNS::MAX_TYPE)
            buttonType = t;
    }
    // Display text str in MessageDialog
    void print(const std::string &str);
    // Checks for Close event
    void update();
    // Call when graphics device is lost
    void onLostDevice();
    // Call when graphics device is reset
    void onResetDevice();
};
#endif
```

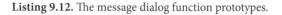

Listing 9.12. The message dialog function prototypes.

The messageDialog.cpp file contains the code for the constructor and destructor. As with all of our previous code, the constructor is limited to simple variable initialization (Listing 9.13).

The initialize function saves the pointers to Graphics and Input objects and the window handle. It also initializes the DirectX font that is used to display the text in the dialog (Listing 9.14).

```
// Programming 2D Games
// Copyright (c) 2011 by:
// Charles Kelly
// messageDialog.cpp v1.0
#include "messageDialog.h"
//=============================================================================
// Constructor
//=============================================================================
MessageDialog::MessageDialog()
{
    initialized = false;            // Set true when successfully initialized
    graphics = NULL;
    visible = false;                // Not visible
    fontColor = messageDialogNS::FONT_COLOR;
    borderColor = messageDialogNS::BORDER_COLOR;
    backColor = messageDialogNS::BACK_COLOR;
    buttonColor = messageDialogNS::BUTTON_COLOR;
    buttonFontColor = messageDialogNS::BUTTON_FONT_COLOR;
    x = messageDialogNS::X;         // Starting position
    y = messageDialogNS::Y;
    height = messageDialogNS::HEIGHT;
    width = messageDialogNS::WIDTH;
    textRect.bottom = messageDialogNS::Y + messageDialogNS::HEIGHT -
                      messageDialogNS::MARGIN;
    textRect.left = messageDialogNS::X + messageDialogNS::MARGIN;
    textRect.right = messageDialogNS::X + messageDialogNS::WIDTH -
                     messageDialogNS::MARGIN;
    textRect.top = messageDialogNS::Y + messageDialogNS::MARGIN;
    dialogVerts = NULL;
    borderVerts = NULL;
    buttonVerts = NULL;
    button2Verts = NULL;
    buttonType = 0;        // OK/Cancel
}
//=============================================================================
// Destructor
//=============================================================================
MessageDialog::~MessageDialog()
{
    onLostDevice();                 // Call onLostDevice() for every graphics item
}
```

Listing 9.13. The message dialog constructor and destructor.

```
//=============================================================================
// Initialize the MessageDialog
//=============================================================================
bool MessageDialog::initialize(Graphics *g, Input *in, HWND h)
{
    try {
        graphics = g;                   // The Graphics object
        input = in;                     // The Input object
        hwnd = h;
        // Initialize DirectX font
        if(dxFont.initialize(graphics, messageDialogNS::FONT_HEIGHT, false,
```

```
                         false, messageDialogNS::FONT) == false)
            return false;                    // If failed
        dxFont.setFontColor(fontColor);
    } catch(...) {
        return false;
    }
    initialized = true;
    return true;
}
```

Listing 9.14. The message dialog `initialize` function.

The `prepareVerts` function creates four vertex buffers: one for the dialog border, another for the text area of the dialog, and two more for the buttons. The code is rather lengthy and repetitive so we will only list the part that creates the first vertex buffer in Listing 9.15.

```
//==================================================================
// Prepare the vertex buffers for drawing dialog background and button
//==================================================================
void MessageDialog::prepareVerts()
{
    SAFE_RELEASE(dialogVerts);
    SAFE_RELEASE(borderVerts);
    SAFE_RELEASE(buttonVerts);
    SAFE_RELEASE(button2Verts);
    // Border top left
    vtx[0].x = x;
    vtx[0].y = y;
    vtx[0].z = 0.0f;
    vtx[0].rhw = 1.0f;
    vtx[0].color = borderColor;
    // Border top right
    vtx[1].x = x + width;
    vtx[1].y = y;
    vtx[1].z = 0.0f;
    vtx[1].rhw = 1.0f;
    vtx[1].color = borderColor;
    // Border bottom right
    vtx[2].x = x + width;
    vtx[2].y = y + height;
    vtx[2].z = 0.0f;
    vtx[2].rhw = 1.0f;
    vtx[2].color = borderColor;
    // Border bottom left
    vtx[3].x = x;
    vtx[3].y = y + height;
    vtx[3].z = 0.0f;
    vtx[3].rhw = 1.0f;
    vtx[3].color = borderColor;
    graphics->createVertexBuffer(vtx, sizeof vtx, borderVerts);
//... repeated three more times to create dialogVerts and buttonVerts
```

Listing 9.15. Creating the vertex buffers for the dialog and buttons.

The draw function displays the dialog to the screen. The dialog border is created by displaying a larger quad and then displaying a smaller quad on top of it. The smaller quad will contain the dialog text. The text is displayed using the dxFont.print function where the parameters textRect and DT_CENTER|DT_WORDBREAK cause the text to be displayed inside the boundaries defined by textRect with the text centered and word wrapped. We define textRect to be smaller than the inner quad of the dialog. The MARGIN constant we defined earlier specifies how much smaller the textRect is to provide a margin between the text and the edge of the inner dialog quad. The button text is displayed using the dxFont.print function where the parameters DT_SINGLELINE|DT_CENTER|DT_VCENTER cause the text to be in one line, and centered horizontally and vertically (Listing 9.16).

The update method is used to check for a button click. We chose to accept a key press or a mouse click to press the left button (1). The constant DIALOG_CLOSE_KEY was defined as the "Enter" key earlier in messageDialog.h.

Before we check for a mouse click on the buttons, we calculate the screen width and height ratios in case the window has been resized. The coordinates of the mouse click are compared to the edges of the buttonRect to determine if the mouse click is inside the button.

The buttonClicked variable is set to 1 when the left button is clicked and set to 2 when the right button is clicked. Any button click sets the dialog visible property to false to hide the dialog (Listing 9.17).

```
//=============================================================================
// Draw the MessageDialog
//=============================================================================
const void MessageDialog::draw()
{
    if (!visible || graphics == NULL || !initialized)
        return;
    graphics->drawQuad(borderVerts);          // Draw border
    graphics->drawQuad(dialogVerts);          // Draw backdrop
    graphics->drawQuad(buttonVerts);          // Draw button
    graphics->drawQuad(button2Verts);         // Draw button2
    graphics->spriteBegin();                  // Begin drawing sprites
    if(text.size() == 0)
        return;
    // Display text on MessageDialog
    dxFont.setFontColor(fontColor);
    dxFont.print(text,textRect,DT_CENTER|DT_WORDBREAK);
    // Display text on buttons
    dxFont.setFontColor(buttonFontColor);
    dxFont.print(messageDialogNS::BUTTON1_TEXT[buttonType],buttonRect,
            DT_SINGLELINE|DT_CENTER|DT_VCENTER);
    dxFont.print(messageDialogNS::BUTTON2_TEXT[buttonType],button2Rect,
            DT_SINGLELINE|DT_CENTER|DT_VCENTER);
    graphics->spriteEnd();                    // End drawing sprites
}
```

Listing 9.16. The draw function displays the message dialog.

```
//=============================================================================
// Checks for DIALOG_CLOSE_KEY and mouse click on OK button
//=============================================================================
void MessageDialog::update()
{
    if (!initialized || !visible)
        return;
    if (input->wasKeyPressed(messageDialogNS::DIALOG_CLOSE_KEY))
    {
        visible = false;
        buttonClicked = 1;                   // Button1 was clicked
        return;
    }
    if (graphics->getFullscreen() == false) // If windowed
    {
        // Calculate screen ratios in case window was resized
        RECT clientRect;
        GetClientRect(hwnd, &clientRect);
        screenRatioX = (float)GAME_WIDTH / clientRect.right;
        screenRatioY = (float)GAME_HEIGHT / clientRect.bottom;
    }
    if (input->getMouseLButton())            // If mouse left button
    {
        // If mouse clicked inside button1 (OK)
        if (input->getMouseX()*screenRatioX >= buttonRect.left &&
            input->getMouseX()*screenRatioX <= buttonRect.right &&
            input->getMouseY()*screenRatioY >= buttonRect.top &&
            input->getMouseY()*screenRatioY <= buttonRect.bottom)
        {
            visible = false;                 // Hide message dialog
            buttonClicked = 1;               // Button1 was clicked
            return;
        }
        // If mouse clicked inside button2 (cancel)
        if (input->getMouseX()*screenRatioX >= button2Rect.left &&
            input->getMouseX()*screenRatioX <= button2Rect.right &&
            input->getMouseY()*screenRatioY >= button2Rect.top &&
            input->getMouseY()*screenRatioY <= button2Rect.bottom)
        {
            visible = false;                 // Hide message dialog
            buttonClicked = 2;               // Button2 was clicked
        }
    }
}
```

Listing 9.17. The message dialog update function.

The text to display in the dialog is set using the print function. The print function sets the size of the textRect to provide a margin for the text as we described earlier. The bottom of the textRect is then adjusted to fit the current text string by calling the dxFont.print function with the parameters DT_CENTER|DT_WORDBREAK|DT_

CALCRECT. The DT_CALCRECT flag tells DirectX to adjust textRect.bottom to the size required to hold the text but it does not display anything. We use this feature to adjust the vertical size of the dialog to the precise size required to contain the text. After setting the height of the dialog, we call prepareVerts to initialize the vertex buffers used to display the quads for the border, background, and buttons (Listing 9.18).

```
//=============================================================================
// Set text string, size dialog bottom to fit text and set visible = true
//=============================================================================
void MessageDialog::print(const std::string &str)
{
    if (!initialized || visible)        // If not initialized or already in use
        return;
    text = str + "\n\n\n\n";            // Leave some room for buttons
    // Set textRect to text area of dialog
    textRect.left   = (long)(x + messageDialogNS::MARGIN);
    textRect.right  = (long)(x + messageDialogNS::WIDTH -
    messageDialogNS::MARGIN);
    textRect.top    = (long)(y + messageDialogNS::MARGIN);
    textRect.bottom = (long)(y + messageDialogNS::HEIGHT -
    messageDialogNS::MARGIN);
    // Set textRect.bottom to precise height required for text
    // No text is printed with DT_CALCRECT option
    dxFont.print(text,textRect,DT_CENTER|DT_WORDBREAK|DT_CALCRECT);
    height = textRect.bottom - (int)y + messageDialogNS::BORDER +
            messageDialogNS::MARGIN;
    prepareVerts();                     // Prepare the vertex buffers
    buttonClicked = 0;                  // Clear buttonClicked
    visible = true;
}
```

Listing 9.18. The print function displays text in the dialog.

9.5.1 Adding a MessageDialog Pointer to the Game Engine

Adding the MessageDialog to our game engine will make it easier to use it in our games. A MessageDialog pointer is added to the Game class in game.h (Listing 9.19).

```
class Game
{
protected:
    // Common game properties
    Graphics *graphics;              // Pointer to Graphics
    Input    *input;                 // Pointer to Input
    Audio    *audio;                 // Pointer to Audio
    Console *console;                // Pointer to Console
    MessageDialog *messageDialog;    // Pointer to MessageDialog
```

Listing 9.19. Adding a MessageDialog pointer to game.h.

```
// Initialize messageDialog
messageDialog = new MessageDialog();
messageDialog->initialize(graphics, input, hwnd);
```

Listing 9.20. Initializing the `MessageDialog` object.

```
input->readControllers();    // Read state of controllers
messageDialog->update();     // Check for button clicks
audio->run();                // Perform periodic sound engine tasks
```

Listing 9.21. Checking for button clicks.

The `MessageDialog` is initialized in the `Game::initialize` function (Listing 9.20). We need to call the dialog's update method to check for a button click. The code is added to the `run` function in the `Game` class (Listing 9.21). A call to the dialog's `draw` method is added to the end of the `Game` class's `renderGame` function (Listing 9.22). And lastly, we need to include the message dialog in our code that handles a lost graphics device and releases reserved memory (Listing 9.23).

```
console->draw();        // Console is drawn here so it appears on
                        // top of game
messageDialog->draw();  // Dialog is drawn on top
// Stop rendering
graphics->endScene();
```

Listing 9.22. Drawing the dialog.

```
//=============================================================================
// The graphics device was lost.
// Release all reserved video memory so graphics device may be reset.
//=============================================================================
void Game::releaseAll()
{
    SAFE_ON_LOST_DEVICE(messageDialog);
    SAFE_ON_LOST_DEVICE(console);
    dxFont.onLostDevice();
    return;
}
//=============================================================================
// Recreate all surfaces and reset all entities
//=============================================================================
void Game::resetAll()
{
    dxFont.onResetDevice();
    SAFE_ON_RESET_DEVICE(console);
```

```
    SAFE_ON_RESET_DEVICE(messageDialog);
    return;
}
//=============================================================================
// Delete all reserved memory
//=============================================================================
void Game::deleteAll()
{
    releaseAll();              // Call onLostDevice() for every graphics
                               // item
    SAFE_DELETE(audio);
    SAFE_DELETE(graphics);
    SAFE_DELETE(input);
    SAFE_DELETE(console);
    SAFE_DELETE(messageDialog);
    initialized = false;
}
```

Listing 9.23. Adding message dialog code to `releaseAll`, `resetAll`, and `deleteAll` in `game.cpp`.

To display a message from the game, just call the `messageDialog->print` function, as is shown in Listing 9.24. The `MessageDialog` will be drawn on top of all other items and it will remain visible until a button is clicked. Only one dialog may be displayed at a time. Attempting to display a dialog if one is currently visible has no effect.

```
    messageDialog->print("Ship1 says \"Ouch, stupid planet!\"");
```

Listing 9.24. Displaying a message dialog.

9.5.2 Message Dialog Demo

The message dialog demo sets the border color and background color of the dialog and displays a message as part of the `initialize` function. The following code is in `message demo.cpp` (Listing 9.25).

```
//=============================================================================
// Initializes the game
// Throws GameError on error
//=============================================================================
void MessageDemo::initialize(HWND hwnd)
{
    Game::initialize(hwnd); // Throws GameError
    reset();                // Reset all game variables
    fpsOn = true;           // Display frames per second
    messageDialog->setBorderColor(graphicsNS::LTGRAY);
    messageDialog->setBackColor(SETCOLOR_ARGB(255,50,50,90));
    messageDialog->print("This is a test message. This is only a test. If"
```

```
                       "this were an actual message it would contain some useful"
                       "information instead of this meaningless dribble.");
}
```

Listing 9.25. Setting the border and background color of a dialog and displaying a message.

When a button on the dialog is clicked, a new dialog is displayed with a message that indicates which button was just clicked. This code is in the `update` function in the `messagedemo.cpp` file (Listing 9.26).

```
//==============================================================================
// Move all game items
// frameTime is used to regulate the speed of movement
//==============================================================================
void MessageDemo::update()
{
    messageDialog->update();    // Check for button events
    if(messageDialog->getButtonClicked() == 1)
    {
        messageDialog->setButtonType(1);
        messageDialog->print("Button 1 clicked");
    }
    else if(messageDialog->getButtonClicked() == 2)
    {
        messageDialog->setButtonType(0);
        messageDialog->print("Button 2 clicked");
    }
}
```

Listing 9.26. Checking for button clicks on the message dialog.

9.6 Input Dialog

An *input dialog* may be used to get user input. We can create an input dialog by adding the ability to accept text input to our message dialog (see Figure 9.12).

Inheritance will be used to create an `InputDialog` class that extends the features of the `MessageDialog` class. The `InputDialog` class will start with everything that is in the `MessageDialog` class. We can use the inherited features as is, overwrite them to change

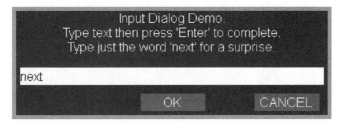

Figure 9.12. The input dialog.

their behavior, or create entirely new features that are unique to the InputDialog. The InputDialog class is declared in the inputDialog.h file. New constants for the colors of the text input area are added to the inputDialogNS namespace (Listing 9.27).

```
// Programming 2D Games
// Copyright (c) 2011 by:
// Charles Kelly
// inputDialog.h v1.0
#ifndef _INPUTDIALOG_H          // Prevent multiple definitions if this
#define _INPUTDIALOG_H          // file is included in more than one place
#define WIN32_LEAN_AND_MEAN
#include <string>
#include "constants.h"
#include "textDX.h"
#include "graphics.h"
#include "input.h"
#include "messageDialog.h"
namespace inputDialogNS
{
    const COLOR_ARGB TEXT_BACK_COLOR = graphicsNS::WHITE;    // Input text
                                                             // background
    const COLOR_ARGB TEXT_COLOR = graphicsNS::BLACK;         // Input text
                                                             // color
}
```

Listing 9.27. Color constants for text input in inputDialog.h.

The syntax that indicates inheritance is highlighted in Listing 9.28. The syntax : public MessageDialog indicates that the InputDialog class inherits from the MessageDialog class. The additional variable required for the text input area is added to the private section of the class. This new variable is in addition to the variables inherited from the MessageDialog (Listing 9.29).

```
// Input Dialog, inherits from Message Dialog
class InputDialog : public MessageDialog
{
```

Listing 9.28. The InputDialog is derived from the MessageDialog.

```
private:
    std::string inText;                 // Input text
    RECT        inTextRect;
    RECT        tempRect;
    COLOR_ARGB  textBackColor;          // Text area background color
    COLOR_ARGB  textFontColor;          // Text area font color
    LP_VERTEXBUFFER inTextVerts;        // Text area vertex buffer
```

Listing 9.29. Additional variables in the InputDialog class.

```
public:
    // Constructor
    InputDialog();
    // Destructor
    virtual ~InputDialog();
    // Prepare vertex buffers
    void prepareVerts();
    // Display the InputDialog
    const void draw();
```

Listing 9.30. New or overridden functions in the `InputDialog` class.

Any functions from the `MessgeDialog` class may be modified by writing the new code in the `InputDialog` class. If a function is not modified it may still be called as part of the `InputDialog` (Listing 9.30).

The `getText` function returns the user-entered text if the input dialog is not visible. If the dialog is still visible, it means no button has been clicked, so an empty string is returned. When the user presses the "Enter" key or clicks the left button, the dialog's visible property is set to `false`. If the user clicks the right button, the input text is cleared and then the visible property is set to `false` (Listing 9.31). The font color and background color of the text area may be set during runtime with the following functions (Listing 9.32).

The `print`, `update`, and `onLostDevice` functions perform the same tasks as their message dialog counterparts, but require some changes to work with the input dialog (Listing 9.33).

```
// Return input text
std::string getText()
{
    if(!visible)
        return inText;
    else
        return "";
}
```

Listing 9.31. The `getText` function from `inputDialog.h`.

```
// Set input text font color
void setTextFontColor(COLOR_ARGB fc)    {textFontColor = fc;}
// Set input text background color
void setTextBackColor(COLOR_ARGB bc)    {textBackColor = bc;}
```

Listing 9.32. Functions for setting the colors of the text area.

```
    // Display text str in InputDialog
    void print(const std::string &str);
    // Checks for Close event
    void update();
    // Call when graphics device is lost
    void onLostDevice();
};
#endif
```

Listing 9.33. Overridden functions in the `InputDialog` class.

Sometimes an overridden function in the derived class needs to call the existing function in the base class. The `prepareVerts` function does just that. The syntax is `BaseClass::function();` and can be seen in Listing 9.34. The `inputDialog.cpp` file contains the remaining code, which we will leave for the reader to explore.

```
//=============================================================================
// Prepare the vertex buffers for drawing dialog background and button
//=============================================================================
void InputDialog::prepareVerts()
{
    MessageDialog::prepareVerts();   // Call perpareVerts in base class
    SAFE_RELEASE(inTextVerts);
```

Listing 9.34. Calling the `perpareVerts` function in the `MessageDialog` base class.

9.7 Windows Dialogs in Fullscreen DirectX Applications

As was mentioned earlier, it is possible to display Windows dialogs in fullscreen DirectX applications. Our inclusion of this code is an effort to provide complete coverage of the subject and should not be considered as a recommendation for this method. We'll just say it is for the adventurous among us who like to explore every avenue of programming. The Direct3D method that allows the use of GDI dialogs in fullscreen mode applications is:

```
IDirect3DDEvice9::SetDialogBoxMode
HRESULT SetDialogBoxMode(
    BOOL bEnableDialogs
);
```

In order to use `SetDialogBoxMode`, we would need to enable lockable back buffers by adding the line of code in Listing 9.35 to our `Graphics::initD3Dpp() function.`

```
d3dpp.Flags = D3DPRESENTFLAG_LOCKABLE_BACKBUFFER;   // Required for GDI
                                                    // dialog boxes
```

Listing 9.35. Enabling GDI dialogs.

Using lockable back buffers may result in a performance loss on some graphics hardware.

The call to `SetDialogBoxMode` would be added to the end of our `Graphics::initial ize` function (Listing 9.36).

```
result = device3d->SetDialogBoxMode(true);
if (FAILED(result))
{
    MessageBox(hwnd, "Error setting Dialog Box Mode", "Error", MB_OK);
    releaseAll();    // Free resources before exit
    return false;
}
```

Listing 9.36. Calling the `SetDialogBoxMode` function.

9.8 Dashboard

In this section, we will create some examples of user interface elements that may be used to enhance the appearance of our games. We refer to this section as "Dashboard" because the displays and controls we are going to create resemble those found on dashboards or instrument panels. Figure 9.13 shows the "Dashboard" demo in action.

We are using bitmap images to create these dashboard elements as opposed to drawing graphics primitives, which we did when creating the dialog box earlier. Using bitmaps allows us to easily replace the rather generic gauges with something that has more detail.

The size of the controls and displays may be adjusted with the scale parameter. A scale number less than 1.0 reduces the size and a scale number greater than 1.0 increases the size. The `draw` function is used to display a control. The controls and displays we will create include:

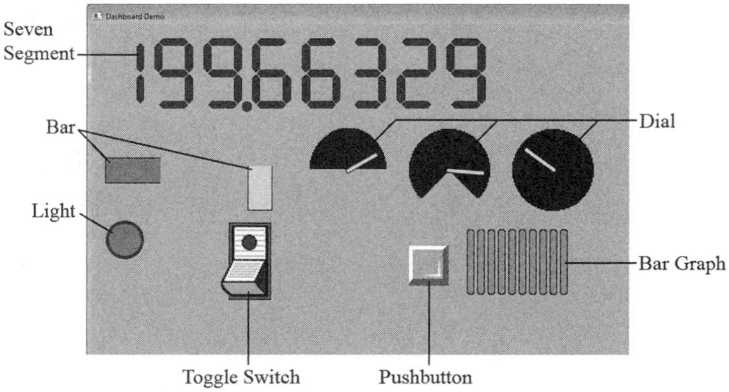

Figure 9.13. The "Dashboard" demo.

- *A multiple-digit, seven-segment display.* The number of digits and color of the digits are adjustable. The `set` function is used to change the display value.

- *An adjustable length bar.* The direction of the bar and color are adjustable. The `set` function is used to change the length of the bar. Accepted values range from 0 to 100, where 0 makes the bar invisible and 100 sets the bar to full length.

- *A dial gauge.* Three variations of the dial gauge are supported. The dial may be rotated to any angle. The color of the dial and pointer are adjustable. The set function is used to set the pointer position. Accepted values range from 0 to 100, where 0 places the pointer at the far left and 100 places the pointer at the far right.

- *A simple flashing light.* The color and flash rate are adjustable. The set function is used to adjust the flash rate. A flash rate < 0 turns the light on. A flash rate = 0 turns the light off. A flash rate > 0 is the flash delay in seconds.

- *A toggle switch.* The switch may be toggled with mouse clicks. The on/off state of the switch may be read.

- *A push button switch.* The switch may be pushed with mouse clicks. The on/off state of the switch may be read.

- *A bar graph or VU meter.* The maximum number of bars and the bar color are adjustable. The set function is used to set the percentage of the bars displayed. Accepted values range from 0 to 100, where 0 is no bars and 100 is the maximum number of bars.

Each control and display will be described by a class. The various constants and classes are declared in the dashboard.h file. The implementation code is in dashboard.cpp. The files may be included into a project as is, or only the desired classes may be copied and used in a project. If changes are made to the textures, be sure to update the corresponding constants in dashboard.h. Each control is displayed with the draw function. Some of the controls have specialized draw functions and some use the draw function inherited from the Image class.

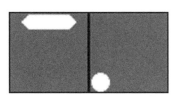

Figure 9.14. The textures used to create the seven-segment display.

9.8.1 Seven-Segment Display

The seven-segment display is drawn by using two simple bitmap images (see Figure 9.14). One image is used to draw each segment and the other is used to draw the decimal point.

The initialize function, in the dashboard.cpp file, sets the screen location, scale, number of digits, and color (Listing 9.37).

```
//=============================================================================
// Initialize the seven-segment display
// Pre: *graphics = pointer to Graphics object
//      *textureM = pointer to TextureManager object
//      left, top = screen location
//      scale = scaling (zoom) amount
//      digits = number of digits
//      color = color of digits
// Post: returns true on success, false on error
//=============================================================================
bool SevenSegment::initialize(Graphics *graphics, TextureManager *textureM,
                    int left, int top, float scale, UINT digs,
                    COLOR_ARGB color)
```

```
{
    try {
        Image::initialize(graphics, dashboardNS::IMAGE_SIZE,
        dashboardNS::IMAGE_SIZE, dashboardNS::TEXTURE_COLS, textureM);
        setCurrentFrame(dashboardNS::SEGMENT_FRAME);
        spriteData.x = (float)left;
        spriteData.y = (float)top;
        spriteData.scale = scale;
        colorFilter = color;
        if(digs < 1)
            digs = 1;
        digits = digs;
        decimal.initialize(graphics, dashboardNS::IMAGE_SIZE,
                           dashboardNS::IMAGE_SIZE,
                           dashboardNS::TEXTURE_COLS, textureM);
        decimal.setCurrentFrame(dashboardNS::DECIMAL_FRAME);
        decimal.setColorFilter(color);
    }
    catch(...)
    {
        return false;
    }
    // Return okay
    return true;
}
```

Listing 9.37. The `SevenSegment` class `initialize` function.

The segments in a real seven-segment display are usually referred to with letters. "A" is the top segment, "B" is the vertical segment to the right of "A," etc. The diagram in the example code in Listing 9.38 identifies the letter of each segment. We have used the typical lettering sequence in our `drawDigit` function. The `drawDigit` function receives the character to display and segment color as parameters. Each segment position is tested to see if it should be displayed as part of the current character. Before a segment is displayed, it is rotated and positioned.

```
//=============================================================================
// Display 7 segment digit 0-9, and -
//          A
//        -----
//      F|     |B
//       |  G  |
//        -----
//      E|     |C
//       |  D  |
//        -----
//=============================================================================
void SevenSegment::drawDigit(char n, COLOR_ARGB color)
{
    float lowerY = spriteData.y + spriteData.height * spriteData.scale * 0.75f;
    float saveY = spriteData.y;
    // Segment A
    if(n=='0' || n=='2' || n=='3' || n=='5' || n=='6' || n=='7' || n=='8'
       || n=='9')
    {
        setDegrees(0);
```

```
        Image::draw(color);
    }
    // Segment B
    if(n=='0' || n=='1' || n=='2' || n=='3' || n=='4' || n=='7' || n=='8'
       || n=='9')
    {
        setDegrees(90);
        Image::draw(color);
    }
    // Segment G
    if(n=='-' || n=='2' || n=='3' || n=='4' || n=='5' || n=='6' || n=='8'
       || n=='9')
    {
        setDegrees(180);
        Image::draw(color);
    }
    // If segment F
    if(n=='0' || n=='4' || n=='5' || n=='6' || n=='8' || n=='9')
    {
        setDegrees(270);
        Image::draw(color);
    }
    spriteData.y = lowerY;  // Set Y for lower half of digit
    // If segment E
    if(n=='0' || n=='2' || n=='6' || n=='8')
    {
        setDegrees(270);
        Image::draw(color);
    }
    // If segment D
    if(n=='0' || n=='2' || n=='3' || n=='5' || n=='6' || n=='8' || n=='9')
    {
        setDegrees(180);
        Image::draw(color);
    }
    // If segment C
    if(n=='0'||n=='1'||n=='3'||n=='4'||n=='5'||n=='6'||n=='7'||n=='8'
       ||n=='9')
    {
        setDegrees(90);
        Image::draw(color);
    }
    spriteData.y = saveY;
}
```

Listing 9.38. The `drawDigit` function from the `SevenSegment` class.

```
//=============================================================================
// Draw the decimal point
//=============================================================================
void SevenSegment::drawDecimal(COLOR_ARGB color)
{
    float saveX = spriteData.x;
    float saveY = spriteData.y;
```

```
    setDegrees(0);
    spriteData.x -= spriteData.width * spriteData.scale * 0.25f;
    spriteData.y += spriteData.height * spriteData.scale * 0.80f;
    decimal.draw(spriteData, color);
    spriteData.x = saveX;
    spriteData.y = saveY;
}
```

Listing 9.39. The drawDecimal function from the SevenSegment class.

```
//=============================================================================
// Set the number on the seven-segment display
//=============================================================================
void SevenSegment::set(double value)
{
    number = value;
}
```

Listing 9.40. The set function from the SevenSegment class.

The SevenSegment::drawDecimal function displays the decimal point in the specified color (Listing 9.39). The set function is used to set the number on the seven-segment display (Listing 9.40).

The SevenSegment::draw function displays the contents of the number variable using the seven-segment display. The number variable is converted to a fixed-point string using a stringstream. The string is displayed by digits until all of the digits have been displayed or the display is full (Listing 9.41).

```
//=============================================================================
// Draw the Seven Segment display
// The number variable contains float value to display
//=============================================================================
void SevenSegment::draw(COLOR_ARGB color)
{
    float saveX = spriteData.x;
    float saveY = spriteData.y;
    char ch;
    if(digits == 0)
        return;
    // Convert number to string
    std::stringstream strstm;
    strstm.precision(digits);
    strstm.flags(std::ios_base::fixed);
    strstm << number;          // Convert number to string
    std::string str = strstm.str();
    UINT digitN = str.length(); // Get digits in string
    if (digitN > digits)        // If string has more digits than 7-seg display
        digitN = digits;
```

```
        // The x location of left-most digit
        spriteData.x += spriteData.width * spriteData.scale * 1.2f *
                        (digits - digitN);
        UINT n=0;
        ch = str.at(n++);              // Get first digit from number
        while(digitN > 0)              // While digits remain to be displayed
        {
            if(ch == '.')              // If decimal point
                drawDecimal(color);
            else
            {
                drawDigit(ch, color);    // Display digit
                // Next digit position onscreen
                spriteData.x += spriteData.width * spriteData.scale * 1.2f;
            }
            if(n < str.length())
                ch = str.at(n++);       // Get next digit
            else
                ch = '0';              // If string ends with '.' pad with 0 digit
            if(ch != '.')              // If not decimal point
                digitN--;              // Decrement digit count
        }
        spriteData.x = saveX;
}
```

Listing 9.41. The `draw` function from the `SevenSegment` class.

9.8.2 Bar

A *progress bar* is a typical description of a Windows control that displays a single bar that varies in length in response to changes in an input value. Progress bars have many uses in games. A simple bar is a good way to display a player's health or shield strength. We could give our progress bar some real character by replacing the simple bitmap of a rectangle with a picture of a sword or stalk of corn if we wanted a progress bar for a weapon upgrade or for resource gathering, and so forth.

The bar gauge `initialize` function sets the screen location, scale, and bar color (Listing 9.42).

```
//=============================================================================
// Initialize the Bar
// Pre: *graphics = pointer to Graphics object
//      *textureM = pointer to TextureManager object
//      left, top = screen location
//      scale = scaling (zoom) amount
//      color = color of bar
// Post: returns true on success, false on error
//=============================================================================
bool Bar::initialize(Graphics *graphics, TextureManager *textureM, int
                     left, int top, float scale, COLOR_ARGB color)
{
    try {
```

```
        Image::initialize(graphics, dashboardNS::IMAGE_SIZE,
                           dashboardNS::IMAGE_SIZE,
                           dashboardNS::TEXTURE_COLS, textureM);
        setCurrentFrame(dashboardNS::BAR_FRAME);
        spriteData.x = (float)left;
        spriteData.y = (float)top;
        spriteData.scale = scale;
        colorFilter = color;
    }
    catch(...)
    {
        return false;
    }
    // Return okay
    return true;
}
```

Listing 9.42. The `initialize` function from the `Bar` class.

The length of the bar is adjusted with the `set` function. The `set` function works by changing `spriteData.rect.right`. Recall that `spriteData.rect` is used by the `Graphics::drawSprite` function to select the portion of the bitmap image to display. By changing `spriteData.rect.right`, we have a bar that is fixed at the left edge and has a moving right edge. If we wanted the right edge to be fixed and the left edge to move, we could rotate it by 180 degrees with the `setDegrees` function. The vertical bar is created by rotating the bar with the `setDegrees` function. Rotating 90 degrees produces a vertical bar that is fixed at the top and has a moving bottom edge, while rotating 270 degrees produces a vertical bar that is fixed at the bottom and has a moving top edge (Listing 9.43).

```
//============================================================================
// Set the Bar size
//============================================================================
void Bar::set(float p)
{
    if (p < 0)
        p = 0;
    else if(p > 100)
        p = 100;
    spriteData.rect.right = spriteData.rect.left +
                            (LONG)(spriteData.width*p/100);
}
```

Listing 9.43. The `set` function from the `Bar` class is used to set the length of the bar.

9.8.3 Dial Gauge

The dial gauge has three possible dial types: a 360-degree dial, a 270-degree dial, and a 180-degree dial. The screen location, scale, type of dial, zero angle, dial color, and pointer color are specified in the `initialize` function. The dial is rotated clockwise by `zeroAngle` degrees. The valid dial types are defined in `dashboardNS` as `DIAL360`, `DIAL270`, or `DIAL180` (Listing 9.44).

```cpp
//==============================================================================
// Initialize Dial Gauge
// Pre: *graphics = pointer to Graphics object
//      *textureM = pointer to TextureManager object
//      left, top = screen location
//      scale = scaling (zoom) amount
//      type = dial type
//      zeroAngle = where zero is on dial
//      dialColor = color of dial
//      pointerColor = color of pointer
// Post: returns true on success, false on error
//==============================================================================
bool DialGauge::initialize(Graphics *graphics, TextureManager *textureM,
                           int left, int top, float scale,
                           dashboardNS::DialType type, float zeroAngle,
                           COLOR_ARGB dialColor, COLOR_ARGB
                           pointerColor)
{
    try {
        Image::initialize(graphics, dashboardNS::IMAGE_SIZE,
                          dashboardNS::IMAGE_SIZE,
                          dashboardNS::TEXTURE_COLS, textureM);
        dialType = type;
        switch(type)
        {
        case dashboardNS::DIAL360:
            setCurrentFrame(dashboardNS::DIAL360_FRAME); break;
        case dashboardNS::DIAL270:
            setCurrentFrame(dashboardNS::DIAL270_FRAME); break;
        case dashboardNS::DIAL180:
            setCurrentFrame(dashboardNS::DIAL180_FRAME); break;
        }
        spriteData.x = (float)left;
        spriteData.y = (float)top;
        spriteData.scale = scale;
        colorFilter = dialColor;
        setDegrees(zeroAngle);
        pointer.initialize(graphics, dashboardNS::IMAGE_SIZE,
                           dashboardNS::IMAGE_SIZE,
                           dashboardNS::TEXTURE_COLS, textureM);
        pointer.setCurrentFrame(dashboardNS::POINTER_FRAME);
        pointer.setColorFilter(pointerColor);
    }
    catch(...)
    {
        return false;
    }
    // Return okay
    return true;
}
```

Listing 9.44. The `initialize` function from the `DialGauge` class.

The `set` function positions the pointer on the dial gauge. A value of 0 sets the pointer to the 0 position and a value of 100 sets the pointer to the maximum position. The pointer rotates clockwise from 0 to 100 (Listing 9.45). The `draw` function is overloaded to draw the dial and the pointer (Listing 9.46).

```
//===========================================================================
// Set the DialGauge pointer
//===========================================================================
void DialGauge::set(float p)
{
    if (p < 0)
        p = 0;
    else if(p > 100)
        p = 100;
    switch(dialType)
    {
    case dashboardNS::DIAL360:
        pointer.setDegrees(p * 360/100.0f + getDegrees()); break;
    case dashboardNS::DIAL270:
        pointer.setDegrees(p * 270/100.0f + getDegrees() - 135); break;
    case dashboardNS::DIAL180:
        pointer.setDegrees(p * 180/100.0f + getDegrees() - 90); break;
    }
}
```

Listing 9.45. The `set` function from the `DialGuage` class is used to set the position of the pointer.

```
//===========================================================================
// Draw the DialGauge and pointer
//===========================================================================
void DialGauge::draw(COLOR_ARGB color)
{
    Image::draw(color);
    float dialAngle = spriteData.angle;
    spriteData.angle = pointer.getRadians();
    pointer.draw(spriteData, graphicsNS::FILTER);
    spriteData.angle = dialAngle;
}
```

Listing 9.46. The `draw` function from the `DialGauge` class.

9.8.4 Light

The light can be on, off, or flashing. The `initialize` function sets the screen location, scale, flash rate, color of the light when on, and color of the light when off (Listing 9.47). The `set` function changes the flash rate. A negative flash rate turns the light on. A flash rate of 0 turns the light off. A flash rate that is greater than 0 sets the number of flashes per second (Listing 9.48).

```
//=============================================================================
// Initialize the Light
// Pre: *graphics = pointer to Graphics object
//      *textureM = pointer to TextureManager object
//      left, top = screen location
//      scale = scaling (zoom) amount
//      flashRate = on/off/flash delay, <0 On, =0 Off, >0 flashes per second
//      colorOn = the color of the light when on
//      colorOff = the color of the light when off
// Post: returns true on success, false on error
//=============================================================================
bool Light::initialize(Graphics *graphics, TextureManager *textureM,
                       int left, int top, float scale, float flashRate,
                       COLOR_ARGB colorOn, COLOR_ARGB colorOff)
{
    try {
        Image::initialize(graphics, dashboardNS::IMAGE_SIZE,
                          dashboardNS::IMAGE_SIZE,
                          dashboardNS::TEXTURE_COLS, textureM);
        setCurrentFrame(dashboardNS::LIGHT_FRAME);
        spriteData.x = (float)left;
        spriteData.y = (float)top;
        spriteData.scale = scale;
        colorFilter = colorOff;
        offColor = colorOff;
        onColor = colorOn;
        if(flashRate > 0)
            flashDelay = flashRate/2.0f;     // 50 % duty cycle
        else
            flashDelay = flashRate;
    }
    catch(...)
    {
        return false;
    }
    // Return okay
    return true;
}
```

Listing 9.47. The `initialize` function from the `Light` class.

```
//=============================================================================
// Set flashRate: <0 On, =0 Off, >0 cycle rate
//=============================================================================
void Light::set(float flashRate)
{
    if(flashRate > 0)
        flashDelay = flashRate/2.0f;     // 50% duty cycle
    else
        flashDelay = flashRate;
}
```

Listing 9.48. The `set` function from the `Light` class is used to change the flash rate.

The `update` function flashes the light by changing the value of the `colorFilter` variable to the on or off color (Listing 9.49).

```cpp
//=============================================================================
// Update the light
//=============================================================================
void Light::update(float frameTime)
{
    if(flashDelay > 0)   // >0 flashing light
    {
        flashTimer += frameTime;
        if(flashTimer >= flashDelay)
        {
            flashTimer -= flashDelay;
            if(colorFilter == onColor)
                colorFilter = offColor;
            else
                colorFilter = onColor;
        }
    }
}
```

Listing 9.49. The `update` function from the `Light` class.

9.8.5 Toggle Switch

The toggle switch may be on or off. The screen location and scale are set in the `initialize` function. The `initialize` function also receives a pointer to the `Input` object and a handle to the window so mouse clicks may be processed (Listing 9.50).

```cpp
//=============================================================================
// Initialize the toggle switch
// Pre: *graphics = pointer to Graphics object
//      *textureM = pointer to TextureManager object
//      *in = pointer to Input object
//      hwnd = handle to window
//      left, top = screen location
//      scale = scaling (zoom) amount
// Post: returns true on success, false on error
//=============================================================================
bool ToggleSwitch::initialize(Graphics *graphics, TextureManager *textureM,
                              Input *in, HWND h, int left, int top, float
                              scale)
{
    try {
        Image::initialize(graphics, dashboardNS::IMAGE_SIZE,
                          dashboardNS::IMAGE_SIZE,
                          dashboardNS::TEXTURE_COLS, textureM);
        setCurrentFrame(dashboardNS::SWITCH_OFF_FRAME);
        spriteData.x = (float)left;
        spriteData.y = (float)top;
```

```
            spriteData.scale = scale;
            hwnd = h;                        // Handle to the window
            input = in;                      // The input object
            switchRect.left = left;
            switchRect.top  = top;
            switchRect.right = (long)(left + (dashboardNS::SWITCH_WIDTH *
                                          spriteData.scale));
            switchRect.bottom = (long)(top + (spriteData.height *
                                          spriteData.scale));
        }
    catch(...)
    {
        return false;
    }
    // Return okay
    return true;
}
```

Listing 9.50. The `initialize` function from the `ToggleSwitch` class.

The `update` function checks for mouse clicks on the button. The current window size is compared to the desired game window size and saved as `screenRatioX` and `screenRatioY`. If the left mouse button is clicked, the mouse coordinates are adjusted by the screen ratios and compared with the edges of the button rectangle. A click inside the button changes the state of the `switchOn` Boolean (Listing 9.51).

```
//=============================================================================
// Checks for mouse click on switch
//=============================================================================
void ToggleSwitch::update(float frameTime)
{
    if (!initialized || !visible)
        return;
    // Calculate screen ratios in case window was resized
    RECT clientRect;
    GetClientRect(hwnd, &clientRect);
    float screenRatioX = (float)GAME_WIDTH / clientRect.right;
    float screenRatioY = (float)GAME_HEIGHT / clientRect.bottom;
    if (input->getMouseLButton())          // If mouse left button
    {
        // If mouse clicked inside switch
        if (input->getMouseX()*screenRatioX >= switchRect.left &&
            input->getMouseX()*screenRatioX <= switchRect.right &&
            input->getMouseY()*screenRatioY >= switchRect.top &&
            input->getMouseY()*screenRatioY <= switchRect.bottom)
        {
            if(mouseClick)
            {
                mouseClick = false;
                switchOn = !switchOn;       // Toggle the switch
                if(switchOn)
                    setCurrentFrame(dashboardNS::SWITCH_ON_FRAME);
                else
```

```
                    setCurrentFrame(dashboardNS::SWITCH_OFF_FRAME);
                }
            }
        } else
            mouseClick = true;
}
```

Listing 9.51 The update function from the ToggleSwitch class.

The on/off state of the switch may be read with the getSwitchOn function and may be set with the setSwitch function (Listing 9.52).

```
// Get switch state
bool getSwitchOn()    {return switchOn;}
// Set switch state
void setSwitch(bool on) {switchOn = on;}
```

Listing 9.52. Functions to read or set the state of the toggle switch.

9.8.6 Push Button

The push button switch may be a momentary type (default) or toggle type. The initialize function sets the screen location, scale, and type. The initialize function also receives a pointer to the Input object and a handle to the window so mouse clicks may be processed. In our example, the push button is scaled to one-half its normal size (Listing 9.53).

```
//=============================================================================
// Initialize the push button
// Pre: *graphics = pointer to Graphics object
//      *textureM = pointer to TextureManager object
//      *in = pointer to Input object
//      hwnd = handle to window
//      left, top = screen location
//      scale = scaling (zoom) amount
//      type = true for momentary, false for toggle
// Post: returns true on success, false on error
//=============================================================================
bool PushButton::initialize(Graphics *graphics, TextureManager *textureM,
                            Input *in, HWND h, int left, int top, float
                            scale, bool type)
{
    try {
        Image::initialize(graphics, dashboardNS::IMAGE_SIZE,
                          dashboardNS::IMAGE_SIZE,
                          dashboardNS::TEXTURE_COLS, textureM);
        setCurrentFrame(dashboardNS::BUTTON_UP_FRAME);
        spriteData.x = (float)left;
        spriteData.y = (float)top;
```

```
        spriteData.scale = scale;
        hwnd = h;                               // Handle to the window
        input = in;                             // The input object
        switchRect.left = left;
        switchRect.top  = top;
        switchRect.right = (long)(left + spriteData.width *
                                        spriteData.scale);
        switchRect.bottom = (long)(top + spriteData.height *
                                        spriteData.scale);

        momentary = type;
    }
    catch(...)
    {
        return false;
    }
    // Return okay
    return true;
}
```

Listing 9.53. The <code>initialize</code> function from the <code>PushButton</code> class.

The update function checks for mouse clicks on the button. The current window size is compared to the desired game window size and saved as screenRatioX and screenRatioY. If the left mouse button is down, the mouse coordinates are adjusted by the screen ratios and compared with the edges of the button rectangle. A click inside the button sets the switchOn Boolean to true for a momentary switch or to the opposite state for a toggle switch. If the mouse button is not pressed and the switch type is momentary, the switchOn Boolean is set to false and the current frame is set to BUTTON_UP_FRAME (Listing 9.54).

```
//=============================================================================
// Checks for mouse click on pushbutton
//=============================================================================
void PushButton::update(float frameTime)
{
    if (!initialized || !visible)
        return;
    // Calculate screen ratios incase window was resized
    RECT clientRect;
    GetClientRect(hwnd, &clientRect);
    float screenRatioX = (float)GAME_WIDTH / clientRect.right;
    float screenRatioY = (float)GAME_HEIGHT / clientRect.bottom;
    if (input->getMouseLButton())              // If mouse left button
    {
        // If mouse clicked inside switch
        if (input->getMouseX()*screenRatioX >= switchRect.left &&
            input->getMouseX()*screenRatioX <= switchRect.right &&
            input->getMouseY()*screenRatioY >= switchRect.top &&
            input->getMouseY()*screenRatioY <= switchRect.bottom)
        {
            if(mouseClick)
            {
```

```
                    mouseClick = false;
                    if(momentary)                 // If momentary switch
                        switchOn = true;
                    else
                        switchOn = !switchOn;   // Toggle the switch
                    if(switchOn)
                        setCurrentFrame(dashboardNS::BUTTON_DOWN_FRAME);
                    else
                        setCurrentFrame(dashboardNS::BUTTON_UP_FRAME);
                }
            }
        }
        else
        {
            mouseClick = true;
            if(momentary)
            {
                switchOn = false;
                setCurrentFrame(dashboardNS::BUTTON_UP_FRAME);
            }
        }
    }
}
```

Listing 9.54. The update function from the PushButton class.

9.8.7 Bar Graph

The bar graph, which is sometimes referred to as a VU meter, displays a sequence of bars
from 0 to the maximum number. The screen location, scale, number of bars in the meter,
and bar color is specified in the initialize function (Listing 9.55).

```
//================================================================================================
// Initialize the Bar Graph
// Pre: *graphics = pointer to Graphics object
//      *textureM = pointer to TextureManager object
//      left, top = screen location
//      scale = scaling (zoom) amount
//      bars = number of bars in meter
//      color = color of bars
// Post: returns true on success, false on error
//================================================================================================
bool BarGraph::initialize(Graphics *graphics, TextureManager *textureM,
                          int left, int top, float scale, UINT bars,
                          COLOR_ARGB color)
{
    try {
        Image::initialize(graphics, dashboardNS::IMAGE_SIZE,
                          dashboardNS::IMAGE_SIZE,
                          dashboardNS::TEXTURE_COLS, textureM);
        setCurrentFrame(dashboardNS::BAR_GRAPH_FRAME);
        spriteData.x = (float)left;
        spriteData.y = (float)top;
        spriteData.scale = scale;
```

```
            colorFilter = color;
        if(maxBars > 0)
            maxBars = bars;
    }
    catch(...)
    {
        return false;
    }
    // Return okay
    return true;
}
```

Listing 9.55. The `initialize` function from the `BarGraph` class.

The percentage of visible bars is changed with the `set` function. Valid percentages range from 0 through 100, where 0 turns off all of the bars and 100 turns them all on (Listing 9.56). The bar graph overrides the `draw` function to display the number of bars specified in the `barsOn` variable (Listing 9.57).

The "Dashboard" demo example (Figure 9.13) displays all of the various controls. The `update` function in `dashboardDemo.cpp` demonstrates how to read the state of the switches and adjust the display properties of the other controls (Listing 9.58).

```
//=============================================================================
// Set barsOn count to the number of bars to display
// The parameter p is a percent from 0 to 100
//=============================================================================
void BarGraph::set(float p)
{
    if (p < 0)
        p = 0;
    else if(p > 100)
        p = 100;
    barsOn = (int)(p * 0.01f * maxBars + 0.5);
}
```

Listing 9.56. The `set` function from the `BarGraph` class.

```
//=============================================================================
// Draw the Bar Graph
// barsOn contains the number of bars to display
//=============================================================================
void BarGraph::draw(COLOR_ARGB color)
{
    float saveX = spriteData.x;
    for (int i=barsOn; i > 0; i--)
    {
        // Next bar position onscreen
        spriteData.x += dashboardNS::BAR_GRAPH_WIDTH * spriteData.scale;
```

```
        Image::draw(color);
    }
    spriteData.x = saveX;
}
```

Listing 9.57. The draw function from the BarGraph class.

```
//============================================================================
// Move all game items
// frameTime is used to regulate the speed of movement
//============================================================================
void DashboardDemo::update()
{
    if(toggleSwitch.getSwitchOn())  // If toggle switch on
    {
        horizontal += frameTime*20; // Increase horizontal
        vertical += frameTime*30;   // Increase vertical
        dial += frameTime*10;       // Increase dial
    }
    if(horizontal > 100)            // Reset when 100 is reached
        horizontal -= 100;
    if(vertical > 100)
        vertical -= 100;
    if(dial > 100)
        dial -= 100;
    horizontalBar.set(horizontal);  // Set horizontal bar size
    verticalBar.set(vertical);      // Set vertical bar size
    dial180.set(dial);              // Set dial positions
    dial270.set(dial);
    dial360.set(dial);
    light.update(frameTime);        // Update the controls
    toggleSwitch.update(frameTime);
    pushButton.update(frameTime);
    sevenSegment.set(fps);          // Display fps in seven segment
    if(pushButton.getSwitchOn())    // If push button switch on
        vu += frameTime*100;        // Increase vu
    if(vu > 100)
        vu -= 100;
    barGraph.set(vu);               // Set bar graph with vu
}
```

Listing 9.58. Reading switch states and adjusting display properties of dashboard controls.

Chapter Review

This chapter was about polish and refinement. We explored several techniques to enhance the appearance of our games. Applying these techniques will add that extra something that separates great games from good. This chapter wasn't just about appearance. We also included something practical when we added a message dialog to our game engine. Some of the key topics from the chapter are the following:

- *Continuous background.* Scrolling images that seamlessly wrap at the edges to provide a continuous background.

- *Simulating depth.* The painter's algorithm helps us simulate depth with 2D graphics.

- *Parallax scrolling.* Parallax scrolling uses different movement speeds for distant objects to further enhance the appearance of depth.

- *Shadows and reflections.* Shadows and reflections not only look good but they can be helpful to players in determining object positions.

- *Displaying messages.* A modal message dialog in the game engine provides an always-available way to display messages to the player.

- *Dashboard elements.* The `Dashboard` class contains several dashboard elements that we can use to create a user interface in our games.

Review Questions

1. What characteristics are important when choosing a picture that will be used to create a scrolling background that wraps the image horizontally and vertically?

2. With a scrolling background, if the spaceship is flying to the right, what direction does the background move?

3. How many drawing scenarios must be considered when drawing a scrolling background image?

4. Describe the painter's algorithm.

5. With parallax scrolling, which objects move faster on the screen: those that are closer to the viewer or those that are farther away? Why?

6. How does the positioning of a shadow and reflection differ?

7. What possible player benefit would a shadow provide?

8. The message dialog we added to the game engine is a modal dialog. What are the properties of a modal dialog?

9. Write one line of code that would display the message "Hello World" in the message dialog.

10. What does the "seven" refer to in "seven-segment display"?

11. Which function is used to change the number on the seven-segment display?

12. The bar graph has one moving edge. How many degrees of rotation would need to be applied to a bar graph for it to have a moving left edge?

13. What could we do to transform the simple bar graph into a graph that represented a weapon upgrade status?

14. What are the three possible dial types of dial gauges?

15. What is the valid range of values to use when setting the pointer position of a dial gauge?

16. What is the zero angle property of the dial gauge used for?

17. What value of the `flashRate` property for the dashboard light will set it to flash five times per second?

18. Which function is used to read the state of the dashboard toggle switch?

19. The push button defaults to a momentary type, which means as soon as the mouse button is released, the switch opens. How do we configure the push button to be a toggle switch?

20. What are the valid range of numbers that may be used to set the number of bars in the bar graph?

Exercises

1. Modify the "Scrolling Bitmap" example to use your own background image.

2. Combine the techniques from parallax scrolling with the "Scrolling Bitmap" example. Add a second background image of stars that is drawn on top of the space background. Make the stars image scroll at a faster speed than the background image to increase the illusion of depth.

3. Create a program that contains one seven-segment display and one momentary push button. Display the number of button clicks on the seven-segment display.

4. Add a second plane to the "Shadow" demo. (Hint: The shadows for both planes must be drawn before the planes are drawn.)

Examples

The following examples are available for download from www.programming2dgames.com.

- *Scrolling Bitmap.* A spaceship remains in the center of the screen as the stars behind it scroll.

  - Demonstrates scrolling an image that wraps around at the edges to allow infinite scrolling in any direction.

- *Parallax Scroll.* A spaceship remains in the center of the screen. The planets behind the ship and the stars scroll at different speeds to provide the illusion of depth.

  - Demonstrates parallax scrolling to create the illusion of depth.

- *Shadow.* An airplane flies over the ocean with its shadow visible on the surface of the water.

  – Demonstrates using alpha transparency to create a shadow.

- *Reflection.* An airplane flies over the ocean with its reflection visible on the surface of the water.

  – Demonstrates using alpha transparency to create a reflection.

- *Message Dialog Demo.* A message dialog is displayed on the screen with a test message and an "OK" button. Clicking a button or pressing the "Enter" key closes the dialog.

  – Demonstrates how to display the message dialog.

- *Input Dialog Demo.* An input dialog is displayed on the screen with a message and a text input region. Entering the word "next" displays a second dailog.

  – Demonstrates how to use the input dialog.

- *Dashboard Demo.* A dashboard of gauges is displayed.

  – Demonstrates how to display each dashboard element.

10 Tiled Games

In this chapter, we examine tiled games. Tiled games play on a map comprised of individual tiles. Each tile contains all or part of an image (see Figure 10.1). The tiles are arranged to form the game world, or *map,* as we will refer to it (Figure 10.2).

Many of the "platform" games on the various game consoles use tiles. Tiled games come in several forms including side scroll, top-down, and isometric view. We will begin by examining the advantages of a tiled game. Then we will explore how to create tile sets and edit game maps. Lastly, we will see how to draw our tiled game screen in different ways. By the end of this chapter, readers will be able to create their own platform-style games.

▮▮ 10.1 Why Tiled?

Defining a map comprised of individual tiles is simply a matter of assigning a number to represent each tile and arranging the numbers to form the map. The maps may be any size we wish with only the currently visible portion displayed on the screen. By reusing tiles, we are able to create very large maps with limited textures. This makes tile-based games a good choice for developing games on platforms that have limited memory, such as some of the hand-held gaming devices.

Our tiles from Figure 10.1 may be defined using the numbers in Figure 10.3. These numbers are the same way we identified individual textures in a larger texture image in previous chapters. That will allow us to select an individual tile image using the same code we have already written to select a texture.

The tiles are arranged into a map that looks like the array in Figure 10.4. We can clearly see in Figure 10.4 that a simple array of numbers is all that is required to represent our entire game world.

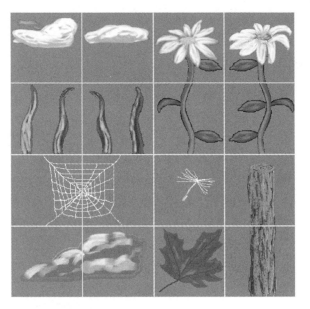

Figure 10.1. The textures used for game tiles.

Figure 10.2. Individual tiles arranged to create a game world.

	0		1			12	13				0	
						11						
		2				15	3				3	2
5	4	5	6	4	4	5	15	4	7	5		14	5	7	6

Figure 10.4. The tile numbers arranged to form a map.

0	1	2	3
4	5	6	7
8	9	10	11
12	13	14	15

Figure 10.3. Numbers used to represent each tile.

Building our game world with numbered tiles presents us with some interesting possibilities, such as changing the background by doing a simple tile substitution; adding random elements to the background; creating the entire game world dynamically; using multiple tile layers with parallax scrolling; and using the tile numbers to determine different player interactions.

10.2 Creating a Tile Set

Tiles may be used over and over, so an important point to consider when creating a tile is how it will appear when drawn next to itself and next to any other tiles. If an image spans multiple tiles, we need to make sure the edges line up correctly.

Each tile is simply a texture, so any tools used to create game textures may be used to create tiles. There are applications dedicated to the creation of game tiles. One example can be found at http://tilestudio.sourceforge.net/.

Thanks to the generosity of some talented artists, there are some free tile sets available on the Internet, such as this great looking set by *Yar*, available at http://opengameart.org/content/isometric-64x64-outside-tileset; the artwork (see Figure 10.5) can be distributed under the Creative Commons license http://creativecommons.org/licenses/by/3.0/.

10.3 Creating Levels

Arranging the tiles into a map or level may be done manually or with the aid of a map editor. Once again, talented programmers have shared their work for our benefit. Here is a partial list of some free map editors:

- http://www.mapeditor.org/

- http://tilemap.co.uk/mappy.php

- http://tilemapeditor.com/

- http://www.codeproject.com/KB/edit/TileEditor.aspx

For the examples in this chapter, we will simply include the map in the source as a 2D array.

Figure 10.5. Free tile set created by *Yar*.

10.4 Displaying the Tiles

We have several choices when it comes to displaying our tiles. All of the techniques we will examine use parallel projection to create the viewable image. In parallel projection, the projection lines are parallel to each other. They do not converge on a distant point. This results in distant objects and near objects having the same projected size. Typically, the angle of the viewer is such that more distant objects appear higher on the screen. Parallel projection is useful with 2D rendering techniques because it is not necessary to change the size of objects as their distance from the viewer changes.

▮ 10.5 Orthogonal Projection

The map of the flowers and grass in Figure 10.2 is drawn using *orthogonal projection*. Orthogonal projection is a type of parallel projection where the projection lines are orthogonal (perpendicular) to the screen. This is the type of projection used for "top down" and "side scroll" games.

The `render` function gets the tile number from the map and displays the appropriate tile image at the correct screen position. Notice that we are able to reuse the `setCurrentFrame` function to set the texture for a tile (Listing 10.1).

Two nested `for` loops are used to access each tile in the map. If a tile is present at the current map coordinate, the tile texture is set by calling `tile.setCurrentFrame(tile Map[row][col])`. The `tile.setX((float)(col*TEXTURE_SIZE) + mapX)` function call sets the tile's *x* screen coordinate to the current column number times the texture size of each tile plus the *x* offset of the map. The tile's *x* position is checked to determine if the tile is currently visible. If the tile is visible, it is drawn with a call to `tile.draw()`.

```
//=============================================================================
// Render game items
//=============================================================================
void FlowerPower::render()
{
    graphics->spriteBegin();
    for(int row=0; row<MAP_HEIGHT; row++)      // For each row of map
    {
        tile.setY( (float)(row*TEXTURE_SIZE) );  // Set tile Y
        for(int col=0; col<MAP_WIDTH; col++)    // For each column of map
        {
            if(tileMap[row][col] >= 0)          // If tile present
            {
                tile.setCurrentFrame(tileMap[row][col]);      // Set tile
                                                              // texture
                tile.setX( (float)(col*TEXTURE_SIZE) + mapX );// Set tile X
                // If tile onscreen
                if(tile.getX() > -TEXTURE_SIZE && tile.getX() < GAME_WIDTH)
                    tile.draw();                // Draw tile
            }
        }
    }
    // Draw butterfly
    butterfly.draw();
    if(menuOn)
        menu.draw();
    graphics->spriteEnd();
}
```

Listing 10.1. The `render` function from the `FlowerPower` class.

Our little example program "FlowerPower" includes an animated butterfly. The butterfly may be controlled with the arrow keys. If the butterfly reaches the right edge of the screen, the map will scroll to the left until the end of the map is reached. Likewise, if the butterfly reaches the left edge of the screen, the map will scroll to the right. The code that moves the butterfly is in `butterfly.cpp` and looks like Listing 10.2.

The butterfly texture contains a sequence of images of the butterfly facing to the right (Figure 10.6). It was created using a simple paint program. The wings were drawn once and scaled vertically to create the different images before pasting them to the butterfly's body. To make the butterfly fly to the left, we flip the image horizontally in our code (see the highlighted lines of code in Listing 10.2).

The butterfly's `update` function is called from the `FlowerPower`'s `update` function, which then scrolls the map left or right based on the current position of the butterfly (Listing 10.3).

```
//=============================================================================
// Update
// Typically called once per frame
// frameTime is used to regulate the speed of movement and animation
//=============================================================================
void Butterfly::update(float frameTime)
{
    Entity::update(frameTime);
    if (input->isKeyDown(UP_KEY))          // If up arrow
    {
        spriteData.y = spriteData.y - frameTime * CLIMB_RATE;
        if (spriteData.y < 0)
            spriteData.y = 0;
    }
    if (input->isKeyDown(DOWN_KEY))        // If decrease altitude
    {
        spriteData.y = spriteData.y + frameTime * DROP_RATE;
        if (spriteData.y > GAME_HEIGHT - HEIGHT)
            spriteData.y = GAME_HEIGHT - HEIGHT;
    }
    if (input->isKeyDown(LEFT_KEY))        // If left
    {
        this->flipHorizontal(true);
        velocity.x -= frameTime * SPEED;
        if(velocity.x < -MAX_SPEED)
            velocity.x = -MAX_SPEED;
    }
    if (input->isKeyDown(RIGHT_KEY))       // If right
    {
        this->flipHorizontal(false);
        velocity.x += frameTime * SPEED;
        if(velocity.x > MAX_SPEED)
            velocity.x = MAX_SPEED;
    }
    spriteData.x += velocity.x * frameTime;
}
```

Listing 10.2. The `update` function from the `Butterfly` class.

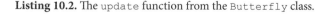

Figure 10.6. Texture image of an animated butterfly.

```
//==============================================================================
// Update all game items
//==============================================================================
void FlowerPower::update()
{
    float butterflyX;
    if (menuOn)
    {
        if (input->anyKeyPressed())
        {
            menuOn = false;
            input->clearAll();
        }
    }
    butterfly.update(frameTime);        // Fly the butterfly
    butterflyX = butterfly.getX();
    if(butterflyX < 0)                  // If butterfly offscreen left
    {
        mapX -= butterfly.getVelocity().x * frameTime;  // Scroll map right
        butterfly.setX(0);              // Put butterfly at left edge
    }
    // If butterfly offscreen right
    else if(butterflyX > GAME_WIDTH - butterfly.getWidth())
    {
        mapX -= butterfly.getVelocity().x * frameTime;  // Scroll map left
        // Put butterfly at right edge
        butterfly.setX((float)(GAME_WIDTH - butterfly.getWidth()));
    }
    if(mapX > 0)        // If map past left edge
    {
        mapX = 0;       // Stop at left edge of map
        butterfly.setVelocityX(0);  // Stop butterfly
    }
    // If map past right edge
    else if(mapX < (-MAP_WIDTH * TEXTURE_SIZE) + GAME_WIDTH)
    {
        // Stop at right edge of map
        mapX = (-MAP_WIDTH * TEXTURE_SIZE) + GAME_WIDTH;
        butterfly.setVelocityX(0);  // Stop butterfly
    }
}
```

Listing 10.3. The `update` function from the `FlowerPower` class.

■ 10.6 Oblique Projection

An *oblique projection* is performed by projecting the shapes using parallel projection, where the projection lines are oblique to the screen (Figure 10.7).

Figure 10.8 represents a checkerboard viewed from a player's position using oblique projection. It appears as a rectangle of uniform width but the height is reduced. Note that the squares and the checkers at the top of the board are the same size as those at the bottom.

The drawing order is important. The more distant objects must be drawn first. In our checkerboard, the more distant checkers are those at the top of the board, so we can simply draw the board and checkers from top to bottom and all is well—or is it? Notice the reflections of the checkers on the board. If we simply draw each board square and the checker on it from top to bottom, we will get the result as shown in Figure 10.9(a). Notice the reflections of the bottom checkers are missing. The proper reflections are shown in Figure 10.9(b). In order to achieve this result, we not only need to draw the objects from back to front but also by layer. First, we draw the checkerboard layer followed by the checker layer.

Our drawing order will be to draw the checkerboard layer from back to front then draw the checkers and reflections layer from back to front. It should be noted that the simple technique we are using here to draw the reflections would not have the correct appearance if the reflections from two or more objects were overlapping. The drawing of the checkerboard is performed in the `render` function of the `checkers.cpp` file located in the "Oblique" example (Listing 10.4).

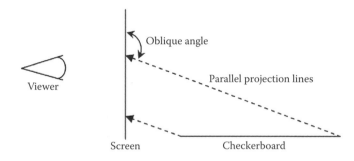

Figure 10.7. Parallel projection lines of oblique projection.

Figure 10.8. An example of oblique projection.

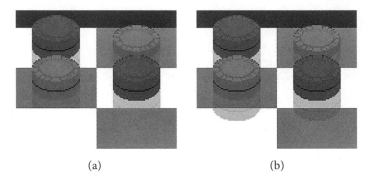

(a)   (b)

Figure 10.9. (a) The checkerboard drawn as one layer obscures the reflections. (b) Drawing the checkerboard layer followed by the reflections and checkers.

```cpp
//===========================================================================
// Render game items
//===========================================================================
void Checkers::render()
{
    float checkerY=0;
    graphics->spriteBegin();
    // Draw checkerboard
    for(int row=0; row<BOARD_SIZE; row++)
    {
        for(int col=0; col<BOARD_SIZE; col++)
        {
            // Orthogonal Grid draw
            boardSquare.setX((float)( BOARD_X + (col*TEXTURE_SIZE) ));
            boardSquare.setY((float)( BOARD_Y + (row*TEXTURE_SIZE/2) ));
            if((row + col)%2)        // Rows and cols are alternating colors
                boardSquare.draw(graphicsNS::GRAY);
            else
                boardSquare.draw(graphicsNS::WHITE);
        }
    }
    // Draw checkers
    for(int row=0; row<BOARD_SIZE; row++)
    {
        for(int col=0; col<BOARD_SIZE; col++)
        {
            checker.setX((float)( BOARD_X + (col*TEXTURE_SIZE) ));
            king.setX((float)( BOARD_X + (col*TEXTURE_SIZE) ));
            checkerY = (float)(BOARD_Y + (row*TEXTURE_SIZE/2) );
            switch(board[row][col])
            {
            case 'r':
                // Draw reflection
                checker.setY((float)(checkerY + TEXTURE_SIZE/7));
                checker.draw(checkersNS::RED_COLOR & graphicsNS::ALPHA25);
                // Draw checker
                checker.setY(checkerY);
                checker.draw(checkersNS::RED_COLOR);
                break;
```

```
        case 'R':
            // Draw reflection
            king.setY((float)(checkerY + TEXTURE_SIZE/4));
            king.draw(checkersNS::RED_COLOR & graphicsNS::ALPHA25);
            // Draw king
            king.setY(checkerY);
            king.draw(checkersNS::RED_COLOR);
            break;
        case 'b':
            // Draw reflection
            checker.setY((float)(checkerY + TEXTURE_SIZE/7));
            checker.draw(checkersNS::BLUE_COLOR & graphicsNS::ALPHA25);
            // Draw checker
            checker.setY(checkerY);
            checker.draw(checkersNS::BLUE_COLOR);
            break;
        case 'B':
            // Draw reflection
            king.setY((float)(checkerY + TEXTURE_SIZE/4));
            king.draw(checkersNS::BLUE_COLOR & graphicsNS::ALPHA25);
            // Draw king
            king.setY(checkerY);
            king.draw(checkersNS::BLUE_COLOR);
            break;
        }
    }
    }
    graphics->spriteEnd();
}
```

Listing 10.4. The `render` function from the `Checkers` class.

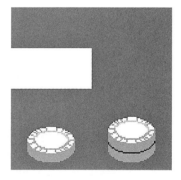

The individual squares of the checkerboard are drawn by specifying the color as `boardSquare.draw( graphicsNS::GRAY )` or `boardSquare.draw( graphicsNS::WHITE )`. The colors of the checkers are also specified in the code. We are using the ability of our `Image` class to apply a color filter to a texture as it is drawn. The textures of the board squares and checkers are drawn in white with gray for shading (Figure 10.10).

The reflection is created by simply drawing the checker image at a lower position on the screen and with an alpha filter value of `graphicsNS::ALPHA25` to make it semitransparent.

Figure 10.10. The texture image used to create the oblique projection checkboard.

▌▌ 10.7 Isometric Projection

An *isometric projection* is performed by using parallel projection with a viewing angle that is the same for the x,y,z-axes. Figure 10.11 shows a checkerboard drawn using isometric projection. The squares and checkers are all the same size. The more distant checkers are those on row 0.

Our checkerboard is drawn using a diamond texture image, as shown in Figure 10.12. The drawing order will once again be by rows, from row 0 through row 7 and by layer, from

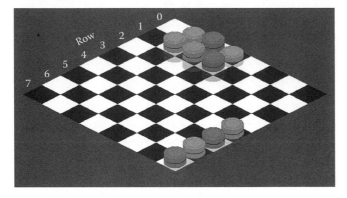

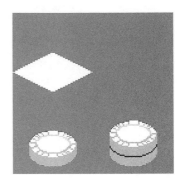

Figure 10.11. A checkerboard drawn using isometric projection.

Figure 10.12. The texture image used to create the isometric projection checkerboard.

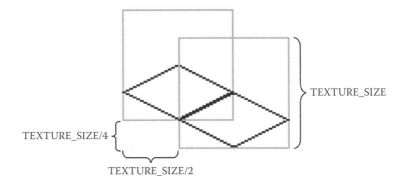

Figure 10.13. The position of each isometric square.

bottom to top. The screen position of each tile is calculated as follows:

$$\text{tile X} = \text{BOARD\_X} - (\text{row*TEXTURE\_SIZE/2}) + (\text{col*TEXTURE\_SIZE/2}),$$
$$\text{tile Y} = \text{BOARD\_Y} + (\text{row*TEXTURE\_SIZE/4}) + (\text{col*TEXTURE\_SIZE/4}),$$

where (`BOARD_X`, `BOARD_Y`) is the screen location of the tile at row 0, column 0.

The formula used to calculate the *x* and *y* tile positions can be explained by observing Figure 10.13. The tile that is drawn one column to the right is located `TEXTURE_SIZE/2` pixels to the right and `TEXTURE_SIZE/4` pixels down from the current tile. The code that draws the checkerboard is in the `render` function in `checkers.cpp` from the "Isometric Diamond" example (Listing 10.5).

```
// Draw checkerboard
for(int row=0; row<BOARD_SIZE; row++)
{
    for(int col=0; col<BOARD_SIZE; col++)
```

```
{
    // Isometric Diamond draw
    if((row + col) % 2)
    {
        boardSquare.setX((float)( BOARD_X -
                            (row*TEXTURE_SIZE/2) +
                            (col*TEXTURE_SIZE/2) ));
        boardSquare.setY((float)( BOARD_Y +
                            (row*TEXTURE_SIZE/4) +
                            (col*TEXTURE_SIZE/4) ));
        boardSquare.draw(graphicsNS::BLACK);
    }
    else
    {
        boardSquare.setX((float)( BOARD_X -
                            (row*TEXTURE_SIZE/2) +
                            (col*TEXTURE_SIZE/2) ));
        boardSquare.setY((float)( BOARD_Y +
                            (row*TEXTURE_SIZE/4) +
                            (col*TEXTURE_SIZE/4) ));
        boardSquare.draw(graphicsNS::WHITE);
    }
    }
}
```

Listing 10.5. The code that draws an isometric checkerboard.

The position of the checkers is determined using the same formula that we used to position the tiles.

10.7.1 Isometric Stagger

If we maintain the diamond shape for each tile but arrange them in a rectangular fashion, we get the tile pattern shown in Figure 10.14. At first glance it might appear as if the tiles are not drawn in the proper order. What happened to the checkerboard pattern we observed when the board was diamond shaped? The answer lies in the way the rows of tiles are arranged. If we remove the checkers from the board and draw an outline around row 0, we can see that across the row the color of tiles alternate between light and dark, just as it did in the diamond configuration (Figure 10.15).

The drawing order will once again be by rows, from row 0 through row 7 and by layer, from bottom to top. The screen position of each tile is calculated as follows:

tile X = BOARD_X + (col*TEXTURE_SIZE/2),
if odd column: tile Y = BOARD_Y + (row*TEXTURE_SIZE/2),
if even column: tile Y = BOARD_Y + (row*TEXTURE_SIZE/2) + TEXTURE_SIZE/4,

where (BOARD_X, BOARD_Y) is the screen location of the tile at row 0 column 0.

The code that draws the checkerboard is in the render function in checkers.cpp from the "Isometric Stagger" example. The code in Listings 10.6 and 10.7 has been edited for clarity.

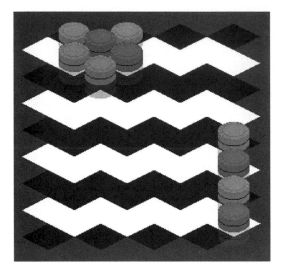

Figure 10.14. The checkerboard drawn using isometric stagger.

Figure 10.15. One row of the checkerboard outlined.

```cpp
// Draw checkerboard in Isometric Stagger
for(int row=0; row<BOARD_SIZE; row++)
{
    for(int col=0; col<BOARD_SIZE; col++)
    {
        // Set tile position
        boardSquare.setX((float)( BOARD_X + (col*TEXTURE_SIZE/2) ));
        if(col % 2)                 // If odd col
            boardSquare.setY((float)( BOARD_Y + (row*TEXTURE_SIZE/2) ));
        else                        // Even col
            boardSquare.setY((float)( BOARD_Y + (row*TEXTURE_SIZE/2 +
                                              TEXTURE_SIZE/4) ));
        // Determine tile color
        black = (row + col)%2;
        if(black)
            boardSquare.draw(graphicsNS::BLACK);
        else
            boardSquare.draw(graphicsNS::WHITE);
    }
}
```

Listing 10.6. The code that draws the checkerboard using isometric stagger.

The checkers must be drawn from back to front. Because of the staggered order of the tiles, the odd-column tiles are drawn behind the even-column tiles. In order to draw the checkers from back to front, we will draw them by alternating from odd column to even column to odd column, etc.

```
// Draw checkers back to front
// The odd column squares are drawn behind the even column squares
// Draw the checkers by columns, odd, even, odd, etc.
for(int row=0; row<BOARD_SIZE; row++)
{
    for(int col=1; col<BOARD_SIZE; col+=2)  // For odd columns
        drawOneChecker(row,col);
    for(int col=0; col<BOARD_SIZE; col+=2)  // For even columns
        drawOneChecker(row,col);
}
```

Listing 10.7. Drawing the checkers on an isometric stagger checkerboard.

■ 10.8 Isometric Terrain

Isometric tiles may be used to create some very nice terrain maps. The terrain may have changes in elevation, so we need some way to represent that when we draw the tiles. If we change a tile's y screen location to represent its elevation, we might get something like Figure 10.16.

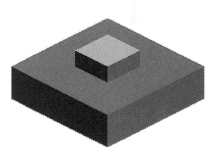

Figure 10.16. Isometric tiles with elevation changes.

This does give the appearance of an increase in elevation, but the change is very abrupt. To make the elevation change look more natural, we can create some transition tiles to draw around the raised tile. In Figure 10.17, we see a raised tile in the center with our transition tiles drawn around it. We have separated the tiles slightly so it is easier to identify each tile.

A lowered tile may be represented in a similar fashion. Figure 10.18 represents a lowered tile with our transition tiles drawn around it. If we add in a special tile for creating a wall and some trees, we can create a terrain as shown in Figure 10.19. The elevation tile set used to create Figure 10.19 is shown in Figure 10.20. The tile set in Figure 10.20 uses tiles that are 64 × 64 pixels with an elevation change of 16 pixels (Figure 10.21). If we use some of the tiles from Figure 10.5, we get the results shown in Figure 10.22. The tile set from Figure 10.5 uses 64 × 64 pixel tiles with an elevation change of 32 pixels.

Figure 10.17. Isometric transition tiles to a raised elevation.

The map for the elevated terrain is contained in three 2D arrays: tileMap, heightMap, and objectMap, which are all located in the elevations.h file. The tileMap array (Listing 10.8) contains a number that represents each tile. The tiles are numbered, as shown in Figure 10.23. As we described earlier in this chapter, these numbers allow us to select an individual tile image using the same function we use to select an individual texture from a larger image.

The heightMap array (Listing 10.9) contains the height of each tile from 0 to the maximum height. The height of the transition tiles is specified as the height of the highest side of the tile. In other words, if all of the tiles are at height 1 and a raised tile is at height 2, then the transition tiles around the raised tile will also be at height 2.

Figure 10.18. Isometric transition tiles to a lowered elevation.

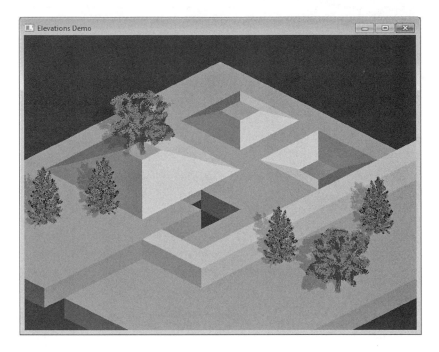

Figure 10.19. An isometric terrain with elevations and surface objects.

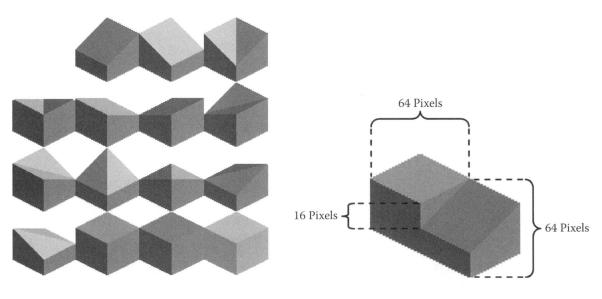

Figure 10.20. An isometric tile set.

Figure 10.21. Tile size and elevation changes.

Figure 10.22. Isometric terrain created using tiles from Figure 10.5.

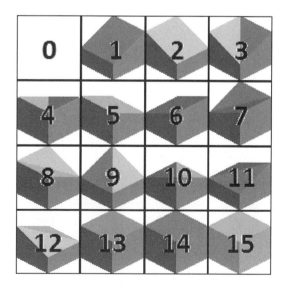

Figure 10.23. The number assigned to represent each tile.

```
// Map
const int tileMap[MAP_SIZE][MAP_SIZE] = {
    13,13,13,13,13,13,13,13,13,13,15,13,13,13,13,13,
    13,13,10, 5,12,13, 3, 1, 7,13,15,13,13,13,13,13,
    13,13, 6,13, 2,13, 2,14, 6,13,15,13,13,13,13,13,
    13,13,11, 1, 9,13, 8, 5, 4,13,15,13,13,13,13,13,
    13,13,13,13,13,13,13,13,13,13,15,13,13,13,13,13,
    13,10, 5, 5, 5,12,13,13,13,15,13,13,13,13,13,
    13, 6,10, 5,12, 2,13,13,13,15,13,13,13,13,13,
    13, 6, 6,13, 2, 2, 0, 0,13,13,15,13,13,13,13,13,
    13, 6,11, 1, 9, 2,13, 0,13,13,15,13,13,13,13,13,
    13,11, 1, 1, 1, 9,13, 0,13,13,15,13,13,13,13,13,
    13,13,13,13,13,13,13, 0,13,13,15,13,13,13,13,13,
    13,13,13,13,13,13,13, 0,15,15,15,13,13,13,13,13,
    13,13,13,13,13,13,13, 0,13,13,13,13,13,13,13,13,
    13,13,13,13,13,13,13, 0,13,13,13,13,13,13,13,13,
    13,13,13,13,13,13,13, 0,13,13,13,13,13,13,13,13,
    13,13,13,13,13,13,13, 0,13,13,13,13,13,13,13,13
};
```

Listing 10.8. The tile map used to describe Figures 10.19 and 10.22.

```
const int heightMap[MAP_SIZE][MAP_SIZE] = {
    1, 1, 1, 1, 1, 1, 1, 1, 1, 1, 2, 1, 1, 1, 1, 1,
    1, 1, 2, 2, 2, 1, 1, 1, 1, 1, 2, 1, 1, 1, 1, 1,
    1, 1, 2, 2, 2, 1, 1, 0, 1, 1, 2, 1, 1, 1, 1, 1,
    1, 1, 2, 2, 2, 1, 1, 1, 1, 1, 2, 1, 1, 1, 1, 1,
    1, 1, 1, 1, 1, 1, 1, 1, 1, 1, 2, 1, 1, 1, 1, 1,
    1, 2, 2, 2, 2, 2, 1, 1, 1, 1, 2, 1, 1, 1, 1, 1,
    1, 2, 3, 3, 3, 2, 1, 1, 1, 1, 2, 1, 1, 1, 1, 1,
    1, 2, 3, 3, 3, 2, 1, 1, 1, 1, 2, 1, 1, 1, 1, 1,
    1, 2, 3, 3, 3, 2, 1, 1, 1, 1, 2, 1, 1, 1, 1, 1,
    1, 2, 2, 2, 2, 2, 1, 1, 1, 1, 2, 1, 1, 1, 1, 1,
    1, 1, 1, 1, 1, 1, 1, 1, 1, 1, 2, 1, 1, 1, 1, 1,
    1, 1, 1, 1, 1, 1, 1, 1, 2, 2, 2, 1, 1, 1, 1, 1,
    1, 1, 1, 1, 1, 1, 1, 1, 1, 1, 1, 1, 1, 1, 1, 1,
    1, 1, 1, 1, 1, 1, 1, 1, 1, 1, 1, 1, 1, 1, 1, 1,
    1, 1, 1, 1, 1, 1, 1, 1, 1, 1, 1, 1, 1, 1, 1, 1,
    1, 1, 1, 1, 1, 1, 1, 1, 1, 1, 1, 1, 1, 1, 1, 1
};
```

Listing 10.9. The height map for Figures 10.19 and 10.22.

The objectMap array (Listing 10.10) contains the location of objects on the map. In our simple example, the only objects we have are two types of trees.

The terrain image is drawn from back to front and layer by layer, from bottom to top, just as we did with the checkerboard. A tile's *x* screen position is determined just as it was in our isometric projection example from Listing 10.5:

tile x = SCREEN_X − (row*TEXTURE_SIZE/2) + (col*TEXTURE_SIZE/2).

```
// 0=empty, 1=Tree0, 2=Tree1
const int objectMap[MAP_SIZE][MAP_SIZE] = {
    0, 0, 0, 0, 0, 0, 0, 0, 0, 0, 0, 0, 0, 0, 0, 0,
    0, 0, 0, 0, 0, 0, 0, 0, 0, 0, 0, 0, 0, 0, 0, 0,
    0, 0, 0, 0, 0, 0, 0, 0, 0, 0, 0, 0, 0, 0, 0, 0,
    0, 0, 0, 0, 0, 0, 0, 0, 0, 0, 0, 0, 0, 0, 0, 0,
    0, 0, 0, 0, 0, 0, 0, 0, 0, 0, 0, 0, 2, 0, 0, 0,
    0, 0, 0, 0, 0, 0, 0, 0, 0, 0, 0, 0, 0, 0, 0, 0,
    0, 0, 0, 0, 0, 0, 0, 0, 0, 0, 0, 0, 0, 0, 0, 0,
    0, 0, 0, 1, 0, 0, 0, 0, 0, 0, 0, 0, 0, 0, 0, 0,
    0, 0, 0, 0, 0, 0, 0, 0, 0, 0, 2, 0, 0, 1, 0,
    0, 0, 0, 0, 0, 0, 0, 0, 0, 0, 0, 0, 0, 0, 0, 0,
    0, 0, 0, 0, 2, 0, 0, 0, 0, 0, 0, 0, 0, 0, 0, 0,
    0, 0, 0, 0, 0, 0, 0, 0, 0, 0, 0, 0, 0, 0, 0, 0,
    0, 0, 0, 2, 0, 0, 0, 0, 0, 0, 0, 0, 0, 0, 0, 0,
    0, 0, 0, 0, 0, 0, 0, 0, 0, 0, 0, 0, 0, 0, 0, 0,
    0, 0, 0, 0, 0, 0, 0, 0, 0, 0, 0, 0, 0, 0, 0, 0,
    0, 0, 0, 0, 0, 0, 0, 0, 0, 0, 0, 0, 0, 0, 0, 0
};
```

Listing 10.10. The object map defining the position of the trees for Figures 10.19 and 10.22.

The y screen position of a tile is also calculated as it was in our isometric projection example and then the tile is moved up the screen by the value in the heightMap multiplied by the height of one elevation change:

$$\text{tile } y = \text{SCREEN\_Y} + (\text{row*TEXTURE\_SIZE}/4) + (\text{col*TEXTURE\_SIZE}/4) - \text{heightMap[row][col]} * \text{HEIGHT\_CHANGE},$$

where (SCREEN_X, SCREEN_Y) is the screen location of the tile at row 0 column 0.

The code that draws the terrain map is in the render function of the elevations.cpp file in this chapter's "Isometric Elevations" example (Listing 10.11).

```
//=============================================================================
// Render game items
//=============================================================================
void Elevations::render()
{
    graphics->spriteBegin();
    // Draw map in Isometric Diamond
    for(int row=0; row<MAP_SIZE; row++)
    {
        for(int col=0; col<MAP_SIZE; col++)
        {
            mapTile.setCurrentFrame(tileMap[row][col]);
            mapTile.setX((float)( SCREEN_X -
                              (row*TEXTURE_SIZE/2) + (col*TEXTURE_SIZE/2) ));
            mapTile.setY((float)( SCREEN_Y +
                              (row*TEXTURE_SIZE/4) + (col*TEXTURE_SIZE/4) -
                               heightMap[row][col] * HEIGHT_CHANGE));
```

```
                mapTile.draw();
        }
}
// Draw Objects,  0=empty, 1=Tree0, 2=Tree1
float treeX = 0, treeY = 0;
for(int row=0; row<MAP_SIZE; row++)
{
    for(int col=0; col<MAP_SIZE; col++)
    {
        switch(objectMap[row][col])
        {
        case 1:      // Tree0
            tree.setX((float)( SCREEN_X -
                (row*TEXTURE_SIZE/2) + (col*TEXTURE_SIZE/2) ) +
                 TREE_OFFSET_X);
            tree.setY((float)( SCREEN_Y +
                (row*TEXTURE_SIZE/4) + (col*TEXTURE_SIZE/4) -
                 heightMap[row][col] * HEIGHT_CHANGE) + TREE_OFFSET_Y);
            if(col%2)
                tree.flipHorizontal(true);
            // Draw shadow
            tree.setCurrentFrame(TREE0_SHADOW);
            tree.setDegrees(TREE_SHADOW_DEGREES);
            treeX = tree.getX();
            treeY = tree.getY();
            tree.setX(treeX + TREE_SHADOW_X);
            tree.setY(treeY + TREE_SHADOW_Y);
            tree.draw(graphicsNS::ALPHA25 & graphicsNS::BLACK);
            tree.setX(treeX);    // Restore X
            tree.setY(treeY);    // Restore Y
            // Draw tree
            tree.setDegrees(0);
            tree.setCurrentFrame(TREE0_FRAME);
            tree.draw();
            tree.flipHorizontal(false);
            break;
        case 2:     // Tree1
            tree.setX((float)( SCREEN_X -
                (row*TEXTURE_SIZE/2) + (col*TEXTURE_SIZE/2) ) +
                 TREE_OFFSET_X);
            tree.setY((float)( SCREEN_Y +
                (row*TEXTURE_SIZE/4) + (col*TEXTURE_SIZE/4) -
                 heightMap[row][col] * HEIGHT_CHANGE) + TREE_OFFSET_Y);
            if(col%2)
                tree.flipHorizontal(true);
            // Draw shadow
            tree.setCurrentFrame(TREE1_SHADOW);
            tree.setDegrees(TREE_SHADOW_DEGREES);   // Rotate shadow
            treeX = tree.getX();                    // Save tree x,y
            treeY = tree.getY();
            tree.setX(treeX + TREE_SHADOW_X);       // Position shadow
            tree.setY(treeY + TREE_SHADOW_Y);
            tree.draw(graphicsNS::ALPHA25 & graphicsNS::BLACK); // Draw
                                                                // shadow
            tree.setX(treeX);                       // Restore tree x,y
            tree.setY(treeY);
            // Draw tree
```

```
            tree.setDegrees(0);
            tree.setCurrentFrame(TREE1_FRAME);
            tree.draw();
            tree.flipHorizontal(false);
            break;
        }
    }
    }
    graphics->spriteEnd();
}
```

Listing 10.11. The code that draws Figures 10.19 and 10.22.

For ease in rendering, each tile in a set should be the same size. If we need to use different size tiles, we will create multiple sets where each tile in a set is the same size.

In this example, the terrain tiles are all 64 × 64 pixels. The tree textures are 128 × 128 pixels. The constants TREE_OFFSET_X and TREE_OFFSET_Y are added to the tile's X, Y coordinate to position the tree texture at the proper screen coordinates. The tree shadow is rotated by TREE_SHADOW_DEGREES. It is positioned in the correct screen location relative to the tree by adding TREE_SHADOW_X and TREE_SHADOW_Y to the current tree location. The tree shadow constants are all defined in elevations.h.

To add extra variety, the tree image is flipped horizontally if the tree is drawn in an odd column. The large tree on the top of the hill in Figures 10.19 and 10.22 is flipped.

Another way to add variety is to apply random textures to the more commonly used tiles. The tile set created by *Yar* (in Figure 10.5) has a number of textures for this very purpose.

■ 10.9 Elevation Layers

If we add additional layers to our map, we can create structures of any height by stacking tiles one on top of the other. Our example program "Isometric Elevations Layers" does just that. We have added an extra layer to our wall to create the raised sections shown in Figure 10.24.

With this technique, we are using a separate map array for each elevation. The heightMap is no longer used to adjust the *y* position of each tile; it is used only to position objects on the map—in this case, the trees. This example contains four layers of elevation maps. The top layer looks like Listing 10.12. The top layer of the wall is made up of tile number 15 and is highlighted in Listing 10.12. The top of the hill under the large tree is also part of the top layer and is also highlighted.

The render function in elevations.cpp draws the map layer by layer. The *y* screen position of the tiles is calculated by multiplying the map layer number by the height of one layer and subtracting the resulting number from the tile's *y* position. For layer 0, HEIGHT_CHANGE*0 obviously subtracts 0 and is simply in the source to emphasize how the tile's *y* position is calculated (Listing 10.13).

Figure 10.24. An isometric terrain with multiple layers as demonstrated here with vertical wall segments.

```
const int tileMap3[MAP_SIZE][MAP_SIZE] = {
    0,  0,  0,  0,  0,  0,  0,  0,  0,  0,  0,  0,  0,  0,  0,  0,
    0,  0,  0,  0,  0,  0,  0,  0,  0,  0,  0,  0,  0,  0,  0,  0,
    0,  0,  0,  0,  0,  0,  0,  0,  0,  0, 15,  0,  0,  0,  0,  0,
    0,  0,  0,  0,  0,  0,  0,  0,  0,  0,  0,  0,  0,  0,  0,  0,
    0,  0,  0,  0,  0,  0,  0,  0,  0,  0,  0,  0,  0,  0,  0,  0,
    0,  0,  0,  0,  0,  0,  0,  0,  0,  0, 15,  0,  0,  0,  0,  0,
    0,  0, 10,  5, 12,  0,  0,  0,  0,  0,  0,  0,  0,  0,  0,  0,
    0,  0,  6, 13,  2,  0,  0,  0,  0,  0,  0,  0,  0,  0,  0,  0,
    0,  0, 11,  1,  9,  0,  0,  0,  0,  0, 15,  0,  0,  0,  0,  0,
    0,  0,  0,  0,  0,  0,  0,  0,  0,  0,  0,  0,  0,  0,  0,  0,
    0,  0,  0,  0,  0,  0,  0,  0,  0,  0,  0,  0,  0,  0,  0,  0,
    0,  0,  0,  0,  0,  0,  0,  0, 15,  0, 15,  0,  0,  0,  0,  0,
    0,  0,  0,  0,  0,  0,  0,  0,  0,  0,  0,  0,  0,  0,  0,  0,
    0,  0,  0,  0,  0,  0,  0,  0,  0,  0,  0,  0,  0,  0,  0,  0,
    0,  0,  0,  0,  0,  0,  0,  0,  0,  0,  0,  0,  0,  0,  0,  0,
    0,  0,  0,  0,  0,  0,  0,  0,  0,  0,  0,  0,  0,  0,  0,  0,
};
```

Listing 10.12. The top layer of elevation maps.

```
// Layer0
for(int row=0; row<MAP_SIZE; row++)
```

```
{
    for(int col=0; col<MAP_SIZE; col++)
    {
        mapTile.setCurrentFrame(tileMap0[row][col]);
        mapTile.setX((float)( SCREEN_X - (row*TEXTURE_SIZE/2) +
                            (col*TEXTURE_SIZE/2) ));
        mapTile.setY((float)( SCREEN_Y + (row*TEXTURE_SIZE/4) +
                            (col*TEXTURE_SIZE/4) - HEIGHT_CHANGE*0));
        mapTile.draw();
    }
}
// Layer1
for(int row=0; row<MAP_SIZE; row++)
{
    for(int col=0; col<MAP_SIZE; col++)
    {
        mapTile.setCurrentFrame(tileMap1[row][col]);
        mapTile.setX((float)( SCREEN_X - (row*TEXTURE_SIZE/2) +
                            (col*TEXTURE_SIZE/2) ));
        mapTile.setY((float)( SCREEN_Y + (row*TEXTURE_SIZE/4) +
                            (col*TEXTURE_SIZE/4) - HEIGHT_CHANGE*1));
        mapTile.draw();
    }
}
... continued for remaining layers
```

Listing 10.13. The `render` function draws the map layer by layer.

Chapter Review

In this chapter, we covered techniques for using tiles to create game environments. Any of these tile environments may be used in combination with the graphic techniques we have already covered to create games. From the classic side scroll to isometric projections with elevation changes, tile-based games provide lots of options for game graphics. Some of the key topics from the chapter are the following:

- *Reuse tiles.* Tiles may be reused to create very large maps with limited texture memory usage.

- *Using arrays.* Tile numbers are stored in a 2D array to create a map of the game environment.

- *Random selection.* Tiles may be randomly selected.

- *Parallax scrolling.* Multiple tile layers may be used in conjunction with parallax scrolling.

- *Tile numbers.* Tile numbers may be used to determine player interaction.

- *Orthogonal projection.* Orthogonal projection uses projection lines that are parallel to each other and perpendicular to the screen.

- *Oblique projection.* Oblique projection uses projection lines that are parallel to each other and intersect the screen at an oblique angle.

- *Isometric projection.* Isometric projection uses parallel projection lines with a viewing angle that is the same for the x,y,z-axes.

- *Object rendering.* Object rendering is done from back to front for oblique and isometric projections.

- *Grid formation.* Isometric stagger arranges the tiles in a grid instead of using a diamond formation.

- *Changes in elevation.* Isometric terrain uses unique tile patterns to represent changes in elevation.

- *Multiple map layers.* Using multiple map layers permits stacking the tiles to create structures that are taller than one tile.

Review Questions

1. What is one advantage of using tiles to create a game world?

2. What projection type is used with tile games that are viewed from the side?

3. How can using tiles to represent a game world reduce the amount of video memory required?

4. When using oblique projection, how do distant objects differ from closer objects when displayed?

5. Why is the drawing order important when using oblique and isometric projections?

6. In the checkerboard examples from this chapter, only one white square was used as a texture. How were the black squares drawn?

7. How many different tile shapes are required to draw an isometric terrain with elevation changes?

8. What is the last thing to be drawn when drawing an isometric terrain?

9. What height is used for the transition tiles that surround a higher tile?

10. What advantage is there in using multiple layers of tiles?

Exercises

1. Modify the "FlowerPower" example to make the game map larger.

2. Add a second map layer of background elements to the "FlowerPower" example to display clouds with parallax scrolling.

3. Add more terrain tiles to the "Isometric Elevations Layers" example.

4. Create a two-player checker game.

Examples

The following examples are available for download from www.programming2dgames.com.

- *FlowerPower.* A butterfly flies over grass and flowers.

  - Demonstrates a tile-based game using orthogonal projection.

  - The butterfly is controlled by the player.

  - The map scrolls when the butterfly reaches the screen edge.

- *Oblique.* A checkerboard is drawn using oblique projection.

  - Demonstrates oblique projection.

  - The checkers have a reflection.

  - The board and checkers are drawn from back to front.

- *Isometric Diamond.* A checkerboard is drawn using isometric projection.

  - Demonstrates isometric projection.

  - The checkers have a reflection.

  - The board and checkers are drawn from back to front.

- *Isometric Stagger.* A checkerboard is drawn using isometric projection with the tiles drawn in a grid pattern.

  - Demonstrates isometric projection.

  - Demonstrates how to position the tiles to form different patterns.

  - Different row and column drawing orders may be selected.

- *Isometric Elevations.* A terrain map is drawn using isometric projection.

  - Demonstrates isometric projection.

- The tiles are drawn to represent different elevations.

- Demonstrates how to incorporate third party tile sets.

- *Isometric Elevations Layers.* A terrain map is drawn that uses multiple map layers.

  - Demonstrates isometric projection.

  - Multiple map layers permit structures that are taller than one tile.

11 Building a Complete Game

In this chapter, we are going to create a complete game. The game we have chosen to create is Spacewar. We chose Spacewar as a way of paying homage to the pioneers of computer games.

Spacewar is one of the earliest known computer games. It was created by Steve "Slug" Russell, Martin "Shag" Graetz, and Wayne Witaenem in 1961–1962.

Actually, we have been building parts of the Spacewar game throughout the previous chapters. In this chapter, we will put all the pieces together to create a finished game. Before we get into the actual creation process, we need to spend some time looking at techniques for project management and software development.

∎ 11.1 Evolutionary Prototyping

Many different development models exist in software engineering. The model described here is a variation of *evolutionary prototyping*. In evolutionary prototyping, a prototype is constructed early in the design process. As the development progresses, the prototype is refined until eventually the finished product is created. At each stage of development, before the refinements are applied to the prototype, the entire project folder is saved. A copy is made of the project folder and given a new version number. The modifications are applied to the new project folder. With this method, a history of prototypes is created.

Several advantages exist with this model. In a learning environment, there is a documented history of student work. This can be especially helpful if project time requirements are underestimated and the game is not completed. The older versions can also be helpful as a reference during the development process. Occasionally, when we make changes in one area of a program, we can inadvertently cause unexpected behavior somewhere else. Having the previous version as a reference allows us to do a comparison of project folders using the WinMerge application. From the comparison, we can see the differences between versions, which can be very helpful in determining the cause of the unexpected behavior.

▉ 11.2 Project Management

Most commercially-produced games are large projects involving many talented people. Just start up one of the latest AAA games and find the credits; then sit back and watch as page after page of names are displayed. The games we create in a learning environment may also be created in groups. Working in a group provides excellent opportunities to develop our project management skills.

Comprehensive project management discussion would easily fill an entire book. We are going to limit our discussion to two aspects of managing a game project: time management and resource management.

The first step is to break our project down into smaller components. For game projects, the base components might be along these lines:

- Planning

- Graphics

- Audio

- Programming

- Writing (story, character dialogs, etc.)

- Quality assurance

- Production

- Documentation

Additional categories might be required or subcategories might be created depending on complexity. Ideally, we would like individual components that are small enough to easily estimate the time and resources required. A component's estimated completion time should be approximately one week or less. Any longer than that and the amount of time that has elapsed before a problem is detected would be too great.

11.2.1 Time Management

The overall goal of time management is to keep our project on schedule. Estimated completion times are assigned to the individual categories we came up with in the previous section. The estimated times are scheduled so the completion of tasks follows a logical order, and we must make sure that all prerequisite tasks are completed before they are

Spacewar
Two players on one computer.
Professor: Kelly
Team:

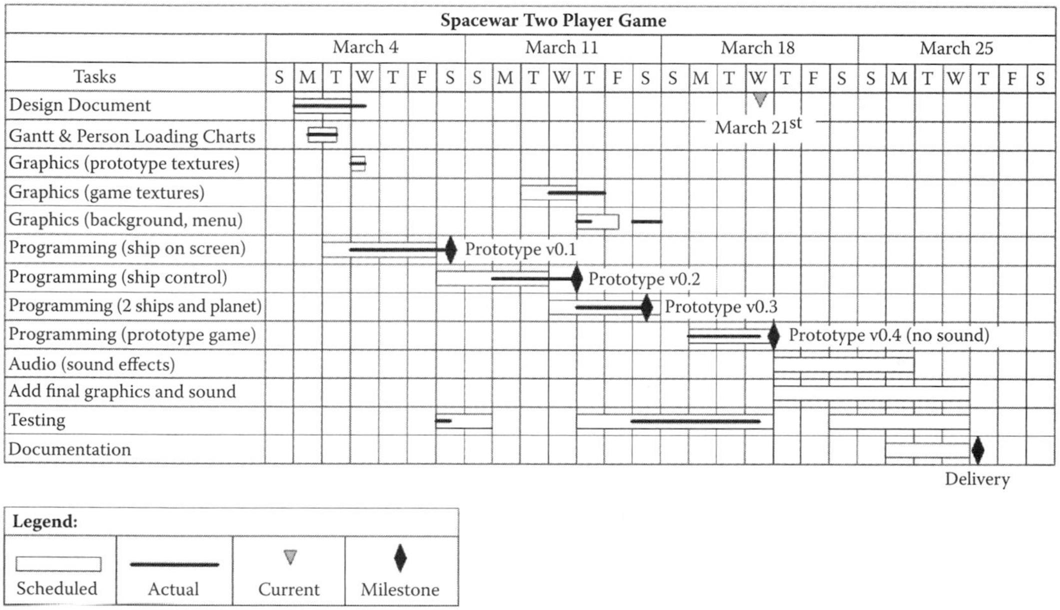

Figure 11.1. Gantt chart of the Spacewar game.

required by later tasks. As our project progresses, we track our progress in relation to the original estimates.

Gantt chart. A good tool for scheduling and tracking is a *Gantt chart*. An example is shown in Figure 11.1. The individual tasks are on the left. The horizontal axis is time divided into months and days. Estimated times are shown as an open rectangle. Actual times are shown as a solid line (refer to the legend). In addition to times, we may place milestone marks on the Gantt chart. In this example, we have milestones for each prototype and the delivery of the final game. We also indicate the current date on the chart.

11.2.2 Resource Management

The resources we need to manage may be people and/or shared equipment. Equipment management involves setting up a schedule so that time conflicts between users are minimized. Managing the people on a project is done by assigning individuals to tasks in discrete time blocks. A good way to assign and track people is a person loading table.

Person loading table. A *person loading table* is simply a table that contains tasks on one axis and people on the other axis. Two numbers are entered into each location separated

Spacewar Two Player Game				
Task Description	**Dave**	**Chuck**	**Marty**	**Total**
Design Document	4/4.5	4/4.5	4/4.5	12/13.5
Gantt & Person Loading Charts	0/0	4/3	0/0	4/3
Graphics (prototype textures)	2/2	0/0	0/0	2/2
Graphics (game textures)	2/1	2/0	3/4	7/5
Graphics (background, menu)	4/1	0/0	4/4	8/5
Programming (ship on screen)	0/0	8/9	8/4	16/13
Programming (ship control)	0/0	16/16	8/8	24/24
Programming (2 ships and planet)	0/0	12/8	12/4	24/12
Programming (prototype game)	0/0	12/10	12/10	24/20
Audio (sound effects)	16/0	0/0	0/0	16/0
Add final graphics and sound	2/0	24/0	24/0	50/0
Testing	10/6	70/32	70/20	150/58
Documentation	4/0	8/0	8/0	20/0

Table 11.1. Person loading table for the Spacewar game.

by a slash (/). The first number represents the estimated time to complete the task (usually in hours) and the second number is the actual time spent up to this point. For example, a table entry of 10/7.5 indicates that 10 hours were estimated and 7.5 hours have been spent. The tasks used for the table may be taken directly from the Gantt chart. See Table 11.1 for an example.

As the project progresses, we can shift the allocation of people between tasks, where possible, to evenly divide the work load and provide extra resources to tasks that may be falling behind schedule.

◧ 11.3 Design Document

A game design document is a description of the game. It may include text, images, drawings, or other media. The primary purpose of a design document is to provide each team member with a clear understanding of the overall project. It is the single reference upon which all other game design decisions are based. The design document provides a high-level description of the game. It does not get into details about implementation. The following is our design document:

Spacewar: A two-player game that runs on a single computer. Each player will have one spaceship he or she controls using either keyboard or game controller inputs. Each ship will have one torpedo that it may fire. A firing delay will be used to prevent more than one torpedo per ship from being active at the same time. The torpedo will damage the other ship with a direct hit. The torpedo will not damage its own ship. A planet in the center of the screen will have mass and gravitational attraction of the ships and torpedoes. Collision detection between the ships, the planet, and the enemy torpedo will be supported. The game will also include sounds for collisions and explosions. A player is awarded one point when the other ship is destroyed in any way, including accidental crashes into the planet. Each player's score will be displayed.

▮▮ 11.4 Prototype Textures

Three texture files will be used for the game: a background, a title screen, and a file that contains all the other game textures. With early prototyping, we are only concerned with creating textures that are the proper size. Our goal is not to create fancy graphics, just some simple textures for use in our prototype. Many of the examples from the earlier chapters contained a more detailed version of the game textures shown here. The examples presented here are meant to be representative of the typical level of detail used for prototyping.

Any Windows paint program will work for this purpose. The following are the textures we created. Figure 11.2 is our title page. The title page is 640 × 480 pixels with white letters on a magenta background. Magenta will be our transparent color. Figure 11.3 is our background image. It is a solid blue with a few white dots thrown in to represent stars. The background image is also 640 × 480 pixels.

Figure 11.4 contains all the other game textures. The background color of the title and game texture images is magenta, which will be specified as the transparent color when the images are displayed.

The game texture image has a visible grid. This helps position individual textures in the larger image. We will remove the grid in the final version. The spaceship and torpedo images will be animated, so we have drawn four of each image. To specify the `Planet` texture location, we can visualize the texture image as being divided into two columns and two rows. The planet is in frame 1.

Figure 11.2. Prototype title.

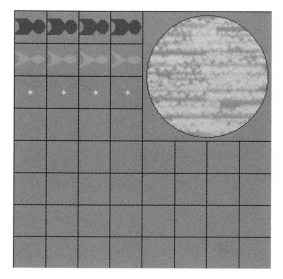

Figure 11.4. Prototype game textures.

Figure 11.3. Prototype background texture.

▌ 11.5 Spacewar Tasks

11.5.1 Ship Onscreen

From our Gantt chart in Figure 11.1, we see that the next phase of our project is drawing a ship on the screen. This task was completed in Chapter 5 in our "Spaceship" example. After we have thoroughly tested the code, we give it a version number (such as Spacewar v0.1) and we save it.

11.5.2 Ship Control

The next task on our schedule is to add user control to the ship. We make a copy of v0.1 and rename it v0.2 before we make any modifications. This task was partially completed in Chapter 5 in the "Spaceship control" example. In that example, the ship stopped moving as soon as the user released a key. In exercise 5.3, we gave the ship momentum so it would keep moving.

11.5.3 Two Ships and a Planet

Spacewar v0.3 is two ships and a planet. The "Planet collision" example from Chapter 6 fulfills this task. In exercise 6.4, we added user control of the two ships.

11.5.4 Prototype Game

Spacewar v0.4 is a prototype game. We need to add the ability for a player to fire a torpedo that can collide with the other ship and the planet. A working game is always a great accomplishment even if it is still a prototype. It's hard to resist having a little fun by playing it. Oh, wait! We don't call it playing—we call it testing. After all, there is a category called "Testing" on the Gantt chart.

11.5.5 Audio (Sound Effects)

Obtaining the sound effects we want to use in our game can be more time-consuming than writing the code to include them. Find something that works and use it. We can always go back and refine the sounds later if we have the time. Recall that one of the advantages of using the XACT sound engine was the ability to modify the game sounds without making modifications to the game code.

11.5.6 Add Final Graphics and Sounds

At this point, our Spacewar game is nearly complete. We have included the code to play our sound effects and added our final graphics.

11.5.7 Testing

Testing should be a part of the entire development process, not just something that is done at the end and only if there is enough time. For one thing, there is never enough time. A common saying in software development circles is, "A program is never complete, it just ships." Make sure adequate time is allocated for testing in the software development plan.

The earlier in the development cycle that defects are detected, the less costly it is to correct them.

11.5.8 Documentation

Documentation can be in several forms. Comments in the source code are a form of documentation meant for internal use. It helps explain the code to other developers or serves as a reminder for future use. Documentation intended for end users can be displayed in help screens or system prompts. End user documentation should be created in files that are separate from the game code. This will make it easier to modify or translate into different languages.

11.6 Spacewar v1.0

With our early prototypes complete and working, it is time to create version 1.0 of our game. The following are the key parts of the game code. The spaceships, planet, and torpedo may all collide with other objects. Any object that needs collision detection should be part of a class that inherits from the `Entity` class. The `Planet` class is the simplest of the three, so let's examine it first.

11.6.1 Planet Class

The `planet.h` file contains constants that define the size, screen position, mass, and texture information (Listing 11.1).

```cpp
// Programming 2D Games
// Copyright (c) 2011 by:
// Charles Kelly
// planet.h v1.0
#ifndef _PLANET_H              // Prevent multiple definitions if this
#define _PLANET_H              // file is included in more than one place
#define WIN32_LEAN_AND_MEAN

#include "entity.h"
#include "constants.h"
namespace planetNS
{
    const int    WIDTH = 128;                    // Image width
    const int    HEIGHT = 128;                   // Image height
    const int    COLLISION_RADIUS = 120/2;       // For circular collision
    const int    X = GAME_WIDTH/2 - WIDTH/2;     // Location onscreen
    const int    Y = GAME_HEIGHT/2 - HEIGHT/2;
    const float  MASS = 1.0e14f;                 // Mass
    const int    TEXTURE_COLS = 2;               // Texture has 2 columns
    const int    START_FRAME = 1;                // Starts at frame 1
    const int    END_FRAME = 1;                  // No animation
}
class Planet : public Entity                     // Inherits from Entity class
{
public:
    // Constructor
    Planet();
```

```
        void  disable() {visible = false; active = false;}
        void  enable()  {visible = true; active = true;}
};
#endif
```

Listing 11.1. The Planet class.

```
// Programming 2D Games
// Copyright (c) 2011 by:
// Charles Kelly
// planet.cpp v1.0
#include "planet.h"
//=======================================================================
// Default constructor
//=======================================================================
Planet::Planet() : Entity()
{
    spriteData.x     = planetNS::X;                   // Location onscreen
    spriteData.y     = planetNS::Y;
    radius           = planetNS::COLLISION_RADIUS;
    mass             = planetNS::MASS;
    startFrame       = planetNS::START_FRAME;         // First frame of ship
                                                      // animation
    endFrame         = planetNS::END_FRAME;           // Last frame of ship
                                                      // animation
    setCurrentFrame(startFrame);
}
```

Listing 11.2. The Planet class constructor.

The Planet inherits from Entity, which contains all of the necessary collision code. The only new code we need to create for the Planet class is the constructor. It simply initializes the location and animation properties (Listing 11.2).

11.6.2 Torpedo Class

The Torpedo class also inherits from Entity. The torpedo.h file contains the constants used to initialize the torpedo's properties; the file also contains the prototypes for member functions (Listing 11.3).

```
// Programming 2D Games
// Copyright (c) 2011 by:
// Charles Kelly
// Version 1.0
#ifndef _TORPEDO_H              // Prevent multiple definitions if this
#define _TORPEDO_H              // file is included in more than one place
#define WIN32_LEAN_AND_MEAN
#include "entity.h"
```

```
#include "constants.h"
namespace torpedoNS
{
    const int    WIDTH = 32;                 // Image width
    const int    HEIGHT = 32 ;               // Image height
    const int    COLLISION_RADIUS = 4;       // For circular collision
    const float  SPEED = 200;                // Pixels per second
    const float  MASS = 300.0f;              // Mass
    const float  FIRE_DELAY = 4.0f;          // 4 seconds between torpedo firing
    const int    TEXTURE_COLS = 8;           // Texture has 8 columns
    const int    START_FRAME = 40;           // Starts at frame 40
    const int    END_FRAME = 43;             // Animation frames 40,41,42,43
    const float  ANIMATION_DELAY = 0.1f;// Time between frames
}
class Torpedo : public Entity               // Inherits from Entity class
{
private:
    float    fireTimer;                      // Time remaining until fire enabled
public:
    // Constructor
    Torpedo();
    // Inherited member functions
    void update(float frameTime);
    float getMass()      const {return torpedoNS::MASS;}
    // New member functions
    void fire(Entity *ship);                 // Fire torpedo from ship
};
#endif
```

Listing 11.3. The Torpedo class.

The Torpedo constructor initializes the properties using the constants defined in torpedo.h (Listing 11.4).

```
// Programming 2D Games
// Copyright (c) 2011 by:
// Charles Kelly
// torpedo.cpp v1.0
#include "torpedo.h"
//=============================================================================
// Default constructor
//=============================================================================
Torpedo::Torpedo() : Entity()
{
    active = false;                                   // Torpedo starts
                                                      // inactive
    spriteData.width       = torpedoNS::WIDTH;        // Size of 1 image
    spriteData.height      = torpedoNS::HEIGHT;
    spriteData.rect.bottom = torpedoNS::HEIGHT;       // Select part of an
                                                      // image
    spriteData.rect.right  = torpedoNS::WIDTH;
    cols          = torpedoNS::TEXTURE_COLS;
    frameDelay    = torpedoNS::ANIMATION_DELAY;
```

```
startFrame        = torpedoNS::START_FRAME;        // First frame of ship
                                                   // animation
endFrame          = torpedoNS::END_FRAME;          // Last frame of ship
                                                   // animation
currentFrame      = startFrame;
radius            = torpedoNS::COLLISION_RADIUS;   // For circular
                                                   // collision
visible           = false;
fireTimer         = 0.0f;
mass = torpedoNS::MASS;
collisionType = entityNS::CIRCLE;
}
```

Listing 11.4. The `Torpedo` class constructor.

The `Torpedo::update` function keeps track of the elapsed time since the torpedo was fired. If enough time has elapsed, the torpedo is made inactive. The `update` function also moves the torpedo and wraps it around at the screen edges (Listing 11.5).

A torpedo may only be fired if `fireTimer` is less than 0. This prevents a torpedo from being fired until the previously fired torpedo has timed out. The firing ship is passed in as a parameter. The initial velocity of the torpedo is based on the current angle of the firing ship (Listing 11.6).

```
//=====================================================================
// Update
// Typically called once per frame
// frameTime is used to regulate the speed of movement and animation
//=====================================================================
void Torpedo::update(float frameTime)
{
    fireTimer -= frameTime;                       // Time remaining until fire
                                                  // enabled
    if (visible == false)
        return;
    if(fireTimer < 0)                             // If ready to fire
    {
        visible = false;                          // Old torpedo off
        active = false;
    }
    Image::update(frameTime);
    spriteData.x += frameTime * velocity.x;       // Move along X
    spriteData.y += frameTime * velocity.y;       // Move along Y
    // Wrap around screen edge
    if (spriteData.x > GAME_WIDTH)                 // If off right screen edge
        spriteData.x = -torpedoNS::WIDTH;         // Position off left screen
                                                  // edge
    else if (spriteData.x < -torpedoNS::WIDTH)    // Else if off left screen
                                                  // edge
        spriteData.x = GAME_WIDTH;                // Position off right
                                                  // screen edge
    if (spriteData.y > GAME_HEIGHT)               // If off bottom screen
                                                  // edge
```

```
        spriteData.y = -torpedoNS::HEIGHT;          // Position off top screen
                                                      // edge
    else if (spriteData.y < -torpedoNS::HEIGHT)  // Else if off top screen
                                                      // edge
        spriteData.y = GAME_HEIGHT;                 // Position off bottom
                                                      // screen edge
}
```

Listing 11.5. The update function from the Torpedo class.

```
//=============================================================================
// Fire
// Fires a torpedo from ship
//=============================================================================
void Torpedo::fire(Entity *ship)
{
    if(fireTimer <= 0.0f)                        // If ready to fire
    {
        velocity.x = (float)cos(ship->getRadians()) * torpedoNS::SPEED;
        velocity.y = (float)sin(ship->getRadians()) * torpedoNS::SPEED;
        spriteData.x = ship->getCenterX() - spriteData.width/2;
        spriteData.y = ship->getCenterY() - spriteData.height/2;
        visible = true;                          // Make torpedo visible
        active = true;                           // Enable collisions
        fireTimer = torpedoNS::FIRE_DELAY;       / Delay firing
        audio->playCue(TORPEDO_FIRE);
    }
}
```

Listing 11.6. The Torpedo::fire function.

11.6.3 Ship Class

The ship.h file contains the constants for two ships, the engine, the shield, and the explosion animations. The engine, shield, and explosion are declared in the Ship class as three Image objects (Listing 11.7).

```
// Programming 2D Games
// Copyright (c) 2011 by:
// Charles Kelly
// ship.h v1.0
#ifndef _SHIP_H                    // Prevent multiple definitions if this
#define _SHIP_H                    // file is included in more than one place
#define WIN32_LEAN_AND_MEAN
#include "entity.h"
#include "constants.h"
namespace shipNS
{
    const int   WIDTH = 32;                    // Image width (each frame)
```

```
    const int   HEIGHT = 32;                    // Image height
    const int   X = GAME_WIDTH/2 - WIDTH/2;      // Location onscreen
    const int   Y = GAME_HEIGHT/6 - HEIGHT;
    const float ROTATION_RATE = (float)PI;       // Radians per second
    const float SPEED = 100;                     // 100 pixels per second
    const float MASS = 300.0f;                   // Mass
    enum DIRECTION {NONE, LEFT, RIGHT};          // Rotation direction
    const int   TEXTURE_COLS = 8;                // Texture has 8 columns
    const int   SHIP1_START_FRAME = 0;           // Ship1 starts at frame 0
    const int   SHIP1_END_FRAME = 3;             // Ship1 animation frames
                                                 // 0,1,2,3
    const int   SHIP2_START_FRAME = 8;           // Ship2 starts at frame 8
    const int   SHIP2_END_FRAME = 11;            // Ship2 animation frames
                                                 // 8,9,10,11
    const float SHIP_ANIMATION_DELAY = 0.2f;// Time between frames
    const int   EXPLOSION_START_FRAME = 32;  // Explosion start frame
    const int   EXPLOSION_END_FRAME = 39;    // Explosion end frame
    const float EXPLOSION_ANIMATION_DELAY = 0.2f; // Time between frames
    const int   ENGINE_START_FRAME = 16;         // Engine start frame
    const int   ENGINE_END_FRAME = 19;           // Engine end frame
    const float ENGINE_ANIMATION_DELAY = 0.1f;   // Time between frames
    const int   SHIELD_START_FRAME = 24;         // Shield start frame
    const int   SHIELD_END_FRAME = 27;           // Shield end frame
    const float SHIELD_ANIMATION_DELAY = 0.1f;   // Time between frames
    const float TORPEDO_DAMAGE = 46;             // Amount of damage
                                                 // caused by torpedo
    const float SHIP_DAMAGE = 10;                // Damage caused by
                                          // collision with another ship
}
// Inherits from Entity class
class Ship : public Entity
{
private:
    float   oldX, oldY, oldAngle;
    float   rotation;                 // Current rotation rate (radians/
                                      // second)
    shipNS::DIRECTION direction;      // Direction of rotation
    float   explosionTimer;
    bool    explosionOn;
    bool    engineOn;                 // True to move ship forward
    bool    shieldOn;
    Image   engine;
    Image   shield;
    Image   explosion;
public:
    // Constructor
    Ship();
    // Inherited member functions
    virtual void draw();
    virtual bool initialize(Game *gamePtr, int width, int height,
                        int ncols, TextureManager *textureM);
    // Update ship position and angle
    void update(float frameTime);
    // Damage ship with WEAPON
    void damage(WEAPON);
    // New member functions
```

```
    // Move ship out of collision
    void toOldPosition()
    {
        spriteData.x = oldX;
        spriteData.y = oldY,
        spriteData.angle = oldAngle;
        rotation = 0.0f;
    }
    // Returns rotation
    float getRotation() {return rotation;}
    // Returns engineOn condition
    bool getEngineOn()  {return engineOn;}
    // Returns shieldOn condition
    bool getShieldOn()  {return shieldOn;}
    // Sets engine on
    void setEngineOn(bool eng)  {engineOn = eng;}
    // Set shield on
    void setShieldOn(bool sh)   {shieldOn = sh;}
    // Sets Mass
    void setMass(float m)       {mass = m;}
    // Set rotation rate
    void setRotation(float r)   {rotation = r;}
    // Direction of rotation force
    void rotate(shipNS::DIRECTION dir) {direction = dir;}
    // Ship explodes
    void explode();
    // Ship is repaired
    void repair();
};
#endif
```

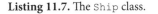

Listing 11.7. The `Ship` class.

The `Ship`'s constructor initializes the properties (Listing 11.8).

```
// Programming 2D Games
// Copyright (c) 2011 by:
// Charles Kelly
// ship.cpp v1.0
#include "ship.h"
//=============================================================================
// Default constructor
//=============================================================================
Ship::Ship() : Entity()
{
    spriteData.width = shipNS::WIDTH;           // Size of Ship1
    spriteData.height = shipNS::HEIGHT;
    spriteData.x = shipNS::X;                    // Location onscreen
    spriteData.y = shipNS::Y;
    spriteData.rect.bottom = shipNS::HEIGHT;    // Select parts of an image
    spriteData.rect.right = shipNS::WIDTH;
    oldX = shipNS::X;
    oldY = shipNS::Y;
    oldAngle = 0.0f;
```

```
    rotation = 0.0f;
    velocity.x = 0;                             // Velocity X
    frameDelay = shipNS::SHIP_ANIMATION_DELAY;
    startFrame = shipNS::SHIP1_START_FRAME;     // First frame of ship
                                                // animation
    endFrame   = shipNS::SHIP1_END_FRAME;       // Last frame of ship
                                                // animation
    currentFrame = startFrame;
    radius = shipNS::WIDTH/2.0;
    collisionType = entityNS::CIRCLE;
    direction = shipNS::NONE;                   // Direction of rotation
                                                // thruster

    engineOn = false;
    shieldOn = false;
    explosionOn = false;
    mass = shipNS::MASS;
}
```

Listing 11.8. The Ship class constructor.

The initialize function prepares the engine, shield, and explosion images
before it calls the Entity::initialize function to initialize the ship (Listing 11.9).

```
//=============================================================================
// Initialize the Ship
// Post: returns true if successful, false if failed
//=============================================================================
bool Ship::initialize(Game *gamePtr, int width, int height, int ncols,
                       TextureManager *textureM)
{
    engine.initialize(gamePtr->getGraphics(), width, height, ncols,
                      textureM);
    engine.setFrames(shipNS::ENGINE_START_FRAME, shipNS::ENGINE_END_FRAME);
    engine.setCurrentFrame(shipNS::ENGINE_START_FRAME);
    engine.setFrameDelay(shipNS::ENGINE_ANIMATION_DELAY);
    shield.initialize(gamePtr->getGraphics(), width, height, ncols,
                      textureM);
    shield.setFrames(shipNS::SHIELD_START_FRAME, shipNS::SHIELD_END_FRAME);
    shield.setCurrentFrame(shipNS::SHIELD_START_FRAME);
    shield.setFrameDelay(shipNS::SHIELD_ANIMATION_DELAY);
    shield.setLoop(false);                  // Do not loop animation
    explosion.initialize(gamePtr->getGraphics(), width, height, ncols,
                         textureM);
    explosion.setFrames(shipNS::EXPLOSION_START_FRAME,
                        shipNS::EXPLOSION_END_FRAME);
    explosion.setCurrentFrame(shipNS::EXPLOSION_START_FRAME);
    explosion.setFrameDelay(shipNS::EXPLOSION_ANIMATION_DELAY);
    explosion.setLoop(false);               // Do not loop animation
    return(Entity::initialize(gamePtr, width, height, ncols, textureM));
}
```

Listing 11.9. The initialize function from the Ship class.

The draw function checks the explosionOn Boolean. If it is true, the explosion. draw function is called to draw the explosion animation. If the ship is not exploding, it is drawn with Image::draw. The engine and shield are also drawn if their corresponding Boolean is true. The explosion, engine, and shield are drawn using the Image:: draw function with the ship's SpriteData structure passed as a parameter. This draws them at the same screen position and orientation as the ship (Listing 11.10).

The update function updates the explosion, shield, and engine images. If the engine is on, the ship's velocity is increased along the direction of the current ship angle. The ship animation is performed by the Entity::update call. Next, the ship rotation rate is adjusted if the player is pressing a rotation key as specified by the direction property. Finally, the ship's angle is increased by the rotation rate and the ship's screen position is set (Listing 11.11).

```
//===========================================================================
// Draw the ship
//===========================================================================
void Ship::draw()
{
    if(explosionOn)
        explosion.draw(spriteData);  // Draw explosion using current
                                      // spriteData
    else
    {
        Image::draw();                // Draw ship
        if(engineOn)
            engine.draw(spriteData);// Draw engine rocket
        if(shieldOn)
            // Draw shield using colorFilter 25% alpha
            shield.draw(spriteData, graphicsNS::ALPHA50 & colorFilter);
    }
}
```

Listing 11.10. The draw function from the Ship class.

```
//===========================================================================
// Update
// Typically called once per frame
// frameTime is used to regulate the speed of movement and animation
//===========================================================================
void Ship::update(float frameTime)
{
    if(explosionOn)
    {
        explosion.update(frameTime);
        if(explosion.getAnimationComplete())   // If explosion animation
                                                // complete
        {
            explosionOn = false;                // Turn off explosion
            visible = false;
            explosion.setAnimationComplete(false);
            explosion.setCurrentFrame(shipNS::EXPLOSION_START_FRAME);
```

```
        }
    }
    if(shieldOn)
    {
        shield.update(frameTime);
        if(shield.getAnimationComplete())
        {
            shieldOn = false;
            shield.setAnimationComplete(false);
        }
    }
    if(engineOn)
    {
        velocity.x += (float)cos(spriteData.angle) * shipNS::SPEED *
                      frameTime;
        velocity.y += (float)sin(spriteData.angle) * shipNS::SPEED *
                      frameTime;
        engine.update(frameTime);
    }
    Entity::update(frameTime);
    oldX = spriteData.x;                        // Save current position
    oldY = spriteData.y;
    oldAngle = spriteData.angle;
    switch (direction)                          // Rotate ship
    {
    case shipNS::LEFT:
        rotation -= frameTime * shipNS::ROTATION_RATE;  // Rotate left
        break;
    case shipNS::RIGHT:
        rotation += frameTime * shipNS::ROTATION_RATE;  // Rotate right
        break;
    }
    spriteData.angle += frameTime * rotation;   // Apply rotation
    spriteData.x += frameTime * velocity.x;     // Move ship along X
    spriteData.y += frameTime * velocity.y;     // Move ship along Y
    // Wrap around screen edge
    if (spriteData.x > GAME_WIDTH)              // If off right screen edge
        spriteData.x = -shipNS::WIDTH;          // Position off left screen
                                                // edge
    else if (spriteData.x < -shipNS::WIDTH)     // Else if off left screen
                                                // edge
        spriteData.x = GAME_WIDTH;              // Position off right
                                                // screen edge
    if (spriteData.y > GAME_HEIGHT)             // If off bottom screen
                                                // edge
        spriteData.y = -shipNS::HEIGHT;         // Position off top screen
                                                // edge
    else if (spriteData.y < -shipNS::HEIGHT)    // Else if off top screen
                                                // edge
        spriteData.y = GAME_HEIGHT;             // Position off bottom
                                                // screen edge
}
```

Listing 11.11. The Ship::update function.

```
//=============================================================================
// Damage
//=============================================================================
void Ship::damage(WEAPON weapon)
{
    if (shieldOn)
        return;
    switch(weapon)
    {
    case TORPEDO:
        audio->playCue(TORPEDO_HIT);
        health -= shipNS::TORPEDO_DAMAGE;
        break;
    case SHIP:
        audio->playCue(COLLIDE);     // Play sound
        health -= shipNS::SHIP_DAMAGE;
        break;
    case PLANET:
        health = 0;
        break;
    }
    if (health <= 0)
        explode();
    else
        shieldOn = true;
}
```

Listing 11.12. The `Ship::damage` function.

The `Entity` class's `damage` function is overridden in the `Ship` class. The ship may be damaged by a `TORPEDO`, a `SHIP`, or the `PLANET`. If the ship is damaged but not destroyed, the `shieldOn` Boolean is set to true (Listing 11.12). Torpedo and ship damage play the appropriate sound effect. Planet damage destroys the ship. The explosion sound is played by the `Ship::explode` function (Listing 11.13). The `repair` function repairs a damaged ship or brings a dead ship back to life (Listing 11.14).

```
//=============================================================================
// Explode
//=============================================================================
void Ship::explode()
{
    audio->playCue(EXPLODE);
    active = false;
    health = 0;
    explosionOn = true;
    engineOn = false;
    shieldOn = false;
    velocity.x = 0.0f;
    velocity.y = 0.0f;
}
```

Listing 11.13. The `Ship::explode` function.

```
//==============================================================================
// Repair
//==============================================================================
void Ship::repair()
{
    active = true;
    health = FULL_HEALTH;
    explosionOn = false;
    engineOn = false;
    shieldOn = false;
    rotation = 0.0f;
    direction = shipNS::NONE;            // Direction of rotation thruster
    visible = true;
}
```

Listing 11.14. The repair function from the Ship class.

11.6.4 Spacewar Class

The Spacewar class is the heart of the game. It inherits from the Game class and it is where
the bulk of the game logic is located. The spacewar.h file starts with some game constants
(Listing 11.15(a)).

```
// Programming 2D Games
// Copyright (c) 2011 by:
// Charles Kelly
// spacewar.h v1.0
#ifndef _SPACEWAR_H                  // Prevent multiple definitions if this
#define _SPACEWAR_H                  // file is included in more than one place
#define WIN32_LEAN_AND_MEAN
#include <string>
#include "game.h"
#include "textureManager.h"
#include "image.h"
#include "dashboard.h"
#include "planet.h"
#include "ship.h"
#include "torpedo.h"
namespace spacewarNS
{
    const char FONT[] = "Arial Bold";  // Font
    const int FONT_BIG_SIZE = 256;     // Font height
    const int FONT_SCORE_SIZE = 48;
    const COLOR_ARGB FONT_COLOR = graphicsNS::YELLOW;
    const COLOR_ARGB SHIP1_COLOR = graphicsNS::BLUE;
    const COLOR_ARGB SHIP2_COLOR = graphicsNS::YELLOW;
    const int SCORE_Y = 10;
    const int SCORE1_X = 60;
    const int SCORE2_X = GAME_WIDTH-80;
    const int HEALTHBAR_Y = 30;
    const int SHIP1_HEALTHBAR_X = 40;
    const int SHIP2_HEALTHBAR_X = GAME_WIDTH-100;
    const int COUNT_DOWN_X = GAME_WIDTH/2 - FONT_BIG_SIZE/4;
```

```
        const int COUNT_DOWN_Y = GAME_HEIGHT/2 - FONT_BIG_SIZE/2;
        const int COUNT_DOWN = 5;              // Count down from 5
        const int BUF_SIZE = 20;
        const int ROUND_TIME = 5;              // Time until new round starts
}
```

Listing 11.15(a). Spacewar game constants.

Following the constants is the class declaration. The `Spacewar` class includes `Texture Manager` objects for the `menu`, `nebula`, and `game` textures. It also contains objects for the ships, torpedoes, planet, nebula, menu, health bar, and fonts, plus some additional variables, as you can see in Listing 11.15(b). As shown in Listing 11.15(c), the class definition wraps up with prototypes for the member functions.

```
// Spacewar is the class we create; it inherits from the Game class
class Spacewar : public Game
{
private:
    // Game items
    TextureManager menuTexture, nebulaTexture, gameTextures;   // Textures
    Ship    ship1, ship2;        // Spaceships
    Torpedo torpedo1, torpedo2;  // Torpedoes
    Planet  planet;              // The planet
    Image   nebula;              // Backdrop image
    Image   menu;                // Menu image
    Bar     healthBar;           // Health bar for ships
    TextDX  fontBig;             // DirectX font for game banners
    TextDX  fontScore;
    bool    menuOn;
    bool    countDownOn;         // True when count down is displayed
    float   countDownTimer;
    char    buffer[spacewarNS::BUF_SIZE];
    bool    ship1Scored, ship2Scored;  // True if ship scored during round
    bool    roundOver;           // True when round is over
    float   roundTimer;          // Time until new round starts
    int     ship1Score, ship2Score;    // Scores
```

Listing 11.15(b). Spacewar objects and variables.

```
public:
    // Constructor
    Spacewar();
    // Destructor
    virtual ~Spacewar();
    // Initialize the game
    void initialize(HWND hwnd);
    void update();      // Must override pure virtual from Game
    void ai();          // "
    void collisions();  // "
```

```
    void render();        // "
    void consoleCommand(); // Process console command
    void roundStart();    // Start a new round of play
    void releaseAll();
    void resetAll();
};
#endif
```

Listing 11.15(c). Spacewar prototypes.

The spacewar.cpp file starts with the constructor and destructor (Listing 11.16). The initialize function prepares all of the game's objects. An exception is thrown if errors occur. The two ships are started on opposite sides of the planet in a stable clockwise orbit (Listing 11.17).

```
// Programming 2D Games
// Copyright (c) 2011 by:
// Charles Kelly
// spacewar.cpp v1.0
// This class is the core of the game
#include "spacewar.h"
//=============================================================================
// Constructor
//=============================================================================
Spacewar::Spacewar()
{
    menuOn = true;
    countDownOn = false;
    roundOver = false;
    ship1Score = 0;
    ship2Score = 0;
    ship1Scored = false;
    ship2Scored = false;
    initialized = false;
}
//=============================================================================
// Destructor
//=============================================================================
Spacewar::~Spacewar()
{
    releaseAll();          // Call onLostDevice() for every graphics item
}
```

Listing 11.16. Spacewar constructor and destructor.

```
//=============================================================================
// Initializes the game
// Throws GameError on error
//=============================================================================
```

```
void Spacewar::initialize(HWND hwnd)
{
    Game::initialize(hwnd); // Throws GameError
    // Initialize DirectX fonts
    fontBig.initialize(graphics, spacewarNS::FONT_BIG_SIZE, false, false,
                       spacewarNS::FONT);
    fontBig.setFontColor(spacewarNS::FONT_COLOR);
    fontScore.initialize(graphics, spacewarNS::FONT_SCORE_SIZE, false,
                         false, spacewarNS::FONT);
    // Menu texture
    if (!menuTexture.initialize(graphics,MENU_IMAGE))
        throw(GameError(gameErrorNS::FATAL_ERROR,
                "Error initializing menu texture"));
    // Nebula texture
    if (!nebulaTexture.initialize(graphics,NEBULA_IMAGE))
        throw(GameError(gameErrorNS::FATAL_ERROR,
                "Error initializing nebula texture"));
    // Main game textures
    if (!gameTextures.initialize(graphics,TEXTURES_IMAGE))
        throw(GameError(gameErrorNS::FATAL_ERROR,
                "Error initializing game textures"));
    // Menu image
    if (!menu.initialize(graphics,0,0,0,&menuTexture))
        throw(GameError(gameErrorNS::FATAL_ERROR,
                "Error initializing menu"));
    // Nebula image
    if (!nebula.initialize(graphics,0,0,0,&nebulaTexture))
        throw(GameError(gameErrorNS::FATAL_ERROR,
                "Error initializing nebula"));
    // Planet
    if (!planet.initialize(this, planetNS::WIDTH, planetNS::HEIGHT, 2,
                           &gameTextures))
        throw(GameError(gameErrorNS::FATAL_ERROR,
                "Error initializing planet"));
    // Ship1
    if (!ship1.initialize(this, shipNS::WIDTH, shipNS::HEIGHT,
        shipNS::TEXTURE_COLS, &gameTextures))
        throw(GameError(gameErrorNS::FATAL_ERROR,
                "Error initializing ship1"));
    ship1.setFrames(shipNS::SHIP1_START_FRAME, shipNS::SHIP1_END_FRAME);
    ship1.setCurrentFrame(shipNS::SHIP1_START_FRAME);
    // Light blue, used for shield
    ship1.setColorFilter(SETCOLOR_ARGB(255,230,230,255));
    ship1.setMass(shipNS::MASS);
    // Ship2
    if (!ship2.initialize(this, shipNS::WIDTH, shipNS::HEIGHT,
                          shipNS::TEXTURE_COLS, &gameTextures))
        throw(GameError(gameErrorNS::FATAL_ERROR,
                "Error initializing ship2"));
    ship2.setFrames(shipNS::SHIP2_START_FRAME, shipNS::SHIP2_END_FRAME);
    ship2.setCurrentFrame(shipNS::SHIP2_START_FRAME);
    // Light yellow, used for shield
    ship2.setColorFilter(SETCOLOR_ARGB(255,255,255,64));
    ship2.setMass(shipNS::MASS);
    // Torpedo1
    if (!torpedo1.initialize(this, torpedoNS::WIDTH, torpedoNS::HEIGHT,
                             torpedoNS::TEXTURE_COLS, &gameTextures))
```

```
        throw(GameError(gameErrorNS::FATAL_ERROR,
               "Error initializing torpedo1"));
    torpedo1.setFrames(torpedoNS::START_FRAME, torpedoNS::END_FRAME);
    torpedo1.setCurrentFrame(torpedoNS::START_FRAME);
    torpedo1.setColorFilter(SETCOLOR_ARGB(255,128,128,255));     // Light
                                                                 // blue
    // Torpedo2
    if (!torpedo2.initialize(this, torpedoNS::WIDTH, torpedoNS::HEIGHT,
                             torpedoNS::TEXTURE_COLS, &gameTextures))
        throw(GameError(gameErrorNS::FATAL_ERROR,
               "Error initializing torpedo2"));
    torpedo2.setFrames(torpedoNS::START_FRAME, torpedoNS::END_FRAME);
    torpedo2.setCurrentFrame(torpedoNS::START_FRAME);
    torpedo2.setColorFilter(SETCOLOR_ARGB(255,255,255,64));      // Light
                                                                 // yellow
    // Health bar
    healthBar.initialize(graphics, &gameTextures, 0,
                         spacewarNS::HEALTHBAR_Y, 2.0f, graphicsNS::WHITE);
    // Start ships on opposite sides of planet in stable clockwise orbit
    ship1.setX(GAME_WIDTH/4 - shipNS::WIDTH);
    ship2.setX(GAME_WIDTH - GAME_WIDTH/4);
    ship1.setY(GAME_HEIGHT/2 - shipNS::HEIGHT);
    ship2.setY(GAME_HEIGHT/2);
    ship1.setVelocity(VECTOR2(0,-shipNS::SPEED));
    ship2.setVelocity(VECTOR2(0,shipNS::SPEED));
    return;
}
```

Listing 11.17. The `Spacewar::initialize` function.

The `Spacewar::update` function is called repeatedly by the game loop. If the menu is currently displayed, the input is checked for a key press. If a key is pressed, the menu is turned off and a new round of play is started.

A new round begins with a countdown from 5 to 1. The `countDownOn` Boolean is true if the `countDownTimer` should be reduced. When the timer reaches 0, the countdown display is turned off.

The player keyboard and gamepad inputs are applied to each ship. If the forward key is pressed, the engine animation is enabled.

The gravity force of the planet is applied to both ships and both torpedoes and then all of the game entities are updated (Listing 11.18).

```
//=============================================================================
// Update all game items
//=============================================================================
void Spacewar::update()
{
    if (menuOn)
    {
        if (input->anyKeyPressed())
        {
            menuOn = false;
```

```
            input->clearAll();
            roundStart();
        }
    }
    else if(countDownOn)
    {
        countDownTimer -= frameTime;
        if(countDownTimer <= 0)
            countDownOn = false;
    }
    else
    {
        if (ship1.getActive())
        {
            // If engine on
            if (input->isKeyDown(SHIP1_FORWARD_KEY) ||
                input->getGamepadDPadUp(0))
            {
                ship1.setEngineOn(true);
                audio->playCue(ENGINE1);
            }
            else
            {
                ship1.setEngineOn(false);
                audio->stopCue(ENGINE1);
            }
            ship1.rotate(shipNS::NONE);
            // If turn ship1 left
            if (input->isKeyDown(SHIP1_LEFT_KEY) ||
                input->getGamepadDPadLeft(0))
                ship1.rotate(shipNS::LEFT);
            // If turn ship1 right
            if (input->isKeyDown(SHIP1_RIGHT_KEY) ||
                input->getGamepadDPadRight(0))
                ship1.rotate(shipNS::RIGHT);
            // If ship1 fire
            if (input->isKeyDown(SHIP1_FIRE_KEY) || input->getGamepadA(0))
                torpedo1.fire(&ship1);                    // Fire torpedo1
        }
        if (ship2.getActive())
        {
            // If engine on
            if (input->isKeyDown(SHIP2_FORWARD_KEY)  ||
                input->getGamepadDPadUp(1))
            {
                ship2.setEngineOn(true);
                audio->playCue(ENGINE2);
            }
            else
            {
                ship2.setEngineOn(false);
                audio->stopCue(ENGINE2);
            }
            ship2.rotate(shipNS::NONE);
            // If turn ship2 left
            if (input->isKeyDown(VK_LEFT) || input->getGamepadDPadLeft(1))
                ship2.rotate(shipNS::LEFT);
            // If turn ship2 right
```

```
        if (input->isKeyDown(VK_RIGHT) ||
            input->getGamepadDPadRight(1))
            ship2.rotate(shipNS::RIGHT);
        // If ship2 fire
        if (input->isKeyDown(SHIP2_FIRE_KEY) || input->getGamepadA(1))
            torpedo2.fire(&ship2);                    // Fire torpedo2
    }
    if(roundOver)
    {
        roundTimer -= frameTime;
        if(roundTimer <= 0)
            roundStart();
    }
}
ship1.gravityForce(&planet, frameTime);
ship2.gravityForce(&planet, frameTime);
torpedo1.gravityForce(&planet, frameTime);
torpedo2.gravityForce(&planet, frameTime);
// Update the entities
planet.update(frameTime);
ship1.update(frameTime);
ship2.update(frameTime);
torpedo1.update(frameTime);
torpedo2.update(frameTime);
}
```

Listing 11.18. The `Spacewar::update` function.

A new round resets the position of each ship and starts the countdown timer (Listing 11.19). Collision detection is performed in the `Spacewar` class. Every combination of possible collisions must be tested. If a ship is involved in the collision, its `damage` function is called with the parameter specifying the item collided with. The collision code also updates the scores. In this version of the game, a player scores only when the other ship is destroyed (Listing 11.20).

```
//=============================================================================
// Start a new round of play
//=============================================================================
void Spacewar::roundStart()
{
    // Start ships on opposite sides of planet in stable clockwise orbit
    ship1.setX(GAME_WIDTH/4 - shipNS::WIDTH);
    ship2.setX(GAME_WIDTH - GAME_WIDTH/4);
    ship1.setY(GAME_HEIGHT/2 - shipNS::HEIGHT);
    ship2.setY(GAME_HEIGHT/2);
    ship1.setVelocity(VECTOR2(0,-shipNS::SPEED));
    ship2.setVelocity(VECTOR2(0,shipNS::SPEED));
    ship1.setDegrees(0);
    ship2.setDegrees(180);
    ship1.repair();
    ship2.repair();
    countDownTimer = spacewarNS::COUNT_DOWN;
```

```
        countDownOn = true;
        roundOver = false;
        ship1Scored = false;
        ship2Scored = false;
}
```

Listing 11.19. The `Spacewar::roundStart` function.

```
//=============================================================================
// Handle collisions
//=============================================================================
void Spacewar::collisions()
{
    VECTOR2 collisionVector;
    // If collision between ship1 and planet
    if(ship1.collidesWith(planet, collisionVector))
    {
        ship1.toOldPosition();        // Move ship out of collision
        ship1.damage(PLANET);
        // Vibrate controller 0, 100%, 1.0 sec
        input->gamePadVibrateLeft(0,65535,1.0);
    }
    // If collision between ship2 and planet
    if(ship2.collidesWith(planet, collisionVector))
    {
        ship2.toOldPosition();   // Move ship out of collision
        ship2.damage(PLANET);
        // Vibrate controller 1, 100%, 1.0 sec
        input->gamePadVibrateLeft(1,65535,1.0);
    }
    // If collision between ship1 and ship2
    if(ship1.collidesWith(ship2, collisionVector))
    {
        // Bounce off other ship
        ship1.bounce(collisionVector, ship2);
        ship2.bounce(collisionVector*-1, ship1);
        ship1.damage(SHIP);
        ship2.damage(SHIP);
        input->gamePadVibrateRight(0,30000,0.5);
        input->gamePadVibrateRight(1,30000,0.5);
    }
    // If collision between torpedos and ships
    if(torpedo1.collidesWith(ship2, collisionVector))
    {
        ship2.damage(TORPEDO);
        torpedo1.setVisible(false);
        torpedo1.setActive(false);
        input->gamePadVibrateRight(1,20000,0.5);
    }
    if(torpedo2.collidesWith(ship1, collisionVector))
    {
        ship1.damage(TORPEDO);
        torpedo2.setVisible(false);
        torpedo2.setActive(false);
```

```
            input->gamePadVibrateRight(0,20000,0.5);
    }
    // If collision between torpedos and planet
    if(torpedo1.collidesWith(planet, collisionVector))
    {
        torpedo1.setVisible(false);
        torpedo1.setActive(false);
        audio->playCue(TORPEDO_CRASH);
    }
    if(torpedo2.collidesWith(planet, collisionVector))
    {
        torpedo2.setVisible(false);
        torpedo2.setActive(false);
        audio->playCue(TORPEDO_CRASH);
    }
    // Check for scores
    if(ship1.getActive() == false && ship2Scored == false)
    {
        ship2Score++;
        ship2Scored = true;
        if(roundOver == false)
        {
            roundTimer = spacewarNS::ROUND_TIME;
            roundOver = true;
        }
    }
    if(ship2.getActive() == false && ship1Scored == false)
    {
        ship1Score++;
        ship1Scored = true;
        if(roundOver == false)
        {
            roundTimer = spacewarNS::ROUND_TIME;
            roundOver = true;
        }
    }
}
```

Listing 11.20. The Spacewar::collisions function.

The render function draws all of the game items (Listing 11.21). Just for fun, we have added a few console commands. The gravity of the planet may be turned on or off and the entire planet may be disabled (Listing 11.22).

```
//=============================================================================
// Render game items
//=============================================================================
void Spacewar::render()
{
    graphics->spriteBegin();                    // Begin drawing sprites
    nebula.draw();                              // Display Orion nebula
```

```
        planet.draw();                          // Draw the planet
        // Display scores
        fontScore.setFontColor(spacewarNS::SHIP1_COLOR);
        _snprintf_s(buffer, spacewarNS::BUF_SIZE, "%d", (int)ship1Score);
        fontScore.print(buffer,spacewarNS::SCORE1_X,spacewarNS::SCORE_Y);
        fontScore.setFontColor(spacewarNS::SHIP2_COLOR);
        _snprintf_s(buffer, spacewarNS::BUF_SIZE, "%d", (int)ship2Score);
        fontScore.print(buffer,spacewarNS::SCORE2_X,spacewarNS::SCORE_Y);
        // Display health bars
        healthBar.setX((float)spacewarNS::SHIP1_HEALTHBAR_X);
        healthBar.set(ship1.getHealth());
        healthBar.draw(spacewarNS::SHIP1_COLOR);
        healthBar.setX((float)spacewarNS::SHIP2_HEALTHBAR_X);
        healthBar.set(ship2.getHealth());
        healthBar.draw(spacewarNS::SHIP2_COLOR);
        ship1.draw();                            // Draw the spaceships
        ship2.draw();
        torpedo1.draw(graphicsNS::FILTER);       // Draw the torpedoes using
                                                 // colorFilter
        torpedo2.draw(graphicsNS::FILTER);
        if(menuOn)
            menu.draw();
        if(countDownOn)
        {
            _snprintf_s(buffer, spacewarNS::BUF_SIZE, "%d", (int)
                    (ceil(countDownTimer)));
            fontBig.print(buffer,spacewarNS::COUNT_DOWN_X,
                        spacewarNS::COUNT_DOWN_Y);
        }
        graphics->spriteEnd();                   // End drawing sprites
}
```

Listing 11.21. The Spacewar::render function.

```
//=============================================================================
// Process console commands
//=============================================================================
void Spacewar::consoleCommand()
{
    command = console->getCommand();    // Get command from console
    if(command == "")                   // If no command
        return;
    if (command == "help")              // If "help" command
    {
        console->print("Console Commands:");
        console->print("fps - toggle display of frames per second");
        console->print("gravity off - turns off planet gravity");
        console->print("gravity on - turns on planet gravity");
        console->print("planet off - disables planet");
        console->print("planet on - enables planet");
        return;
    }
    if (command == "fps")
    {
```

```
        fpsOn = !fpsOn;                     // Toggle display of fps
        if(fpsOn)
            console->print("fps On");
        else
            console->print("fps Off");
    }
    if (command == "gravity off")
    {
        planet.setMass(0);
        console->print("Gravity Off");
    }else if (command == "gravity on")
    {
        planet.setMass(planetNS::MASS);
        console->print("Gravity On");
    }else if (command == "planet off")
    {
        planet.disable();
        console->print("Planet Off");
    }else if (command == "planet on")
    {
        planet.enable();
        console->print("Planet On");
    }
}
```

Listing 11.22. Console commands added to the Spacewar game.

The Spacewar class concludes with the releaseAll and resetAll functions (Listing 11.23).

```
//==============================================================================
// The graphics device was lost
// Release all reserved video memory so graphics device may be reset
//==============================================================================
void Spacewar::releaseAll()
{
    menuTexture.onLostDevice();
    nebulaTexture.onLostDevice();
    gameTextures.onLostDevice();
    fontScore.onLostDevice();
    fontBig.onLostDevice();
    Game::releaseAll();
    return;
}
//==============================================================================
// The grahics device has been reset
// Recreate all surfaces
//==============================================================================
void Spacewar::resetAll()
{
    fontBig.onResetDevice();
```

```
fontScore.onResetDevice();
gameTextures.onResetDevice();
nebulaTexture.onResetDevice();
menuTexture.onResetDevice();
Game::resetAll();
return;
}
```

Listing 11.23. The `releaseAll` and `resetAll` functions from the `Spacewar` class.

That concludes the code we created for the Spacewar game. The files that comprise the game engine contain the rest. They are all included in the project. The complete source is available for download at www.programming2dgames.com.

▐ 11.7 Saving and Loading

Our Spacewar game did not include the ability to save or load a game in progress. This is not a feature that is typically included in a two-player game of this nature. If we were creating a single-player game that required the player to complete a series of quests, we should provide some way to save the player's progress. This could be in the form of automatic saves at key points in the game or something that the player would select. The only data that needs to be saved are those variables that are changed by the player's activity.

In order to demonstrate saving and loading of games, we have created a single-player game that reuses most of the Spacewar code.

11.7.1 Space Pirates

The premise behind the game is that space pirates have stolen Earth's cows. Apparently, the pirates learned about ice cream during a recent scouting mission to our planet and decided to steal the cows to make their own (and who could blame them?). The player must round up the stolen cows and return them to earth (see Figure 11.5).

The game features `saveGame` and `loadGame` functions. The `saveGame` function is called automatically when the game is exited. When a new game is started, a third function, `foundGame`, is used to check for the presence of a saved game. If a saved game is found, the player is asked if he or she would like to load the previously saved game.

The `saveGame` function creates a text file. The name of the file to create is defined by the constant `SAVE_NAME` as `SpacePiratesSave.txt`. No path name is specified, which means the file will be created in the same folder as the game executable (Listing 11.24).

Using a text file for saved games is good for development purposes because it allows us to easily examine the file's contents. It would also make it easier for a player to make modifications to the file in order to cheat. If cheating is something we wanted to prevent, we could use a binary file instead. We might even take steps to obfuscate the data within the file.

Loading a game looks like the code in Listing 11.25. We use local variables `n`, `x`, and `y` to load the values from the file and then as parameters to the `set` functions to set the actual game variables.

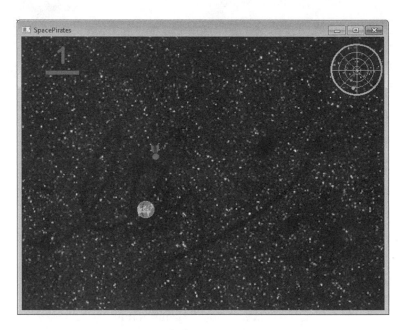

Figure 11.5. The Space Pirates game.

```
//============================================================================
// Save game
// Does not save torpedoes. Saves only ship1 velocity.
//============================================================================
void SpacePirates::saveGame()
{
    std::ofstream outFile(SAVE_NAME);
    if(outFile.fail())                      // Error creating save file
    {
        messageDialog->print("Error creating save file.");
        return;
    }
    outFile << ship1Score << '\n'
            << ship1.getX() << '\n'
            << ship1.getY() << '\n'
            << ship1.getHealth() << '\n'
            << ship1.getVelocity().x << '\n'
            << ship1.getVelocity().y << '\n';
    for(int i=0; i<MAX_PIRATES; i++)
    {
        outFile << ship2[i].getX() << '\n'
                << ship2[i].getY() << '\n'
                << ship2[i].getHealth() << '\n'
                << cow[i].getX() << '\n'
                << cow[i].getY() << '\n';
    }
}
```

Listing 11.24. The `saveGame` function from the `SpacePirates` class.

```
//============================================================================
// Load game
//============================================================================
void SpacePirates::loadGame()
{
    std::ifstream inFile(SAVE_NAME);
    float n, x, y;
    if(inFile.fail())                    // Error opening save file
    {
        messageDialog->print("Error opening save file.");
        return;
    }
    inFile >> ship1Score;
    inFile >> n;
    ship1.setX(n);
    inFile >> n;
    ship1.setY(n);
    inFile >> n;
    ship1.setHealth(n);
    inFile >> x;
    inFile >> y;
    ship1.setVelocity(D3DXVECTOR2(x,y));
    for(int i=0; i<MAX_PIRATES; i++)
    {
        inFile >> n;
        ship2[i].setX(n);
        inFile >> n;
        ship2[i].setY(n);
        inFile >> n;
        ship2[i].setHealth(n);
        inFile >> n;
        cow[i].setX(n);
        inFile >> n;
        cow[i].setY(n);
    }
}
```

Listing 11.25. The `loadGame` function from the `SpacePirates` class.

The `foundGame` function checks for the presence of a saved game by attempting to open the file for input (Listing 11.26). The `saveGame` function is called from the game's destructor, so it will run when the game is exited (Listing 11.27).

```
//============================================================================
// Check for saved game file
// Post: returns true if saved game found, false if not
//============================================================================
bool SpacePirates::foundGame()
{
    std::ifstream inFile(SAVE_NAME);
    if(inFile.fail())                    // Error opening save file
        return false;                    // No saved game found
```

```
        inFile.close();
        return true;                        // Saved game found
}
```

Listing 11.26. The `foundGame` function from the `SpacePirates` class.

```
//=========================================================================
// Destructor
//=========================================================================
SpacePirates::~SpacePirates()
{
    saveGame();               // Save game state
    releaseAll();             // Call onLostDevice() for every graphics item
}
```

Listing 11.27. Calling the `saveGame` function.

The `foundGame` function is called at the end of the `initialize` function. The code checks for the presence of a saved game and uses a `messageDialog` to ask the user if he or she would like to load the last saved game. A `loadGameDialog` Boolean is set to true to indicate that we are waiting for the player to click "Yes" or "No" on the `messageDialog` (Listing 11.28).

The `loadGameDialog` Boolean is used in the update function. If the player clicks the "Yes" button on the `messageDialog`, the `loadGame` function is called to load the saved game (Listing 11.29).

```
    // Load game?
    if(foundGame())                 // If saved game found
    {
        messageDialog->setButtonType(messageDialogNS::YES_NO);
        messageDialog->print("Load last saved game?");
        loadGameDialog = true;
    }
```

Listing 11.28. Using the `foundGame` function to check for a saved game.

```
//=========================================================================
// Update all game items
//=========================================================================
void SpacePirates::update()
{
    if(loadGameDialog)
    {
        if(messageDialog->getButtonClicked() == 1)  // If Yes
```

```
        loadGame();                                    // Load saved game
    if(messageDialog->getVisible() == false)
        loadGameDialog = false;
}
```

Listing 11.29. Handling the button clicks from the load game dialog.

The complete source for Space Pirates is available for download from www.programming
2dgames.com.

Chapter Review

We began this chapter by studying some project management techniques. A software development model was chosen. We introduced techniques for time and resource management,
and we broke the job of creating our Spacewar game into smaller tasks, then described how
those tasks were completed throughout the previous chapters. Then we put it all together
and described the final version of our game. The last topic we discussed was saving and
loading a game. Some of the key topics from the chapter are the following:

- *Evolutionary prototyping.* Evolutionary prototyping is a software development
  model that involves the creation of prototypes early in the design process.

- *SAVE.* SAVE, SAVE, SAVE the early prototypes. Use a different version number for
  each one.

- *Learn the skills.* Project management skills are crucial in game development.

- *Gantt chart.* A Gantt chart is a good tool for time management.

- *Person loading table.* A person loading table is a good tool for resource management.

- *Design document.* Each project should begin with a design document to provide the
  team members with a common reference point.

- *Be quick.* Prototype textures and sound effects should be created quickly.

- *Be logical.* Arrange the completion of tasks in a logical order so that prerequisite
  tasks are completed before they are required.

- *TEST.* TEST, TEST, TEST.

- *Comment.* Write good descriptive comments in the source code.

- *Document.* User documentation should be in separate files for ease in modification
  and translation.

- *Break it down*. Creating a game is an evolutionary process. Many first-time game programmers can be overwhelmed when confronted by the complexity of a finished game for the first time. Break the job down into smaller manageable tasks.

Review Questions

1. What is one advantage of evolutionary prototyping?

2. What is the longest estimated time we would like for any one task in our game project?

3. What is the overall goal of time management in a game project?

4. What is a Gantt chart used for?

5. What happens in a Gantt chart when the actual time required to complete a task exceeds the estimated time?

6. What aspect of project management is a person loading table used for?

7. How do the task descriptions in a person loading table compare to those in a Gantt chart?

8. What is the purpose of a design document?

9. What is important in prototype textures?

10. Why is early testing important?

11. What form of documentation is meant for internal use?

12. Game objects that collide are all derived from which game engine class?

13. Which line of code applies the force of gravity between the planet and ship1?

14. When two spaceships collide, both are damaged. What does the function call look like that damages ship1?

15. How does the `foundGame` function check for the presence of a saved game file?

Exercises

1. Create a Gantt chart for your own game project.

2. Create a person loading table for your own game project.

3. Create a design document for your own game project.

4. Make a change in the game play of the Spacewar game. Describe the rationale for the change and the code changes necessary.

5. Add a new console command to the Spacewar game that reverses the gravity of the planet so that ships and torpedoes are repelled.

Examples

The following examples are available for download from www.programming2dgames.com:

- *Spacewar Gantt Chart.* A Microsoft Visio Gantt chart for the Spacewar game.

- *Spacewar v1.0.* A complete version of the Spacewar game.

  - Demonstrates most of the game programming aspects from the previous chapters.

- *Space Pirates.* A single player variation on the Spacewar theme that includes saving and loading a game.

  - Demonstrates how to save and load a game state.

  - Demonstrates how to check for the presence of a file.

  - Demonstrates most of the game programming aspects from the previous chapters.

12 Network Programming

12.1 Network Overview

"Look, good against remotes is one thing. Good against the living? That's something else."
—Han Solo

Who are we to argue with Han Solo? Unfortunately, our human opponents are not always nearby when we want to play against them. If our computer is connected to a network, we can play against other human opponents who are on the other side of the room or even on the other side of the world.

In the network world, we hear the terms *client* and *server*. With networked games, the client is the device the player is using, and the server is the device the clients are communicating with. The client accepts input from the player and sends it to the server. The server typically runs the game, receives input data from the client, applies it to the game, and sends the state of the game back to the client. The clients use the state information received from the server to display the game as seen by the player. This is the typical client/server model used by most games.

The Internet and most local area networks use *Internet protocol* (IP). The Internet protocol is a set of rules that define how information and hardware are to be configured so that data may be sent from one location to another. However, IP does not define specific rules about how large files are to be sent and what should happen if an error occurs during transmission. For those scenarios, there are higher-level protocols that work in conjunction with IP.

TCP. *Transmission control protocol* (TCP) provides the reliable delivery of data. Large messages are automatically broken into smaller IP-sized packets, transmitted, received, and reassembled in order by the receiver. Packets that are lost during transmission are automatically retransmitted. The reliability of TCP message delivery can result in long delays (on the order of seconds) if packets are lost and must be retransmitted. For this reason, TCP is typically not considered suitable for the delivery of real-time data. TCP establishes a connection between the two devices; this connection is maintained until broken by one or both devices. In our implementation, only one TCP connection is permitted at a time. If the other device breaks the connection, an error will result when attempting to send or receive data.

UDP. *User datagram protocol* (UDP) is a connectionless protocol. A connectionless protocol supports communicating with multiple devices from a single interface. UDP provides no guarantee of data delivery. Data packets may arrive out of order, may be duplicated, or may not be delivered at all. UDP is typically used for time sensitive applications where the timely delivery of data is more important than reliability.

12.1.1 Addresses

Each device on the network must have a unique IP address. The original addressing scheme, known as IPv4, uses a 32-bit number for each address. This allows for 2^{32} (4,294,967,296) addresses. Because of the large number of devices now connected to the Internet and the way these addresses are allocated, we are quickly running out of unused addresses. A new addressing scheme, known as IPv6, has been introduced. IPv6 uses a 128-bit number for each address. This allows for 2^{128} (approximately 3.4×10^{38}) addresses—to put it in perspective, with IPv6 there are enough addresses to give every grain of sand on the earth its own IP address and still have a bunch left over. The IPv4 addressing scheme is still the most widely used, so we will be using it in this book.

12.1.2 Port

Each addressable device also has a range of port numbers that are used. A port number is a 16-bit number. This yields 2^{16} (65,536) port numbers. We might equate the IP address with the address of a building and the port number with a room in the building. Port numbers 0–1023 are predefined for use in well-known services and should be avoided. Port numbers 1024–65535 may be freely used.

12.1.3 Socket

In network programming, a *socket* is an interface to the network. For this reason, *network programming* is often referred to as *socket programming*. For Windows programming, *Winsock* is the API that supports the creation of sockets that support TCP/IP and UDP/IP. Sockets may be configured as *blocking* or *nonblocking*. A blocking socket does not return from function calls to send or receive data until the operation is complete. A nonblocking socket always returns immediately, even if no data was sent or received. Given the real-time nature of many games, we cannot afford to wait for socket operations to complete. If blocking sockets were used, we would need to write a multithreaded application with a separate thread to handle communications. Writing multithreaded programs requires additional complexity, which we would like to avoid, so we will be using nonblocking sockets.

12.2 The Net Class

In order to add network support to our game engine, we will create a new Net class. The Net class will contain the code to create a nonblocking Winsock socket that we may use to send and receive data. The socket will be configured to use either TCP/IP or UDP/IP network communications. The Network class is contained in two files: net.h and net.cpp. The net.h file includes winsock2.h. There is also an older winsock.h file. If these two header files are included in the same project, errors will occur. Unfortunately, windows.h automatically, and perhaps incorrectly, includes winsock.h. The statement #define WIN32_LEAN_AND_MEAN prevents windows.h from loading several header files, including winsock.h. When working with the Net class, make sure all of the project's header files define WIN32_LEAN_AND_MEAN prior to any include statements.

12.3 Initialize the Network

The first step in using Winsock is to call the WSAStartup function. This function allows the application to call additional Winsock functions. When finished using Winsock, an application must call WSACleanup to free the resources allocated by WSAStartup. The WSACleanup function must be called for every call made to WSAStartup.

```
int WSAStartup(
    WORD wVersionRequested,
    LPWSADATA lpWSAData
);
```

The parameters are:

- wVersionRequested. The highest version of Windows sockets that may be used. We will be using version 2.2. The Winsock DLL, Ws_32.dll, supports applications that use Winsock specifications from version 1.0 through 2.2.

- lpWSAData. A pointer to a WSAData structure that receives information about the Windows sockets implementation.

The return value is 0 on success or an error code on failure. We will examine the error codes in more detail later in this chapter. WSAStartup is called as part of our initialize function, as seen in Listing 12.1(a).

```
//=============================================================================
// Initialize network
// Protocol = UDP or TCP
// Called by netCreateServer and netCreatClient
// Pre:
//   port = Port number
```

```
//   protocol = UDP or TCP
// Post:
//   Returns two-part int code on error
//      The low 16 bits contains Status code as defined in net.h
//      The high 16 bits contains "Windows Socket Error Code"
//============================================================================
int Net::initialize(int port, int protocol)
{
    unsigned long ul = 1;
    int             nRet;
    int status;
    if(netInitialized)                  // If network currently initialized
        closeSockets();                 // Close current network and start over
    mode = UNINITIALIZED;
    status = WSAStartup(0x0202, &wsd);  // Initiate the use of winsock 2.2
    if (status != 0)
        return ( (status << 16) + NET_INIT_FAILED);
```

Listing 12.1(a). Calling WSAStartup in the Net::initialize function.

12.3.1 Create the Socket

After Winsock is initialized, the next step is to create a network socket. The socket function creates a socket of the specified address family, type, and protocol.

```
SOCKET WSAAPI socket(
    int af,
    int type,
    int protocol
);
```

The parameters are:

- af. The address family. The possible values are defined in the Winsock2.h header file or in the Ws2def.h header file on the Windows SDK released for Windows Vista and later. We want the Internet address family for IPv4, which is AF_INET. The supported types are:

    - AF_UNSPEC. Unspecified.

    - AF_INET. Internet protocol version 4 (IPv4).

    - AF_INET6. Internet protocol version 6 (IPv6).

    - AF_IPX. The IPX/SPX address family; not supported on Windows Vista and later.

    - AF_APPLETALK. The AppleTalk address family; not supported on Windows Vista and later.

    - AF_NETBIOS. The NetBIOS address family; not supported on 64-bit versions of windows.

- AF_IRDA. The Infrared Data Association (IrDA) address family.

- AF_BTH. The Bluetooth address family.

- type. The type of socket to create. The supported types are:

    - SOCK_STREAM. Reliable connection-based byte stream. Uses TCP with the Internet address family (AF_INET or AF_INET6).

    - SOCK_DGRAM. A socket that supports datagrams, which are connectionless and unreliable. Uses UDP with the Internet address family (AF_INET or AF_INET6).

    - SOCK_RAW. A raw socket that allows an application to manipulate the protocol header.

    - SOCK_RDM. Reliable datagram message socket.

    - SOCK_SEQPACKET. A reliable sequence packet.

- protocol. The protocol used. Many types are supported. The only two types we are interested in are:

    - IPPROTO_TCP. The af parameter must be either AF_INET or AF_INET6, and the type parameter must be SOCK_STREAM.

    - IPPROTO_UDP. The af parameter must be either AF_INET or AF_INET6 and the type parameter must be SOCK_DGRAM.

The return value is a socket reference unless an error occurred, in which case INVALID_SOCKET is returned. A detailed error code may be obtained by calling the WSA GetLastError function.

Our initialize function accepts a protocol parameter that is used to determine which parameters to use when creating the socket (Listing 12.1(b)).

```
switch (protocol)
{
case UDP:      // UDP
    // Create UDP socket and bind it to a local interface and port
    sock = socket(AF_INET, SOCK_DGRAM, IPPROTO_UDP);
    if (sock == INVALID_SOCKET)
    {
        WSACleanup();
        status = WSAGetLastError();         // Get detailed error
        return ( (status << 16) + NET_INVALID_SOCKET);
    }
    type = UDP;
    break;
case TCP:      // TCP
    // Create TCP socket and bind it to a local interface and port
```

```
        sock = socket(AF_INET, SOCK_STREAM, IPPROTO_TCP);
    if (sock == INVALID_SOCKET)
    {
        WSACleanup();
        status = WSAGetLastError();          // Get detailed error
        return ( (status << 16) + NET_INVALID_SOCKET);
    }
    type = UNCONNECTED_TCP;
    break;
default:     // Invalid type
    return (NET_INIT_FAILED);
}
```

Listing 12.1(b). Creating the network socket.

If an error is detected as part of the socket creation, WSACleanup is called to end Windows socket operations and free resources. The function WSAGetLastError is called to retrieve the error code, which is combined with our own error code and returned. The code return ((status << 16) + NET_INVALID_SOCKET); shifts the error code number to the left by 16 bits and inserts our error code. The returned error code contains the Winsock error number in the upper 16 bits and our own error code in the lower 16 bits. The getError function (covered later in this chapter) will return a detailed error message from our two-part error code.

12.3.2 Put the Socket in Nonblocking Mode

A socket may be made nonblocking with the ioctlsocket function.

```
int ioctlsocket(
    SOCKET s,
    long cmd,
    u_long *argp
);
```

The parameters are:

- s. The socket.

- cmd. The command to perform on the socket. The supported commands are:

    - FIONBIO. If *argp points to an unsigned long of 0, nonblocking mode is disabled. If *argp points to a nonzero value, nonblocking mode is enabled.

    - FIONREAD. Gets the amount of data pending that may be read with the recv function. Stores the size into the unsigned long pointed to by *argp.

    - SIOCATMARK. Used to determine if all out of band (OOB) data has been read.

- argp. A pointer to the command parameters.

```
// Put socket in nonblocking mode
nRet = ioctlsocket(sock, FIONBIO, (unsigned long *) &ul);
if (nRet == SOCKET_ERROR)
{
    WSACleanup();
    status = WSAGetLastError();              // Get detailed error
    return ( (status << 16) + NET_INVALID_SOCKET);
}
```

Listing 12.1(c). Putting the socket in nonblocking mode.

The function returns 0 on success or SOCKET_ERROR on error. The specific error code may be retrieved by calling WSAGetLastError, as shown in Listing 12.1(c).

12.3.3 Set Family and Port

Before we can send or receive data, we need to set up a SOCKADDR_IN structure. The structure looks like this:

```
typedef struct sockaddr_in {
    ADDRESS_FAMILY sin_family;
    USHORT         sin_port;
    IN_ADDR        sin_addr;
    CHAR           sin_zero[8];
} SOCKADDR_IN, *PSOCKADDR_IN;
```

The members are:

- sin_family. The address family to use; always set to AF_INET.

- sin_port. The port number we are using. If more than one application running on a computer uses the same port, a conflict will result.

- sin_addr. An IN_ADDR structure that contains an IPv4 address. This is the address of the server in the client code and the address to listen for in the server code.

- sin_zero. Reserved for system use.

We set the sin_family and sin_port portion of the structure in our initialization code, as seen in Listing 12.1(d). The rest of the structure will be filled in as needed.

```
// Set local family and port
localAddr.sin_family = AF_INET;
localAddr.sin_port = htons((u_short)port);    // Port number
// Set remote family and port
remoteAddr.sin_family = AF_INET;
remoteAddr.sin_port = htons((u_short)port);   // Port number
```

```
    netInitialized = true;
    return NET_OK;
}
```

Listing 12.1(d). Setting the socket's family and port.

▌ 12.4 Creating a Server

To create a server, we need to know the port number to use and the protocol (UDP or TCP). Our `createServer` function of the `Net` class sets up a server.

```
int createServer
(
    int port,
    int protocol
);
```

The parameters are:

- `port`. The port number to listen on. Port numbers 0–1023 are used for well-known services and should not be used for a game. Port numbers 1024–65535 may be freely used.

- `protocol`. UDP or TCP. The `net.h` file defines UDP and TCP as constants for use as parameters values.

The return value is `NET_OK` on success or a two-part error code. The error code may be expanded into a detailed error message by the `getError` function (covered later in this chapter).

The first step in the `createServer` function is to call the previously described `initialize` function, as shown in Listing 12.2(a). A server can communicate with multiple clients and so it must listen for incoming communications from any address. We configure the server to listen on any address by setting the `sin_addr` member of the `local Addr` structure to `INADDR_ANY` (Listing 12.2(b)).

```
//===========================================================================
// Setup network for use as server
// May not be configured as Server and Client at the same time
// Pre:
//   port = Port number to listen on
//      Port numbers 0-1023 are used for well-known services
//      Port numbers 1024-65535 may be freely used
//   protocol = UDP or TCP
// Post:
//   Returns NET_OK on success
//   Returns two-part int code on error
//      The low 16 bits contains Status code as defined in net.h
//      The high 16 bits contains "Windows Socket Error Code"
//===========================================================================
```

```
int Net::createServer(int port, int protocol)
{
    int status;
    // ----- Initialize network stuff -----
    status = initialize(port, protocol);
    if (status != NET_OK)
        return status;
```

Listing 12.2(a). Creating a network server.

```
localAddr.sin_addr.s_addr = htonl(INADDR_ANY);    // Listen on all
                                                  // addresses
```

Listing 12.2(b). Setting the server to listen on all addresses.

12.4.1 Winsock bind Function

Next, we use the Winsock bind function to associate the socket with the localAddr structure. An unconnected socket must be bound before the Winsock listen function may be called to listen for an incoming connection. We only need to make an explicit call to bind for a server socket. A client socket is implicitly bound when it is used to send data. The bind function looks like this:

```
int bind(
    SOCKET s,
    const struct sockaddr *name,
    int namelen
);
```

The parameters are:

- s. The socket.

- name. A pointer to the localAddr structure.

- namelen. The length of the name in bytes.

The return value is 0 if no errors or SOCKET_ERROR if error. A specific error code may be retrieved by calling the WSAGetLastError function.

We call the bind function, then return an error code if there is an error or set the bound property to true and mode to SERVER on success, as seen in Listing 12.2(c).

```
    // Bind socket
    if (bind(sock, (SOCKADDR *)&localAddr, sizeof(localAddr)) ==
                SOCKET_ERROR)
```

```
        {
            status = WSAGetLastError();           // Get detailed error
            return ((status << 16) + NET_BIND_FAILED);
        }
        bound = true;
        mode = SERVER;
        return NET_OK;
    }
```

Listing 12.2(c). Binding the server socket with the `localAddr` structure.

▮ 12.5 Creating a Client

To create a client, we need to know the IP address of the server to connect to, the port number to use, and the protocol (UDP or TCP) to use. Our `createClient` function of the `Net` class sets up a client.

```
int createClient
(
    char *server,
    int port,
    int protocol
);
```

The parameters are:

- `server`. A pointer to the IP address of the server to connect to as a `NULL`-terminated string (e.g., "192.168.1.100") or a `NULL`-terminated string containing the host name (e.g., "www.programming2dgames.com").

- `port`. The port number to listen on. Port numbers 0–1023 are used for well-known services and should not be used for a game. Port numbers 1024–65535 may be freely used.

- `protocol`. UDP or TCP. The `net.h` file defines UDP and TCP as constants for use as parameters values.

The return value is `NET_OK` on success or a two-part error code. The error code may be expanded into a detailed error message by the `getError` function (covered later in this chapter).

The first step in the `createClient` function is to call the previously described `initialize` function. After allocating some local variables, the `initialize` function is called (Listing 12.3(a)).

```
//==========================================================================
// Setup network for use as a Client
// Pre:
//    *server = IP address of server to connect to as null-terminated
```

```
//        string (e.g. "192.168.1.100") or null-terminated host name
//        (e.g. "www.programming2dgames.com")
//     port = Port number. Port numbers 0-1023 are used for well-known
//     services
//        Port numbers 1024-65535 may be freely used
//     protocol = UDP or TCP
// Post:
//     Returns NET_OK on success
//     Returns two-part int code on error
//        The low 16 bits contains Status code as defined in net.h
//        The high 16 bits contains "Windows Socket Error Code"
//     *server = IP address connected to as null-terminated string
//=============================================================================
int Net::createClient(char *server, int port, int protocol)
{
    int status;
    char localIP[IP_SIZE];   // IP as string (e.g. "192.168.1.100");
    ADDRINFOA host;
    ADDRINFOA *result = NULL;
    // ----- Initialize network stuff -----
    status = initialize(port, protocol);
    if (status != NET_OK)
        return status;
```

Listing 12.3(a). Creating a network client.

12.5.1 Get an IP Address from the Name

Next, the `*server` parameter is examined to see if it contains an IP address in the dotted
quad form "nnn.nnn.nnn.nnn." If it does not, we assume it must contain a host name. The
Winsock `getaddrinfo` function is used to retrieve the IP address of the host name.

```
int WSAAPI getaddrinfo(
    PCSTR pNodeName,
    PCSTR pServiceName,
    const ADDRINFOA *pHints,
    PADDRINFOA *ppResult
);
```

The parameters are:

- pNodeName (optional). A pointer to a NULL-terminated string that contains the
  host name or a string that contains the IP address in dotted quad form. We will
  always use the host name.

- pServiceName (optional). A pointer to a NULL-terminated string that contains a
  port number or a service name. We are not interested in retrieving this information so we will use NULL for this parameter value. Only one of the pNodeName or
  pServiceName parameters must be provided; the other is optional.

- pHints. A pointer to an ADDRINFO structure that contains information about the
  type of socket.

- ppResult. A pointer to a linked list of one or more ADDRINFO structures that contains the results.

The return value is 0 on success. An error returns a Windows sockets error code.

If the address is found, it is used to continue the setup of the remoteAddr address structure. We also save the address in dotted quad string form in the server parameter, as shown in Listing 12.3(b). The final step in the createClient function is to get the IP address of the client and add it to the localAddr structure. Our getLocalIP function returns the IP address of the local computer; see Listing 12.3(c) for an example.

```
// If server does not contain a dotted quad IP address nnn.nnn.nnn.nnn
if ((remoteAddr.sin_addr.s_addr = inet_addr(server)) == INADDR_NONE)
{
    // Setup host structure of use in getaddrinfo() function
    ZeroMemory(&host, sizeof(host));
    host.ai_family = AF_INET;
    host.ai_socktype = SOCK_STREAM;
    host.ai_protocol = IPPROTO_TCP;
    // Get address information
    status = getaddrinfo(server,NULL,&host,&result);
    if(status != 0)                    // If getaddrinfo failed
        status = WSAGetLastError();
        return ((status << 16) + NET_DOMAIN_NOT_FOUND);
    }
    // Get IP address of server
    remoteAddr.sin_addr = ((SOCKADDR_IN *) result->ai_addr)->sin_addr;
    strncpy_s(server, IP_SIZE, inet_ntoa(remoteAddr.sin_addr),
            IP_SIZE);
}
```

Listing 12.3(b). Getting the IP address of the server name.

```
    // Set local IP address
    getLocalIP(localIP);            // Get local IP
    localAddr.sin_addr.s_addr = inet_addr(localIP);   // Local IP
    mode = CLIENT;
    return NET_OK;
}
```

Listing 12.3(c). Adding the IP address of the client to the localAddr structure.

▌ 12.6 Get the Local IP Address

The address of the local computer may be specified several ways. The IP address 127.0.0.1 refers to the local computer, as does the host name *localhost*. To determine the specific IP address of the local computer, we use the Winsock gethostname function to get the host name of the local computer. Then we use the Winsock `gethostbyname` function to get the IP address, just like we did in the `createClient` function when we retrieved the IP address of a server. The `gethostname` function syntax is:

```
int gethostname(
    char *name,
    int namelen
);
```

The parameters are:

- `name`. A pointer to a buffer that will receive the name.

- `namelen`. The length of the buffer in bytes.

The return value is 0 on success and `SOCKET_ERROR` on error. Specific error information may be retrieved with the `WSAGetLastError` function.

We use these two functions in our `getLocalIP` function:

```
int getLocalIP(
    char *localIP
);
```

The parameter is:

- `localIP`. A pointer to the buffer that will receive the IP address of the local computer as a `NULL`-terminated string.

The return value is `NET_OK` on success or a two-part error code on error (Listing 12.4).

```
//==========================================================================
// Get the IP address of this computer as a string
// Post:
//    *localIP = IP address of local computer as null-terminated string on
//    success
//    Returns two-part int code on error
//       The low 16 bits contains Status code as defined in net.h
//       The high 16 bits contains "Windows Socket Error Code"
//==========================================================================
int Net::getLocalIP(char *localIP)
{
    char host name[40];
    ADDRINFOA host;
    ADDRINFOA *result = NULL;
    int status;
    gethostname(hostname,40);
    // Setup host structure for use in getaddrinfo() function
    ZeroMemory(&host, sizeof(host));
    host.ai_family = AF_INET;
    host.ai_socktype = SOCK_STREAM;
    host.ai_protocol = IPPROTO_TCP;
```

```
    // Get address information
    status = getaddrinfo(host name,NULL,&host,&result);
    if(status != 0)                          // If getaddrinfo failed
    {
        status = WSAGetLastError();          // Get detailed error
        return ( (status << 16) + NET_ERROR);
    }
    // Get IP address of server
    IN_ADDR in_addr = ((SOCKADDR_IN *) result->ai_addr)->sin_addr;
    strncpy_s(localIP, IP_SIZE, inet_ntoa(in_addr), IP_SIZE);
    return NET_OK;
}
```

Listing 12.4. The `getLocalIP` function gets the IP address of the local computer.

▌ 12.7 Sending

Data is sent with the Winsock function `sendto`. Before we can call the `sendto` function, we will need to finish configuring the socket. The socket configuration is different for a client or a server. It also depends on if we are using TCP or UDP. Our `sendData` function configures the socket based on the current mode of operation and then calls `sendto`.

```
int sendData(
    const char *data,
    int &size,
    const char *remoteIP
);
```

The parameters are:

- `data`. A pointer to a buffer containing the data to send.

- `size`. The number of bytes to send. Upon return, `size` contains the number of bytes sent or 0 if no data was sent.

- `remoteIP`. A pointer to the destination IP address as a `NULL`-terminated string.

If the application is a server, the `remoteAddr` structure is filled in with the `remoteIP` address. We must set the remote address each time because a server may be talking to multiple clients at different addresses (Listing 12.5(a)).

```
//=======================================================================
// Send data
// Pre:
//   *data = Data to send
//   size = Number of bytes to send
//   *remoteIP = Destination IP address as null-terminated char array
// Post:
```

```
//    Returns NET_OK on success. Success does not indicate data was sent
//    Returns two-part int code on error
//      The low 16 bits contains Status code as defined in net.h
//      The high 16 bits contains "Windows Socket Error Code"
//    size = Number of bytes sent, 0 if no data sent
//==========================================================================
int Net::sendData(const char *data, int &size, const char *remoteIP)
{
    int status;
    int sendSize = size;
    size = 0;          // Assume 0 bytes sent, changed if send successful
    if (mode == SERVER)
        remoteAddr.sin_addr.s_addr = inet_addr(remoteIP);
```

Listing 12.5(a). The `sendData` function sets the `remoteAddr` structure when the mode is SERVER.

12.7.1 Winsock connect Function

If the application is a client with an unconnected TCP socket, a call is made to the Winsock `connect` function. The `connect` function attempts to connect the socket with the remote destination. Once a socket is connected, it may be used to send and receive data. The `connect` function syntax is:

```
int connect(
    SOCKET s,
    const struct sockaddr *name,
    int namelen
);
```

The parameters are:

- `s`. The socket.

- `name`. A pointer to a `sockaddr` structure that describes the destination to connect with.

- `namelen`. The length of the name `sockaddr` structure in bytes.

The return value is 0 on success or SOCKET_ERROR on error. A detailed error code may be obtained by calling the `WSAGetLastError` function.

Our code calls `connect` and then checks the error code. If the error code is WSAEIS CONN, it means the socket is already connected, in which case we clear the error code and set `type` to CONNECTED_TCP. We are using nonblocking sockets so we need to test for two more error conditions that may occur. An error code of WSAEWOULDBLOCK indicates that the operation cannot be completed immediately and an error code of WSAEALREADY indicates an operation is already in progress on the socket. Both of these errors are normal when using nonblocking sockets, so we return NET_OK (Listing 12.5(b)).

```
if(mode == CLIENT && type == UNCONNECTED_TCP)
{
    ret = connect(sock,(SOCKADDR*)(&remoteAddr),sizeof(remoteAddr));
    if (ret == SOCKET_ERROR) {
        status = WSAGetLastError();
        if (status == WSAEISCONN)    // If connected
        {
            ret = 0;                 // Clear SOCKET_ERROR
            type = CONNECTED_TCP;
        }
        else
        {
            if ( status == WSAEWOULDBLOCK || status == WSAEALREADY)
                return NET_OK;       // No connection yet
            else
                return ((status << 16) + NET_ERROR);
        }
    }
}
```

Listing 12.5(b). The `connect` function is called for unconnected TCP clients.

12.7.2 Winsock sendto Function

The Winsock `sendto` function sends the data to the destination. The function syntax is:

```
int sendto(
    SOCKET s,
    const char *buf,
    int len,
    int flags,
    const struct sockaddr *to,
    int tolen
);
```

The parameters are:

- `s`. The socket.

- `buf`. A pointer to a buffer containing the data to send.

- `len`. The number of bytes to send.

- `flags`. Options for how the data should be sent. We will always use 0 for this parameter.

- `to`. A pointer to a `sockaddr` structure that contains the destination address.

- `tolen`. The size of the `to` parameter's `sockaddr` structure.

The return value is the number of bytes sent or SOCKET_ERROR if an error occurred. The number of bytes sent can be less than the value specified in the len parameter. A detailed error may be obtained by calling the WSAGetLastError function.

The sendto function implicitly binds the socket if it is not already bound. Our function calls sendto, returns any errors that occur or sets bound to true, sets size to the number of bytes transmitted, and returns NET_OK (Listing 12.5(c)).

```
    ret = sendto(sock, data, size, 0, (SOCKADDR *)&remoteAddr,
        sizeof(remoteAddr));
    if (ret == SOCKET_ERROR)
    {
        status = WSAGetLastError();
        return ((status << 16) + NET_ERROR);
    }
    bound = true;           // Automatic binding by sendto if unbound
    size = ret;             // Number of bytes sent, may be 0
    return NET_OK;
}
```

Listing 12.5(c). The sendto function is called to send the data.

■ 12.8 Receiving

Our function readData reads incoming data and stores it in a buffer. The function syntax is:

```
int readData
(
    char *data,
    int &size,
    char *senderIP
);
```

The parameters are:

- data. A pointer to a buffer that will receive the incoming data.

- size. The number of bytes to receive. On return, size is set to the number of bytes received. If no data is received, size is set to 0.

- senderIP. A pointer to a buffer where the sender's IP address will be saved in dotted quad form as a NULL-terminated string (e.g., "192.168.1.100").

The return value is NET_OK on success or a two-part error code.

If the socket is not currently bound, then it may not be used for reading, so the function returns NET_OK (Listing 12.6(a)).

```
//============================================================================
// Read data
// Pre:
//    *data = Buffer for received data
//    size = Number of bytes to receive
//    *senderIP = NULL
// Post:
//    Returns NET_OK on success
//    Returns two-part int code on error
//      The low 16 bits contains Status code as defined in net.h
//      The high 16 bits contains "Windows Socket Error Code"
//    size = Number of bytes received, may be 0
//    *senderIP = IP address of sender as null-terminated string
//============================================================================
int Net::readData(char *data, int &size, char *senderIP)
{
    int status;
    int readSize = size;
    size = 0;              // Assume 0 bytes read, changed if read successful
    if(bound == false)  // No receive from unbound socket
        return NET_OK;
```

Listing 12.6(a). The readData function returns NET_OK if the socket is not bound.

12.8.1 Winsock listen Function

If the application is a server with an unconnected TCP socket, the Winsock listen function is called. The listen function configures a socket to wait for incoming connections.

```
int listen(
    SOCKET s,
    int backlog
);
```

The parameters are:

- s. The socket.

- backlog. The maximum length of the backlog of pending connections.

The return value is 0 on success or SOCKET_ERROR on error. A detailed error may be obtained by calling the WSAGetLastError function, as seen in the code in Listing 12.6(b).

```
    if(mode == SERVER && type == UNCONNECTED_TCP)
    {
        ret = listen(sock,1);
        if (ret == SOCKET_ERROR)
        {
            status = WSAGetLastError();
            return ((status << 16) + NET_ERROR);
        }
    }
```

Listing 12.6(b). Unconnected TCP servers call the listen function to wait for incoming connections.

12. Network Programming

12.8.2 Winsock accept Function

After the socket is configured to `listen`, we call the Winsock `accept` function, which accepts the first pending connection and creates a new socket to handle the connection (Listing 12.6(c)). The syntax for `accept` is:

```
SOCKET accept(
    SOCKET s,
    struct sockaddr *addr,
    int *addrlen
);
```

The parameters are:

- `s`. The socket that is in the listen state.

- `addr`. An optional pointer to a `sockaddr` structure where the address of the connected device will be stored.

- `addrlen`. An optional pointer to the length in bytes of the `addr sockaddr` structure.

The return value on success is a newly connected socket that should be used for all future communications with the destination device. If there is an error, `INVALID_SOCKET` is returned.

Our code calls the `accept` function and checks for errors. With the nonblocking sockets we are using, it is common to get a `WSAEWOULDBLOCK` error that indicates no connections are waiting to be accepted. We ignore the `WSAEWOULDBLOCK` error and return `NET_OK`. If `accept` was successful, we close the old socket and replace it with `tempSock` created by `accept`.

If `readData` is called from a client with an unconnected TCP socket, then there is no connection to read data from. In this case, the function simply ignores the read request and returns `NET_OK` (Listing 12.6(d)).

```
    SOCKET tempSock;
    tempSock = accept(sock,NULL,NULL);
    if (tempSock == INVALID_SOCKET)
    {
        status = WSAGetLastError();
        if ( status != WSAEWOULDBLOCK) // Don't report WOULDBLOCK error
            return ((status << 16) + NET_ERROR);
        return NET_OK;          // No connection yet
    }
    closesocket(sock);          // Don't need old socket
    sock = tempSock;            // TCP client connected
    type = CONNECTED_TCP;
}
```

Listing 12.6(c). The `accept` function is called after calling the `listen` function.

```
if(mode == CLIENT && type == UNCONNECTED_TCP)
    return NET_OK;  // No connection yet
```

Listing 12.6(d). NET_OK is returned when attempting to read from an unconnected TCP client.

12.8.3 Winsock recvfrom Function

The actual reading of data is performed with the Winsock recvfrom function. The syntax is:

```
int recvfrom(
    SOCKET s,
    char *buf,
    int len,
    int flags,
    struct sockaddr *from,
    int *fromlen
);
```

The parameters are:

- s. The socket.

- buf. A buffer where the incoming data will be stored.

- len. The length of the buffer in bytes.

- flags. Options.

- from. An optional pointer to a sockaddr structure where the sending address will be stored.

- fromlen. An optional pointer to the length of the sockaddr structure pointed to by the from parameter.

The return value on success is the number of bytes received. When there is an error, SOCKET_ERROR is returned. Zero is returned if the connection was properly closed. A detailed error may be obtained by calling the WSAGetLastError function.

Our code uses the optional parameters to obtain the address of the sender, which we store in the remoteAddr structure. A detailed error is returned if an error is detected. The error code REMOTE_DISCONNECT is returned if the socket was closed. If no errors occurred, the IP address of the sender is written to senderIP as a NULL-terminated string in dotted quad form (e.g., "192.168.1.100"). The number of bytes read is saved in the size parameter and NET_OK is returned, as shown in Listing 12.6(e).

```
if(sock != NULL)
{
    remoteAddrSize = sizeof(remoteAddr);
```

```
            ret = recvfrom(sock, data, readSize, 0, (SOCKADDR *)&remoteAddr,
                           &remoteAddrSize);
        if (ret == SOCKET_ERROR) {
            status = WSAGetLastError();
            if ( status != WSAEWOULDBLOCK)  // Don't report WOULDBLOCK
                                            // error
                return ((status << 16) + NET_ERROR);
            ret = 0;                // Clear SOCKET_ERROR
        // If TCP connection did graceful close
        } else if(ret == 0 && type == CONNECTED_TCP)
            // Return Remote Disconnect error
            return ((REMOTE_DISCONNECT << 16) + NET_ERROR);
        if (ret)
            // IP of sender
            strncpy_s(senderIP, IP_SIZE, inet_ntoa(remoteAddr.sin_addr),
                    IP_SIZE);
        size = ret;             // Number of bytes read, may be 0
    }
    return NET_OK;
}
```

Listing 12.6(e). The `recvfrom` function reads the data.

■ 12.9 Closing a Socket

Closing a socket releases any resources used by the socket. It also discards any pending `send` and `receive` operations and discards any queued data. We should always close each socket we create. Our `closeSocket` function closes the socket. The syntax is:

```
int closeSocket();
```

We only have one open socket in our class, so there is no need for parameters. The `close Socket` function is called automatically by the class destructor. The return value is `NET_OK` on success or a two-part error code, as seen in Listing 12.7(a). Our function calls the Winsock `closesocket` function to perform the close.

```
//==============================================================================
// Close socket
// Post:
//    Socket is closed
//    Returns two-part int code on error
//      The low 16 bits contains Status code as defined in net.h
//      The high 16 bits contains "Windows Socket Error Code"
//==============================================================================
int Net::closeSocket()
{
    int status;
    type = UNCONNECTED;
    bound = false;
    netInitialized = false;
```

Listing 12.7(a). Our function that closes the socket.

12.9.1 Winsock closesocket Function

The Winsock `closesocket` function closes a socket. The syntax is:

```
int closesocket(
    SOCKET s
);
```

The parameter is:

- s. The socket to close.

The return value is 0 on success or `SOCKET_ERROR` on error. A detailed error may be obtained by calling the `WSAGetLastError` function, as you can see in Listing 12.7(b).

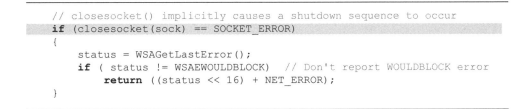

```
// closesocket() implicitly causes a shutdown sequence to occur
if (closesocket(sock) == SOCKET_ERROR)
{
    status = WSAGetLastError();
    if ( status != WSAEWOULDBLOCK)   // Don't report WOULDBLOCK error
        return ((status << 16) + NET_ERROR);
}
```

Listing 12.7(b). The Winsock `closesocket` function performs the close.

12.9.2 Winsock WSACleanup Function

The last step in the cleanup process is to call the Winsock function `WSACleanup`. This function is the counterpart to the `WSAStartup` function we called in our `initialize` function. `WSACleanup` deregisters the application from Windows sockets and frees any resources allocated for the application. The function syntax is:

```
int WSACleanup();
```

There are no parameters. The return value is 0 on success or `SOCKET_ERROR` on error. A detailed error may be obtained by calling the `WSAGetLastError` function. The code for this step is listed in Listing 12.7(c).

```
    if (WSACleanup())
        return NET_ERROR;
    return NET_OK;
}
```

Listing 12.7(c). The `WSACleanup` function is called.

12.10 Get Error

Our final function in the `Net` class is `getError`. This function returns a detailed error message string from a two-part error code. The syntax is:

```
std::string getError(
    int error
);
```

The parameter is:

- `error`. A two-part error code returned from one of our `Net` class functions.

The return value is a string containing a detailed error message. Our error codes are defined as constants in the `net.h` file. They are shown in Listing 12.8. These constants have matching detailed error messages, which are also defined as constants in `net.h`. They are contained in Listing 12.9. Detailed messages for the Winsock error codes are also contained in `net.h` (Listing 12.10).

```
const int NET_OK = 0;
const int NET_ERROR = 1;
const int NET_INIT_FAILED = 2;
const int NET_INVALID_SOCKET = 3;
const int NET_GET_HOST_BY_NAME_FAILED = 4;
const int NET_BIND_FAILED = 5;
const int NET_CONNECT_FAILED = 6;
const int NET_ADDR_IN_USE = 7;
const int NET_DOMAIN_NOT_FOUND = 8;
```

Listing 12.8. Our network error codes.

```
// Network error codes
static const char *codes[ERROR_CODES] = {
    "No errors reported",
    "General network error: ",
    "Network init failed: ",
    "Invalid socket: ",
    "Get host by name failed: ",
    "Bind failed: ",
    "Connect failed: ",
    "Port already in use: ",
    "Domain not found: ",
    "Unknown network error: "
};
```

Listing 12.9. The detailed error messages for our error codes.

```
const int SOCK_CODES = 29;
// Windows Socket Error Codes
static const ErrorCode errorCodes[SOCK_CODES] = {
    {0x2714, "A blocking operation was interrupted"},
    {0x271D, "Socket access permission violation"},
    {0x2726, "Invalid argument"},
    {0x2728, "Too many open sockets"},
    {0x2735, "Operation in progress"},
    {0x2736, "Operation on non-socket"},
    {0x2737, "Address missing"},
    {0x2738, "Message bigger than buffer"},
    {0x273F, "Address incompatible with protocol"},
    {0x2740, "Address is already in use"},
    {0x2741, "Address not valid in current context"},
    {0x2742, "Network is down"},
    {0x2743, "Network unreachable"},
    {0x2744, "Connection broken during operation"},
    {0x2745, "Connection aborted by host software"},
    {0x2746, "Connection reset by remote host"},
    {0x2747, "Insufficient buffer space"},
    {0x2748, "Connect request on already connected socket"},
    {0x2749, "Socket not connected or address not specified"},
    {0x274A, "Socket already shut down"},
    {0x274C, "Operation timed out"},
    {0x274D, "Connection refused by target"},
    {0x274E, "Cannot translate name"},
    {0x274F, "Name too long"},
    {0x2750, "Destination host down"},
    {0x2751, "Host unreachable"},
    {0x276B, "Network cannot initialize, system unavailable"},
    {0x276D, "Network has not been initialized"},
    {0x2775, "Remote has disconnected"},
};
```

Listing 12.10. Detailed error messages for Winsock error codes.

Our `getError` function combines the text messages from each part of the error code in a string and returns it (Listing 12.11).

```
//=========================================================================
// Returns detailed error message from two-part error code
//=========================================================================
std::string Net::getError(int error)
{
    int sockErr = error >> 16;   // Upper 16 bits is sockErr
    std::string errorStr;
    error &= STATUS_MASK;        // Remove extended error code
    if(error > ERROR_CODES-2)    // If unknown error code
        error = ERROR_CODES-1;
    errorStr = codes[error];
    for (int i=0; i< SOCK_CODES; i++)
    {
        if(errorCodes[i].sockErr == sockErr)
```

12. Network Programming

```
        {
            errorStr += errorCodes[i].message;
            break;
        }
    }
    return errorStr;
}
```

Listing 12.11. Our function that returns detailed error messages from a two-part error code.

▌ 12.11 Client/Server Chat

We should test our new Net class by creating a simple client/server chat program (Figure 12.1). To keep this program as simple as possible, we will create it as a Windows console application.

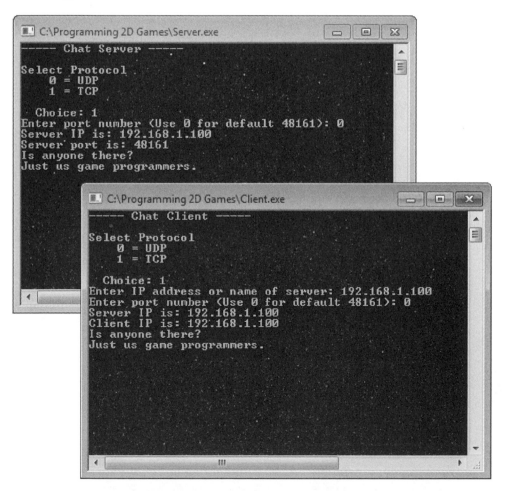

Figure 12.1. The client/server chat demo.

12.11.1   Chat Client

Let's examine the client program first. The main.cpp file begins by including some necessary header files, including our net.h file. Variables and buffers are declared next (Listing 12.12(a)).

```cpp
// Programming 2D Games
// Copyright (c) 2011 by:
// Charles Kelly
// Chat Client v1.0
#include <iostream>
#include <conio.h>
#include "net.h"
using namespace std;
int main()
{
    const int BUFSIZE = 256;
    int port = 48161;
    int newPort = 0;
    int protocol;             // TCP or UDP
    char remoteIP[BUFSIZE];   // Remote IP address or domain name
    char localIP[16];         // Local IP address as dotted quad; nnn.nnn.
                              // nnn.nnn
    char netbuf[BUFSIZE];     // Network receive
    char keybuf[BUFSIZE];     // Keyboard input
    int error    = netNS::NET_OK;
    int lastError = netNS::NET_OK;
    int sizeXmit=0;           // Transmit size
    int sizeRecv=0;           // Receive size
    int size=0;
    Net net;                  // Network communication object
```

Listing 12.12(a). The variables of the chat client.

Next, we get the desired protocol from the user, as you can see in Listing 12.12(b).

```cpp
// ----- create client -----
do
{
    // Display protocol menu
    cout << "----- Chat Client -----\n"
         << "\nSelect Protocol\n"
         << "    0 = UDP\n"
         << "    1 = TCP\n\n"
         << "  Choice: ";
    cin >> protocol;    // Get character
}while(protocol != 0 && protocol != 1);
cin.ignore();
```

Listing 12.12(b). The user selects the client protocol.

```
// Prompt for IP address or name of server
cout << "Enter IP address or name of server: ";
cin.getline(remoteIP, BUFSIZE);      // Read IP address or name
// Get port number
//      Port numbers 0-1023 are used for well-known services
//      Port numbers 1024-65535 may be freely used
do
{
    cout << "Enter port number (Use 0 for default 48161): ";
    cin >> newPort;
}while(newPort < 0 || newPort > 65535);
if(newPort != 0)
    port = newPort;
cin.ignore();
```

Listing 12.12(c). The IP address or server name and the port number are entered.

Now we get the IP address or host name of the server and the port number to use (see Listing 12.12(c)). With all of the required information collected, we proceed to create the client with our net.createClient function. Then we display the IP address of the server and client by using the code in Listing 12.12(d).

```
// Create client
error = net.createClient(remoteIP, port, protocol);
if(error != netNS::NET_OK)            // If error
{
    cout << net.getError(error) << endl;
    system("pause");
    return 1;
}
// Display serverIP
cout << "Server IP is: " << remoteIP << endl;
// Display clientIP
net.getLocalIP(localIP);
cout << "Client IP is: " << localIP << endl;
```

Listing 12.12(d). The client is created.

The program enters an infinite loop. Inside the loop, we check for pending input from the keyboard. We read the input line and save it in keybuf. We also get the number of characters input and save that in sizeXmit. If characters were entered, we send them with our net.sendData function, as shown in Listing 12.12(e).

```
// Send messages to server and display what is sent back
while(true)      // ***** INFINITE LOOP *****
{
    // If keyboard input pending
    if (_kbhit())
```

```
    {
        cin.getline(keybuf,BUFSIZE);      // Get input
        sizeXmit += (int)cin.gcount() + 1;   // Get size of input +
                                             // null
        if(cin.fail())       // If failbit
        {
            cin.clear();      // Clear error
            cin.ignore(INT_MAX,'\n');    // Flush input
        }
    }
    // If data ready to send
    if(sizeXmit > 0)
    {
        size = sizeXmit;
        error = net.sendData(keybuf,size,remoteIP); // Send data
        if(error != netNS::NET_OK)
            cout << net.getError(error) << endl;
        sizeXmit -= size;    // - number of characters sent
        if(sizeXmit < 0)
            sizeXmit = 0;
    }
```

Listing 12.12(e). Keyboard input is sent to the server.

After sending the chat message, we check for a response from the server and display any text received. A call to Sleep(10) at the end of the loop reduces the workload of the CPU. Listing 12.12(f) shows the code for these steps.


```
    // Check for receive
    sizeRecv = BUFSIZE;      // Max chars to read
    error = net.readData(netbuf,sizeRecv,remoteIP);
    if(error != netNS::NET_OK)    // If error
    {
        if(error != lastError)   // If new error
        {
            lastError = error;
            cout << net.getError(error) << endl;
        }
    }
    else
        if(sizeRecv > 0)           // If characters received
            // Display incomming message
            cout << netbuf << endl;
    // Insert short delay to reduce CPU workload
    Sleep(10);
    }
    return 0;
}
```

Listing 12.12(f). Characters received from the server are displayed.

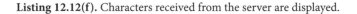

12.11.2 Chat Server

The variables and buffers required for the server are nearly identical to those required for the client (Listing 12.13(a)). After the declarations, we prompt the user for the protocol (Listing 12.13(b)).

```cpp
// Programming 2D Games
// Copyright (c) 2011 by:
// Charles Kelly
// Chat Server v1.0
#include <iostream>
#include <conio.h>
#include "net.h"
using namespace std;
int main()
{
    const int BUFSIZE = 256;
    int port = 48161;
    int newPort = 0;
    int protocol;            // TCP or UDP
    char remoteIP[BUFSIZE];  // Remote IP address or domain name
    char localIP[16];        // Local IP address as dotted quad; nnn.nnn.
                             // nnn.nnn
    char netbuf[BUFSIZE];    // Network receive
    char keybuf[BUFSIZE];    // Keyboard input
    int error    = netNS::NET_OK;
    int lastError - nctNS::NET_OK;
    int sizeXmit=0;          // Transmit size
    int sizeRecv=0;          // Receive size
    int size=0;
    Net net;                 // Network communication object
    netbuf[0] = '\0';
```

Listing 12.13(a). The server's variables and buffers.

```cpp
    // ----- create server -----
    do
    {
        // Display protocol menu
        cout << "----- Chat Server -----\n"
            << "\nSelect Protocol\n"
            << "    0 = UDP\n"
            << "    1 = TCP\n\n"
            << " Choice: ";
        cin >> protocol;    // Get character
    }while(protocol != 0 && protocol != 1);
    cin.ignore();
```

Listing 12.13(b). The user selects the server protocol.

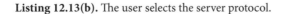

```
// Get port number
//     Port numbers 0-1023 are used for well-known services
//     Port numbers 1024-65535 may be freely used
do
{
    cout << "Enter port number (Use 0 for default 48161): ";
    cin >> newPort;
}while(newPort < 0 || newPort > 65535);
if(newPort != 0)
    port = newPort;
cin.ignore();
```

Listing 12.13(c). The port number is entered.

Next, we get the port number, as listed in Listing 12.13(c). The server is created by calling our net.creatServer function. If the creation is successful, we display the server's IP address and port, as you can see in Listing 12.13(d).

```
// Create server
error = net.createServer(port, protocol);
if(error != netNS::NET_OK)            // If error
{
    cout << net.getError(error) << endl;
    system("pause'');
    return 1;
}

// Display serverIP
net.getLocalIP(localIP);
cout << "Server IP is: " << localIP << endl;
cout << "Server port is: " << port << endl;
```

Listing 12.13(d). The server is created by calling the net.createServer function.

The server also uses an infinite loop. Inside the loop, we check for incoming text with our net.readData function and display it. If an error is detected during the read operation, we display the error message and recreate the server (Listing 12.13(e)).

```
// Display incoming text and send back response
while(true)      // ***** INFINITE LOOP *****
{
    // Check for receive
    sizeRecv = BUFSIZE;      // Max bytes to receive
    error = net.readData(netbuf,sizeRecv,remoteIP);
    if(error != netNS::NET_OK)
    {
        cout << net.getError(error) << endl;
        error = net.closeSocket();      // Close connection
```

12. Network Programming

```
    // Re-create server
    error = net.createServer(port, protocol);
    if(error != netNS::NET_OK)          // If error
    {
        cout << net.getError(error) << endl;
        return 1;
    }
}
if(sizeRecv > 0)            // If characters received
{
    // Display incomming message
    cout << netbuf << endl;
}
```

Listing 12.13(e). The server waits for incoming text and displays it.

After displaying any incoming text, we check for pending input from the keyboard. The input line is saved in the `keybuf` buffer. We also get the number of characters input and save that in `sizeXmit`. If characters were entered, we send them with our `net.send Data` function. A call to `Sleep` again at the end of the loop concludes our server (Listing 12.13(f)).

```
    // If keyboard input pending
    if (_kbhit())
    {
        cin.getline(keybuf,BUFSIZE);    // Get input
        sizeXmit += (int)cin.gcount() + 1;  // Get size of input + null
        if(cin.fail())          // If failbit
        {
            cin.clear();      // Clear error
            cin.ignore(INT_MAX,'\n');   // Flush input
        }
    }
    // If data ready to send
    if(sizeXmit > 0)
    {
        size = sizeXmit;
        error = net.sendData(keybuf,size,remoteIP);  // Send data
        if(error != netNS::NET_OK)
            cout << net.getError(error) << endl;
        sizeXmit -= size;     // - number of characters sent
        if(sizeXmit < 0)
            sizeXmit = 0;
    }
    // Insert short delay to reduce CPU workload
    Sleep(10);
}
return 0;
}
```

Listing 12.13(f). Keyboard input is sent to the client.

▋ 12.12   Client/Server Spacewar

In this section, we are going to add network play to our Spacewar game. Actually, the phrase "add network play" is a little misleading. Creating a network-playable game is not simply a matter of including a new class and making a few function calls. The network code must be integrated into the game to accommodate the unique requirements of the client and server. We are only going to examine the core changes that are necessary to create the server or client. To determine all of the changes that were made, we suggest using the WinMerge application to compare the project files from the network game with those of the original Spacewar.

In our implementation, the game will run on a trusted server. The clients will operate as display and input devices only. This model is the one most often used by commercial games—not because it is the most optimal for performance, but because the clients cannot be trusted. With the game running on a trusted server, the ability for players to cheat is reduced. If the data coming from the clients were trusted, it would make it easier for players to cheat. Players still have the ability to attempt cheating, but with a trusted server it is possible to implement measures to detect their cheating attempts.

The clients will send periodic transmissions to the server that contains the player's game input. The server will respond with the latest state of the game. In the nonnetworked game, when a sound effect was played, both players could hear it because they were both playing on the same computer. In the networked version, the game is running on the server. When the server determines that a sound effect needs to be played, that information must be conveyed to each client as part of the game state. This is typical of the types of issues we need to deal with when creating network playable games.

In a real-time game like Spacewar, the timely delivery of data is more important than reliability. If the server sent the current state of the game to a client and the data was lost, there is no reason to resend it because the next state transmission would render it obsolete anyway. The same is true for client data that is sent to the server. For that reason, our game will use the UDP to communicate.

12.12.1   Bandwidth Requirements

We should take into consideration the volume of data that will need to be delivered by the server. The game state that is sent to each client will consist of all the data required to describe the state of each player's ship and torpedo, plus some additional information about sounds and the game state. For our Spacewar game, approximately 50 bytes must be transmitted to describe each player's state plus a few extra bytes to describe the game state and create an IP packet. The state of every player in the game must be transmitted to every client. If we assume one player per client, then the bandwidth requirements increase by the square of the number of players. If the game state is sent to the clients 30 times per second, we can calculate the upload bandwidth requirements for the server using the following formula:

bits per second = players^2 × bytes per player × 8 bits per byte × 30 transmissions per second.

As we can see from Table 12.1, the upload bandwidth requirements of the server increase rapidly as the number of players increase. These numbers are just an approximation.

We could reduce the bandwidth requirements by taking additional steps to compress the data prior to sending. Our example is limited to two players, so no additional compression is attempted beyond the use of bit flags, as described next.

12.12.2 Bit Flags

To minimize the bandwidth requirements, we will send game state information using bit flags when possible. The bits will be sent as part of a `char`, `short`, or `int` type of variable. Bits may be set in a variable by doing a bitwise OR (|) with a number that contains a 1 in bit position(s) we wish to set. For example:

Players	Upload Bandwidth (bps) (~50 bytes per player)
2	48 K
4	192 K
8	768 K
16	3 M
32	12 M

Table 12.1. The server's upload bandwidth requirements.

```
variable   10100001

OR ( | )   00001111
           _____        Bits set
result     1010 1111
```

Bits may be cleared by doing a bitwise AND (&) with a number that contains all 1s everywhere except for the bit(s) we wish to clear.

```
variable   10100001

AND ( & )  00001111
           _____        Bits cleared
result     0000 0001
```

The current state of a bit may be changed from 0 to 1 or from 1 to 0 by performing a bitwise exclusive OR (^) with a number that contains a 1 in the bit position(s) we wish to change.

```
variable   10100001

XOR ( ^ )  00001111
           _____        Bits inverted
result     0000 1110
```

12.12.3 Sending Momentary Information Reliably with UDP

Some of the events we need to send are momentary in nature, such as telling a client to play the sound effect for two ships colliding; other events are continuous in nature, like telling a client to play the sound effect for a ship's engine. For the continuous information, we can simply use the value of a bit. If the bit is 0, the sound is off, and if the bit is 1, the sound is on. If a data packet is lost during transmission, it will not matter because the next data packet will have the latest bit value anyway. If we sent a momentary event using a single data packet, and the data packet was lost, the client and the server would be out of sync. To send momentary information reliably, we will use the change in a bit's state to convey the information. When the recipient sees the bit's state change, it will know the momentary event has

Sending Momentary Data				
	Using Bit Value		Using Change of Bit	
	Sent	Received	Sent	Received
Packet 0	00000000	00000000	00000000	00000000
Packet 1	00000000	00000000	00000000	00000000
Packet 2	00000010	Packet lost	00000010	Packet lost
Packet 3	00000000	00000000	00000010	00000010
Packet 4	00000000	00000000	00000010	00000010

Table 12.2. The effect of a lost packet when sending momentary data.

occurred. If a data packet is lost, the next packet will still contain the bit in the new state and the momentary information will be received. Table 12.2 illustrates how it works.

When Packet 2 is lost, the information it contained is also lost. If we are sending a momentary event using the value of a bit in one packet, the receiver will not get the update. If, however, we are using a change in the bit's state, the receiver will see the bit change in the next packet received and will be able to update its game state to match the sender.

▮ 12.13 Spacewar Server

The first step in creating our server is to get access to our Net class. We begin by copying our existing Spacewar game into a new folder. To that folder we add our net.cpp and net.h files. Next, we open the Spacewar project and add the same two files to the project's "Source Files" and "Header Files" folders, respectively. Now we add #include "net.h" to our spacewar.h file.

12.13.1 Game Structures

The server maintains the game state, accepts input from the clients, and sends the current game state back to the clients. To help organize the data that flows between the client and server, we will create several structures. The following structures are declared in spacewar.h.

The ToServerStc structure is sent to the server from a client.

```
struct ToServerStc
{
    UCHAR buttons;
    UCHAR playerN;
};
```

The members are:

- buttons. The current state of a player's button presses. A type UCHAR (unsigned char) is a 1-byte (8-bit) value. A bit value of 0 indicates a button is up and a value of 1 indicates a button is pressed. Bit 0 is "Left," bit 1 is "Forward," bit 2 is "Right," and bit 3 is "Fire." Bits 4 through 7 are reserved for future use.

- playerN. The player number 0 through MAX_PLAYERS;.

The ToClientStc structure is sent to a client from the server.

```
struct ToClientStc
{
    Player  player[spaceWarNS::MAX_PLAYERS];
    UCHAR   gameState;
    UCHAR   sounds;
};
```

The members are:

- player[]. An array of player structures.

- gameState. The current game state. A type UCHAR (unsigned char) is a 1-byte (8-bit) value. Bit 0 is used to signal the start of a new round. A value of 1 indicates a new round should be started. Bits 1 through 7 are reserved for future use.

- sounds. The sound effect(s) the client should play. A type UCHAR (unsigned char) is a 1-byte (8-bit) value. The momentary sounds are conveyed using a change in the bits state. Continuous sounds are conveyed as 1 = on, 0 = off. The bits and their corresponding sounds are:

    - Bit 0 = cheer   state change

    - Bit 1 = collide   state change

    - Bit 2 = explode   state change

    - Bit 3 = engine1   1 = on, 0 = off

    - Bit 4 = engine2   1 = on, 0 = off

    - Bit 5 = torpedoCrash state change

    - Bit 6 = torpedoFire   state change

    - Bit 7 = torpedoHit   state change

The Player structure describes the ship and torpedo for one player.

```
struct Player
{
    ShipStc      shipData;
    TorpedoStc   torpedoData;
};
```

The members are:

- shipData. A ShipStc structure that contains state information about the ship.

- torpedoData. A TorpedoStc structure that contains state information about the torpedo.

The ShipStc structure contains the state information for a ship. It is declared in ship.h.

```
struct ShipStc
{
    float X;
    float Y;
    float radians;
    float health;
    VECTOR2 velocity;
    float rotation;
    short score;
    UCHAR playerN;
    UCHAR flags;
};
```

The members are:

- X. The *x* screen coordinate.

- Y. The *y* screen coordinate.

- radians. The rotation angle in radians.

- health. The health from 0 through 100.

- velocity. The velocity vector.

- rotation. The rotation rate in radians per second.

- score. The player's score.

- playerN. The player's number.

- flags:

  - Bit 0. Player state, 0 = inactive, 1 = active.

  - Bit 1. Engine state, 0 = off, 1 = on.

  - Bit 2. Shield state, 0 = off, 1 = on.

The TorpedoStc structure contains the state information for a torpedo. It is declared in torpedo.h.

```
struct TorpedoStc
{
    float X;
    float Y;
    VECTOR2 velocity;
    bool  active;
};
```

The members are:

- X. The *x* screen coordinate.

- Y. The *y* screen coordinate.

- velocity. The velocity vector.

- active. The active state (true or false)

12.13.2 Modifications to the Spacewar Class

The following modifications to the Spacewar class are necessary to convert our game into a server.

One change we made is to create arrays to hold the ships and torpedoes. This step was not necessary, but was done to make it easier for anyone who might wish to expand the game beyond two players in the future.

When the server starts, it needs to initialize the network code and game items. The server initialization will be handled by our new initializeServer function (Listing 12.14).

```
//===========================================================================
// Initialize Server
//===========================================================================
int Spacewar::initializeServer(int port)
{
    std::stringstream ss;
    if(port < netNS::MIN_PORT)
    {
        console->print("Invalid port number");
        return netNS::NET_ERROR;
    }
    // ----- Initialize network stuff -----
    error = net.createServer(port, netNS::UDP);
    if(error != netNS::NET_OK)              // If error
    {
        console->print(net.getError(error));
        return netNS::NET_ERROR;
    }
    for (int i=0; i<MAX_PLAYERS; i++)       // For all players
    {
        ship[i].setActive(false);
        ship[i].setConnected(false);
        ship[i].setScore(0);
```

```
    }
    console->print("----- Server -----");
    net.getLocalIP(localIP);
    ss << "Server IP: " << localIP;
    console->print(ss.str());
    ss.str("");                              // Clear stringstream
    ss << "Port: " << port;
    console->print(ss.str());
    return netNS::NET_OK;
}
```

Listing 12.14. Initializing the Spacewar server.

The server messages are displayed to the console, which is opened automatically after the server menu is displayed (code is not shown). The initializeServer function is called at the end of the initialize function.

The communications with the game clients is handled by the communicate function. This function is called repeatedly as part of the main game loop. It checks for incoming data from clients each time it is called. A netTime value is also calculated. When the proper time has elapsed, the checkNetworkTimeout function is called to check for inactive clients (Listing 12.15).

```
//============================================================================
// Do network communications
//============================================================================
void Spacewar::communicate(float frameTime)
{
    // Communicate with client
    // This function is not delayed so client response is as fast as
    // possible
    doClientCommunication();
    // Calculate elapsed time for network communications
    netTime += frameTime;
    if(netTime < netNS::NET_TIME)        // If not time to communicate
        return;
    netTime -= netNS::NET_TIME;
    // Check for inactive clients, called every NET_TIME seconds
    checkNetworkTimeout();
}
```

Listing 12.15. Communicate with the game clients.

All currently connected players have a timeout counter that is incremented by the checkNetworkTimeout function. Each time a player sends a new data packet, the time-out counter is reset. If the timeout counter exceeds MAX_ERRORS, the player is automatically disconnected from the server (Listing 12.16).

The data the clients send to the server contain either the player's game input or a request by the client to join the server. The doClientCommunication function handles incoming transmissions from all clients. A client requests to join the server by setting `toServer` `Data.playerN` to 255. If a client is requesting to join the server, the `clientWantsTo` `Join` function is called. If the client is already connected, the player's inputs are applied to the game and the latest game state is sent to the client (Listing 12.17).

```
//=============================================================================
// Check for network timeout
//=============================================================================
void Spacewar::checkNetworkTimeout()
{
    std::stringstream ss;
    for (int i=0; i<MAX_PLAYERS; i++)        // For all players
    {
        if (ship[i].getConnected())
        {
            ship[i].incTimeout();            // Timeout++
            // If communication timeout
            if (ship[i].getTimeout() > netNS::MAX_ERRORS)
            {
                ship[i].setConnected(false);
                ss << "***** Player " << i << " disconnected. *****";
                console->print(ss.str());
            }
        }
    }
}
```

Listing 12.16. Checking for client timeouts.

```
//=============================================================================
// Do client communication
// Called by server to send game state to each client
//=============================================================================
void Spacewar::doClientCommunication()
{
    int playN;                       // Player number we are communicating with
    int size;
    prepareDataForClient();          // Prepare data for transmission to clients
    for (int i=0; i<MAX_PLAYERS; i++)    // For all players
    {
        size = sizeof(toServerData);
        if( net.readData((char*) &toServerData, size, remoteIP) ==
            netNS::NET_OK)
        {
            if(size > 0)             // If data received
            {
                playN = toServerData.playerN;
                if (playN == 255)    // If request to join game
                {
                    clientWantsToJoin();
                }
                else
```

```
            {
                if (ship[playN].getConnected())    // If this player is
                                                   // connected
                {
                    if (ship[playN].getActive())   // If this player is
                                                   // active
                        ship[playN].setButtons(toServerData.buttons);
                    size = sizeof(toClientData);
                    // Send player the latest game data
                    net.sendData((char*) &toClientData, size,
                                    ship[i].getNetIP());
                    ship[playN].setTimeout(0);
                    ship[playN].setCommWarnings(0);
                }
            }
        }
        else    // No more incomming data
        {
            break;
        }
    }
}
```

Listing 12.17. Send the game state to each client.

Data is sent to the clients in the `toClientData` structure. The `prepareDataForClient` function loads the structure with data from each ship and torpedo (Listing 12.18).

```
//==============================================================================
// Prepare data to send to client. It contains information on all players.
//==============================================================================
void Spacewar::prepareDataForClient()
{
    for (int i=0; i<MAX_PLAYERS; i++)          // For all players
    {
        toClientData.player[i].shipData = ship[i].getNetData();
        toClientData.player[i].torpedoData = torpedo[i].getNetData();
    }
}
```

Listing 12.18. Preparing the `toClientData` structure to send to the clients.

A client request to join the server is handled by the `clientWantsToJoin` function. If there are no players currently in the game, the `roundOver` flag is set to true and the scores are reset to 0. Next, the function checks each player's position to look for an open spot. If a ship (a player) is found that is not connected, that ship is assigned to the joining player. The server sends the client the `SERVER_ID` and player number to acknowledge the connection. If the server is full, it returns `SERVER_FULL` to the client (Listing 12.19).

12. Network Programming

```
//===========================================================================
// Client is requesting to join game
//===========================================================================
void Spacewar::clientWantsToJoin()
{
    std::stringstream ss;
    int size;
    int status;
    connectResponse.number = 255;          // Set to invalid player number
    if(playerCount == 0)                    // If no players currently in game
    {
        roundOver = true;                   // Start a new round
        for(int i=0; i<MAX_PLAYERS; i++)    // For all players
            ship[i].setScore(0);            // Reset score
    }
    console->print("Player requesting to join.");
    // Find available player position to use
    for(int i=0; i<MAX_PLAYERS; i++)            // Search all player positions
    {
        if (ship[i].getConnected() == false)// If this position available
        {
            ship[i].setConnected(true);
            ship[i].setTimeout(0);
            ship[i].setCommWarnings(0);
            ship[i].setNetIP(remoteIP);     // Save player's IP
            ship[i].setCommErrors(0);       // Clear old errors
            // Send SERVER_ID and player number to client
            strcpy_s(connectResponse.response, netNS::SERVER_ID);
            connectResponse.number = (UCHAR)i;
            size = sizeof(connectResponse);
            status = net.sendData((char*)&connectResponse, size, remoteIP);
            if ( status == netNS::NET_ERROR)
            {
                console->print(net.getError(status)); // Display error
                                                       // message
                return;
            }
            toServerData.playerN = i;       // Clear join request from
                                            // input buffer
            ss << "Connected player as number: " << i;
            console->print(ss.str());
            return;                         // Found available player
                                            // position
        }
    }
    // Send SERVER_FULL to client
    strcpy_s(connectResponse.response, netNS::SERVER_FULL);
    size = sizeof(connectResponse);
    status = net.sendData((char*)&connectResponse, size, remoteIP);
    console->print("Server full.");
}
```

Listing 12.19. Handle a player's request to join the game.

The response to the client is sent in a `connectResponse` structure.

```
struct ConnectResponse
{
    char response[netNS::RESPONSE_SIZE];
    UCHAR  number;
};
```

The members are:

- `response`. A `NULL`-terminated string containing `CLIENT_ID`, `SERVER_ID`, or `SERVER_FULL` strings.

- `number`. The player's number if connected.

12.13.3 Modifications to Ship and Torpedo Classes

The following modifications necessary to convert our game into a server occur in the `Ship` and `Torpedo` classes. A new function is added that returns the ship's data in a `ShipStc` structure. This is the data that is sent from the server to each client to describe the current state of a ship (Listing 12.20).

```
//=======================================================================
// Return current ship state in ShipStc
//=======================================================================
ShipStc Ship::getNetData()
{
    ShipStc data;
    data.X = getX();
    data.Y = getY();
    data.radians = getRadians();
    data.health = getHealth();
    data.velocity = getVelocity();
    data.rotation = getRotation();
    data.score = getScore();
    data.playerN = getPlayerN();
    //-----flags-----
    // Bit0 active
    // Bit1 engineOn
    // Bit2 shieldOn
    data.flags = 0;
    if(getActive())
        data.flags |= 0x01;
    if(getEngineOn())
        data.flags |= 0x02;
    if(getShieldOn())
        data.flags |= 0x04;
    return data;
}
```

Listing 12.20. The `getNetData` function returns the ship state in a `ShipStc` structure.

A similar function is added to the `Torpedo` class to return the current state of a torpedo (Listing 12.21).

```
//=============================================================================
// Return Torpedo state in TorpedoStc
//=============================================================================
TorpedoStc Torpedo::getNetData()
{
    TorpedoStc data;
    data.X = getX();
    data.Y = getY();
    data.velocity = getVelocity();
    data.active = active;
    return data;
}
```

Listing 12.21. The `getNetData` function returns the torpedo state in a `TorpedoStc` structure.

12.13.4 Modifications to the Game Class

The final parts of the integration that we will examine are the changes to the `Game` class. Inside the `run` function of the `Game` class, we have placed a call to the `communicate` function. We also prevented the game from being paused when the console is visible (Listing 12.22).

```
// update(), ai(), collisions() and render() are pure virtual functions
// You must override these functions in your code when you inherit from
// game.h
if (!paused)                         // If not paused
{
    update();                        // Update all game items
    ai();                            // Artificial intelligence
    collisions();                    // Handle collisions
    input->vibrateControllers(frameTime); // Handle controller
                                          // vibration
}
renderGame();                        // Draw all game items
communicate(frameTime);              // Do network communication
// Check for console key
if (input->wasKeyPressed(CONSOLE_KEY))
{
    console->showHide();
    // Paused = console->getVisible(); // Pause game when console is
                                       // visible
}
consoleCommand();                    // Process user entered console command
```

Listing 12.22. Modifications required to the `Game` class for network play.

▌ 12.14 Spacewar Client

Creating the `Spacewar` client begins with the same steps we used to create the server. We copy our existing Spacewar game into a new folder. To that folder we add our `net.cpp` and `net.h` files. Next, we open the Spacewar project and add the same two files to the project's "Source Files" and "Header Files" folders, respectively. Now we add `#include "net.h"` to our `spacewar.h` file.

12.14.1 Modifications to the Spacewar Class

We created arrays to hold the ships and torpedoes just like we did in the server code. Again, this was done to make it easier for anyone who might wish to expand the game beyond two players in the future. The client contains the same structures described in the server section earlier. In addition, we have added the functions described in the next paragraph.

The `communicate` function is called as part of the game loop. It performs the network communications with the server. If the client is currently connected, the `getInfoFromServer` function is called to get any pending game state data sent by the server. Next, a `netTime` value is calculated. This value is used to regulate the frequency of transmissions to the server. If it is time to transmit to the server and `tryToConnect` is true, the `connectToServer` function is called. If the client is already connected, the `checkNetworkTimeout` function is called to check for a server timeout and then the `sendInfoToServer` function is called to send the player input (Listing 12.23).

Connecting to the server requires multiple steps with interaction between the user, client, and server. We can't simply wait in a loop for each step to complete because the game loop must continue to run in order for the game screen to be drawn. We will use a `step` variable to keep track of which step we are currently at. The `connectToServer` function will continue to be called as long as the `tryToConnect` Boolean is true. As each step in the connection process is complete, the `step` variable will be set to the next step to perform.

```
//=============================================================================
// Do network communications
//=============================================================================
void Spacewar::communicate(float frameTime)
{
    if(clientConnected)
        getInfoFromServer();            // Get game state from server
    // Calculate elapsed time for network communications
    netTime += frameTime;
    if(netTime < netNS::NET_TIME)       // If not time to communicate
        return;
    if(tryToConnect)
        connectToServer();          // Attempt to connect to game server
    else if(clientConnected)        // If connected
    {
        checkNetworkTimeout();  // Check for disconnect from server
        sendInfoToServer();     // Send player input to server
    }
    netTime -= netNS::NET_TIME;
}
```

Listing 12.23. Client communications with the server.

If the client is already connected, `tryToConnect` is set to false and the function returns. Theoretically, this should never happen, but theory and practice are two different things. If the client is not connected, a switch statement is used to select the current step. In step 0, a menu is displayed on the console requesting the user to enter the IP address or the name of the server, and the `step` variable is set to 1, as seen in Listing 12.24(a).

In step 1, we wait for the user input. Once we have the user input, we save it in `remoteIP`. A prompt is displayed asking the user to enter the port number and then `step` is set to 2, as seen in the code in Listing 12.24(b).

```
//=============================================================================
// Attempt to connect to the game server
// When a connection is established the game begins
//=============================================================================
void Spacewar::connectToServer()
{
    static int step = 0;
    static float waitTime;   // Seconds we have waited for a response from
                             // server
    int size;
    int newPort;
    std::string str;
    std::stringstream ss;
    if(clientConnected)      // If connected
    {
        tryToConnect = false;
        console->print("Currently connected");
        return;
    }
    switch(step)
    {
    case 0:
        console->print("----- Spacewar Client -----");
        console->print("Enter IP address or name of server:");
        console->clearInput();              // Clear input text
        console->show();
        step = 1;
        break;
```

Listing 12.24(a). Step 0 in connecting to a server.

```
    case 1:
        str = console->getInput();
        if(str == "")                       // If no address entered
            return;
        strcpy_s(remoteIP, str.c_str());    // Copy address to remoteIP
        console->clearInput();              // Clear input text
        console->print("Enter port number, 0 selects default: ");
        step = 2;
        break;
```

Listing 12.24(b). Step 1 in connecting to a server.

```
case 2:
    str = console->getInput();
    if (str == "")
        return;
    newPort = atoi(str.c_str());
    if(newPort == 0)
        newPort = netNS::DEFAULT_PORT;
    if(newPort > netNS::MIN_PORT && newPort < 65536)
    {
        port = newPort;
        step = 3;
    }
    else
        console->print("Invalid port number");
    console->clearInput();
    break;
```

Listing 12.24(c). Step 2 in connecting to a server.

In step 2, we wait for the user to enter the port number. If they enter a valid number, we save it in newPort and set the step variable to 3. These steps are listed in Listing 12.24(c). In step 3, we attempt to create a UDP client. If an error occurs, an error message is displayed, tryToConnect is set to false, and the step variable is reset to 0. If a UDP client is created, we send a request to join to the server and set the step variable to 4, as seen in Listing 12.24(d).

In step 4, we wait for the server to respond to our request to join. The waitTime timer is incremented by netTime. If the time waited exceeds CONNECT_TIMEOUT, we assume that the request to join was lost. The step variable is set to 3, an error message is displayed, and tryToConnect is set to false. If the server responds with the proper ID, we save our player

```
case 3:
    // Create UDP client
    error = net.createClient(remoteIP, port, netNS::UDP);
    if(error != netNS::NET_OK)             // If error
    {
        console->print(net.getError(error)); // Display error message
        tryToConnect = false;
        step = 0;
        return;
    }
    // Send request to join the server
    console->print("Attempting to connect with server."); // Display
                                                            // message
    toServerData.playerN = 255;    // PlayerN=255 is request to join
    size = sizeof(toServerData);
    console->print("'Request to join' sent to server.");
    error = net.sendData((char*) &toServerData, size, remoteIP);
    console->print(net.getError(error));
    waitTime = 0;
    step = 4;
    break;
```

Listing 12.24(d). Step 3 in connecting to a server.

number and set `clientConnected` to true. If any other response is received, we display an error message and set `tryToConnect` to false and the `step` variable to 0 (Listing 12.24(e)).

```
case 4:
    waitTime+=netTime;         // Add time since last call to connect
    // If we timed out with no reponse to our request to join
    if (waitTime > CONNECT_TIMEOUT)
    {
        step = 3;                // Send request again
        console->print("'Request to join' timed out.");
        tryToConnect = false;
    }
    // Read ConnectResponse from server
    size = sizeof(connectResponse);
    error = net.readData((char*)&connectResponse, size, remoteIP);
    if (error == netNS::NET_OK)      // If read was OK
    {
        if(size == 0)   // If no data received
            return;
        // If the server sent back the proper ID then we are connected
        if (strcmp(connectResponse.response, netNS::SERVER_ID) == 0)
        {
            if (connectResponse.number < MAX_PLAYERS)  // If valid
                                                       // player number
            {
                playerN = connectResponse.number;       // Set my player
                                                         // number
                ss << "Connected as player number: " << playerN;
                console->print(ss.str());
                clientConnected = true;
                commErrors = 0;
                commWarnings = 0;
            }
            else
                console->print(
                        "Invalid player number received from server.");
        }
        else if (strcmp(connectResponse.response, netNS::SERVER_FULL)
                == 0)
            console->print("Server Full");
        else
        {
            console->print("Invalid ID from server. Server sent:");
            console->print(connectResponse.response);
        }
    }
    else        // Read error
    {
        console->print(net.getError(error));
    }
    tryToConnect = false;
    step = 0;
}
}
```

Listing 12.24(e). Step 4 in connecting to a server.

```
//===================================================================
// Check for network timeout
//===================================================================
void Spacewar::checkNetworkTimeout()
{
    if (!clientConnected)
        return;
    commErrors++;                           // Increment timeout count
    if (commErrors > netNS::MAX_ERRORS)     // If communication timeout
    {
        clientConnected = false;
        console->print("***** Disconnected from server. *****'');
        console->show();
    }
}
```

Listing 12.25. Checking for a network timeout.

The checkNetworkTimeout function increments commErrors each time it is called. If commErrors exceeds MAX_ERRORS, then the connection to the server is assumed to be lost. The clientConnected Boolean is set to false and a message is displayed (Listing 12.25).

The player's game inputs are sent to the server by the sendInfoToServer function. The button state and player number are placed in a toServerData structure, which is sent using the net.sendData function (Listing 12.26).

The game state sent by the server is read by the getInfoFromServer function. The net.readData function is called to read the incoming data. If the read was successful, the data is loaded into each ship and torpedo. The gameState flags are checked to see if a new round has been started. Finally, the sounds flags are used to play the appropriate sound effects on the client (Listing 12.27).

```
//===================================================================
// Send the keypress codes to the server
//===================================================================
void Spacewar::sendInfoToServer()
{
    int size;
    // Prepare structure to be sent
    toServerData.buttons = buttonState;
    toServerData.playerN = playerN;
    // Send data from client to server
    size = sizeof(toServerData);
    error = net.sendData((char*) &toServerData, size, remoteIP);
}
```

Listing 12.26. Sending player inputs to the server.

```cpp
//=============================================================================
// Get toClientData from server
// Called by client to get game state from server
//=============================================================================
void Spacewar::getInfoFromServer()
{
    int size;
    size = sizeof(toClientData);
    int readStatus = net.readData((char *)&toClientData, size, remoteIP);
    if( readStatus == netNS::NET_OK && size > 0)
    {
        for(int i=0; i<MAX_PLAYERS; i++)        // Search all player positions
        {
            // Load new data into each ship and torpedo
            ship[i].setNetData(toClientData.player[i].shipData);
            ship[i].setScore(toClientData.player[i].shipData.score);
            torpedo[i].setNetData(toClientData.player[i].torpedoData);
            // Game state
            // Bit 0 = roundStart
            // Bits 1-7 reserved for future use
            if((toClientData.gameState & ROUND_START_BIT) &&
                countDownOn == false)
                roundStart();
            gameState = toClientData.gameState; // Save new game state
            // Play sounds as indicated by server
            // Momentary sounds are indicated by a state change. With a
            // state change from 0 to 1 or 1 to 0 the sound is played
            // one time. Other sounds are indicated with 1=on, 0=off.
            // Bit 0 = cheer         state change
            // Bit 1 = collide       state change
            // Bit 2 = explode       state change
            // Bit 3 = engine1       1=on, 0=off
            // Bit 4 = engine2       1=on, 0=off
            // Bit 5 = torpedoCrash  state change
            // Bit 6 = torpedoFire   state change
            // Bit 7 = torpedoHit    state change
            if((toClientData.sounds & CHEER_BIT) !=
                (soundState & CHEER_BIT))
                audio->playCue(CHEER);
            if((toClientData.sounds & COLLIDE_BIT) !=
                (soundState & COLLIDE_BIT))
                audio->playCue(COLLIDE);
            if((toClientData.sounds & EXPLODE_BIT) !=
                (soundState & EXPLODE_BIT))
                audio->playCue(EXPLODE);
            if(toClientData.sounds & ENGINE1_BIT)
                audio->playCue(ENGINE1);
            else
                audio->stopCue(ENGINE1);
            if(toClientData.sounds & ENGINE2_BIT)
                audio->playCue(ENGINE2);
            else
                audio->stopCue(ENGINE2);
            if((toClientData.sounds & TORPEDO_CRASH_BIT) !=
                (soundState & TORPEDO_CRASH_BIT))
                audio->playCue(TORPEDO_CRASH);
            if((toClientData.sounds & TORPEDO_FIRE_BIT) !=
                (soundState & TORPEDO_FIRE_BIT))
```

```
                audio->playCue(TORPEDO_FIRE);
            if((toClientData.sounds & TORPEDO_HIT_BIT) !=
               (soundState & TORPEDO_HIT_BIT))
                audio->playCue(TORPEDO_HIT);
            soundState = toClientData.sounds;         // Save new sound states
            commErrors = 0;
            commWarnings = 0;
        }
    }
}
```

Listing 12.27. Getting the game state from the server.

12.14.2 Modifications to the Ship and Torpedo Classes

The following modifications that convert our game into a client are located in the Ship and Torpedo classes. A new function is added that sets the ship's data from a ShipStc structure. This is the data that is sent from the server to each client to describe the current state of a ship (Listing 12.28). The Torpedo class contains a similar function that sets the state of a torpedo (Listing 12.29).

```
//================================================================================
// Sets all ship data from ShipStc sent from server to client
//================================================================================
void Ship::setNetData(ShipStc ss)
{
    setX(ss.X);
    setY(ss.Y);
    setRadians(ss.radians);
    setHealth(ss.health);
    setVelocity(ss.velocity);
    setRotation(ss.rotation);
    setActive((ss.flags & 0x01) == 0x01);
    if(active)
        visible = true;
    setEngineOn((ss.flags & 0x02) == 0x02);
    setShieldOn((ss.flags & 0x04) == 0x04);
    if(health <= 0 && explosionOn == false && visible) // If ship destroyed
        explode();
}
```

Listing 12.28. Updating a client ship with data sent from the server.

```
//================================================================================
// Sets all torpedo data from TorpedoStc sent from server to client
//================================================================================
void Torpedo::setNetData(TorpedoStc ts)
{
    setActive(ts.active);
```

```
    if(active)
        setVisible(true);
    else
        setVisible(false);
    setX(ts.X);
    setY(ts.Y);
    setVelocity(ts.velocity);
}
```

Listing 12.29. Updating a client torpedo with data sent from the server.

12.14.3 Modifications to the Game Class

The Game class run function includes a call to the communicate function just as the server code did (Listing 12.30).

```
// update(), ai(), collisions() and render() are pure virtual functions
// You must override these functions in your code when you inherit from
// game.h
if (!paused)                            // If not paused
{
    update();                           // Update all game items
    ai();                               // Artificial intelligence
    collisions();                       // Handle collisions
    input->vibrateControllers(frameTime); // Handle controller
                                          // vibration
}
renderGame();                           // Draw all game items
communicate(frameTime);                 // Do network communication
```

Listing 12.30. Modifications made to the client's Game class.

Chapter Review

In this chapter, we covered how to write UPD/IP and TCP/IP socket code using Winsock. We created a new Net class to hold our network code. We used the Net class to create a client/server chat program and we created a network playable version of our Spacewar game. Some of the key topics from the chapter are the following:

- Han Solo knows what he's talking about.

- *Client device.* In a client/server game, the player uses the client device.

- *Running the game.* The server typically runs the game.

- *IP.* Most networks support the Internet protocol (IP).

- *TCP.* Transmission control protocol (TCP) provides reliable delivery of data.

- *UDP.* User datagram protocol (UDP) does not guarantee the delivery of data.

- *Unique addresses.* Each device on an IP network must have a unique IP address.

- *IPv4 and IPv6.* IPv4 uses a 32-bit address and IPv6 uses a 128-bit address.

- *Ports.* Each IP addressable device also has 65,536 possible ports.

- *Sockets.* A socket is an interface to the network.

- *Winsock.* Winsock is Microsoft's socket API for Windows.

- *Initiation of Winsock.* Winsock's `WSAStartup` function initiates the use of Winsock.

- *Creating a socket.* Winsock's `socket` function creates a socket.

- *Nonblocking mode.* Winsock's `ioctlsocket` function may be used to put a socket in nonblocking mode.

- *Creating a server.* The `Net::createServer` function may be used to create a UDP or TCP server.

- *Connecting sockets with addresses.* Winsock's `bind` function associates a socket with an address.

- *Bound sockets.* Only bound sockets may listen for incoming connections.

- *Creating a client.* The `Net::createClient` function may be used to create a UDP or TCP client.

- *Returning IP addresses.* Winsock's `getaddrinfo` function returns the IP address of a host name.

- *Returning the host name.* Winsock's `gethostname` function returns the host name of the local computer.

- *Sending data.* The `Net` class's `sendData` function sends data to the specified IP address.

- *Connection between sockets.* Winsock's `connect` function establishes a connection between TCP sockets.

- *Socket to socket.* Winsock's `sendto` function sends data from socket to socket.

- *Reading network data.* The `Net::readData` function reads network data.

- *TCP server socket configuration.* Winsock's `listen` function configures a TCP server socket to wait for incoming connections.

- *Creating a new socket.* Winsock's `accept` function creates a new socket that is connected to an incoming connection.

- *Reading data.* Winsock's `recvfrom` reads data from the network.

- *Closing and releasing.* The `Net::closeSocket` function closes a socket and releases its resources.

- *Closing a socket.* Winsock's `closesocket` function closes a socket.

- *Deregistering.* Winsock's `WSACleanup` function deregisters an application from Windows sockets.

- *Error messages.* The `Net::getError` function returns a detailed error message from a two-part error code.

- *Bandwidth requirements.* The bandwidth requirements of a game server increase by the number of players squared.

- *State changes.* Using state changes is a more reliable way to send momentary data on a UDP network.

Review Questions

1. What is the Internet protocol?

2. How do TCP and UDP differ?

3. How many bytes are in an IPv4 address?

4. What range of port numbers is acceptable to use?

5. What is a network socket?

6. Show an example of creating a TCP socket with the Winsock `socket` function.

7. Describe the difference between a blocking and nonblocking socket.

8. From which addresses does a server listen for incoming communications?

9. Which socket type must be explicitly bound?

10. Which `Net` class function is used to create a client?

11. What does the Winsock `getaddrinfo` function do?

12. What host name always refers to the local computer?

13. What does the `size` parameter contain after a successful call to the `Net::sendData` function?

14. Which Winsock function is used to send data?

15. What does the `size` parameter contain after a successful call to the `Net::read Data` function?

16. What does the Winsock `listen` function do?

17. Describe the steps required to use the Winsock `accept` function.

18. What will the `from` parameter contain after a successful call of Winsock's `recvfrom` function?

19. Which Winsock function deregisters the application from Windows sockets?

20. Give an example of using the `Net::getError` function to display a detailed error message from a two-part error code.

Exercises

1. Create a console-based application that prompts the user for a host name and displays the corresponding IP address.

2. Modify the server in the client/server chat program so the server will echo the client messages back to the client.

3. Modify the client/server chat program so that up to ten clients may connect to the server. All messages should be sent to all clients.

4. Modify the Spacewar client/server game to support more than two players.

Examples

The following examples are available for download from www.programming2dgames.com.

- *Client/Server Chat.* A console program that allows users to send messages back and forth across a network.

  - Demonstrates using Winsock to send and receive data across a network.

  - Demonstrates how to use the game engine's `Net` class.

- *Client/Server Spacewar.* A network-playable version of the Spacewar game. It includes a dedicated server that supports two client connections.

  - Demonstrates using Winsock to send and receive data across a network.

  - Demonstrates a client/server game configuration with a dedicated server.

The Journey

The journey we began back in Chapter 1 has taken us through many aspects of game programming. I do hope the reading has been as rewarding as the writing. Please consider joining the forum at www.programming2dgames.com. It is a great place to ask questions and share your latest creation.

Index

pitch 198
pitch var. 199
planets 132–135
Planet class 333–334
playCue 191, 196
Player 397
PostQuitMessage 24
prepareDataForClient 402
Present 44
primitives 81–82
progress bar 288–289
projection 155
projectionsOverlap 156
pSrcRect 113
pure virtual functions 6, 75–76, 85
push button 295–297

Q

quad 240–241
QueryPerformanceCounter 79
QueryPerformanceFrequency 79

R

rasterization 41
RAWINPUTDEVICE 88
readControllers 84, 98
readData 379
reciprocal homogenous w (rhw) 246
recvfrom 382
reflections 265–268, 311
releaseAll 49, 134
remoteAddr 374
render 81–83, 85, 103, 118, 134
renderGame 82, 84, 117
resetAll 134
ROTATED_BOX 163
rotated box and circle collision 157–160
rotated box collision 152–157
rotatedBoxReady 154
rotatedX 154
rotatedY 154
rotation 140–141
run 83–84, 98, 102
runtime library 54

S

SAFE_DELETE 46
SAFE_RELEASE 46
saving 355–359
saveGame 355
scaling 140–141

scope resolution operator 5
SDKVersion 40
sendData 376
sendInfoToServer 410
sendto 376, 378
server 363, 370–371
setCurrentFrame 129, 137, 139
setFrameDelay 137
setFrames 137
setMouseButton 94
setRect 129, 139
setTransform 119
seven-segment display 284–288
shadows 265–268
shields 171–174, 341
shieldOn 174
Ship class 165–166
    draw 173
    initialize 172
    update 165, 176
ShipStc 398, 404, 412
showBackbuffer 51, 57
sleepTime 84
socket 364–366
    blocking 364
    nonblocking 364
    programming 364–366
sound bank 185–187
SOUND_BANK 191
sound cues 191–193
source file 3
Space Pirates 355–359
Spacewar 103–105, 327–329, 344
    client 406
    server 396
    update 176
spriteCenter 121
spriteData 120, 128, 139
spriteEnd 134
sprites 111–124
startFrame 137
Stencil 43
stopCue 192
struct 9
SUCCEEDED 43
SwapEffect 44
switchOn 296

T

TestCooperativeLevel 80
testing 332